UPHOLSTERY

— A Complete Course —

UPHOLSTERY

- A Complete Course -

Chairs, sofas, ottomans, screens and stools

Written and illustrated by

David James

Guild of Master Craftsman Publications

Dedication
To E, R, C and P

First published 1990
by Guild of Master Craftsman Publications Ltd,
Castle Place, 166 High Street, Lewes, East Sussex BN7 1XU

Reprinted 1997

© David James 1990

ISBN 0 946 81919 X

Front cover photograph by Philip McCarthy

The fabric used as a background for the cover is Padua Damask
by Parkertex

Back cover photographs:

Top right – Gerald Hutchinson and Richard Levene for
J.C. and M.P. Smith Ltd 1989

Bottom left – Helen Moss at Buckinghamshire College

Bottom right – Dinah Phillips, 'By Design', High Wycombe

The plate from Didérot's *Encyclopédie* on page 14 is reproduced by
kind permission of the Brotherton Library, Leeds University

The photograph of the House of Commons on page 17 is
reproduced by kind permission of Dunlopillo

Designed by Robert and Jean Wheeler Design Associates

Printed and bound in Great Britain by
Hillman Printers (Frome) Ltd, Frome, Somerset

Contents

Foreword   7
Introduction   9

 1   History   11
 2   Development   18
 3   The Workshop   24
 4   Tools and Power Tools   31
 5   Machines and Mechanisation   48
 6   Materials   64
 7   Fabrics and Covers   87
 8   Leather   101
 9   Preparation of Materials   110
10   Foams   125
11   Frames and Structures   138
12   Springs and Suspension Systems   151
13   Traditional Techniques   166
14   Modern Techniques   188
15   The Traditional Chair   207
16   Hand-sprung Upholstery   228
17   Settees and Other Pieces   237
18   Beds and Bedding   253
19   Restoration   265
20   The Furniture Industry: opportunities, training, associations, useful addresses and publications   275

Colour Sections
Project 1   Loose Seat for a Dining Chair
Project 2   Piped Scatter Cushion
Project 3   Hall or Lounge Stool
Project 4   Mid-Victorian Dining Chair with Buttoned Seat

Bibliography   282
Glossary   283
Metric Conversion Table   287
Index   288

Acknowledgements

My sincere and grateful thanks to my wife Eirlys, and to Richard, Christine and Philip whose patience, understanding and support have allowed me to complete a worthwhile and somewhat lengthy project. I can't promise that there won't be another. Eric Bruton of Ipswich started me off scribbling and writing with a quiet chat and a glass of beer one winter's evening. His encouragement is remembered with gratitude.

I am indebted to many colleagues and friends with whom I have worked and long been associated. Their experience and knowledge, which was freely given, has been of tremendous value both directly and indirectly.

I would particularly like to thank the following for the contributions they have made, and for allowing me to use their work and their expertise: Len Rentmore, John Turner, the late Ted Hudson, David Edgar, Phil Birtles, Ed Wilson, Dennis Hatt, Cyril Dawes, Dr Hew Reid, Allan Hill, Ray Chapel, John Lees, Bryon Baron, Julia Shields, Mark Dennis and Greg Jones.

My thanks especially to Angela Burgin, whose workshops in Tring have been my 'Aladdin's cave'.

The companies and institutions listed I acknowledge with grateful thanks for access to their products and information supplied. Singer Company UK Ltd, Parker Knoll Ltd, G-Plan Furniture Ltd, Tetrad Associates, Horatio Myer and Co. Ltd, Dunlopillo, Vitafoam Ltd, British Vita, Conolly Bros Ltd, The Bridge of Weir Leather Co., Beaverfoam Ltd, Pullman Flexolators, Devilbis, Senco Pneumatics UK Ltd, Rapid Tools, Bosch Tools, Eastman Machine Co., Samco Presses, J. & P. Coats UK Ltd, Matramatic, J. DeWalleg Ltd, Fibertex, A. & C. Fabrics, Fogarty Fillings, ICI Chemicals UK, Dupont UK, Bedding and Upholstery Supplies, Chiltern Springs, Adler UK, Pirelli, Heals Bedding, A. Ornstin Ltd, Fanghangel & Co., A. V. Lancashire, Pfaff Machines, Spuhl Ltd, Selectus Ltd, Hypnos Ltd, Astor Berning, Fisco Nails, The Furniture Industries Research Association, and the Buckinghamshire College of Higher Education.

Lastly, a very sincere thank you to the Guild of Master Craftsmen – particularly Bernard Cooper – and my editor Elizabeth Inman, for her enthusiasm, understanding and much-needed support.

Foreword

Of all the furniture we use, that which is upholstered relates to us most intimately. Because of this it has, throughout history, expressed most directly the status, the outlook and aspirations of its users. Undoubtedly it is upholstery and soft furnishings that are most significant in creating the ambience of an interior, and the more they are in evidence, the more skilfully they are used, then the more stately and imposing, or informal and homely, will be the room.

So the upholsterer's art is an important one, and it is vital therefore that the multiplicity of skills that have been developed over the centuries, and the new ones made necessary by today's technology, should be recorded and made available to us all.

David James' book represents the practical experience of a working life – in industry, in his own practice, and from years of teaching – that has honed his ability to explain and to solve the infinite variety of problems that only students know how to find. This book is the summation of that experience. It is a comprehensive account of practical upholstery from its historical development to the use of present day methods and materials. Its scope includes the layout of the workshop; the equipment, tools and machinery used; both traditional and modern materials and fillings; springing; suspension systems; covers and frame construction. Traditional and modern techniques are described and illustrated using a multitude of very varied pieces as examples.

This book must surely establish itself as the most authoritative and comprehensive account of the upholsterer's art for the beginner, the amateur and the experienced professional alike.

Philip Hussey, BA, NDD, MCSD
High Wycombe, 1990

Introduction

Upholstery is a universal craft – one which knows no language barriers, as I discovered quite by chance some years ago when I came across an upholsterer's workshop in the back streets of Venice. Peeping through the open door the warm glow of familiarity was immediate and I felt instantly at home. The atmosphere – the jumble, the well-worn tools, and the half-finished chair standing proudly on the trestles – was just as it would be anywhere in the world.

Some years later I had a similar experience in a small bustling town in central France. A row of chairs stood outside a small shop and the sign 'Tapissier' caught my attention. Chairs and stools in the French style were colourfully displayed around the shop, and new wood frames hung from the wall. It was 2 o'clock on a warm, sunny summer's afternoon, and the doors and windows were all wide open, but there was no sign of the upholsterer (tapissier), or the apprentice whose bicycle stood in the corner of the workshop.

And again, quite recently I was fortunate to meet a man from Rhode Island, USA, who is also a practising upholsterer. He was a big gentle fellow with strong arms and hands, and he proudly showed us photographs of some of his recent work. It was mostly eighteenth and nineteenth century American upholstery which he had faithfully restored for his clients. He was a man of long experience, and his work was clean and well executed. I had no doubt that he too would be capable of practising his craft anywhere in the world.

Of course upholstery in the traditional sense is a vast and fascinating subject, describing the use of fabrics and textiles in the complete furnishing of a house or building. Broadly speaking this splits into four separate areas: seating, bedding, drapery, and floor coverings. The upholsterers of the eighteenth and nineteenth centuries dealt with all these areas and provided a complete furnishing service. It was their job to survey and appraise their clients' house furnishings and interiors, and work of this nature in many very large houses was almost continuous. The service included the maintenance and care of all fabrics and covered furnishings, and these were often in need of cleaning or replacement, either annually or at the end of the summer or winter seasons.

Today the word upholstery has become synonymous with chairs and seating, and the soft furnisher deals with all other fixed fabric furnishings, in particular drapery and detachable coverings for windows and beds. This book concentrates mainly on the upholstery of furniture and seating both large and small, and is intended as a practical companion and a reference book both for those learning the craft and for those who may already be knee deep in curled hair, cotton felt, sheets of foam and all the other paraphernalia of the trade. It will appeal particularly to those who have already mastered the basic skills and wish to advance their technical knowledge, and at the same time take on work of a more adventurous kind. Particular emphasis is placed on the fact that traditional skills are easily adapted to new and modern techniques.

There is of course no substitute for practical experience, and I would encourage anyone seriously involved in the craft to travel as widely as possible to learn both modern and traditional methods and skills. Spend time in an upholstering factory environment, if only as a visitor. Arrange to see upholstery foam being cut and fabricated. Watch a weaver and a screen printer at work. Learn about frame-making and watch a chair-maker building a frame. Above all, share your knowledge and your skills with others in different areas of the craft.

It is hoped that you will also be encouraged to record your work, and the work of other upholsterers, by taking photographs and making drawings and notes. Every piece of upholstery you do may be unique to you and may include a technique which is new to you.

Short courses and master classes are available to everyone, so when possible try some loose cover cutting or some simple drapery. Textiles are an integral part of the upholstery process, so using a variety of skills will add scope and interest to your upholstery. Use colour, form, texture and pattern to make the work interesting and exciting.

Finally, always take pleasure in all the upholstery you do. Take as much as you need, and give back as much as you can to the craft that you inherit, and remember that an awareness of history can add immensely to the enjoyment of this very old skill.

Design and make new pieces, using the best materials and techniques, if that is your preference. Or reproduce faithfully, with as much care as you are able. Conserve and restore sympathetically, and your work will give pleasure for many years to come.

Chapter One

History

*Wh_en the upholsterers and carpenters of the sixteenth and
seventeenth centuries began the craft of covering chairs, fixing drapes
and making cushions and mattresses with a few simple hand tools,
they enjoyed a certain freedom of inventiveness and experimentation
as they discovered new ways to adorn the living areas of their houses.*

Their work then, as it is today, was a combination of manipulating, trimming and fixing a variety of fabrics. They must have learned quickly how to deal with the finest silks and stretch the heavy leathers that were available at that time. Records show clearly that upholstery construction was very simple and, in many cases, crude, but the covering materials, which were mostly handmade, were of excellent quality.

Early upholstery consisted of fabrics and leathers nailed directly to wood frames with very little or no stuffing. The seat of a chair or day bed was made reasonably comfortable with a stuffed cushion filled with wool, feathers or rags. These were usually supported by strips of nailed hide or rope. From the end of the sixteenth century well-upholstered chairs and sofas were produced for many of the great houses in England.

Unfortunately, much of this work has disappeared because of its perishable nature, and the influence of events such as a change of monarch, feuds and wars, which all have an unsettling effect on domestic life. However, an amazing number of good examples have survived and most of the great houses in the United Kingdom have maintained their own collections of period upholstery, though very few still have their original coverings.

The upholsterer was referred to as an artisan who made and finished articles of furniture using textiles

Winchester X-frame Oak Chair c. 1590

Upholstered and decorated chairs of this kind display fixed upholstery rarely seen before 1600. Several recorded examples illustrate the desire for more comfortable seating at a time when timber boards and panelling were the norm for most people.

Upholstery Hair, wool or feathers would provide suitable fillings inside cases of linen and cotton. Although fixed upholstery showed very little evidence of padding, the seat squab or loose cushion was well filled and provided warmth and comfort.

Coverings Heavily embroidered velvets were fixed with ornamented nails, and the whole chair heavily decorated with long fringe and corner tassels.

For some time after, the X-frame chair was produced for use in halls and churches, usually with little or no upholstery.

and stuffings. The Upholders' Guild was in existence before 1460, but was always closely linked with the Carpenters' Company and the Skinners' Company. At the time of the restoration of the monarchy in 1660 an upholsterer was appointed to the office of King's Upholsterer. Many early catalogues, inventories and wills make reference to work being carried out by the upholsterer. The work was varied and included curtains, bed-making and drapes, wall hangings and chair work. Many rooms of early-seventeenth-century houses relied on rich upholstery for effects of colour and fashionable design.

During the Tudor period coverings such as plain and embroidered velvets, satin tapestry and needlework were the main furnishing materials. During and after the reign of Charles II a much wider range of coverings became available. Among these were some particularly interesting fabrics, such as brocatelle, painted silks, horsehair cloth, mohair, damasks and chintz used for bedrooms. Apart from during the brief Cromwellian period, trimmings and decoration were widely used to

Fig 1.1 Illustrations from Daniel Marot's eighteenth-century book of designs. These styles of upholstery were fashionable amongst the very wealthy in the late seventeenth and early eighteenth centuries.

SECTION II. PLATE XIV.

enrich upholstered furniture. Fringes and wide braids, combined with festoon drapes, appear on most large beds and around windows. These elaborate handmade trimmings were a feature of seventeenth-century upholstery and often covered ornate carved framework.

Hand-embroidered fabrics were used a great deal for furnishing purposes. Crewel-stitch needlework was used to produce wall hangings and curtains, and *petit-point*, which is a slanting stitch, was more suitable for chair seats. Turkey work, also called set work, was another favourite furnishing enmbroidery which consisted of a knotted woollen pile on a base linen, and was evidently a technique copied from oriental carpet-making. Produced in bright coloured wools, Turkey work was an extremely durable furniture covering.

Stuffed and fixed upholstery of the seventeenth and early eighteenth centuries consisted mainly of curled hair and sheep's wool supported and covered by linens and webbings.

During the reign of William and Mary in the late seventeenth century, large tall-back chairs with scroll arms and wings covered in Genoese velvets or handmade needlework were typical. Squab cushions were the normal treatment for seats, and where fixed upholstery appeared, backs and seats were finished with fringes of small balls and tassels. Running above this a wide braid was fixed, or rows of handmade brass-headed nails.

Upholsterers working during this period produced some very interesting and beautiful furnishings. Examples shown in drawings from Daniel Marot's eighteenth-century book of designs illustrate some of the window, bed and chair treatments which were popular during the early part of the eighteenth century.

From about 1750 onwards upholstery techniques improved when designers and architects demanded a change from the tightly pulled, simple domed shapes to more rectangular seats and backs. Stuffings were arranged more evenly over seats, and edges were built up by rolling amounts of stuffing in linen scrim and stitching them in place. This provided a more durable seat edge and allowed covers to last longer.

Upholsterers realised that stuffings of all kinds could be stabilised and held in place by running linen thread or twine through a seat, either before the coverings were applied or after. This tying-in or bridling technique was particularly suited to cushions and mattress-making. Tufts of wool, silk or leather were often tied at intervals all over the surface of the chair back or seat cushions.

The loose seat or drop-in seat, which was popular during the Queen Anne period (1702–14) because it could be easily removed and re-covered, was mostly ignored during the eighteenth century. Chairs and sofas produced during the so-called age of the designer

were neatly upholstered, with well-stitched edges. Coverings were relatively light in weight and style. Heavy braids and fringes were replaced by rows of fine brass nails. Close nailing around arm rails and legs matched the delicate coverings and sharp outlines.

At various times during the eighteenth century several books were published by the leading furniture designers. This has provided us with a link which enables us to relate particular pieces of furniture to specific periods.

The most popular furnishing and covering fabric of the mid- and late-Georgian period (1730–1800) was silk damask, woven with symmetrical patterns of flowers, scrolls and wildlife. Deep-coloured Spanish hides were also specified for chair work, and embroidery still flourished as a hand craft and a pastime for ladies and their servants. Imported velvets were individualised with embroidered crests and motifs. Needlework panels for cushions and chair upholstery were usually produced on linen foundations.

The upholsterer was in great demand at this time and it was not unusual to use as much as a hundred yards of various fabrics to furnish a particular room. Rooms so treated were often described by naming the fabric predominantly used.

Bedrooms were particularly well furnished by the upholsterers. The large beds were hung with velvets, damasks and printed cottons. Embroidery and tapestries were to be found in the less important bedrooms.

By the end of the eighteenth century the upholsterer had become the leading tradesmen in the business of furnishing houses. In many instances he emloyed other craftsmen to assist him in carrying out schemes of work for his customers. Firms and partnerships of cabinet-makers and upholsterers had been set up to deal with the interiors designed by Chippendale, Sheraton and Adam.

In the Regency period, from 1811 until 1820, upholstery styles became less fussy and very simple in outline. Long-seated sofas and couches with their generous scroll ends were scattered with circular cushions and bolsters. The window seat and backless box ottoman upholstered in plain and striped silks and brocades had long hair-filled seat cushions. Stools which were well designed and made were also a feature of this period. Fabrics were carefully pleated and gathered at corners and cushions piped to give uncluttered classical lines.

Design in seating, as in most types of furniture, was soon to be influenced by the development of machines and the Industrial Revolution. However, it is probably true to say that upholstery construction was influenced more directly by the invention of the coil spring early in the Victorian period. The demand for furniture was greater at that time than ever before. The struggle to provide comfort outweighed, for a time, the desire for

Fig 1.2 An eighteenth-century upholsterer's workroom. The stairs on the right lead up to the shop and the upholsterer stands in the bottom left-hand corner inspecting a finished chair while young girls sew curtains or hangings. Chair frames waiting to be upholstered hang from the ceiling. The room also contains bedding, mirrors and a bureau, reminders that the upholsterer was also an interior decorator.

good design. Seating generally became larger and deeper to accommodate the new springing. Show-wood disappeared and the making of fully upholstered stuffover chairs and settees led us into what might be called the age of the upholsterer.

The production of textiles for all kinds of furnishings increased at a tremendous rate, and the range of fabrics available was very wide. The early Victorians favoured silk and wool plush and horsehair fabric which they improved by adding linen and cotton to its foundation. Printed linens and cottons depicted framed scenes of a variety of subjects. Berlin wool work, produced by hand in bright Merino wool, was particularly fashionable for small pieces of upholstery, such as foot stools, gout stools, prayer chairs and nursing chairs.

Later in the period, sofas and chairs filled with springs and heavily buttoned were covered in American cloth, wool plush, chenille and a variety of velvets. At the same time designs for corner seats, conversation seats and ottomans became popular, many upholstered in American cloth and hide.

The Victorian craftsmen were responsible for many of the techniques which form the basis of the trade today. Tufting was developed further and the tufts were exchanged for buttons and pulled deeply into well-filled seats and backs and arms.

The button-back chair was the 'cosy chair' of the Victorian period. Firmly upholstered and elegant, it was found in the most comfortable middle-class homes. The technique of buttoning had been introduced in the second half of the eighteenth century as a device to give fresh decorative character to upholstered chairs, and also to increase comfort. It was during this period that the technique known as buttoning was used to attach various upholstery materials and fabrics to shaped surfaces, both in furniture and coach-building. Although buttoning was introduced primarily as an ornamental device it was soon recognised in coach-building as a practical method for securing hard-wearing resilient material, and was called quilting. Victorian upholsterers used the technique of quilting to furnish and upholster the first-class areas of railway carriages and horse-drawn carriages.

Fluting or channel work which had appeared earlier was combined with button work to produce the heavy and rather fussy Victorian sofas and ottomans. Pieces of cane and whale bone were used for spring edge work, shaped and lashed to form bow fronts and serpentine shapes, all requiring a good deal of skill.

As the period progressed small workshops expanded to become factories, turning out great numbers of hand-built pieces. Towards the end of the nineteenth century two machines became available which were to assist the upholsterer – the carding machine and the sewing machine – both of which had to be manually operated. At a time when the cutting and shaping of timber and metal was fast becoming mechanised in all other industries, the assembly of a piece of furniture and the subsequent polishing of the wood and the upholstering was still a hand-craft business and remained so well into the present century. During the long Victorian era many new materials and techniques were tried and experimented with. These new ideas were often interesting and successful. Metals were cast and bent and riveted to produce chairs and tables for indoor and outdoor use. Papier-mâché was formed and inlaid and lacquered, but generally timber remained the basic material for furniture making, except perhaps in the production of bed frames and bedsteads.

To fulfil the increasing demand for upholstery fillings, several alternatives were used to supplement a dwindling supply of hair and wool. Shredded seaweed and grass fibre dyed black made reasonable first stuffings. Cotton-mill puff and rag flocks, though poor in bulk and resilience, were found to be suitable second or top stuffings for padding out the type of heavy upholstery being produced. However, in the better bespoke upholstery, good-quality curled horsehair and cotton waddings were still the best fillings available, with down and feathers for loose cushions. A variety of trimmings in wool and silk, which had been machine made for some time, was evident during the mid- and late-Victorian period. Silk cords particularly were cleverly used to hold down and trim the elegantly shaped upholstered work.

Many of the Victorian styles continued to be produced during the relatively short Edwardian era. However, upholstered chairs, sofas and beds became less clumsy and there was a clear influence in design from the Arts and Crafts Movement begun by William Morris and friends around 1870. The ideals of this movement were continued by designers such as C. F. Voysey, Charles Rennie Mackintosh and Ernest Gimson on into the twentieth century. The Art Nouveau style of 1900 was considered quaint and arty and was often slim and spindly in construction. Hence the upholstery produced during the early twentieth century was a mixture of factory-made copies of various styles, and handmade commissions which indicated the trend towards a modern style.

Materials and methods became more sophisticated during the Art Deco period of the 1930s and indicated much lighter treatments in upholstery, with seats

Knole Settee
c. 1600

The Knole settee is one of three sofas at Knole House in Kent, all of which are fully upholstered in rich crimson velvets and well decorated with fringe and copper nails. Frame joints are tenoned and pinned and the adjustable ends work on a rack mechanism.

Upholstery Various fillings of vegetable fibre, wool and hair are supported by linen cloth and webbing. Fixed pillows are made an integral part of the tilting settee ends.

The settees and matching side chairs are some of the oldest existing upholstery work.

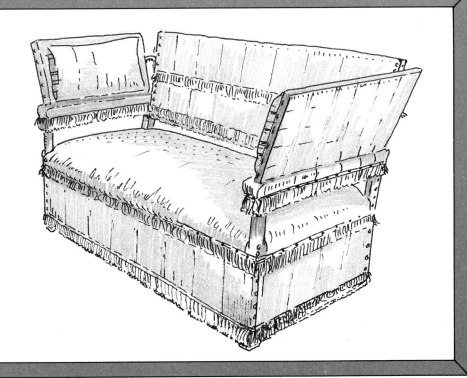

generally higher from the floor. New designs featured the use of steel tube, usually chromed, and painted timber which was often inlaid or lined in. The wood machinist produced interesting rebated and chamfered show-wood rails. Upholstery coverings of leather and the new leather cloths were used side-by-side and often together on the same piece. Lightweight modern tapestry with splashes of colour and small all-over patterns were popular from World War I and onwards into the 1930s. Chair design particularly was influenced by notable German, French and American designers who specialised in furniture.

Industrial areas such as London, Nottingham, Leeds and Glasgow had particular localities that became noted for upholstery work, and many of these still remain today.

The Art Deco period produced many exciting and outstanding furniture designs which were symetrical and angular and influenced particularly by the architecture of the day. Coverings of blue, brown and grey tapestry and moquette were combined with veneered plywood surfaces. Sunray effects were produced by fluting for chair backs and arms. Seats for chairs and sofas were sprung with machine-made spring units using single and double cone springs often in double-decker formation.

The development of latex foam in 1929 was to give new significance to the word 'comfort'. Latex-foam cushioning originated with a team of scientists in the Dunlop laboratories and the new cushioning material was found to possess immense advantages, and its use over the next twenty years was to confirm this. Moulded units in solid or cavity foam could be produced to suit almost any application. Cavity sheet could be applied easily to chair arms and backs and reversible latex cushion interiors soon replaced the spring-unit interiors which had to be hand-built.

Soon after World War II, production of the new foam increased and its use spread to vehicle seating, aircraft, shipping and bed production. On 26 October 1950 the reconstructed Chamber of the House of Commons was opened, and every foot of seating throughout the historic building was upholstered with Dunlopillo latex foam.

During the war years certain furniture companies were licensed to produce Utility furniture. Others joined the war effort and turned out more essential items such as glider parts, airscrews, ammunition boxes and specialised furniture for the Ministry of Defence. In 1951 the Festival of Britain provided the opportunity for designers and craftsmen in all industries to demonstrate their abilities with a fresh look at their products.

New materials and the techniques to deal with them resulted in many exciting products. A large percentage of these new materials for furniture were plastic in various forms. Plastic fibres, and foams, both rigid and flexible, that could be moulded, expanded and easily fabricated were soon to find a place in furniture making and upholstery in particular. Commercial development of the new polyurethane foams for cushioning and synthetic fibres for textiles took place in America, Germany and Britain during the 1950s. Methods of springing also changed during the late 1940s and early '50s. Chair designs with shallow seats and foam cushions did not need deep-spring units using compression-type springs. Lateral suspension using close-coiled tension springs or sinuous zig-zag wires provided the answer. These systems were lightweight and easily assembled and fixed.

At the same time many of the traditional materials and fillings were being converted and preformed to fulfil the demand for faster and cleaner production methods. Pre-formed fillings in the form of pads and sheet using rubberised animal hair, needled pads of

Fig 1.3 A typical piece of early Victorian furniture.

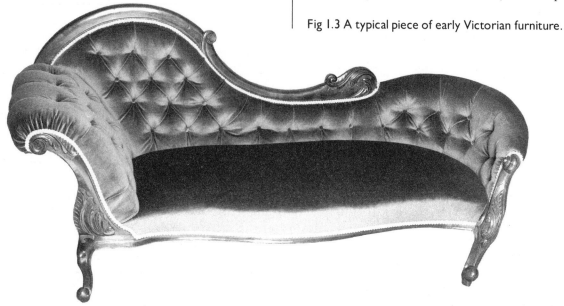

Fig 1.4 The Chamber of the House of Commons. In 1950 every foot of seating was upholstered with Dunlopillo latex foam.

hair and fibres and felts were found to be more economical to produce and to use.

In 1961 Richard Burton, an American chemist, wrote in the magazine *Industrial Design*: 'Of all the plastics vying for attention as design materials in today's market, none enjoys a more advantageous position than polyurethane foam. It is the most versatile of all foamed plastics, capable of doing more different jobs than any other foam, and it is a superbly competent cushioning material and thermal and acoustical insulating medium.

'Four other compounds currently compete with urethane foam. They are latex, styrene, polyurethane and vinyl. All of them can be foamed or expanded. Latex seems unlikely to survive as a major competitor because it ages quickly, is costlier, less engineerable and more vulnerable to chemical deterioration.'

During the 1960s, Pop Art furniture made from coated metals, foamed plastics and board materials gave some relief from the strong influence of Scandinavian design. The availability of urethanes made the upholstery of difficult sculptured shapes a possibility. Upholstery covers were tailored and fitted and, where possible, made detachable for easy cleaning and replacement. The traditional skills of the upholsterer were generally no longer needed except for

high-grade reproduction work and the restoration of period pieces.

The second half of the twentieth century has seen a separation of the upholsterer's work into several distinct craft areas. The interior designer has become the co-ordinator who selects from the areas of bedding, upholstery, floor coverings and soft furnishings to produce interior schemes in the same way that the upholsterer did a century or more ago.

During the past two decades three oil-based plastic materials have played a major role in the development of upholstery. Running alongside the increasing use of polyurethane foams, two synthetic fibres, polyester and acrylics, have been used more and more to provide durable upholstery for the mass market. These materials have changed the look and feel of upholstered seating from the tightly tailored pieces of the post-war years to today's soft, plump designs which offer the buyer of upholstery a luxury and comfort only available to royalty in the sixteenth and seventeenth centuries.

A general knowledge of the history and development of furniture and furnishing provides the craftsman with the ability to recognise a style or period. This can often be done by studying the materials that have been used, and the way in which they have been put together. The chart in Chapter Two gives a general indication of when particular furniture-making materials were introduced or developed, from the seventeenth century to the present day.

— *Chapter Two* —
Development

The following chart shows furniture periods and events which together trace the progress of styles in furniture making, furnishing, and textile manufacture. The dates and periods are approximate, but do give an indication of when an event occurred or a particular design or style became popular.

Furniture Style and Period		Construction	Fabric Coverings
Elizabethan (Renaissance)	1558–1603	Oak, beech	Silk velvets, tapestry
Early Stuart (Jacobean)	1603–1649	Oak, fruit woods	Tapestry
Commonwealth (Cromwellian)	1649–1660	Oak	Silk embroidery, ox hide
Late Stuart (Carolean)	1660–1688	Walnut	Turkey work, cane work

Designer, Event or Development	Examples in Upholstery	
Early fixed upholstery Stuffed cushions	Upholstered oak X-frame chair c.1590 (see page 11)	
Knole House furniture Knole settee	The Knole settee c.1600 (see page 15) Early oak chair c.1600–1640 (see page 26)	
Tapestry factory founded at Mortlake	Nailed upholstery (see pages 29 and 32) Farthingale chair c.1650 (see page 36)	
Huguenot silk weavers settle in England	French armchair c.1660 (see page 50) Walnut framed, winged sleeping chair c.1675 (see page 57, also page 65)	

Furniture Style and Period		Construction	Fabric Coverings
William and Mary (Dutch influence)	1689–1702	Walnut	Damasks
Queen Anne (Baroque)	1702–1714	Walnut, marquetry	Embroidered velvets
Georgian: George I	1714–1727	Mahogany	Brocade, baize
George II	1727–1760	Mahogany	Soho tapestry
George III	1760–1820	Mahogany, painted woods	Printed Indian chintz
Regency	1811–1820	Satinwood, birch	Spanish leather, Berlin woolwork
George IV	1820–1830	Painted and gilded hardwoods	Hair cloth
William IV	1830–1837	Rosewood, metal	Cross stitch, tent stitch

Designer, Event or Development	Examples in Upholstery
Age of the cabinet maker	Walnut upholstered armchair c.1690 (see page 71, also page 81)
William Kent, architect	Queen Anne side chair c.1715 with loose seat upholstery (see page 90)
Daniel Marot, book of designs	Early wing armchair, Georgian style, c.1730 (see page 97)
Thomas Chippendale French and Chinese influence	Walnut and mahogany side chairs c.1730 (see page 103)
Hepplewhite and Adam Bros. Early stitched and shaped upholstery	Hepplewhite settee, mahogany, c.1770 (see page 111)
Empire and Egyptian influences Horsehair upholstery	Danhauser sofa, Vienna c.1820 (see page 121)
Thomas Hope interiors George Smith	Regency couch c.1830 Bolsters and scrolls (see page 127)
Samuel Pratt invents the coil spring	Library seat, buttoned in hide, c.1835 (see page 133)

Furniture Style and Period		Construction	Fabric Coverings
Victorian	1837–1901	All woods, papier-mâché	Holland linen, calico, velour
Art Nouveau	1890–1901	Ash, beech, bentwood	Leathercloth, wool plush
Edwardian	1901–1910	Steel	Chenille, Morocco (goatskin), moquette
Art Deco	1918–1939	Plywoods, early plastics	Modern tapestry, cut moquette
Modern (George VI, Elizabeth II)	1940–1960	Oak, teak	Moquettes, leathercloth
Pop Art	1960–1970	Glass, steel, moulded plastics	PVC cloths, tweeds, corduroy
Modern (Elizabeth II)	1970–	Steel, hardwoods, board materials	Acrylic velvets, tweeds and prints

Designer, Event or Development	Examples in Upholstery
The Great Exhibition 1851 Treadle sewing machines assist production	Walnut ladies' chair, buttoned, *c.*1860 (see page 146, also page 142) *Chaise-longue*, French cabriole legs, *c.*1850 (see page 155, also pages 163, 171, 183)
Arts and Crafts movement William Morris Paris Exhibition 1900	The Morris chair, adjustable, in oak, *c.*1870 (see page 187, also pages 194, 201, 206)
Eastlake and Pugin criticism of upholstery and chair design	Edwardian suite, carpet panels, *c.*1900 (see page 211, also page 222)
Gimson and Mackintosh Latex foams developed	Tub chair, nailed upholstery *c.*1925 Tube chair *c.*1932 (see page 230, also page 240)
Tension springing Utility furniture Festival of Britain, 1951 Pneumatic tools	Fully sprung arm chair *c.*1940 Wing chair buttoned in moquette *c.*1955 (see page 257, also page 261)
Danish influence KD furniture Oil-based materials	Sacco chair *c.*1960 and all-foam chair (see page 269, also page 276)
Italian influence Flamability legislation	Modern settee and chair *c.*1980 (see page 279)

— *Chapter Three* —
The Workshop

In the upholstery workshop space is always at a premium and most practising upholsterers would agree that they never have enough of it. It is therefore essential that every centimetre of space is used to best advantage.

WORKSHOP PROCESSES

Before examining the demands of space, equipment and safety, let us look at the kind of work that goes on in a typical workshop. Work processes in upholstery will generally fall into the following categories and a workshop should be arranged to cope with these jobs:

1 Stripping.
2 Frame repairs or frame making.
3 Discarding large amounts of old upholstery.
4 Cleaning and carding re-usable materials.
5 Bench work, springing and upholstery construction.
6 Marking out and cutting materials and foams, etc.
7 Measure for, mark out and cut new covers.
8 Machine sewing and making up.
9 Making up new cushion interiors.
10 Button making and cushion filling.
11 Finishing, trimming and cleaning.

Many of these processes are described in detail in later chapters, and this list is intended to indicate some of the many jobs that are undertaken, and to help in the planning of work space and the installation of equipment.

SPACE

It becomes extremely difficult to produce good work in an area that is cramped or cluttered and has poor storage facilities.

Approximately thirty-five square metres is the very minimum floor space for one person to work comfortably. If at all possible, long-term storage of materials and work should be arranged in a first-floor room or a partitioned-off area.

The importance of space in upholstery will become clear if we consider first the essential equipment required and secondly the various jobs that will have to be done in the workshop.

The basic equipment needed is not elaborate or expensive, and can normally be made up by the average woodworker or small company. In fact, it is often necessary to make one's own equipment and jigs because their specialist nature means they are not available commercially.

Good lighting in the form of large windows and fluorescent lighting is the ideal, and should be made a priority when considering a possible workspace. Upholstery work and materials must be inspected continually during the production process, so good lighting, which should if possible come from all sides of the workshop, will help to provide a pleasant atmosphere and ensure good workmanship.

Adequate ventilation is also important. By nature upholstery is dusty work and can be very dirty at times. A workshop should have at least one extractor fan, or several opening windows at various levels will assist air circulation. Although the materials used in modern upholstery construction are plastic based and relatively clean, there is often a strong heady smell when quantities of new foam, fillings and fabrics are stored in a confined space. All upholstery work undertaken will produce dust while it is being stripped and prepared for recovering. Many upholstery fabrics, particularly pile fabrics, give off fibre dust while they are being cut and sewn.

While it is seldom possible to provide absolutely perfect working conditions, as much thought and planning as possible should be given to the setting up of a new workshop or the changing of an existing area. Improvements are always possible, and there is no doubt that adequate space, good lighting and clean air help enormously to create an environment which any craftsman should expect and, in fact, deserves.

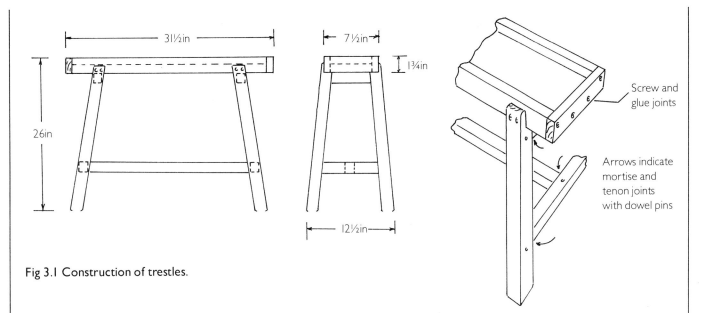

Fig 3.1 Construction of trestles.

EQUIPMENT

Work bench and bench space

There is no better method of supporting pieces of upholstery than a pair of strong, well-made trestles. (Special jigs and fixtures for batch production are dealt with in Chapter 14.) The trestle has been found to be completely versatile – no other method gives such clear access to the work and, at the same time, is adjustable in such a variety of ways. Upholstery work demands all-round access and visibility to a chair or sofa; the trestle support provides this.

Construction of the trestles should be strong and well braced, so that a work piece of any weight or shape is held rigid, but can be rolled over or lowered at any time. Trestles can be made from good-grade softwood or a straight-grained hardwood, e.g. pine or beech. A well should be formed at the top to contain a soft pad and this will stop the work from sliding off. Details of construction are shown in Fig 3.1. Figs 3.2 and 3.3 illustrate some of the ways that the trestle can be used. The experienced upholsterer uses the trestles so that the work is turned or tilted. It is better to move the work often rather than bend awkwardly with poor vision.

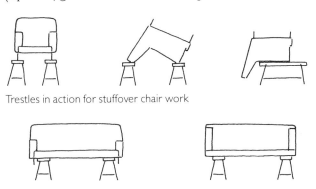

Trestles in action for stuffover chair work

Settees and couches can be heavy and cumbersome

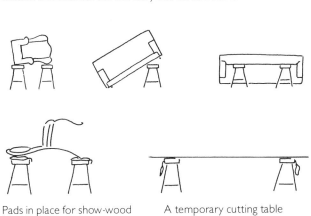

Pads in place for show-wood   A temporary cutting table

Fig 3.2 Using the trestle bench to its best advantage. The work should be moved to give the best and most comfortable working position.

Fig 3.3 Trestles with well pads removed.

Early Oak Chair
c. 1600–40

An oak-framed chair, early seventeenth century. Upholstery of this type had very little stuffing and consisted of handmade coverings supported by two thicknesses of linen or cow hide.

Covering Furnishing embroidery known as 'Turkey work' has been used on this example and was also used to cover tables and floors. The coarse-cut pile was evidently copied from oriental carpets, with similar patterns and motifs. Turkey work had a knotted-wool pile in bright colours on a flax-base cloth.

Bench board

For convenience, when upholstering small items such as loose seats, head boards, and chair components, e.g. wings, KD (knock down) seat frames, etc., a bench board will complement the trestles and allow the upholsterer to sit at the bench, as one would sit at a desk. A useful bench board size is 4ft by 3ft (1m by 1½m). One side of the board should be padded and covered with a strong durable covering, leaving a plywood or hardboard surface on the other. The padding provides a non-slip surface and will deaden noise, besides being kind to show-wood polished surfaces.

To complete the bench equipment a pair of bench blocks will be found useful. These will give support to delicate or long chair rails while tacking, and hold shaped work, especially loose seats and chair backs. The blocks should be padded and covered along their top surfaces. A long, narrow strip of hardwood which can be easily bolted to the surface of a bench board can be used as a stop against which small pieces of work can be pushed during stripping. Bench stops may be

fitted permanently at the edges of the board or made detachable with the use of bolts and wing nuts.

An alternative to the trestle-type bench is the table bench, which is preferred by some upholsterers. The construction is usually of wood and is very similar to a polisher's bench, except that the top is padded to provide the non-slip protective surface. Dimensions are usually about 3ft by 4ft (1m by 1.2m) long and 2ft (0.6m) high. This size will support almost all designs of chair. Settees and sofas will straddle the bench but will need to be moved more often for access to the undersides. Table benches are very rigid and, of course, do not require additional bench boards (see Fig 3.5).

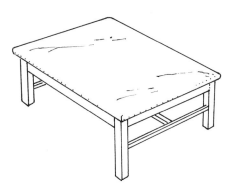

Fig 3.5 The low table bench preferred by some upholsterers, 3ft by 4ft and 2ft high (915mm×1220mm, 610mm).

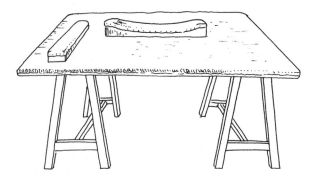

Fig 3.4 The bench set up for small work, and bench blocks ready as needed.

Cutting table

By far the largest piece of equipment in the workshop is the cutting table. The structure and size may vary enormously and will largely depend on the space available and the type of work being done. The table should be of a good weight and have a rigid base or underframe which can be made from metal or timber. The cutting-table surface must be flat, smooth and absolutely square, so that measuring and straight cutting can be taken from the table edge. The most suitable materials for the table top are plywood, blockboard or chipboard, which should be lipped at the edges and have a cutting surface of hardboard, lino or plastic laminate laid over the whole table.

Table-top size should 54–60in (135–150cm) wide to allow for most widths of cover, and at least 8ft (2½m) long. Thickness of the top will depend on the material used but would normally be about 1in (25mm) to give good stability. This size of table will be adequate for the small business. However, cutting tables in larger concerns may be up to 70ft (21m) long, but the width will remain about the same.

The space under the cutting table can be made use of with a shelf fitted above the floor to store linings, hessians and covering fabrics, as well as marking patterns and tools.

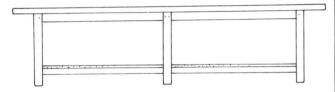

Standard timber frame construction with hardboard or plywood surfaces

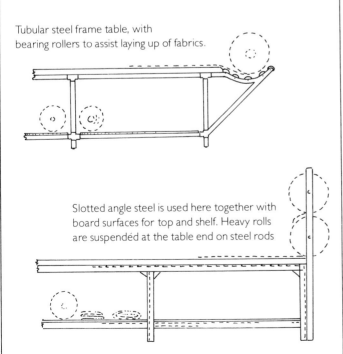

Tubular steel frame table, with bearing rollers to assist laying up of fabrics.

Slotted angle steel is used here together with board surfaces for top and shelf. Heavy rolls are suspended at the table end on steel rods

Fig 3.6 Cutting tables.

The working height of the table is very important as the upholsterer will usually spend some time at the table each day. If set too low, working at the table will be uncomfortable. Also, it is often necessary to be able to reach across the full width during cutting operations. The height should therefore suit the person using the table regularly. A good cutting table has many uses, and if kept clean and clear will be a great asset.

Decisions are often made at the cutting table while studying a drawing, or making a cutting plan. A crucial part of any piece of work is its planning and being able to visualise the construction work during preparation of the materials.

Fig 3.6 shows some of the alternative materials which may be used in the construction of a cutting table – hardwood or steel tube or steel angle. Whichever base is chosen, the table top will be basically the same. Cutting-table accessories are not essential, but certainly help to reduce the effort of lifting and rolling heavy bolts of stock items. Materials which are needed several times a day need not be lifted or moved around unnecessarily if they are stored at the end of the cutting table and suspended on metal rods. The four items most commonly used, particularly in traditional work, are hessian, scrim, calico and a black lining. Platform cloths and polypropylene linings could be included, or stored on the shelf under the cutting table.

A very simple but effective device which helps when heavy bolts of cover or vinyl are being laid out is a pair of slotted wooden blocks. These are triangular in shape and made from 3in (75mm) thick timber. Fig 3.7 illustrates the blocks in use. The blocks depend on the weight of the roll for their stability and are not much use when it has diminished to a few metres.

During the work the upholsterer handles many small items – tools, fixing materials, twines and cords, as well as screws, nails, staples and tacks, etc. Some provision

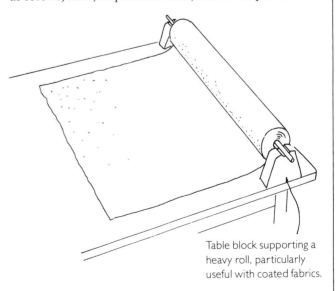

Table block supporting a heavy roll, particularly useful with coated fabrics.

Fig 3.7

must be made to have these all close at hand and clearly visible. A wall space immediately behind the bench is probably the ideal spot, enabling the craftsman to have everything at about chest height just behind him. The stock should be neatly arranged on a pair of deep shelves, or in a purpose-made narrow cupboard or on a table fixed to the wall. This, or a similar arrangement, will save time and the frustration of having to leave the bench space for odd items.

Services to the bench area

Providing power for tools at the bench will, of course, be included in the overall workshop layout. Two different power lines are required; electrical in the form of 13-amp points, and pneumatic for air tools. If possible these should be suspended overhead, one to the right of the bench and one to the left. However, wall-mounted points are equally efficient, but probably a little less safe because of trailing wires and hoses. A hook for each power tool, either overhead or at the wall, will hold them safely and conveniently in place when not in use.

Services to the cutting table are normally only electrical, and for safety reasons should always be overhead – electric cloth-cutters are very sharp and will easily slice through a power cable. The cutting process will extend over a large area of the table and so some form of take-up system for the wiring to the cutters is necessary. This will ensure that lengths of electrical cable do not build up on the cutting area. However, if such a system is not available then the cutter must always be aware of the potential danger.

Gluing foams
If space is available a small area should be kept aside for the gluing of foams, particularly if the glue is to be applied by spray. A small table with standing room for the pressure pot is all that will be needed, and an air-line socket to the power.

Button making
Button-making presses need not take up floor space but can be fixed to any firm surface or may be mounted on a heavy wood base about 2ft by 1ft (60cm by 30cm) and stored under the cutting table until needed.

The main elements are dealt with here, but the setting up and arrangement of any bench area is always a matter of personal preference and will relate to the type of upholstery being done.

A typical workshop layout is shown in Fig 3.8 and includes large items of equipment plus machines. The elevation gives a clearer impression of scale and an upholstery shop generally.

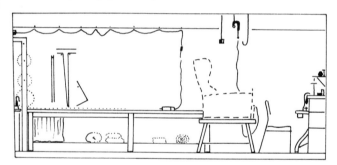

Elevation viewed from the store room.

Fig 3.8 Typical upholstery shop layout.

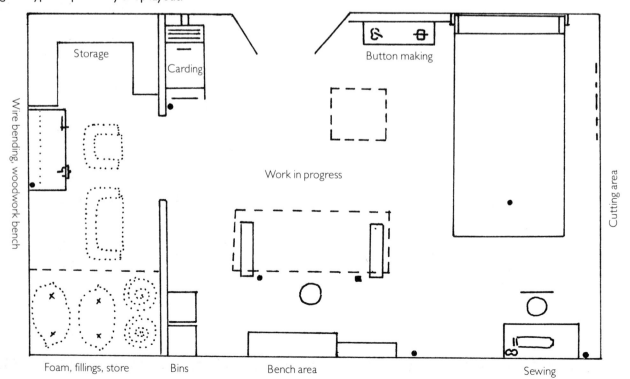

Wire bending, woodwork bench

Storage

Carding

Foam, fillings, store

Bins

Work in progress

Bench area

Button making

Cutting area

Sewing

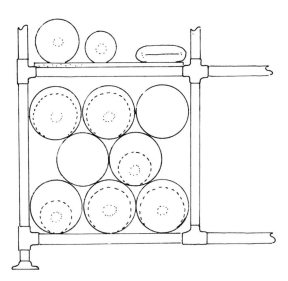

Fig 3.9 Storage rack for upholstery cover. Top: single-layer, free-standing on shelf. Below: rolls housed in large cardboard tubes, which can be stacked to ceiling height.

SAFETY

Safety in the workshop is closely linked to the environment and is generally a matter of common sense. However, safety precautions depend on the size and position of a workshop and especially the number of persons using it or employed there. Details of the Health and Safety at Work Act, 1980, are available from HM Stationery Office or any area Factory Inspectorate.

The following list of safety points is explained in more detail below. It gives the main areas to be considered, but should be expanded or modified to suit particular work spaces for upholstery work.

1 Workshop exits – doorways and windows
2 Clearways and gangways – access and escape
3 Fire-fighting equipment – risks and care
4 Dust and fume extraction
5 First aid
6 Safety apparatus and protective clothing
7 Machines and power tools
8 Facilities and maintenance

Workshop exits or doorways

There should be at least two exits, preferably at opposite ends of the shop. One of these openings should be a double door or a sliding door with a span of 5ft (1½m) minimum. Such a large doorway helps enormously when bringing in or removing pieces of upholstered seating, which at times can be very large.

Clearways

At least one walkway must be kept clear of all materials and work. This is not only a help in the daily running of a workshop, but allows easy escape and access, should that ever be necessary.

Firefighting equipment

Upholstery workshops can be particularly vulnerable to fire risks. This is mainly because of the nature and variety of the materials used. The risk can be minimised easily by good housekeeping, careful storage and having two types of extinguisher available at all

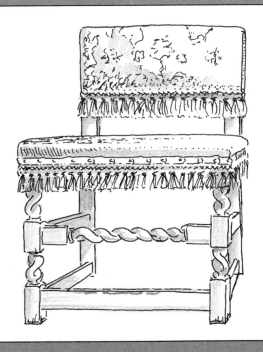

Framed and Turned Chair
c. 1640–60

A broadseated low-back chair, with bobbin and twist turning.

Upholstery Stuffings of wool or tow supported on stretched linen or hide.

Coverings Coarse wool-work tapestry decorated with knotted fringe and handmade braids. Nails were used to fix and decorate.

times in the workshop. A knowledge of how to use them is, of course, essential. Advice is freely available from fire stations.

Dust and fume extraction

An extractor is always worth the initial cost, enabling polluted air to be replaced with fresh. An extractor fan should be fitted close to a carding machine, and where solvents and glues are being used. During the summer months the extractor can also serve to keep temperatures at a pleasant working level.

First aid

Accidents will happen, and although upholstery work does not involve any particularly dangerous processes, any wound, no matter how small, should be dealt with quickly. A box containing basic first-aid equipment should be clearly marked and easily accessible. A sticky plaster applied quickly keeps the wound clean – and may well avoid an expensive piece of fabric being marked.

Safety apparatus and protective clothing

These should be made available in all workshops. The wise craftsman protects his hands by using a stitching glove. Rubber gloves should be worn when glue is being applied in large quantities and barrier creams are a good alternative when a dirtier job has to be done. These assist the easy removal of oil, grease, glue or solvents.

A simple elasticated mask with changeable gauze pads will protect the nose and mouth when very dusty work has to be done. To protect the feet, good shoes should always be worn in any workshop situation. Nails, tacks and metal strips have a nasty habit of sitting on the floor point-uppermost.

The traditional craftsman's apron is, of course, also a form of protective clothing. Made from lightweight canvas or strong calico, its large front pocket provides a convenient place for scissors and hammer, and at the same time protects normal clothing.

Machines and power tools

Upholstery is not a highly mechanised craft, although it is gradually becoming more so. However, the average small workshop will contain only two or three machines, plus hand-power tools for cutting and fixing. As a general rule, moving parts on an industrial machine need to be guarded and the guards painted a bright colour to indicate their function. Some of the old carding machines which are still in use and still give good service are potentially dangerous. These need to be checked and modified, particularly if they are to be motorised.

Most sewing machines are belt-driven from a half-horse-power motor, but do not offer much danger to the operator. Later models of most machines have

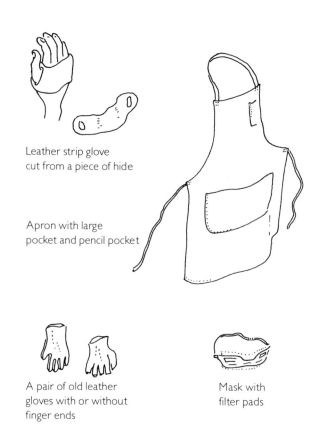

Leather strip glove cut from a piece of hide

Apron with large pocket and pencil pocket

A pair of old leather gloves with or without finger ends

Mask with filter pads

Fig 3.10 Some items of protective clothing.

belt-drive guards. As with all kinds of machines and powered equipment, weekly routine maintenance is the greatest aid to safety. Not only does this prolong the life of any machine, but ensures efficient running and prevents small dangers becoming big ones. Regular maintenance should be carried out in a logical sequence to ensure that nothing is overlooked. The following is a good routine and provides a useful check-list.

1   Remove from power source
2   Check condition of wiring or hose
3   Remove detachable parts, e.g. blades or guards
4   Clean, lubricate and/or sharpen
5   Check levels of lubricants and coolants
6   Reassemble
7   Connect to power and test

Facilities and maintenance

Washing facilities with hot and cold running water are needed if work is to be kept clean. Water can be used to dampen floors before sweeping, or to dampen hides and cane for certain types of work. Generally, the work area should be cleaned down and rubbish removed as often as possible. Upholsterers, by nature, tend to be rather lax in cleaning – they like to hoard and hang on to bits and pieces, a habit that has to be moderated for the sake of cleanliness and safety.

Chapter Four

Tools and Power Tools

The upholsterer's tools range from the most simple and familiar, such as hammers, chisels, scissors and needles, to highly specialised and super-efficient pneumatic and electrical equipment, including staple guns, glue guns, cloth cutters and foam cutters.

HAND TOOLS

The hand tools used by the upholsterer are basically very simple but rather special to the trade. Many are lightweight versions of the cabinet-maker's tools, while others are very similar to those used by the carpet layer and the soft furnisher. Over the past century many have been developed and improved, but in general appearance they all remain basically the same.

The tacking hammer has been the subject of change in that its weight has been increased and the head now has two faces. There are generally three types still available, but the magnetic hammer with two faces is without doubt the most commonly used today. The other two versions are a little lighter and more traditional in their design. A standard tacking hammer has a single face, a claw and a smooth, round handle. Probably the oldest design of these three is the cabriole hammer, which is also used by cabinet makers. It has a fine small face of about 7mm in diameter, and a long pear-shaped handle. A small single-face magnetic hammer may also be found useful. The four types are illustrated in Fig 4.1.

It is not necessary to have all three designs of hammer, but every craftsman tends to make a collection of tools over a period of time. An old hammer is seldom thrown away, and new handles made from hickory or ash can easily be fitted to a favourite head. Owing to the low weight of tacking hammers which are designed especially for upholstery work a heavier medium-sized claw hammer of the kind used by carpenters should be included in the tool kit. This will be needed for frame repairs, wire forming and any heavy work which would put too much strain on the tack hammer.

Upholstery scissors or shears, of which there are several types, must be of high quality and the very best

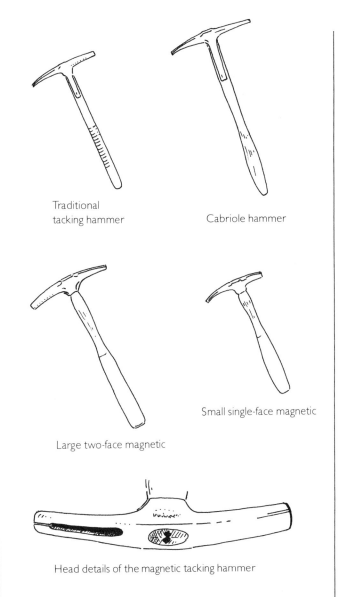

Traditional tacking hammer

Cabriole hammer

Large two-face magnetic

Small single-face magnetic

Head details of the magnetic tacking hammer

Fig 4.1 Tacking hammers.

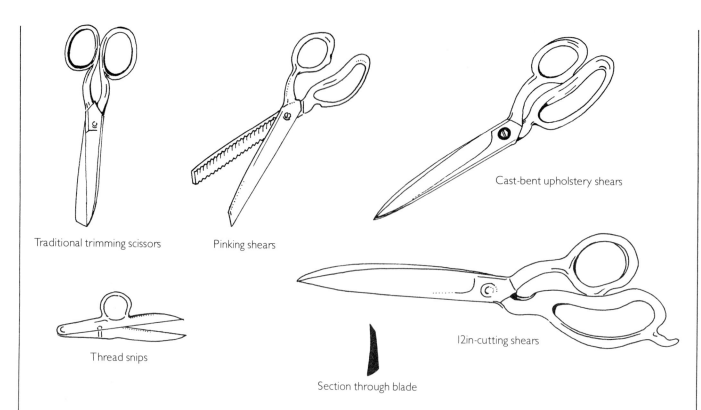

Traditional trimming scissors

Pinking shears

Cast-bent upholstery shears

Thread snips

12in-cutting shears

Section through blade

Fig 4.2 Scissors and shears.

that can be afforded (Fig 4.2). It certainly pays to look around carefully at all the makes and types available, and to try them before buying. As the busy upholsterer will be trimming and cutting all kinds of material for a very large percentage of the workshop time, it is essential that the scissors used at the bench and at the cutting table are always in good condition and kept sharp.

For upholstery work a minimum length of 8in (200mm) for trimming scissors is usual. The traditional design is flat and straight, with a blunt end filed smooth and used for tucking away fabric between chair rails and into corners. If maintained and kept sharp, a pair of these scissors will last many years. The cast-bent shear has proved more popular, almost certainly due to the fact that its comfortable shape and long blade make it easier to work and handle for long periods. These shears have a large and small hand grip, which has

Cromwellian Chair
c. *1650*

Oak frame with bobbin turning.

Upholstery Stout leather covering directly over the framework and the leather held on with large and small brass-headed nails. Cow and ox hide up to $3/16$in (4mm) thick lasted many years, and often as long as the chair itself.

angled edges fitting snugly over the fingers and the base of the thumb. Shear lengths range from 8in (200mm) up to 14in (355mm). A pair of 12-inch (305mm) cutting shears is ideal for cover cutting at the table and may also be used comfortably at the bench.

Modern synthetic fabrics can be extremely tough and do demand a keen edge to the blades. The blade tips particularly must be kept sharp, so that the cutting stroke is the full length of the blade, and trimming away excess after tacking is quick and easy.

Re-grinding should normally be left to an expert, but maintaining an edge to the blades can be done with care, using a fine flat file or stone. Care should be taken to keep the angle of the cutting edge intact. A spot of oil occasionally at the bolt and a smear of oil along the blades is the only lubrication needed.

A good pair of 8-inch or 10-inch scissors can be kept for trimming and miscellaneous cutting of various materials such as rubberised hair, waddings, thin foam, etc., and a pair of 12-inch cutting shears for cover cutting.

Pinking shears and thread snips are of a more specialist nature. A pair of pinking shears is useful for the cutting of fine fabrics and for those types of cloth most likely to fray easily. The blades are serrated and make a zig-zag cut, leaving the edge reasonably clean and less susceptible to fraying. A pair of thread snips is a tool used by the sewing machinist. It is lightweight and usually sprung, so that the blades are held open in readiness to trim thread or snip seams when necessary. The snips are often hung on a lace around the machinist's neck, or tucked into a pocket situated on the machine head. They are obviously much easier to handle at speed during sewing operations than a standard pair of shears. Fig 4.2 shows five types and a sectional view of the cutting blade.

The web strainer or stretcher (Fig 4.3) has not changed in its design or shape since it was first made by early upholsterers. No other tool is quite so simple and yet so effective. The business of fixing and straining webbings is a skill which must be learnt and perfected as early as possible by those entering the trade.

Webbed bases provide the foundation for both traditional and modern work. Good quality beech, which has a close, straight grain with a natural resilience, is the accepted hardwood for web strainers. The timber should be between ⅝in and ¾in (18mm and 25mm) thick, and the dowel peg a diameter of ⅝in (18mm). Most upholsterers use the standard slot-and-dowel type of strainer, but with a little practice the other simpler types are equally effective. In emergency a short wood batten about 3in (80mm) wide will do the job quite well.

The spiked type of strainer is probably the least popular, because of the damage that can be caused to the webbing itself during straining. This strainer is not suitable for pulling the woven polypropylene webbings used in modern production.

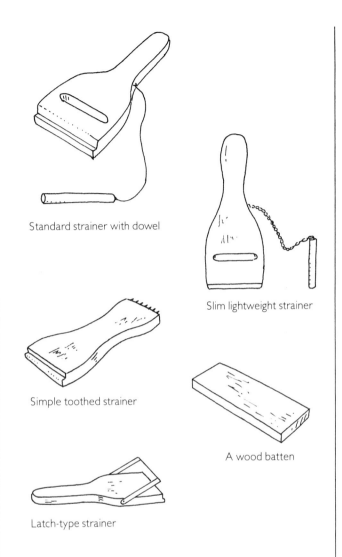

Standard strainer with dowel

Slim lightweight strainer

Simple toothed strainer

A wood batten

Latch-type strainer

Fig 4.3 Wooden web strainers, best made from beech.

A pair of metal strainers, often called iron hands, with jaw widths of 2in (50mm) and 1in (25mm), are useful as a general straining or stretching tool. As they depend on the strength of the user's hand, they are limited for webbing applications, but they are often needed in hide work, and for tightening heavy canvasses and sewn welts, etc. – in fact, in any situation where a cover requires a heavy pull beyond normal tightness. Although expensive, the purchase of a pair of metal strainers will soon be justified, and they should be included in the tool kit as soon as possible (Fig 4.4).

The ripping chisel, or ripper (Fig 4.5), is designed specifically for the fast easy removal of tacks and staples. It should be struck with the wooden mallet, and not with the tacking hammer. The most effective type of ripper, and the kind most used by the professional, is straight bladed. This is a very strong tool with a heavy blade and a built-in shock absorber set in front of the brass ring where the blade is joined to the handle. Hickory and boxwood are used for the turned wood handle and will give good service if used

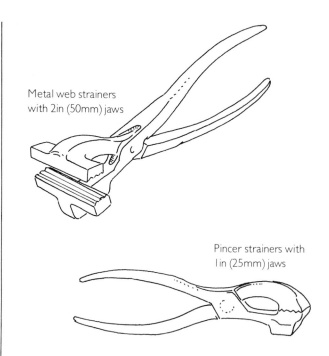

Metal web strainers
with 2in (50mm) jaws

Pincer strainers with
1in (25mm) jaws

Fig 4.4

with respect. The tip of the ripping-chisel blade is ground flat to a near-sharp chisel point. This will require grinding after long periods of heavy use, so that the tack heads and staples can be lifted easily with a sharp tap from the mallet.

Two other types of ripper or tack lifter are available. The cranked-blade chisel usually has a pear-shaped handle and a bevelled tip, and the split-point tack lifter is designed for removing tacks at a more gentle pace. There are occasions when all three types have their advantages. For example, when stripping close to show wood in a rebate, the cranked type will provide better leverage and help to avoid unnecessary splitting at show-wood edges.

Heavy wooden mallets of the type employed by carpenters are not easy to use and will be found too cumbersome. The smaller lightweight versions, either round or square headed are ideal and are easily handled for long periods. Stripping of upholstery work, often done many times before, can be very tiring and hard on the wrists and hands so the tools should be as light as possible and the blades always good. Upholsterers' mallets are almost always made from good-grade beech, with chamfered edges and, most important, a comfortable handle. It is a habit of many craftsmen to cover one face of the mallet head with a piece of hide, which will preserve the face and reduce noise (Fig 4.5).

A selection of trimming and cutting knives will be found in any upholsterer's tool kit. Some have fixed blades which need to be regularly sharpened. Those with removable or retractable blades may be sharpened on an oil stone or the blades replaced when necessary. Whichever type is preferred, the tip of the blade will be

used more than the rest of the blade and so will require constant attention. Although scissors are used regularly for the trimming of fabrics, when hide or vinyl-coated fabrics are being used the knife is more effective. This is particularly so when a clean, straight cut is required or an edge is to be thinned or skived. A hide-skiving knife has a curved bevelled edge on a strong, rigid blade. A sharp knife is invaluable when upholstery is being stripped from an old frame and will often save unnecessary strain on scissors. Fig 4.6 shows a typical range of knives for trimming and skiving.

Now that the staple has become the common fixing medium for upholstery materials, a variety of staple-lifting tools is available. These are mostly produced by the staple-manufacturing companies, who have developed the lifters to assist the users of their products. However, because the holding properties of most frame-making hardwoods are so good, it is extremely difficult to lift and remove a $\frac{3}{8}$in (10mm) staple completely without breaking it. If a staple lifter is used, a pair of small pincers will be needed to lift the bits of staple left in the rails. Those stubborn bits which break off low to the surface should be hammered back in. Fig 4.7 shows some of the staple lifters available, all of which depend on the user's ability to dig the tool into the rail and under the staple crown.

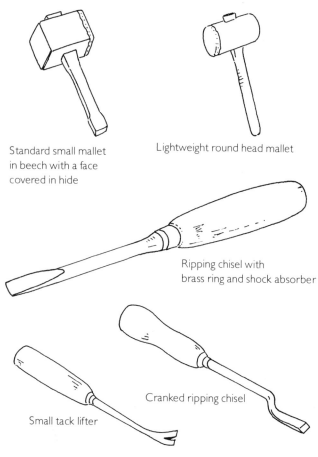

Standard small mallet
in beech with a face
covered in hide

Lightweight round head mallet

Ripping chisel with
brass ring and shock absorber

Cranked ripping chisel

Small tack lifter

Fig 4.5

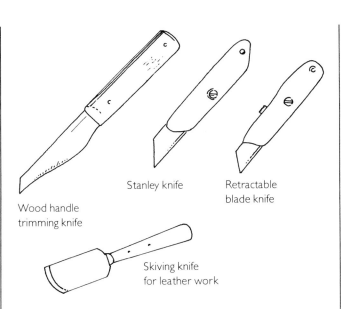

Wood handle
trimming knife

Stanley knife

Retractable
blade knife

Skiving knife
for leather work

Fig 4.6

Most upholsterers would agree that they simply do not
have time to remove all the staples in a chair one by
one, so in practice covers are ripped off using the ripper
and the lifter and then cleaned up and odd bits
removed as quickly as possible.

A range of nine upholstery needles of various types
and sizes provides the basic stitching and sewing
equipment. Additional needles can be added if and
when the variety of work undertaken demands a
greater range of sizes. The use of twine and thread to
join and fix upholstery materials and to form stuffed
shapes applies mainly to traditional upholstery. In
modern production work, such needles will only be
needed for buttoning and the occasional small amount
of slip stitching.

Three straight needles are illustrated in Fig 4.8,
beginning with the 12in (305mm) two-point bayonet
needle, 12- or 19-gauge designed for edge stitching. A
shorter round-point, double-ended needle 10in

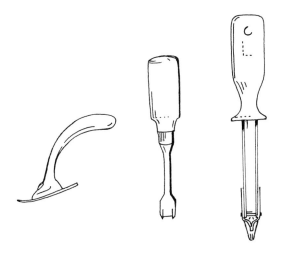

Fig 4.7 Three different types of staple lifters.

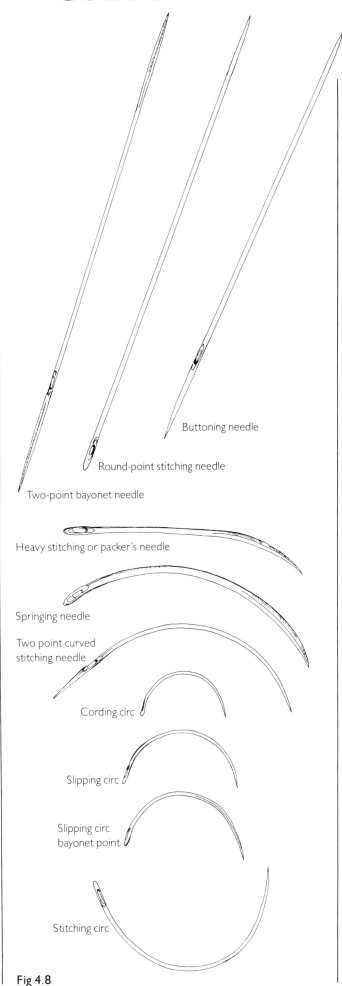

Buttoning needle

Round-point stitching needle

Two-point bayonet needle

Heavy stitching or packer's needle

Springing needle

Two point curved
stitching needle

Cording circ

Slipping circ

Slipping circ
bayonet point

Stitching circ

Fig 4.8

Farthingale Chair
c. 1650

The oak-upholstered farthingale chair became popular during the first half of the seventeenth century, and was later produced in pairs or sets. Sunken seats presupposed the use of a stuffed cushion. Height of the seat and back was varied to suit ladies' and gentlemen's sitting habits and clothing.

Upholstery Lightly stuffed seat and back, occasionally with loose seat cushion. Many were simply upholstered with thick hide for institutional use.

Coverings Tapestry or coarse wool work over leather. Trimmings and lines of nails were used to fix and decorate.

(255mm) by 13-gauge is used for small stitched edges and scroll work.

The buttoning needle has a single round point and a large eye. It may be necessary to use a bayonet point for buttoning if particularly dense fillings or foams prove difficult. Curved and circular needles, as in Fig 4.8, are peculiar to the upholstery trade.

The length of a curved needle is measured around the curve and the gauge is the standard wire gauge (SWG) number indicating the thickness of the wire used to make the needle. The two heavy 8- or 10-gauge needles with four-sided bayonet points are springing needles. Their length is 5in (125mm) and they are used to sew in and fix springs and spring wires.

The half-round, two-point needle is excellent for edge stitching, close up to a show-wood rail, when a straight needle could only be used with great difficulty. This is normally 12 gauge and 5 to 6in (125–150mm). The three rounded-point circular needles each have a different job. The longer 6in (150mm) 16-gauge is used with twine to produce stuffing ties and join hessian and scrims. The 3in (75mm) 18-gauge needle is a 'slipping circ' used with slipping thread to close upholstery covers on chair outsides and cushions, etc. The smallest of the three needles is a 'cording circ' and is used with strong thread to sew in cords and trimmings. Cording circs are usually 2½in (63mm) 18-gauge.

A 10in (255mm) regulator is used to regulate and adjust fillings and manipulate covers. In fact, this tool has many uses, particularly in stitched edge work. Sizes range from 8in (200mm) to 13in (330mm) and the smaller 8in size should be kept for small lighter work.

The wooden dolly stick made from a length of beech is used to help fold and pleat fabrics and leather. The smooth, round point and flat spade-shaped end will be found generally kinder to materials than a steel tool. The stick is 7in (175mm) to 8in (200mm) long.

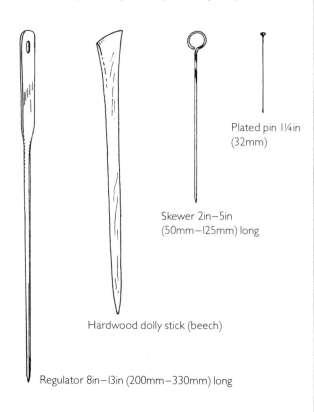

Plated pin 1¼in (32mm)

Skewer 2in–5in (50mm–125mm) long

Hardwood dolly stick (beech)

Regulator 8in–13in (200mm–330mm) long

Fig 4.9

Skewers and pins have obvious uses as holding tools where temporary fixing of materials is needed prior to sewing or stitching (Fig 4.9). Pins are 1¼in (32mm) plated and skewers are normally 3in (75mm) or 4in (100mm).

A medium-sized rasp with a 10in (255mm) blade (Fig 4.10) is an essential wood-working tool for the upholsterer. Sharp edges on timber rails must be removed before upholstery begins, particularly on inside edges before webbings are applied. A well-rasped edge forming a chamfer is needed where scrim is to be turned in and tacked before making a stitched edge. (The rasp cuts only on the forward-pushing stroke and not when it is being drawn back.)

A pair of pincers is the standard tool for gripping and removing nails, pins and staple ends. It may also be used to cut soft wire and to lever out small nails of all kinds using the claw at the end of the hand grip.

Two tube-shaped hole cutters are also illustrated in Fig 4.10 and are used to punch or drill polyurethane foams in preparation for buttoning. One is simply a short length of 1in to 1¼in (25–32mm) steel tube which has been sharpened to a cutting edge at one end. This can be pushed into the foam by hand or hammered, depending on the thickness and density of the foam. The other type is designed for fitting to a power drill and is useful if a lot of foam drilling is done regularly. The power cutter is ground and sharpened from the inside, and has two holes drilled at the top end of the tube to allow air flow, and assist removal of the cut foam.

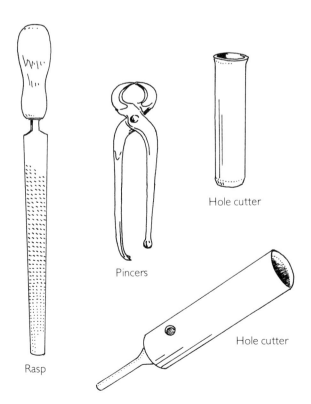

Hole cutter

Hole cutter

Pincers

Rasp

Fig 4.10

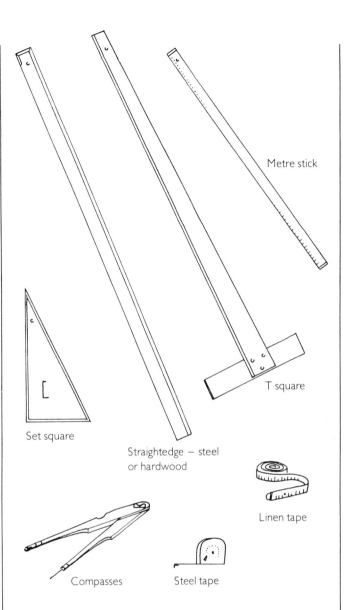

Metre stick

T square

Set square

Straightedge – steel or hardwood

Linen tape

Compasses

Steel tape

Fig 4.11

Tools and equipment for measuring and marking out materials (Fig 4.11) must be accurate and kept in good condition. They can be housed by hanging from hooks in a convenient place close to the cutting table. The metre stick is marked in metric measurements on one side and imperial on the other. It is the tool most used at the cutting table. This is complemented by the T-square and a long straightedge. The T-square is used for marking across the width of the cutting table and will give accurate lines at 90° to the table edge. A straightedge of up to 6ft (2m) in length can be used for marking along the length of the roll or cutting table. A good example is the marking of piping strips which may be straight or bias cut.

A large set square made from plywood, usually at 60°, can be used with the T-square and provides a check for squareness at any time. A large pair of compasses should be included in the range of tools.

Two types of flexible measuring tape, one steel and

one linen, at least 4ft (1.5m) long, are necessary for taking measurements from chairs etc.

The following is a list of marking tools which are suitable for the various surfaces which will be encountered.

1   Tailor's crayon – most fabrics
2   White stick chalk – vinyls, hides
3   Soft pencil (4B) – hides and linings
4   Felt pen – foams
5   French dusting chalk – Kraft paper stencils

Flutes and channels in upholstered chair backs were traditionally hand-formed by stitching fabric down on to a base cloth or scrim in straight and curved lines. The section between the rows of stitching was then filled to form the flute before the next row of stitching was made.

Using a fluting stick or tube (Fig 4.12), a complete panel can be machine sewn to a pre-marked cloth base and then filled afterwards. The tube or stick both work in the same way; they are simply a means of inserting a length of thick filling such as cotton felt, curled hair and wadding or a strip of foam wrapped in polyester into each separate flute. The length of filling is laid on to the stick, the cloth strip pulled tightly down in the form of a sandwich and simply inserted into the open

tube. The tool and the filling is then carefully pushed into the whole length of the flute and the tool removed leaving the filling neatly in place.

The fluting stick is the more versatile of the two types because several widths of stick can be made from ¼ in (6mm) plywood and a matching strip of vinyl cloth fixed at one end very cheaply. The ply strip must be well rounded at its edges and sanded to a fine, smooth finish. This ensures that the stick will slide easily into the flutes, and can be removed without disturbing the fillings. The width of the tool should be approximately ⅜ in (10mm) less than the flute or channel to be filled. A set of fluting sticks of various widths can be kept and used or modified as and when they are needed. If the sticks are made at one metre lengths this will be long enough to deal with any normal-sized panels. Curved sticks to suit curved flutes are made and used in the same way.

The cutting and bending of spring wire is all part of the springing process. With the right tools, shown in Fig 4.13, springs and spring units can be modified and adjusted to fit particular frame types. Edge wires for traditional and modern work can be cut and formed to suit a variety of spring edges and applications. The simplest and quickest way to cut wire of any type is

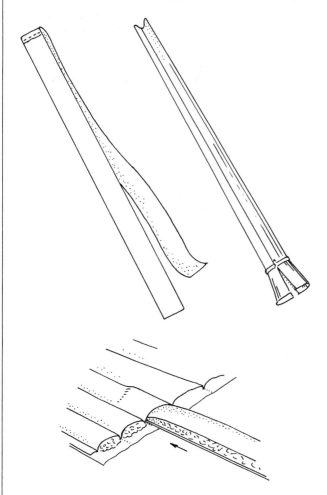

Fig 4.12 Fluting stick and tube.

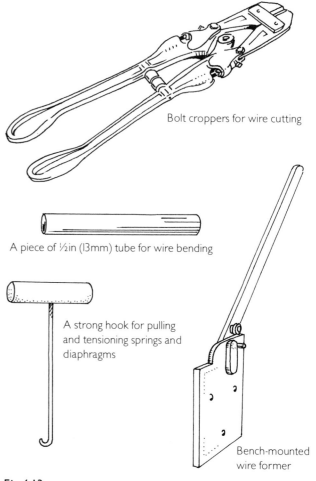

Bolt croppers for wire cutting

A piece of ½in (13mm) tube for wire bending

A strong hook for pulling and tensioning springs and diaphragms

Bench-mounted wire former

Fig 4.13

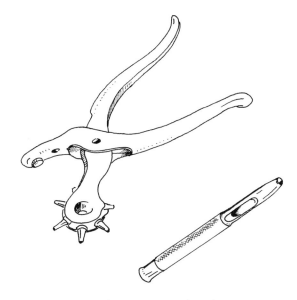

Fig 4.14 Hole punches, six-way and single.

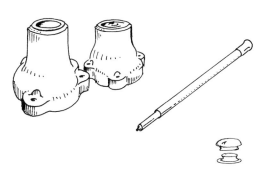

Fig 4.15 Press-stud dies and punch.

with a pair of bolt croppers. These can be adjusted for jaw opening to deal with all gauges of wire, and make the cutting of high-carbon wires a quick and easy business.

A short length of ½in (13mm) steel tube makes the bending of wire reasonably easy. The tube is simply slid along the wire to a point where the wire is to be bent, and then by levering with the hands a right-angle or radius can be formed. A bench vice will also do the job of holding the wire while a bend is formed, particularly when opposing angles are required.

If necessary, the bench-mounted wire former is a device worth having. This works on a similar levering principle, while the wire is held between the metal stud and a small curved former.

A strong wire hook (Fig 4.13) fixed to a wood handle is an extremely useful pulling tool, and can be easily made. The length of the wire hook will depend on the needs of the individual, but between 6in and 10in (150mm–250mm) is usual. The hook will assist with the stretching and insertion of tension springs, rubber platforms and spring units.

Of the variety of hole punches available, the adjustable six-way type is invaluable (Fig 4.14). This will cut neat holes from about ¹⁄₃₂in (1.5mm) up to ¼in (6mm) in diameter in leather, plastics, fabrics, etc. However, there are occasions when a single punch will be needed for cutting holes in the centre of patterns, templates or covers, or when making up a Kraft paper stencil for repetition cutting of covers. Two or three sizes between ⅛in (3mm) and ⅜in (10mm) will be found adequate.

Fig 4.15 shows a typical set of stud dies with a punch for fitting press-stud fasteners to tapes, cushions and detachable upholstery components. The dies may be kept loose in a box or screwed down on to a board. The press fastener has many uses and provides a good detachable fixing between fabrics and leathers and on to timber and metal frames. Press studs are produced in four parts, two to form the top and two to form the base. These have to be punched together to fix them permanently to the covers being used.

The springing balance (Fig 4.16) can be kept handy for checking and weighing fillings of all types, both traditional and modern. To determine how much loose filling has been used in a particular job, a bag or sack of filling whose weight is known can be re-weighed at the end of the job. This gives an indication of the amount of filling used and also provides a form of stock control. Bags of new filling can also be checked for accuracy, and the density of polyurethane foam can be checked by weighing sample pieces and calculating the weight per cubic metre. It is also useful to know how much a

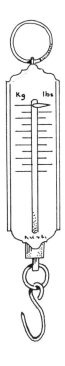

Fig 4.16 Spring balance to weigh out fillings.

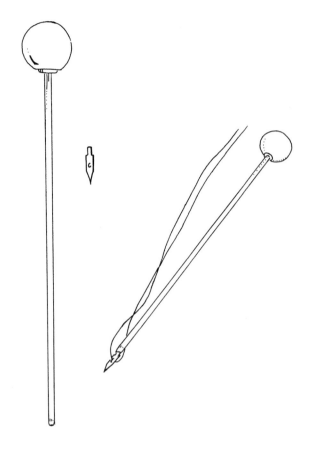

Fig 4.17 Buttoning tool.

particular cushion weighs after it has been filled with feather and down, or kapok, etc. The weights and dimensions of the cushions can be noted and such information used in the future. The weight of the filling may also be needed for costing. The spring balance should give kilogrammes and pounds so that comparisons can be made when necessary.

The buttoning tool (Fig 4.17) is especially designed for replacing upholstery buttons of all types that have come loose or broken out. The loose dart forms an anchor inside the upholstered chair and a button can be retied on to the twine using a slip knot. There are also many instances when this method of button fixing can be used on new work.

POWER TOOLS

A large number of pneumatic and electric power tools is available to the upholsterer. All these assist in the production of upholstery and make the processing of materials much quicker and more efficient. In most cases some power tools are essential, particularly in modern work where foams are being shaped and cut, and materials fixed to boards and to frames.

In the large workshop and the factory, powered hand tools have almost completely replaced the traditional hand tools. For instance, the staple gun (Fig 4.18) is a

very fast and efficient fastener and is a cleaner and less fatiguing tool to use than a hammer and tacks. Fabric cutting is another example where a powered cutter helps to speed up what can be a lengthy operation. The bulk cutting of fabrics and linings is also possible where production demands large amounts of cut parts.

In the small business, a combination of the use of small hand tools and power tools provides the best of both worlds. The upholsterer who works on their own will only purchase expensive power tools where they feel that there is a definite advantage. Initially all these will almost certainly be electric. The decision to install an air compressor and use air-powered tools will depend on the amount and type of work being undertaken. Some craftsmen prefer to specialise in traditional work and stick rigidly to the hand methods associated with this type of upholstery. However, the majority of upholsterers, for obvious reasons, take on all types of work, including some loosecover and curtain making, and power tools can be a great asset in these situations.

Staple guns
The electric staple gun works off the normal 220–240v 13-amp supply. This, of course, makes it very mobile, and its use is not confined to the workshop. The firing mechanism is electro-magnetic which tends to make

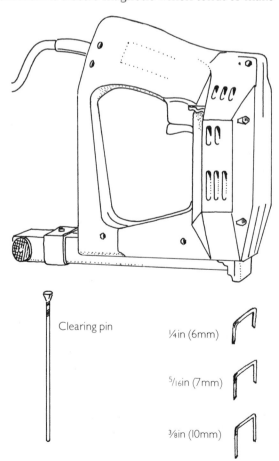

Clearing pin

¼in (6mm)

⁵/₁₆in (7mm)

³/₈in (10mm)

Fig 4.18 Electric staple gun.

the tool relatively heavy and rather cumbersome. However, its firing power is good, provided that the tool is held firmly against the work being fixed. On many models the nose length is rather short and can limit its use in confined spaces, which is often the case on many chair frames. The electric gun has been designed for all kinds of fixing jobs and not specifically for upholstery, so its potential as an upholstery tool must be seen only in general terms.

As with most staple guns, the particular staples recommended for the gun should be adhered to and are not generally interchangeable. The gauge of wire used and the crown width will vary from one make to another. Length of staple leg ranges from ¼in (6mm) up to ⅜in (10mm), which is adequate for most upholstery work.

Most staple guns are bottom loading, which means that the gun must be turned upside down and the magazine slid open for reloading. If jamming occurs, clearing the bent or broken staples should be fairly simple. A clearing pin is supplied with some makes of gun and this can be used if the driver or plunger ever becomes jammed by a broken or bent staple.

The maintenance and safe working of the electric gun is important and is normally a matter of keeping the gun and its wiring clean and in good condition. The driver or hammer may occasionally become burred at the end, and this can be lightly filed so that its return is not impeded. The model illustrated in Fig 4.18 is the Rapid 137b which is provided with two useful features. A safety catch located above the trigger makes the gun safe when not in use and prevents accidental firing. An impact pressure regulator allows a variable pressure at the driver when stapling with short staples or into soft materials. A high-impact pressure should not be used unnecessarily.

General maintenance includes the following:

1 Clean the magazine with a brush or compressed air
2 Protect the gun from damp conditions
3 Lubricate the catch mechanism with a drop of oil from time to time
4 A full service should be carried out by an authorised dealer

The pneumatic stapling gun (Fig 4.19) is a compact and lightweight machine designed specifically for upholstery applications. It is the smallest of a large range of industrial air fasteners, all of which have applications in the furniture industry. The air tacker, as it is sometimes called, requires a miminun air pressure of 70psi (4.9–7.0kg/cm²). Most compressed-air systems provide a constant controlled air flow of around 80psi to 100psi.

Fig 4.19 shows the Senco Model J gun which is typical of the types used for upholstery and allied trades.

Pre-formed lengths of staples are bottom-loaded into the magazine at the base of the gun, and this

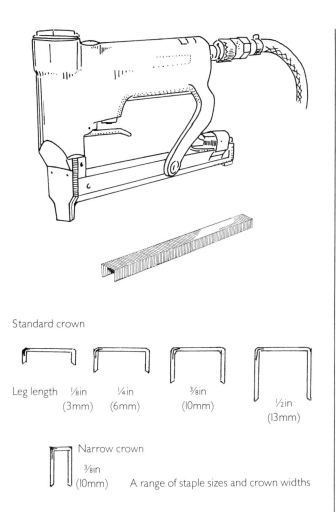

Fig 4.19 Pneumatic staple gun.

bottom-loading function gives easy access to the driver shaft for clearing and cleaning. Variations of the basic gun are available, which provide for specific operations such as repeater firing of staples for long lengths of open work; narrow-crown models fire staples which are coloured along their top surfaces, commonly called 'gimp staples' and used where less visible fixings are required. Long leg lengths of 13mm and above are often required where heavy fixings are needed into soft woods or badly worn chair rails, etc.

The firing action of the air gun is very light and fast compared with the electric types, mainly because of the simplicity of its action and its high power for weight ratio. Staple lengths for the air gun range from as low as ⅛in (3mm) up to ½in (13mm) which will cover almost all possible upholstery requirements, including the fixing of lightweight board materials and minor repairs to frames.

Regular maintenance is essential with all air tools and consists mainly of cleaning and correct lubrication. Detailed servicing and the replacement of worn parts should be carried out by an authorised dealer. However, tool faults and the probable causes can normally be

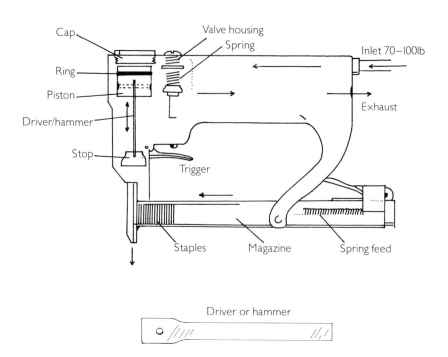

Fig 4.20 An inside view of the staple gun showing the principal parts and workings.

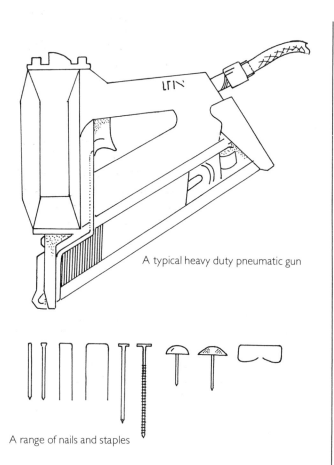

A typical heavy duty pneumatic gun

A range of nails and staples

Fig 4.21

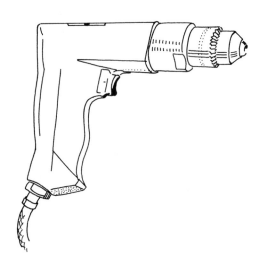

Fig 4.22 Pneumatic power drill.

dealt with by running through a check list supplied by the manufacturer. Remember that, before any repair is attempted, the tool must be disconnected from the power source.

Technical specifications and parts lists are usually supplied with each tool for the help and guidance of the user. Preventative maintenance is always the best way of ensuring that a gun gives long, uninterrupted service.

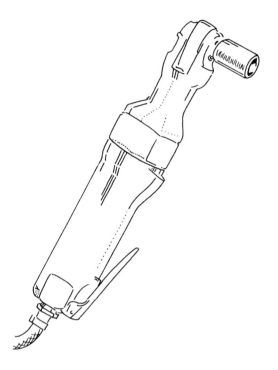

Fig 4.23 Pneumatic spanner/wrench.

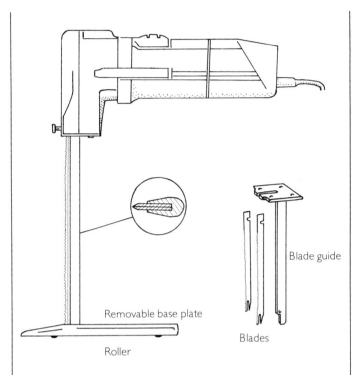

Fig 4.24 Electric foam cutter.

Foam cutters

The Bosch 1575 insulated foam cutter is a versatile twin bladed tool which is capable of cutting and shaping upholstery foams and rubberised hair fillings to a depth of 12in (300mm). The cutter can be used with or without a footplate. The large footplate with rollers allows comfortable handling and correct guidance of the saw. For cutting complicated shapes it is advisable to work without the footplate. The tool is normally used freehand, but can be mounted under a table surface with the blade protruding up through a hole cut in the surface. In this way long straight cuts or angle cuts can be achieved at set dimensions using an adjustable guide or fence.

For general foam cutting, shaping, chamfering etc. simple jigs formed with straight edges and pieces of timber can provide a variety of accurately cut foam parts.

The cutters work off a normal 220–240v 13-amp power supply, or 70–100 psi air lines. Blade lengths available are 2¾in, 5⅛in, 8in and 12in (70mm, 130mm, 200mm and 305mm).

Fig 4.24, shows the electric cutter with a medium size blade and the foot plate fitted. The sectional detail of the two blades shows their correct assembly in the blade guide. The cutting action is a reciprocating motion, controlled by the blade guide stud and run from the gear box above.

Maintenance

The slots for cooling air should be kept free and clear. Damaged cables and plugs should be renewed immediately. It is good practice to clean the saw blade and guide after every ten operating hours. The saw blades can be cleaned with petrol and the guide with a scraper.

Lubrication

The tool should be regreased after every second brush change by an authorised dealer. Saw blades can be sharpened using the recommended blade holder which holds the blades in pairs, while light sharpening of the chamfered face of the tooth setting is carried out with a sharpening stone. A few even strokes over each blade are all that is necessary (Fig 4.25).

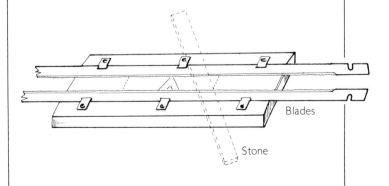

Fig 4.25 Blade holder for sharpening.

Electric hot melt glue gun

This tool is a small lightweight adhesive applicator which has proved to be very useful for upholstery purposes. The heating element liquefies a solid glue stick. This is pushed manually as glue is needed. The gun works off a normal 13-amp electrical supply and is ready for use after a short warming-up period of about seven minutes. Almost any materials in common use (excluding styrenes) may be bonded together using the correct adhesive. The melted adhesive in the pistol is applied to the surfaces to be joined through the nozzle which has a diameter of one millimetre.

The surfaces must be free from grease, dust and damp. Molten glue should be applied in spots or lines and the two surfaces pressed together immediately. The adhesives are odourless, thermoplastic and can be worked at temperatures between 180°C and 230°C.

The glue gun requires no maintenance. If necessary the applicator nozzle can be unscrewed provided that the gun is at operating temperature.

Safety checks should be made regularly for damaged or worn wiring. Only the recommended glue sticks and spares should be used. Touching the hot glue nozzle or molten glue can cause skin burns. Keep easily combustible or heat sensitive materials away from the vicinity of the hot nozzle.

Four types of glue stick are available for use with the gun and should be selected for the particular application. Exposure time or open joint time is 20–60 seconds only, therefore preparation of the materials to be bonded must be done before the glue is applied so that the bond can be made quickly.

Some typical uses in upholstery are: fabric to fabric, e.g. braids, gimps, fringes etc. Fabric to timber and

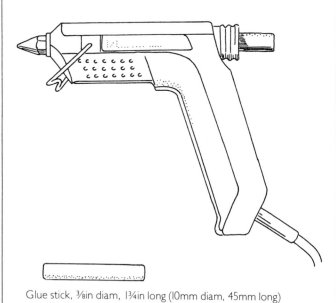

Glue stick, ⅜in diam, 1¾in long (10mm diam, 45mm long)

Fig 4.26 Hot melt glue gun.

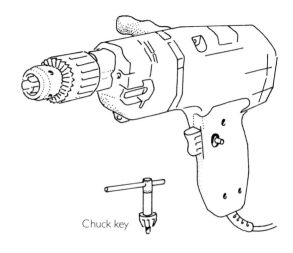

Extension cable 240 volts, 13 amp

Fig 4.27 Electric power drill.

fabric to metal. Cardboard and millboard to wood frames, and some frame repairs. Fig 4.26 shows the Bosch model PKP 15 E.

Electric drill

An electric drill, with the enormous variety of accessories and fittings available, is probably the most popular and most used power tool in any craft workshop. In different weights and types, it has a use in most industrial applications. The upholsterer will use the standard small version, with two speeds and a ⅜in (10mm) chuck size. This can be comfortably held in one hand for a variety of drilling operations in wood and metal. Frame repairs and frame alterations, mainly in wood, using drills for screws and dowels, are the most common uses.

Electric power drills work off the 13-amp domestic supply. Maintenance and safe working are closely linked to each other. If the tool and its wiring are kept clean and in good condition then it will give long and trouble-free service. The chuck mechanism needs a spot of oil at weekly intervals and the air cooling vents must be kept clean and clear at all times. Major servicing and the renewal of motor brushes should be entrusted to an authorised dealer. Fig 4.27 illustrates a typical Black and Decker two speed power drill with chuck key.

Low-pressure adhesive spray gun

Applying glue to foams, frames and fabrics is carried out by brush or scraper if only small amounts are needed. However, where an upholstery business intends to undertake modern work, either new or as reupholstery, then a small pressure pot and a spray gun are well worth the investment. The saving in time and adhesive costs are very high, particularly if an air power supply already exists.

Application of the synthetic contact adhesive is very fast, direct, and bonding is instantaneous. The small spray gun shown in Fig 4.28 is part of the Dunlop low pressure 'easy spray' system. The system includes a pressure pot which takes one five litre can of adhesive, the gun and all necessary hoses and fittings. Pressure in the pot is only 20–30psi and pressure at the gun 5–10psi, all of which are controlled by built-in valves and regulators. The only other equipment required is a bench or table and a wall-mounted air socket close by. Using the spray system, one five litre can of adhesive will give an average coverage of 600-plus square feet. This can be compared with approximately 200 square feet of coverage with glue applied by hand, again using five litres of adhesive.

The gun is held at a distance of about 8in to 12in (200mm–300mm) from the work. Adjustments at the gun are the spray fan or spray design ¼in to 2in (6mm–50mm) and the flow of fluid.

Cleaning and maintenance are obviously of prime importance. Regular daily cleaning with recommended solvent cleaner after use will keep the air cap and fluid tip clear of glue build-up. Two or three spots of a light oil applied by removing the fluid cap will keep the needle moving freely.

Periodic maintenance of the whole gun requires a complete strip-down, cleaning of all moving parts, and renewal of the needle packing. This will ensure trouble-free running and will prevent adhesive creeping along the fluid needle to the air intake and trigger-control mechanisms, Fig 4.29. Safety is again important, and regular checks should be made on the whole system and simple safe working rules applied:

- Storage of solvents and glues should be in a metal cupboard kept at a temperature of 5–10°C.
- Protect the hands and face from glue and strong solvents by using barrier creams and wearing protective gloves and a face mask where necessary.
- Check pressure pot condition and ensure that pressure gauges and safety valve function properly.
- Check that any pressure in the container has been relieved before attempting to remove the container lid.

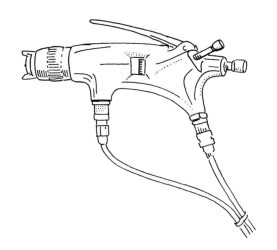

Fig 4.28 Low-pressure adhesive spray.

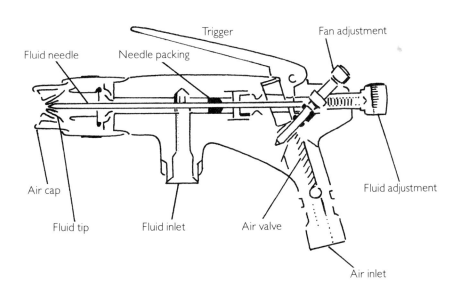

Fig 4.29 The main parts of the spray gun.

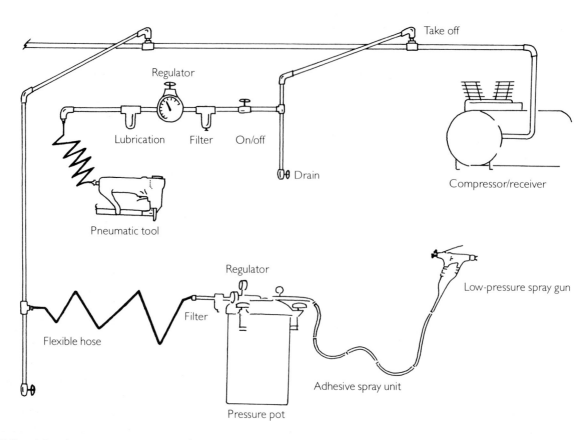

Fig 4.30 Supplying the power – compressed air.

Adhesives normally spray a frosty white colour, but can be pigmented for easier recognition where light colour foams are being used.

Electric cloth cutters

Powered cloth cutters are chiefly used to advantage by the medium to large upholstery manufacturer, where a cutting shop turns out large numbers of cut cover parts on a continuous daily basis. However the small hand-held electric cloth cutter, Fig 4.31, should be considered as an alternative to hand shears, particularly if the cutting of covers includes regular cutting of long lengths of piping strips, or if the upholsterer has a personal preference for mechanisation. The small cutter has a rotary cutting action and is fitted with a 1⅝ in (40mm) blade capable of making very accurate straight and curved cuts. Cloth cutters generally should be powered from overhead 13-amp power sockets, and the tool hung up over the cutting table when not in use. The cutting point is created by the blade running against an adjustable base plate, and the blade is protected by the adjustable

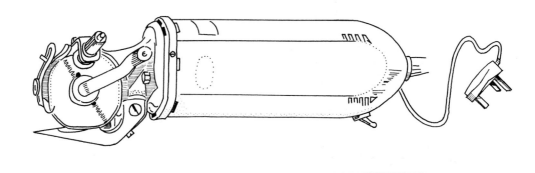

Section through blade

Fig 4.31 Electric cloth cutter.

guard at the front. A sharpening stone is incorporated which allows easy maintenance of the blade while it is running.

To maintain the cutter, daily cleaning with a tool brush is essential to prevent dust and fluff building up around the blade area. The blade, which is easily removable for wiping, is held in place by a spring strip pressing on to the centre block. All vents must be cleaned and kept clear, and wiring checked regularly. Visible moving parts will need a spot of oil after every ten hours of use. The cutter is sealed and earthed, but the usual safety checks should be made regularly.

The model in Fig 4.31 is the 'Hoog Liliput' and a section through the blade is shown with the outer face uppermost.

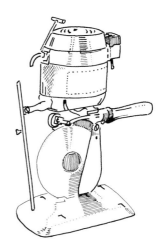

Fig 4.33 Round knife cloth cutter, the Eastman 562.

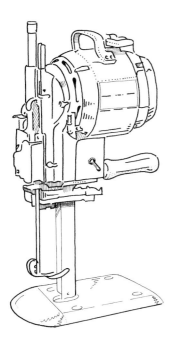

Fig 4.32 Straight knife electric cloth cutter, the Eastman 625.

The heavy duty straight knife and round knife cloth cutters (Figs 4.32 and 4.33) are designed to cope with the bulk cutting of fabrics in layers. The bulk cutting of fabrics stacked in lays on a cutting table is standard practice in the clothing and fashion trade, the motor industry and, to a lesser extent, the furniture industry. Provided that large amounts of standard size pieces of fabric are required regularly, then this sytem of cutting can be adopted. Details of this and other methods are described in Chapters 5 and 9.

The cutting capacity of these machines ranges from 4½in (115mm) up to 13in (330mm) for the straight blade type and up to 6¾in (170mm) for the round knife. The streamlined base plates reduce friction or distortion in the lay and are channelled so that fluff and

lint can escape from the bottom of the machines. The entire power mechanisms are suspended in neoprene rubber, which helps to eliminate vibration. For the cutter's convenience the electric cables are attached at the top and to the rear of the motors, keeping them out of the way when making turns.

Generally the round knife cutter is best employed for straight cuts and cross cuts, and the straight knife cutter for more intricately shaped work.

For straight blade cutters a variety of blades is available, and Fig 4.34 shows four types generally used: straight edge for all round use on standard materials; saw tooth for extremely hard materials and coated fabrics; the wave edge blade eliminates fusing cuts with very little friction; the half wave is used for low lays. Notched edge blades are ideal for packed unbacked plastics.

The size and power of these machines make them potentially dangerous. They should be used and handled with great care, and maintenance and cleaning, together with correct lubrication, are essential. Blades must be kept very sharp using the sharpening devices which are built in to both cutters.

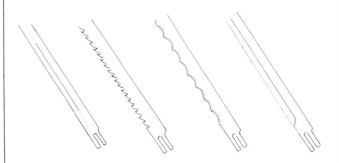

Fig 4.34 Cutting blades.

~ Chapter Five ~
Machines and Mechanisation

The craft of upholstering has been slow and difficult to mechanise. The basic skills required are rather complex and depend largely on the individual upholsterer's ability to apply and fix a great variety of materials to frames and shells, manipulating them to suit each different product.

It was during the 1950s that production methods began to change and lean towards sectionalising the chair and using KD (knock-down) techniques for production purposes. At the same time, prefabricated fillings and moulded foam units relieved the upholsterer of the full responsibility of his craft.

During the years that followed these changes, a number of machines which already existed were developed further and some new ones added. Most were adaptations of those already in use in the car industry and in bedding production. For instance, the production of beds and mattresses particularly has seen the fast growth of mechanised processes, no doubt because of the simple standard shape of the modern bed.

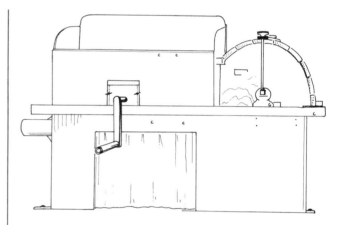

Fig 5.2 Carding machine.

Early upholstery machinery consisted of the industrial sewing machine, which was manual or motor driven, the carding machine, and two other devices, the loose seat press and a hand-operated cushion filler which was developed for use with the spring interior cushion (see Figs 5.1, 5.2, 5.3 and 5.4).

While the craft remained basically a hand skill the use of machines in upholstery was chiefly in the area of industrial sewing, to join and quilt covers and fabrics. However, as chair and seating design has gradually changed and new materials have become available, so hand-based techniques have been replaced by methods which lend themselves to mechanisation. It is clear from present trends that machines in upholstery are being used increasingly to prepare materials. The construction, assembly and finishing of the product, though far less skilled, remains basically a manual operation with the assistance of jigs to hold and line up components.

The preparation of materials for upholstery and

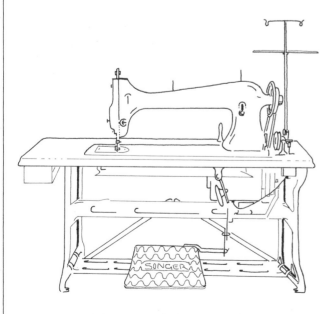

Fig 5.1 Industrial sewing machine.

bedding falls roughly into the following separate areas:

1 Manufacture of springs and suspension
2 Conversion and fabrication of foams
3 Marking out and cutting of covers
4 Sewing and quilting of covers
5 Filling, buttoning and closing of cushions and foam units

It is in these particular areas that machinery will almost certainly continue to be developed, so that components and prefabricated materials can be tailor-made for the upholsterer to build into the product.

The diversity of the market place for upholstered goods does not allow a rigid uniformity of production methods. There is an equal demand for a variety of types, from conventional upholstery on timber frames, to the less rigid moulded or cut 'all-foam' furniture.

It is in the use of metal and plastic structures that machine-produced upholstery is most apparent. Moulded plastic shells have found a place in contract areas of the upholstery market, and metal tube now competes successfully with timber as a material for domestic seating frames. In both of these examples the upholstery is designed with machines in mind, and is made up in the form of pre-shaped foam units and

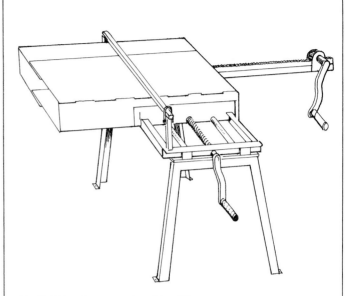

Fig 5.4 Hand-operated cushion filler.

tailored covers which are held in place using zip fasteners, hooks, press fasteners and Velcro fasteners.

The making of springs and rubber suspension systems, and the production and fabrication of foams are both very specialised areas. They are basically engineering functions which provide an essential service to the upholsterer, and are dealt with in Chapters 10 and 12.

The first stage of upholstering new work begins with the marking and cutting of covers, and it is here that a study of machinery is worthwhile beginning.

CLOTH INSPECTION AND MEASURING

New rolls of upholstery fabric with a piece length of up to sixty metres are inspected and measured to provide a check on the cloth design, its colour and quality. At the same time each roll can be labelled and its true length recorded as a means of stock control. Where large quantities of cloth are being bought and used then a machine to carry out these functions is a good investment.

As the fabric is slowly unwound it passes over a well-lit table surface, which allows clear visible inspection. The machine can be stopped at any point for flaws in the cloth to be marked or labelled at the selvedge. While the cloth travels from one side of the table to the other a trumeter measuring device records the accurate length.

Machines of this type are available as horizontal or vertical tables. Most tables are fitted with electric cross cutters, which give the option of producing exact-cut lengths at any time should production necessitate. Typical machines are built to handle pile fabrics and

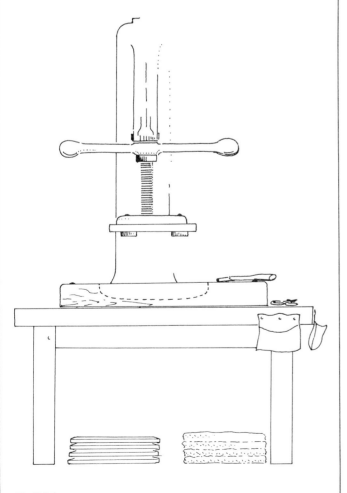

Fig 5.3 Loose seat press.

French Armchair c. 1660

Fauteuils (armchairs) of this period usually had fixed upholstery and backs were straight and flat.

Upholstery Generally thin and flat, with small amounts of animal hair or linen webs.
   Wool upholstery fabrics of this period were called moquettes in France and velours in the rest of Europe. The velours were single colours with embossed or cut patterns. Moquettes were often multi-coloured with small designs.

any stable fabric, and are fitted with variable speed and cut. Rolls may be wound with or without cardboard centre tubes. Fig 5.5 illustrates a typical horizontal version of the cloth-inspection machine.

Taking trouble to inspect cloth before it is marked out or cut can have many advantages, not least the fact

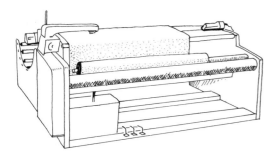

Fig 5.5 Automated cloth-inspection machine.

that goods cannot be returned once they are cut. While the cover manufacturer makes every effort to produce goods of good quality, flaws in fabrics are inevitable. The upholsterer is always aware that once the cover is made up and put on to the chair then any faults in the fabric are his responsibility and may lead to bigger problems later.

Some of the faults that regularly occur are: bad creasing, yarns drifting and not square to the selvedge, large knots, missing yarns or broken yarns, distortion or bareness in pile fabrics, changes in density, and bad registration on printed fabrics.

CLOTH SPREADERS

When rolls of upholstery cover are required for marking and cutting, they are transferred from storage racks or tubes to the cutting room. If a bulk or layered cutting system is being used, a cloth-spreading machine may be employed to layer automatically fabrics on to the cutting table. The machine automatically spreads fabric with the face in one direction only. The operation of the machine, which is mounted on rails over the cutting table, commences when spreading begins at the right-hand end of the lay and travels a predetermined length of the table to the left-hand end. Here it stops and the electrically operated cutter travels across the machine and cross cuts the lay end. The machine then returns to the right-hand end without spreading, clamps the fabric automatically and then continues with the selected laying sequence.

Machines of this type are equipped with an electronic edge-guide and power-driven variable speed. Pile fabrics and one-way pattern fabrics can be laid in the same direction, and the machine operator has the opportunity to check the fabric for face faults. Fully automatic cloth spreaders are also available, and have additional features such as ply counters, stop mechanism when roll runs out, elimination of floating and air pockets, electronic brake and two-directional laying for certain types of fabric.

At present, although fully automatic machines are available, most upholstery manufacturers use manually operated spreaders fitted to existing tables. This is because the system being used must be versatile

Fig 5.6 A semi-automatic cover-laying machine.

enough to handle the great range of cover types used in upholstery manufacture, which is usually dictated by fashion. Quantities of cut covers needed for production will vary enormously from a few sets to batches of thirty or forty sets. These amounts, however, are not large compared with production in the clothing and allied trades. Therefore, a laying-up device, which makes the unrolling of large rolls of fabric easier and facilitates clamping and cross cutting, is all that is needed in most upholstery cutting shops (Fig 5.7).

PRESS CUTTING

The cutting of fabrics and coverings for upholstery is still largely a manual operation, with the use of powered electric cutters, and marking or following jigs. However, the cutting of relatively small batches of covers can be mechanised by press cutting.

A press-cutting machine consists of a series of shaped knives, or upstanding blades, which are set into a base board and form the surface of the cutting table. Fabrics are layered over the knives and clamped into position. When preparation is complete the table is rolled under a hydraulic press, which stamps out the required shapes. It is usual to infill the areas around the blades with foam to the same height as the blades. This keeps the lay flat and also assists with removal of the cut parts.

Providing that space is available for a large mobile table and a press cutter, there are advantages to this system of cutting – it is precise and fast, and the business of marking out is eliminated. A machine of this kind can be used and applied most successfully where small compact layouts of cover parts are required repeatedly, for example, cushion parts, seat squabs and linings, etc. Similar cutting methods are used to cut

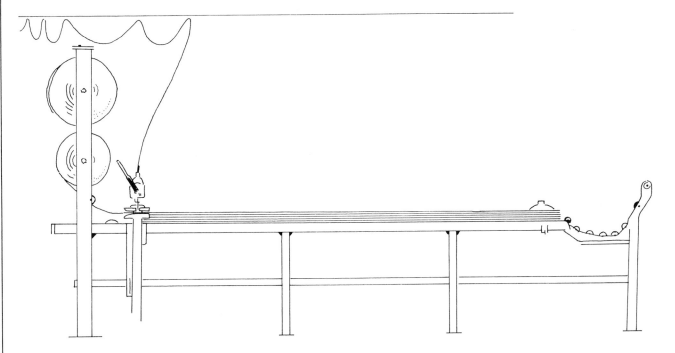

Fig 5.7 A manually operated lay-up and cutting area.

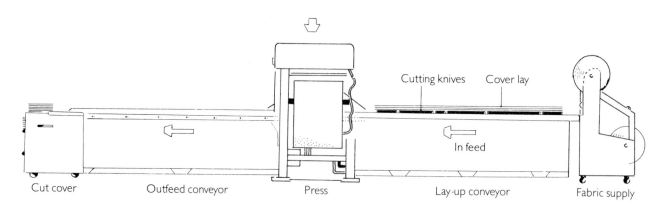

Fig 5.8 Hydraulic press − with lay and knives loaded.

flexible foams for the building and packaging industries, and to some extent for furniture (Fig 5.8).

Fig 5.9 illustrates an alternative and more flexible method of press cutting. A series of cutting blades is made up, with one blade for each shape to be cut. These cutting frames are then arranged on to the cover, usually only one or two layers, in a suitable layout before being rolled to the press. This method of press cutting is ideal where a great variety of different covers is being processed in small batches, such as a

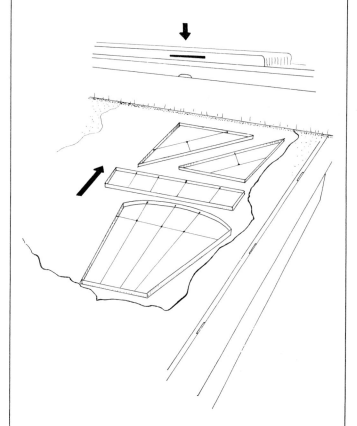

Fig 5.9 Cutters arranged on a hide ready for press cutting.

mixture of patterned and plain fabrics and pile materials.

This method of cutting from above the cover with individual frames is used a great deal for the cutting of upholstery hides. No two hides are ever identical in area or shape, and so are cut one at a time with the cutting frames arranged to suit the different surfaces and outlines. By cutting in this way, full advantage can be taken of the operator's ability to arrange the blades so that scars and rough areas are avoided, with waste kept to the minimum.

When the cutting operator is satisfied with the layout, the table, with the hide and the cutters in place, is rolled under the press.

INDUSTRIAL SEWING MACHINES

The joining and quilting of covers and fabrics is almost certainly one of the most important features of any piece of modern upholstery, and to a lesser extent some traditional work. Sewing-machine design and application has changed and developed over the past forty years, from a standard drop-feed, lock-stitch machine, to a group of very specialised and sophisticated pieces of machinery. The modern machine, though basically still lock-stitch, is designed to deal with specific sewing operations.

However, for the small workshop carrying out a variety of upholstery, one good machine of the right type and fitted with a range of accessories will deal with almost all sewing operations. The range of such a machine is largely dependent on the skill and ability of the operator to manipulate and improvise for the job in hand. The industrial situation is rather different; the making up of sewn covers is generally broken down into a number of smaller simpler operations. A specialised machine is installed to deal with each component, and then assembly of the piece parts is completed quickly and accurately ensuring a uniform product.

The most widely used stitch type, and certainly the best for upholstery purposes, is the lock stitch, British

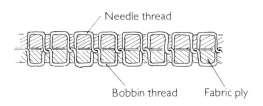

Fig 5.10 Lock-stitch type 301.

Standard stitch type 301. The lock stitch is universal and is almost certainly the strongest seam stitch that can be produced. Two threads are required, a needle thread and a bobbin thread. A loop of the needle thread is pushed through the fabric and is interlaced with the bobbin thread. The upper needle thread is then pulled back, so that the interlacing or locking comes midway between the plies of fabric being sewn. The diagram in Fig 5.10 shows a cross section of a lock stitch type 301.

The drawing in Fig 5.11 shows a general view of a standard industrial sewing machine, indicating the main parts. The top half of the machine, called the machine head, can be easily detached from the table. The two parts are priced and purchased separately, so that there is an interchangeability of various heads with different table designs.

Machine types
Lock-stitch machines are produced as single-needle models and twin-needle models, and are available in three basic forms, flat bed, post bed and cylinder bed. A flat bed is the type for normal sewing operations,

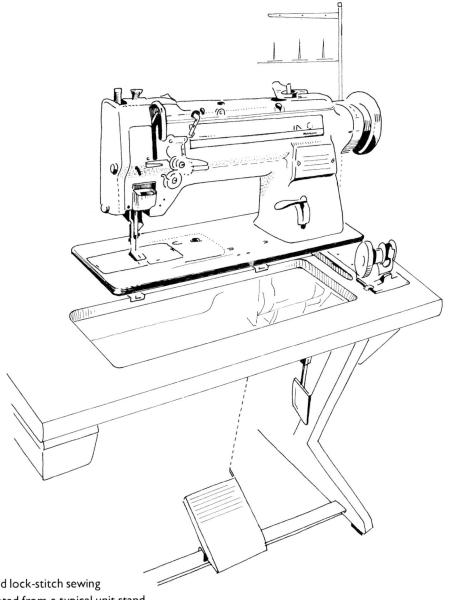

Fig 5.11 Flat-bed lock-stitch sewing machine separated from a typical unit stand.

while the other two are more specialised. Post-bed machines are usually twin needle and the head is elevated above the table and tilted towards the sewer for easier working and vision. As Fig 5.12 shows, the cylinder bed arrangement produces a single-needle stitch at the end of the table, with an extension table to support the work during sewing.

Feed mechanisms

A basic lock-stitch machine may have one of several different feed mechanisms. It is important to appreciate the difference between these work-feed systems, particularly when selecting a sewing machine for a workshop or sewing room.

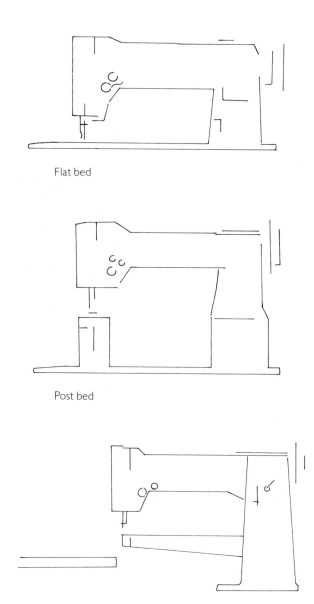

Flat bed

Post bed

Cylinder bed

Fig 5.12

Drop feed

This is a conventional feed system in which the fabric is fed forward by the moving feed dog, with the presser foot held on to the fabric by spring pressure. Needle movement is in a straight line up and down, with feed taking place when the needle is in the up position. The feed dog 'drops' below the throat plate surface on its return motion. Although this system is adequate for most lightweight applications, it is not now recommended for general upholstery sewing which is mainly in the heavy class.

Compound or needle feed

This feed mechanism goes some way to eliminating the problem of fabric plies slipping, which is associated with the drop-feed system. Feed in this case takes place with the needle in the down position, the needle making a forward movement in unison with the feed dog. Resulting seams of two or more thicknesses are more uniform, and puckering of bottom plies much less frequent. Compound feed with a plain presser foot is considered adequate for light and medium upholstery covers.

Compound feed with alternating presser

Where a compound feed is fitted with an alternating presser foot then feed becomes more positive. This combination is very well suited to upholstery sewing. The presser foot in this case is a two-part mechanism arranged to alternate in pressing down of the fabric plies. The two parts of the presser appear to walk over the fabric, with feed being maintained by the inner of the two parts. Commonly called a walking foot in the trade, this feed system is now recommended for general and heavy upholstery work and is particularly suited to hide work and the sewing of heavy tweeds and pile fabrics. It is ideal for the reupholstery business.

Differential feed

This is a machine designed principally for situations where the puckering and gathering of fabrics is required as a feature on a chair or a cushion. Only where large amounts of this type of work are required would the purchase of such a machine be economical. The feed mechanism is basically drop feed, employing two feed dogs working in tandem. These two can be adjusted to work at different rates, thus forming a gathering function in front of the needle. A tape is usually sewn into the seam to set and hold the gather while it is resewn or fixed into other parts.

For the gathering of heavier upholstery fabrics a swing-out pressure plate is used. This has been found to be more effective and sits on the fabric in front of the presser foot. The plate can easily be removed when normal sewing is needed.

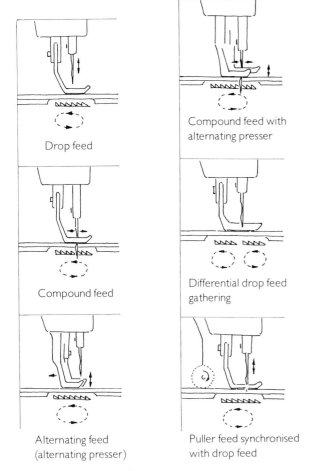

Fig 5.13 Work-feed mechanisms.

Puller feeds

To assist feeding and the control of unstable materials a powered roller puller is available for fitting to most machines, but is mainly used for long runs of border making, zip insertion, and where different types of material are being quilted or laminated together. As these examples indicate, puller-feed systems are designed to assist in the straight sewing of difficult materials, and are standard on automatic seamers.

Specialised lock-stitch machines

Swing needle – zig-zag

A range of machines which are basically lock-stitch and drop feed, but with the added feature of a swinging needle. These will produce plain and decorative seams as required. Their application in upholstery is very small. They are principally used for embroidery and the decoration and finishing of garments. They do, however, have some applications in soft furnishing for both curtain and bed-cover making. Where a decorative quilted effect is incorporated into a chair or cushion cover the zig-zag seam is used to good effect, although it may be susceptible to wear where abrasion is heavy in seat areas. Some seam patterns are illustrated to show its potential (Fig. 5.14).

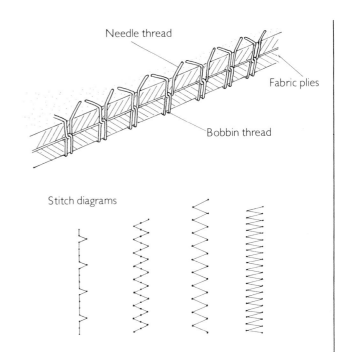

Fig 5.14 Lock-stitch zig-zag, type 304.

Long-arm machines

Where fluted and quilted panels are to be produced in quantity, the long-arm sewing machine is essential. These machines are compound feed, lock-stitch types, with spoon- or boat-shaped presser feet. The main feature of this range is the long machine head arm. While the standard-size lock-stitch machine has a space of about 12in to 15in (305–380mm) to the right of the needle bar, the long-arm machine can have up to 32in (815mm). This provides good, clear working space as the panel being produced builds up on the right-hand side of the needle. The upholsterer who has attempted to produce this kind of work on a standard machine will know the difficulties.

Long-arm machines are classed as heavy duty and are built to deal with multiple plies of fabric and fillings. Stitch lengths and bobbin sizes are all as large as possible to provide effective, strong sewing lines. Additional features on these machines include safety clutches – in case of accidental strain – foot-operated presser bars, compound feed and alternating pressers, and low speed ½hp motors (Fig 5.15).

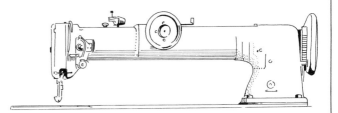

Fig 5.15 Long-arm lock-stitch machine.

Chain-stitch machines

Single- and two-thread chain-stitch machines are used to advantage in a limited number of applications in upholstery production and mattress making, although they are used much more in automotive upholstery and the clothing industry. British Standard stitch type 401 has the advantage of being simply formed by the needle thread and needs no underthread or bobbin. Machines in this category can be run continuously with no stops for bobbin change. Seaming is therefore continuous until the needle thread reel runs out.

However, although this may at first seem ideal, the seam itself does not compare for strength or tightness with the lock stitch. If a chain-stitch seam is put under great strain for any length of time then gaping and seam-opening problems occur. Also, should the seam become fractured at any point in a sewn-up cover, because of its nature the seam will run open far more easily than is likely with the lock-stitch type.

There are some applications to which the chain stitch is well suited in a mass production situation. These are areas of preparation of sewn parts or pre-sewing, with components such as zipped borders, piping, quilted borders and first seams, all of which will later be sewn again into made-up covers. In the small workshop a compound-feed lock-stitch machine could be used to produce the same components if required. Only when it is a definite advantage to do so should a specialised machine of this type be installed (Fig 5.16).

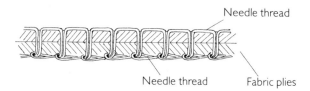

Single-thread chain stitch, BS 101

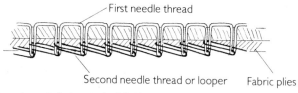

Two-thread chain stitch, BS 401

Fig 5.16

Overedge machines

This group of sewing machines is being used increasingly for upholstery work. The demand for detachable and loose covers, for both traditional and modern seating, has increased the need for seam edges to be overlocked.

Cut edges can be made reasonably fray-proof, which in turn automatically adds to the seam strength in situations where slip covers, arm caps and cushion covers are removable for cleaning. Overedge machines may be two-, three-, or four-thread and single- or two-needle. Stitch formation is very complicated, but is basically a chain stitch with a looper and a needle producing the overlock, a second needle providing the safety stitch alongside the overlocking one. Four-thread overlockers produce seams suitable for stretch covers and, of course, are used a great deal in garment manufacture. Fig 5.17 shows the overedge machine and some seam examples.

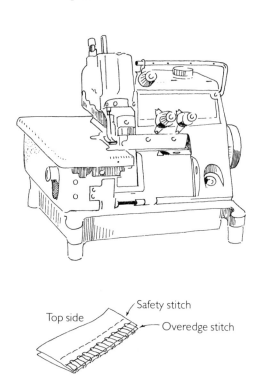

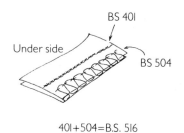

401+504=B.S. 516

Fig 5.17 Overedge and safety-stitch machine.

*Sleeping Chair
Charles II c. 1675*

A walnut-frame wing chair of large
proportions.

Upholstery Fabric-covered rails, wings and
arms provided reasonable comfort. The back
cushion was filled with wool or feathers and
fixed into position. Seat squabs were loose
and supported on leather strips or rope.

Coverings Crimson silk which was brocaded
with metal threads and brightly-coloured
silks. Nails were usually spaced on fringe and
cushion seams decorated with hand stitching
or braids.

A guide to stitch types

The following is a list of those stitch types most
commonly used in upholstery sewing. Approximate
thread consumption ratios are also given, but five per
cent should be added for thread wastage.

Stitch type		Inches of thread to 1in of seam	Length in mm to 25mm of seam
BS 301	Lock stitch	2½	63
BS 101	Single chain stitch	4	100
BS 401	Two-thread chain stitch	5½	138
BS 304	Lock-stitch zig-zag	7	175
BS 504	Overlock, three-thread	14	350
BS 801	Safety stitch, four-thread	17½	425

For lock-stitch sewing on leather and plastic materials
the ratio may be as high as 5½–1.

Specialist sewing machines

This new generation of industrial machines is designed
and produced to meet the needs of the manufacturer
who is willing to invest in a piece of equipment which
will reproduce quickly and accurately a single
component. These machines may be purpose built or
they may be off-the-shelf models, adapted to suit a
purpose.

Adaptations can be made and accessories fitted to
provide the solution to a particular production
problem. Most leading machine manufacturers offer a
product-application service, and will advise on the best
machine for a particular sewing job. Many of the
specialised machines were originally developed for the
clothing and bedding industries, but now there is a
large range available to suit the upholstery
manufacturer.

The need for specialised sewing has grown from the
part-production principle where an upholstery cover,
once produced completely by one operator, is now
broken down into a series of smaller operations carried
out by several people on a variety of machines.
Basically, the product progresses from a number of
prepared components to final assembly by one
machinist on a standard lock-stitch machine.

The following are some good examples of the
machines and their applications.

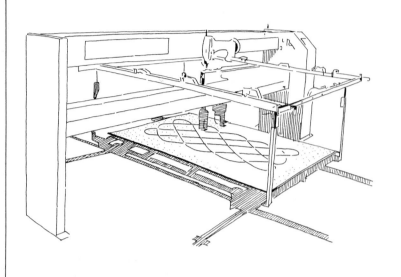

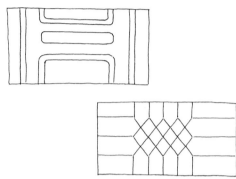

Some chair and settee back panels

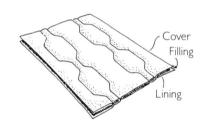

Cover
Filling
Lining

Quilter: May be single or multi needle; will produce flat sewn panels ready for insertion into a mattress or a chair (Fig 5.18).

Fig 5.18 Single-needle quilting machine.

Twin-head boxing or **cushion-boxing machines:** Produce boxed cushions and covers by joining border strips to top and bottom panels simultaneously, and finish the edges plain sewn or with piped or ruched seams (Fig 5.19).

Fig 5.19 Twin-head boxing machine.

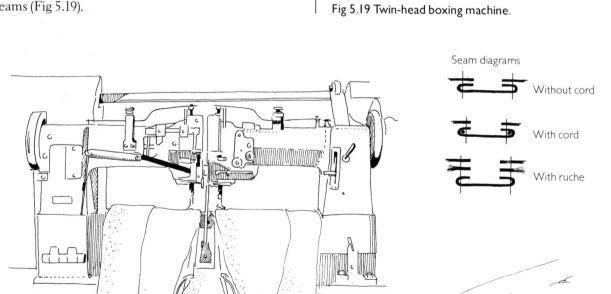

Seam diagrams

Without cord

With cord

With ruche

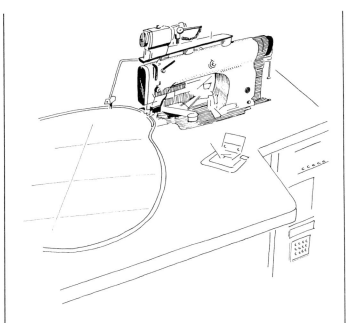

Fig 5.20 Automatic profile seamer.

Profile seamers: Sew together an almost unlimited range of sub-assemblies quickly and accurately. Using an autojig system the machine stitches and trims one or two plys of fabric to the predetermined shape (Fig 5.20).

Automatic straight seamers: Equipped with synchronised puller feeds on top and bottom, a double-chain-stitch head, thread cutters and monitors. These machines have some application where long straight seams are required, such as lengthening or widening of cloth panels, applying linings and flys, and pre-sewing before shaping (Fig 5.21).

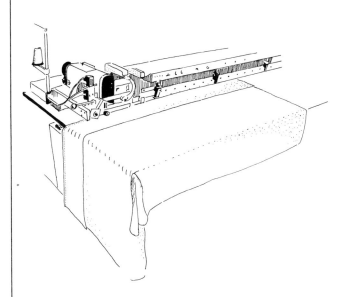

Fig 5.21 Automatic straight-sewing unit.

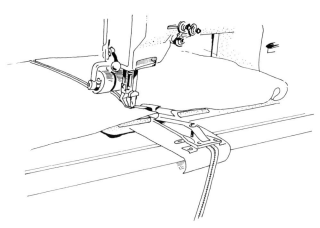

Fig 5.22 Twin-needle continuous zipper with puller feed and folders.

Continuous zippers: Usually two or four needle, and may be chain stitch or lock stitch, designed for the fast production of zipped components and continuous zipped borders. Guides and folders fitted to the bed ensure accurate positioning of the cover parts (Fig 5.22).

BUTTON-MAKING AND BUTTONING MACHINES

Button making and the insertion and fixing of buttons has always been a requirement of certain types of upholstery. During the past decade and in particular during the 1970s it was a design feature of mass-produced upholstery for domestic chairs and sofas to be buttoned in the seat, back and arm areas. Although, at present, fashion demands a less fussy appearance, there is no doubt that buttoning in various

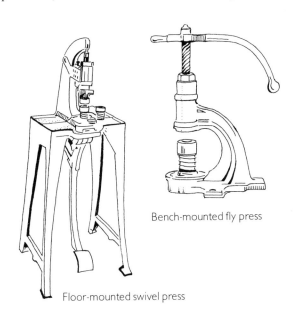

Bench-mounted fly press

Floor-mounted swivel press

Fig 5.23 Button-making presses.

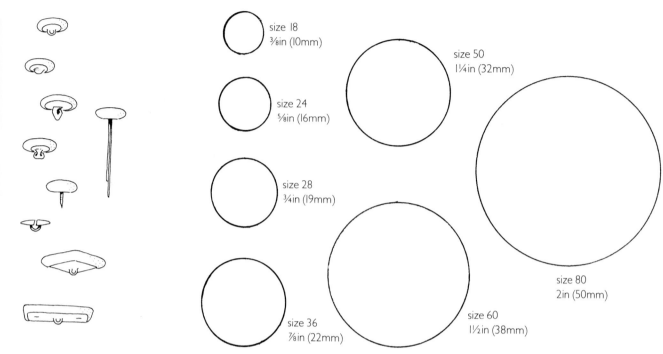

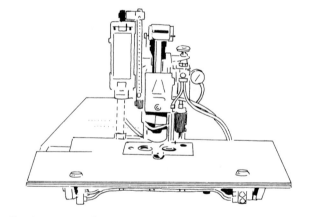

Fig 5.24 Buttons.

forms, either functional or decorative, will remain a part of the upholstery process.

In the smaller workshop where output is not on a large scale, a small manually operated button-making press is quite satisfactory. The machine will accommodate various size dies, to produce small, medium and large fabric-covered buttons with different loop or hook bases to suit the fixings required.

The two-hand-operated machines most commonly used are shown in Fig 5.23. The making process requires discs of fabric to be cut to suit the size of the die, and then the clamping of the upper and lower parts together with the cover moulded around the upper or dome surface. Covered buttons may be produced as conventional round shapes, or square and oblong if needed.

Fig 5.24 shows a small range of the button types that are available and their sizes. A more comprehensive list of all the various types and their special fixings is always available from the manufacturers of button-making equipment.

The automation of the button-making process has progressed rapidly to the point where semi- and fully-automatic machines are available to deal with all the upholsterer's needs. Machines, which are normally pneumatic with electronic functions, will produce from six hundred to three thousand buttons of any type per hour. Cover-cutting presses with multiple banks of disc cutters will cut pneumatically at a rate required for the above machines.

The machine in Fig 5.25 produces one button every stroke, records the number of buttons produced and automatically ejects at a maximum of six hundred per hour.

Semi-automatic button-making machine

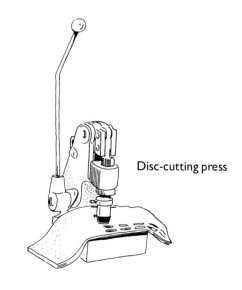

Disc-cutting press

Fig 5.25

Fig 5.26 Automatic hopper-fed button-making machine.

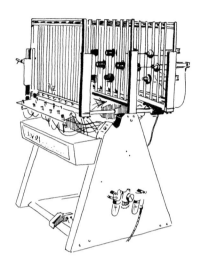

Fig 5.27 Button-fastening machine (pneumatic).

The automatic type in Fig 5.26 boasts automatic hopper feed of the button parts, electro-pneumatic drive and production at three thousand buttons per hour. Both machines require an air pressure of 85psi.

Button-fastening machines use a combination of pneumatic power and steel frames to locate, hold and compress a piece of upholstery in the form of covered cushions, mattresses, squabs, and seat and back units. Machines will normally deal with sizes up to 1m wide and 2m long or larger in special circumstances. All types of anchor or open-hook buttons and tufts may be used, and fastening can be deep or shallow to any design or layout. Single frames of 1m size will usually facilitate up to 24 buttons at one time.

Using the pre-formed nylon twine or tape-loop system, made up to the required buttoning depth, the cylinder-powered needles pierce the upholstery in one single stroke, which then leaves the operator free to attach the second buttons or the fixings before the needles are reversed back through the work to complete the cycle.

Machines may be vertical frames or horizontal, and this is usually dependent on the size of work and the preference of the upholstery manufacturer. Fig 5.27 shows a typical vertical frame machine of single frame size designed to handle average chair-back and seat units, with the option that long pieces can be released and moved through the open sides, relocated and buttoned along their entire length.

The process of buttoning through and fixing can be done manually using a hand needle rather than air cylinders. The same machine in this case would simply hold and compress the upholstery and provide accurate button positions to the design selected. Fig 5.28 shows

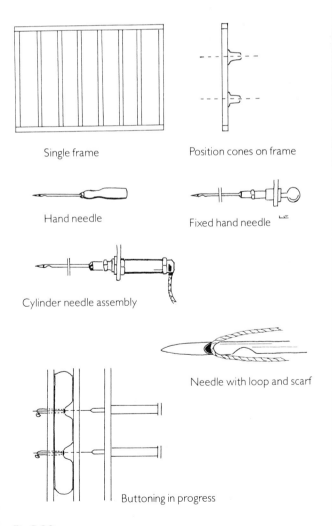

Single frame

Position cones on frame

Hand needle

Fixed hand needle

Cylinder needle assembly

Needle with loop and scarf

Buttoning in progress

Fig 5.28

some machine parts and needles in detail. The business of compression tufting by machine has been used for some time in the bedding industry for mattress making. Upholstery buttoning, however, will always be a more variable process, with the greater variety of shapes and sizes in components and the constant changes in design. For this reason many manufacturers prefer to design and build jigs and fixtures as and when they are required, from timber, metal and plastics and plywood, rather than install machines. However, while a permanent installation will basically hold and compress any size of component, providing the button position cones are always adjustable, mechanisation of this kind will remain feasible. The only mains service required for machine buttoning and tufting operations is a supply of compressed air at 80–100psi.

CUSHION FILLING BY MACHINE

The machine filling of cushions offers many advantages over manual filling. Filling cushions and closing them has traditionally been carried out by women in the industry, the interior being folded and eased into the cover and the opening pinned and sewn up by hand. The whole operation takes perhaps ten to fifteen minutes per cushion. The introduction of machine filling, together with zip closing of the cover, has speeded up the operation and reduced the manual handling of the cushion and its interior, which can be tiring and tedious work. Machine filling allows those employed on this work more time to enjoy a variety of other jobs.

Early types of cushion-filling machines were developed particularly for the filling of spring-unit interior cushions. These were bulky and difficult to handle with their layers of fibre or hair and cotton-felt fillings, and compressing or bending the unit manually was not possible. Most of the early machines of the ram type were manually operated and needed two people, one to operate the ram and the other to hold the cushion cover over the machine opening.

The filling of cushions today is a much cleaner, simpler and less physical job, and can be completed by one person in a fraction of the old time. Interiors are generally lighter in weight, easier to handle, and there are a number of good machines capable of handling almost any size and type of interior. Fig 5.29 illustrates the three main types which all compress and eject the filling in different ways. Fig 5.29(a) uses compressed air to squash the fillings down to the size of the cover opening, after which a ram pushes the filling into the cover while it is held over the mouth of the box. Fig 5.29(b) has eight tubular steel arms which move together to compress the interior. The cover is then pulled over and the arms are retracted leaving the filled case ready for closing. Fig 5.29(c) operates vertically,

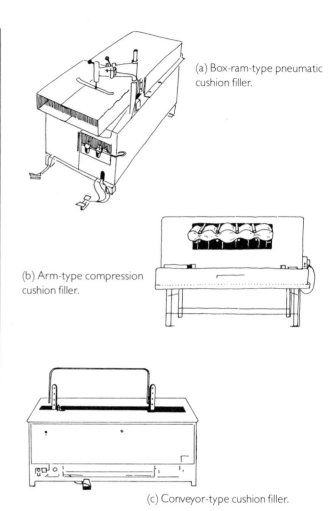

(a) Box-ram-type pneumatic cushion filler.

(b) Arm-type compression cushion filler.

(c) Conveyor-type cushion filler.

Fig 5.29

compressing almost any type of filling inside the cabinet. Ejection into the cushion cover is by means of small conveyors and rollers pushing the interior upwards into the ready made case. All the machines use a mixture of mains electricity and compressed air at 80–100psi.

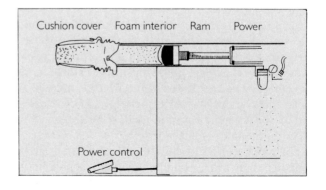

Cushion cover   Foam interior   Ram   Power

Power control

Fig 5.30 Operation of a ram-type filler.

SAFE WORKING IN THE USE OF MACHINE-ASSISTED UPHOLSTERY PRODUCTION

Electric and pneumatic power supply to machinery must be carefully regulated, with built-in safety mechanisms to ensure that the installations are basically sound. All machines will normally be fused and earthed, and a check should be made regularly on wiring, hoses and pipework. Routine maintenance is often the key to safer machinery. Turn-off buttons or switches are fitted to each machine and must be easily accessible and well marked. Similarly, wall-mounted, brightly coloured 'panic buttons', where electrical supply can be stopped quickly, are fitted to all work areas.

Exposed moving parts on any machine are always a potential hazard, and so, as far as possible, these must be guarded or fenced. Those who work with machines must be reminded and made fully aware of potential dangers, by labelling, colouring and the use of warning signs on machines and machine parts. Machine operators will know more about the general condition and efficiency of particular machines than anyone else. They are therefore in a good position to report regularly on working conditions. Unsafe machinery must be reported as a requirement of the Health and Safety at Work Act, 1980.

To ensure the trouble-free running of any well-used machine, a policy of planned preventative maintenance usually pays in the long term. This will mean putting machines out of action for short periods, perhaps monthly, or during holiday periods. Checks of this kind will often reveal small faults and at the same time provide an opportunity for fine tuning and adjustments, which in turn keep efficiency at a high level.

MAIN PRODUCTION AREAS

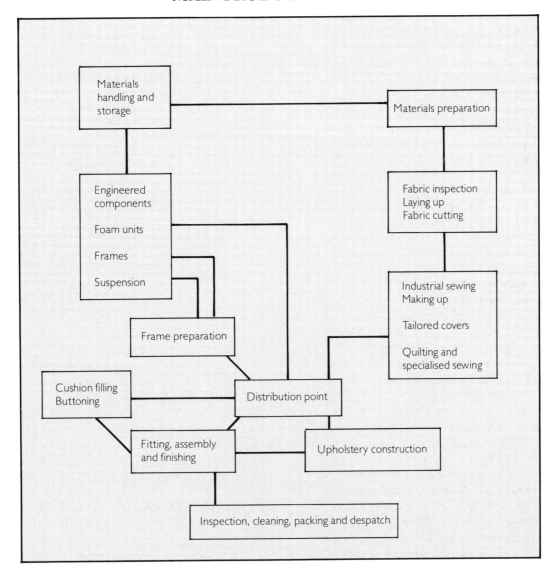

Chapter Six

Materials

The upholsterer uses a very wide range of materials for both traditional and modern work. Many of the materials one would expect to find in a chair made a hundred years ago have of course changed or been replaced – improvements in processing and the introduction of synthetics and new technology make this inevitable.

But there is still a considerable demand for many of the good, naturally based materials such as webbings, natural fillings and woven cloths. Many of these materials have been modified, or their construction changed to improve strength or to make them easier to handle and to use.

It is also interesting that there is still a core of good craftsmen and women who produce new furniture and restore old, using the best natural materials that are available, expensive though this may be. It would not, of course, be possible to mass-produce this kind of hand-built upholstery. It is only right that the modern chair is built using the best of modern materials with the associated technology, to produce a blend of comfort and good design that suits modern living. The two very different areas of the craft continue side by side, balancing and complementing each other and providing a wide range of upholstery for the would-be buyer.

The selection of materials and choosing what to use in a particular job are an important part of the upholsterer's work. The range is very large and the quality enormously varied. Those who work almost entirely on traditional lines will follow a rigid pattern, using the well-tried and tested materials which are known to give good service and suit the type of work they do.

The buyer who is responsible for purchasing new materials for modern work will stay basically with those he has enjoyed using in the past, produced and supplied by reputable companies. To try a new development or material is interesting and tempting, and providing that there is evidence of testing by a research institute or by the manufacturer of the product, then, with caution, prototypes can be made up and tried out by the upholsterer. The Furniture Industries' Research Association is continually assessing new products and will advise and report independently on any aspect of materials quality and use.

SUPPORT MATERIALS AND LININGS

Webbings

Narrow strips of tightly woven fabric made in different widths, from 2in (50mm) to 4in (100mm) wide, have provided the foundation to upholstery for well over 250 years. Woven furniture webbing was probably developed from horse bridle and girth webbings as a follow on from the narrow strips of leather used in early upholstery and seating.

When a chair is stripped for reupholstery, the type and condition of the webbings can often explain a great deal about the age and origin of the chair, or indicate when it was last upholstered.

Continental webbings are usually of the wider type; British generally tends to be the 2in (50mm), narrower kind.

Composition and construction

The fibre composition of webbings has gradually changed over the years. Heavy flax and hemp fibres were followed by more refined flax and cotton, with the introduction of sisal and jute fibre as raw materials. Today, man-made yarns are blended in to improve strength and stability. Rayon, nylon and polypropylene are examples of good synthetics which, when blended with natural fibres, produce strong and durable modern webbings.

Early webbing construction was of simple plain weave, with use of strong heavy warp yarns (those running along the length of the web). A good webbing must have a strong selvedge. Cotton and flax have

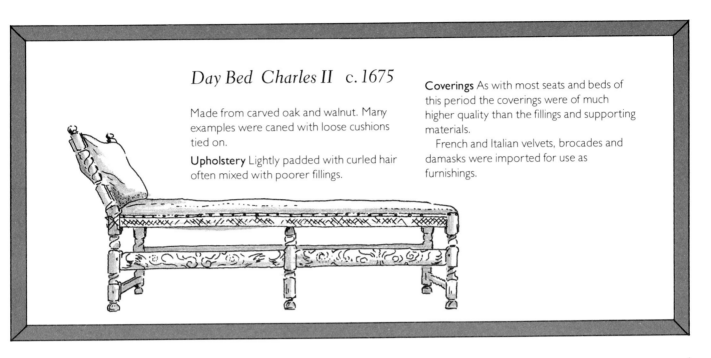

Day Bed Charles II c.1675

Made from carved oak and walnut. Many examples were caned with loose cushions tied on.

Upholstery Lightly padded with curled hair often mixed with poorer fillings.

Coverings As with most seats and beds of this period the coverings were of much higher quality than the fillings and supporting materials.

French and Italian velvets, brocades and damasks were imported for use as furnishings.

---

traditionally been used for this purpose.

During the nineteenth century, twill weaves were introduced and accepted as a stronger method of construction. From that time on the twill types were known as best webbings, and plain weaves as common or standard webs. Today the situation is unchanged, except that it is often difficult to tell which fibres are being used and in what percentages. Black and undyed jute are predominant, with cotton, flax and synthetics added.

Different webbings can be recognised by their colour, weave and weight. There are five colours, pale brown, black and white mixed, brown and white mixed, for the traditional types, and dark brown and black for the purely synthetic types. The quality of a webbing is measured by its weight in pounds per 1 gross yard. Its metric equivalent is measured in kilogrammes per 129.6m. The different types are shown below.

1. Best flax, pale brown colour, double chevron weave, 12–15lb weight.
2. English, black and white colour, double chevron weave, 10lb weight.
3. English, brown and white colour, double chevron weave (twill) 10lb weight.
4. Common jute, pale brown colour, plain weave, 9–11lb weight.
5. Synthetics, brown or black colour, plain weave, very lightweight.

Compositions:
1. 100% pure flax
2. Dyed flax and cotton or 79% jute and 21% cotton, a typical composition
3. Undyed jute, cotton and rayon
4. 100% jute
5. Polypropylene

Fig 6.1 shows three examples, and their weave patterns.

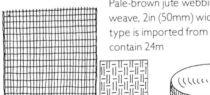

Pale-brown jute webbing, plain weave, 2in (50mm) wide. Much of this type is imported from India. Rolls contain 24m

English or black and white webbing, mainly jute with cotton selvedge. 2in (50mm) wide, rolls contain 18m. Commonly called best webbing, often contains single or double red or green warp yarns

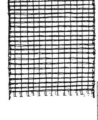

All polypropylene webbing, 2in (50mm) wide and produced from synthetic tape and not spun yarn. Lightweight but very strong, easily identified by its smooth, shiny surface

Fig 6.1 Webbings.

Hessian cloths

Hessians are noted for their strength and rigidity and so are particularly good as lining and support cloths for upholstery. A suitable weight should be chosen for light or heavy use. The cloth qualities range from 7oz (200g) per metre up to 16oz (450g) per metre, and those over 12oz (340g) are called tarpaulins. Widths also vary, 36in (90cm) and 72in (180cm) are the most popular; other widths available are 40in (1m), 48in (120cm) and 54in (135cm).

As an example of their durability hessians have traditionally been used in carpet and lino manufacture, and industrial sacking, and also for wall coverings; these are all very tough applications.

Jute is the raw material for hessian manufacture, by nature a tough, coarse, non-stretch base vegetable fibre, grown as an annual plant in India and Pakistan. The Indian centre of Calcutta, and Dundee in Scotland are traditional jute-processing and weaving centres.

Upholstery hessians are plain-weave constructions, with single yarns in both warp and weft direction. When specifying hessians for upholstery the cloth width is given first, followed by the weight, e.g. 72″, 10oz/sq. yd (180cm, 280g/M^2). Although there are a variety of constructions, standard hessian is made using 12 ends and 13 picks per 10in (25cm), that is 12 weft yarns and 13 warp yarns for every inch of cloth.

As a general rule, the heavier cloths are used for applications over springing and spring units, because of the obvious demands on their strength. The lower weights are more suited to lining over webbings, outside arms and backs, and for chair bottoms.

Spring hessian – 12–16oz (340–450g) per metre × 72in (1.8m) wide
Inner linings – 10oz (280g) per metre × 72in (1.8m) wide
Outer linings – 7–10oz (200–280g) per metre × 72in (1.8m) wide

Bulk purchases may be by the roll or bolt (Fig 6.2).

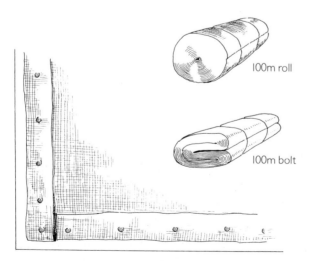

100m roll

100m bolt

Fig 6.2 Hessian tacked and folded on to a timber frame.

Scrims

Scrim is a fine, plain-woven shaping fabric which is used in many different trades. It is used to form and shape and hold in place the basic medium being used. In the building industry scrim strips are used by plasterers in the forming of edges, corners and mouldings. The plaster is built up over and around the scrim-lined base layers. Milliners use stiffened cotton scrim to form shapes in hat making. The fine scrim layers are often pasted to other cloths while three-dimensional shapes are produced.

Fig 6.3 A hair pad shaped up in scrim, bridled and edge-stitched.

Generally, for upholstery work 8oz or 9oz (200 or 230g) jute scrim is used to cover first stuffings in the forming of stitched edges around seats, backs and various shaped facings. Scrim may also be used to build dug rolls and rolled edges. Its density and general construction is similar to that of hessian. However, a close comparison of the yarns of the two materials will show that those for hessian are flat in section and those in scrim are more rounded. The number of yarns per 1in (25mm) of cloth in the warp or weft direction is about fifteen, slightly higher than hessian.

It would be unusual to find scrim used in a modern chair where foams are the predominant filling, but for any traditional work a good scrim provides the first covering over loose, fibrous fillings, bridled in place with ties or twine, while edge shapes are formed on squabs, cushions, small mattresses, and on fixed chair work. Small amounts of cotton scrim, which is finer than jute, can be kept for making up bolsters, small squabs, or where delicate pinstuffed work is required. Weights generally fall between 5½oz and 8oz per square yard (150g and 200g per metre). Widths of cloth for jute scrim — 72in (1.8m) and for cotton 40in and 60in (1m and 1.5m).

Calico

Calico is the name given to woven cotton cloth, produced in various qualities. The weave structure is fine and plain. Calico is used in tailoring, dress making, curtain making and as a lining material in upholstery. The cloth is produced as loomstate, or grey goods, i.e. unbleached and undyed, and is an off-white colour, easily recognised by the very fine bits of cotton seed which appear on the surface. The same cloths, however, may be bought as bleached calico, or dyed black, brown or beige.

The term 'pulled down in calico' refers to a piece of upholstery lined and upholstered over the second stuffing, prior to being top covered. It is common practice to line good quality upholstery with calico.

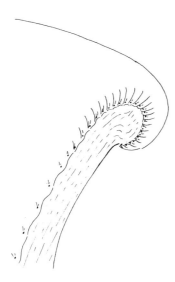

Fig 6.4 A scroll end pulled down in calico, and carefully pleated and tacked.

This allows the calico to take the strain and tension before the cover is applied. The final cover will also give better and longer service when the upholstery is lined.

Cotton calico is produced in many qualities and widths. For upholstery purposes a medium weight of 5oz per sq yd (140g per sq m) is suitable for most work. Occasionally a heavier weight may be chosen for lining or covering, where, for instance, a loose detachable cover is to be made, or where the calico is to remain as the outer cover. Very light muslin-weight calicos may also be used when costs are to be kept to the minimum, or the work will not be subjected to heavy use.

When calico is produced at a weight of 10oz (280g) the term 'cotton duck' is used to describe the cloth; weights above this approach those of canvas. Typical specifications for the purchase of calico are as follows:

1   Loomstate, 2½oz (70g) muslin weight, 54in (137cm) width, 80–100m pieces (rolls).
2   4oz (110g), dyed black, brown, beige, 48in (122cm) wide.
3   Loomstate, 5oz (140g) medium weight, 40in (102cm), 50in (127cm), 72in (180cm) widths, 100m pieces (rolls).
4   Heavyweight 6½oz (180g) unbleached, 54in (135cm) 72in (180cm,) 100–400m pieces (rolls).
5   Cotton duck, 10oz (280g) 72in (180cm) wide, 50m pieces (rolls).

The flame proofing of calico has become normal practice on certain weights of cloth. These are always specified and labelled or printed on the cloth. A flame-proofed grade may be used wherever the type of furniture being produced is covered by the requirements of legislation, which requires the upholstery to be fire-proof to a certain standard. New furniture produced for sale to the general public or for use in public buildings may well fall into this category.

Ticking

Ticking is a strong twill-weave fabric, woven from white cotton with a narrow black stripe in the warp direction. The stripe makes it easily recognisable, and the cloth has a strong, slightly stiff feel. It is reasonably proof against fibrous filling materials, such as feathers, hair, flocks and kapok. The main uses for ticking are in the bedding industry as coverings and linings for mattresses, pillows and beds. However, tickings are available as woven pattern fabrics, produced in great variety on jacquard looms.

The white-with-black-stripe type is a very traditional, close-weave twill fabric, which is often used to advantage in upholstery, particularly where feather- and kapok-filled cases are being incorporated into the seats, backs and ends of chairs and couches.

Weights are in the medium to high range compared with calicos. Widths are 36in (90cm) and 72in (180cm). Ticking wears well and has good drape which makes it an excellent curtain and wall-covering fabric. Linen tickings are available, or as unions of 50% cotton/ 50% linen.

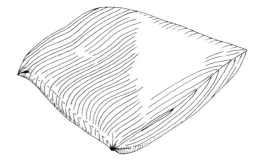

Fig 6.5 A striped ticking pillow case, kapok or feather filled.

Cambric

Another fine, strong, all-cotton fabric, produced mainly for the clothing and fashion industry. Cambric is plain woven from fine bleached cotton, with a very smooth surface and usually glazed. Its construction may well contain as many as 140 yarns per 1in (25mm) of cloth. Cambric is an excellent lining cloth, and for upholstery purposes is down proofed with a waxing process. When made up as a cushion interior and filled, it has a

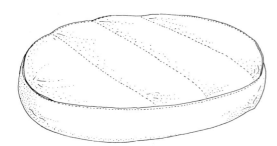

Fig 6.6 A feather-filled cushion made from down-proof cambric.

luxurious feel, and the quiet rustling sound of stiff new cotton.

The cloth works well and can be cut and sewn with good accuracy. Weight compares with medium to better grade calico at about 5oz per sq yd (140g per 25sq mm). Cambric is recognised by its cream colour, semi-glazed surface and crisp, cool feel. Width is 48in (120cm) in rolls of 100m. When making up cambric into cushion cases, the shiny side should be on the inside or filling side, to help movement of fillings.

Platform cloths

Strong, neutral-coloured woven cloths are used for upholstered platforms in chair and settee seats, and inside backs. In a situation where loose or reversible cushions form the main sitting area, a platform cloth is used to cover the base upholstery. The area covered by this cloth is not normally seen unless the cushions are removed. A platform cloth needs to be visually acceptable as an outer cover, but at the same time very durable and able to stand up to constant flexing and movement while the chair is being used. Some upholsterers use one colour and one type of cloth for all purposes, while others prefer a small range of colours which will blend with the upholstery cover being used. There are several types of cloth which are suitable for the job:

A heavy-duty bleached and dyed calico, or a dyed cotton duck are both plain woven and strong.
Linen Holland is another plain, flat cloth, reasonably strong and of medium weight.
Repp is a plain-woven fabric made from all cotton, or a blend of cotton and wool. It has a fine-rib structure running in the warp direction. Repp is strong and is slightly flexible.
Bedford cord is another warp-rib fabric, which makes an excellent platform cloth; it is slightly flexible, has good thickness and the heavy grades may be plain or twill weave.

Ideally, a good platform cloth should have good tear reisistance, and good seam-strength properties.

In some modern upholstery applications a platform

will need to be very stretchy and flexible, particularly when used over a shallow layer of foam on rubber webbing. In this case a knitted fabric made from rayon or nylon with a laminated foam backing for extra strength is ideal. Widths of cloth are normally standard 48in (120cm) to 54in (137cm).

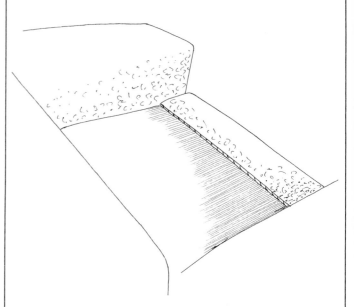

Fig 6.7 A seat platform covered in Bedford cord, a welted seam forms the joint with the cover.

Stockinette

A single jersey fabric, knitted from cotton, rayon or other synthetic yarns on a circular knitting machine. These fabrics are in a continuous sock of about 10in (25cm) diameter, and have tremendous stretch qualities, particularly in the weft direction. A length of stockinette is cut off the roll and stretched over foams, foam-cushion interiors and synthetic fibre fillings. It is simply a lightweight lining cloth used to contain and hold in place, and make handling much easier. When used over foam interiors the flimsy lining reduces the grip and abrasion properties of foam surfaces, and allows easier handling particularly during machine closing and filling. Sealing the ends of the stockinette lining is done by overlock sewing or by heat-sealing equipment.

Fig 6.8 A fibre-filled cushion covered in stockinette and sealed at each end.

Non-woven fabric linings

The non-woven fabrics used in furniture as support cloths and linings are the spun-bonded type. These are produced mainly from polypropylene yarns. Webs of staple fibres are heat pressed and rolled together to form a strong non-woven cloth of different weights. The cloth is easily recognised by its flat, fibrous nature, lightweight feel, and sometimes an embossed perforated surface.

Much of this type of fabric is used for disposable clothing and cleaning cloths, etc. Heavier weights are used for upholstery in place of traditional hessian, and as underlinings for those areas that require a strong fabric and are not normally seen. Non-woven fabric linings are continually being improved and developed further, but because of their nature will only be used as inner linings for upholstery and not as covers. The technique of stitch bonding is also well developed and these fabrics may well be used for upholstery purposes as linings. Pieces are 100m and 200m long in widths of 24in (60cm), 30in (76cm) and 48in (120cm) and up to 100in (2.5m).

There is a range of cloth weights and densities. The following is a typical specification for upholstery applications:

Average weight (g/sqm)	100	125	140	155
Fibre denier	5	5	5	5
Breaking strength (N/cm)	40	50	70	90

Colours are white, grey, brown and black
1lb = 4.5N (Newtons)

Its properties include: good strength for sewing and stapling, dimensionally stable, does not fray, resists insects and mildew, odour-free and non-allergic, air permeable, and has good tear strength. Some particular applications are: insulation over springs, general lining of arms, insides, outsides and bottom, valance linings, base cloths for pad fillings and underlays.

Board materials

Various lightweight board materials are used to line up upholstery chair frames and to support filling in the modern chair. Basically, the boards do the job that was traditionally done by webbings and hessian. However, because of their strength they are often used to help reinforce and strengthen a chair frame, using the principal of box construction.

The three boards used most are thin plywood ⅛–¼in (3–6mm thick), ³/₁₆in (5mm) hardboard, and 2–3mm millboard. Millboard is particularly well suited for use in upholstery. Dark grey or black in colour, it is a high-density fibre board, with good holding properties and pliable enough to be stapled or pinned around shaped framing. All the boards are manufactured in 8 × 4ft (2.4 × 1.2m) sheets.

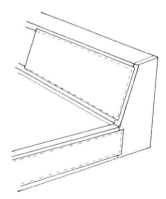

Fig 6.10 An inside arm and seat front lined with millboard.

Buckram

Glue, size and starch are all used to produce a stiffened fabric called buckram. For upholstery work hessian is used as the base material, and is heavily impregnated with glue, usually an animal glue. The glue content is normally not more than 45 per cent of the weight of the finished buckram. The material produced is similar in nature to a heavy cardboard, but with the strength and flexibility of a fabric. Cotton-based cloths are also used to produce a lighter weight buckram stiffened with the same percentage of size or starch.

Buckram is made in short rolls and strips 39in (1m) wide and less. High-quality stiffened all-cotton buckram is made in 100m rolls, 6in (15cm) and 12in (30cm) wide for use in soft furnishing. The making of

Fibretex non-woven lining cloth

Corovin non-woven underlining

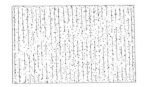

Fibretex non-woven polypropylene

Typar spun-bonded lining cloth

A non-woven cloth used on the underside of a cushion

Fig 6.9

upholstered pelmets is a good example of the use of buckram.

It is one of those traditional materials which has so many different uses in upholstery, and a small stock of odd pieces or short rolls should be kept handy. Buckram can be cut, folded or shaped, used to support corners, reinforce edges, used for back tacking, and for supporting outsides.

The use of animal glue allows for easy fixing of fabric to buckram, by simply heating with an electric iron, which melts the glue and provides a quick bond where required. This process is known as 'ironing on' and is used largely in soft furnishings, but can have its uses in upholstery. Coach trimmers, whose work is chiefly in the field of upholstered vehicle seating, use buckrams to upholster on to, and then apply and fix the panels into seats and vehicle sides. In any situation where the outside of a seat or back is not accessible to the upholsterer the buckram panel principle can be used to good effect (Fig 6.11).

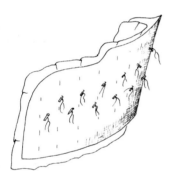

Fig 6.11 A buckram panel used to support fillings and buttoning before being fixed into seating where access is restricted.

FILLINGS, PADS AND INSULATORS

Natural fillings are either animal or vegetable in origin, produced from the seed, leaf or fruit of plants, or as hair and wool from various animals. Apart from foam fillings, which are dealt with in Chapter 10, synthetic fibre fillings add to the wide range that is available to the upholsterer and upholstery manufacturer.

It is important that the filling selected will do the job that it is required to do, and that the filling is pleasant and easy to use. Those fillings that have now become relics of the past were generally the poorer types, and at the same time were very coarse and difficult to use, and tended to be dusty. These were all vegetable materials and can often be found in old chairs pre-1950. Examples such as cotton millpuff, dyed seaweed and wood wool all become dry and brittle with age, and cannot be reused by carding and cleaning. The one notable exception is horsehair, which simply

went out of use because it is no longer available in any quantity and the high cost prohibits its general use.

A good upholstery filling should have high-bulk properties, not be too heavy, and be resilient and strong. The degree of hardness or feel is very important, and it is this quality which makes a filling suitable either as a first or a second stuffing. The stronger, firmer types make good insulators and the softer, lighter ones make better toppings. This principle applies equally to modern as well as traditional work. Foams manufactured for upholstery are regulated and used in exactly the same way, with resilience and density kept as high as possible throughout.

All filling materials are subject to flamability regulations and are tested and treated to conform with the Furniture and Furnishings (Fire) (Safety) Regulations 1988.

Natural filling fibres

Animal fibre

The term curled hair is now widely used to describe a mixture of pig hair and cow hair. Both are by-products of the meat trade, and are available in good quantity. American hog hair is imported to this country and blended with cow hair to produce a reasonably good mixture. A typical blend would be 85 per cent hog and 15 per cent cow, and the mixture left a natural grey colour or dyed completely black.

A better quality hair filling is produced from cow-tail hair; this is softer than hog hair and has a much longer fibre length. It is white in colour and has excellent resilience and bulk. The hair is carefully selected and processed to produce what is now the best available in any quantity. Mane hair is also used and blended in, and will be recognised as the shorter and softest fibres.

Small amounts of horsehair can be obtained, but relatively expensively; few jobs will justify the very high cost. Horsehair is the longest, hardest and most durable of the three types used for upholstery. Curled horsehair is clipped from the mane and tail of wild horses which are rounded up in South America once every year. In some cases small percentages of horsehair are still blended into curled hair mixtures, a maximum of 10 or 12 per cent of the mixture.

By nature animal hair is strong, resilient and durable. Fibre length varies from 1in (25mm) to 20in (500mm). Each tiny fibre acts as a minute spring when packed closely together. If all the hair fibres were left straight in their natural form and not curled, then the resulting filling would soon flatten and would feel rather dead. Curling of the fibre is therefore a very important part of the processing.

The raw material is scoured and deodorised then dried on a revolving platform blown with warm air. When thoroughly dry the blended long and short fibres are tightly twisted into ropes of about ¾in (19mm)

William and Mary Armchair
c. 1690

A walnut-upholstered armchair of fine proportions. The William and Mary period included many fine tall-back and wing-arm chairs, with carved and turned stretchers.

Upholstery Although cane-work seats and backs were still being produced, richly upholstered pieces of furniture became the vogue during this period. Wool and animal hair covered in linen provided a comfortable foundation for the rich heavy fabrics.

Coverings Were in embroidered silk and imported Italian velvets and brocades. Many examples had plain cotton or linen covers on the outside arms and outside backs.

thick and 40ft (12m) long. Great care is taken to ensure the curling of every hair in the mixture. The ends of the ropes are joined together and plaited into 7m strands, which are then boiled in chemically treated water to give the hair a permanent set. Drying is then followed by seasoning for periods up to ninety days in cool, dry conditions.

Curled hair fillings are marketed to the upholsterer in three different forms, and can be selected for different types of work. Loose hair filling, in two qualities, is bought in 56lb (25kg) bags. Hair pads are produced by needling layers of curled hair on to 200g weight hessian, at a density of about 5oz per sq yd (140g per sq m). This produces a dense prefabricated pad about 1in (25mm) thick. Sizes of pad are 24in (60cm), up to 72in (180cm) wide and any length required. Hair pads make good insulators and are used directly over spring units, particularly in the bedding industry in good quality mattress making. The pads have the advantage of being quick and easy to apply, and of even density throughout. The hessian or woven polypropylene backing can be easily clipped or stapled in place. The needling process is done with long comb needles which have hook points, and as they pass through the hair layer small amounts are pushed and tufted into the backing cloth.

Rubberised hair sheet is another way in which curled hair is fabricated into easily used sheeting. A conveyor system is used on to which the short staple hair is sprinkled and then sprayed with a fine spray of liquid latex rubber. Further layers are added until the thickness of sheet required is reached. The sheet is

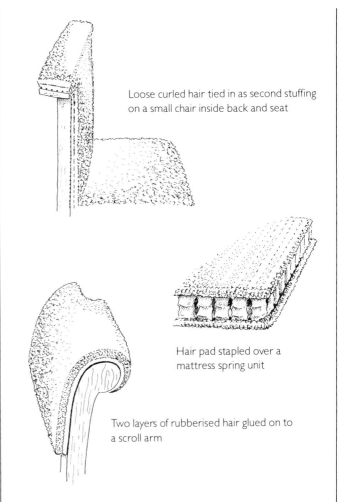

Loose curled hair tied in as second stuffing on a small chair inside back and seat

Hair pad stapled over a mattress spring unit

Two layers of rubberised hair glued on to a scroll arm

Fig 6.12

continuous at about 80in (2m) wide. Heat is applied to vulcanise and cure the latex, which binds the product into a compact hair and rubber composition. One-metre-wide pieces are cut off the continuous layer, and each new sheet is then rolled and trimmed, and stored to age before use. Three densities are produced: light, medium and heavy at 1in (25mm) and 2in (50mm) thicknesses.

Although this material has largely been superseded by foam products in the mass production of upholstery, rubberised hair still offers the upholsterer a less costly flexible filling, easily shaped and fixed, which has special characteristics of its own. Each hair fibre is coated with the latex, which combines the resilience of a rubber product with the durability and feel of curled animal hair. It does have some advantages over plastic foams, particularly to the small-quantity user, and those engaged in reproduction work. It provides an excellent platform for other loose fillings in chair inside arm and back upholstery, and retains the traditional feel of hand-built work.

Its resistance to fire and difficult and slow ignition is said to be equal to fire-retardant polyurethane foams, which are far more costly. Rubberised hair can be successfully moulded, and is produced as moulded components for the specialised packaging industry.

Specifications

> 1in (25mm) sheet, light density, 24oz (670g)
> 1in (25mm) sheet, medium density, 36oz (1000g)
> 2in (50mm) sheet, medium density, 36oz (1000g)
> 1in (25mm) sheet, heavy density, 48oz (1340g)
> Sheet size, all 2m × 1m

Vegetable fibre
Coconut (coir) fibre

The outer husk of the coconut provides the raw material for this tough and durable upholstery filling. It is occasionally dyed black, but mainly left in its natural ginger-brown colour, by which it is easily recognised. Bales of raw coir fibre are shipped to this country from tropical countries, such as Sri Lanka, East Indies, Thailand and East and West Africa. When the very thick layer of fibrous husk is removed from the fruit, it is laid out to dry in the sun, and then shredded into loose fibre and baled. The processing of coir fibre is very similar to that for curled hair fillings. The fibre is cleaned, then all the very short fibres and particles of the outer husk are removed. Very tightly twisted ropes are made up from the long, fresh fibres and the curl is set with mild chemical solutions and steam heat. After drying the ropes are cut into short lengths, and carding produces a mass of curled coir fibre ready for use.

Traditionally, this filling was known as 'ginger fibre' or more often just 'fibre'. More recently, the term coir fibre, and the trade name 'Curlifil', are used to specify this filling. The name Willowed Fly has also been used to describe fillings of this type. This relates to the

A twisted rope of coconut fibre

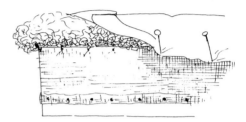

Coir fibre first stuffing tied down over a spring edge

Fig 6.13

spraying of the raw fibre with a mist of white oil, to make processing easier and cleaner.

Loose coir fibre makes an excellent first stuffing, or scrim stuffing for traditional work. By nature it is coarse, strong and reasonably resilient. It packs and forms well, and can be stitched to a firm strong edge. Coir-fibre pads are prefabricated by layering on to hessian or woven polypropylene, in the same way as curled hair pads are produced. A base cloth of 7oz per yd (200g per m) is used, with a fibre density of 5oz (140g) per sq ft. Pads are 27in and 36in (675 and 900mm) wide for upholstery purposes, and up to 1.5m wide for mattress manufacture.

The bedding industry is now the major user of coir fibre in pad form. Its properties as a durable insulator in spring-interior mattress making are excellent. Old coconut fibre fillings which have been stripped from an existing chair can be carded and reused, provided the filling has not become too dry or brittle. If the old fibre is still of good length and is not obviously powdering, then it can be reused, perhaps with the addition of a small amount of new fibre.

Specifications

> Coir fibre, loose, black dyed, in bags of 55lb (25kg)
> Coir fibre, loose, natural ginger, in bags of 55lb (25kg)
> Curlifil, loose, natural colour, in bags of 55lb (25kg)
> Fibre pads, 5oz (140g) per sqft, 27in and 36in (675 and 900mm) wide by 20m rolls, larger or cut sizes to order

Some other uses for coir fibre include woven and bonded door mats, and bristle for brush and broom manufacture.

Algerian fibre

A filling which is not widely used in the industry, but is still available in loose form as a first stuffing. It is usually dyed black, and is slightly softer than coir fibre. Some upholsterers prefer to use Algerian fibre, applied by hand in the traditional manner. The filling is made from the palm leaves of the *Chamereops humilis*, which grows widely in southern Spain and North Africa. The leaves are shredded through a simple teasing machine and the fibre is dried and then curled in the way described for hair fillings.

The fibre in its natural green colour is extensively used in Europe. It can easily be recognised by its strong smell, and is dyed black as a means of sterilisation for use in the UK. It is about the same weight and density as coir fibre, though a little less coarse.

Pre-formed fibre pads are also produced, by needling on to 7oz (200g) hessian cloth. Many upholsterers who produce hand-built work prefer to use Algerian fibre, because it is kinder to the hands and does not pack down as densely as coir fibre fillings. Its resilience is good, but a small disadvantage is that the black dye can make the hands very dirty while the filling is being handled.

Sisal, from the agave plant
Another vegetable fibre which is now little used as an upholstery filling. Sisal is a very strong fibre, creamy white in colour with a lustrous surface. It has good bulk resilience and is much lighter and finer than coir fibre. Most of the sisal we use is grown in East Africa and then processed there mainly for the production of ropes and cords. Some sisal is also used in textile manufacture, blended in with other natural fibres.

A 25kg bag of Algerian vegetable fibre

A roll of needled sisal on 7oz hessian 27in (68.5cm) wide

Fig 6.14

Cotton felt
Cotton felt is a soft, white top stuffing, produced from pure new cotton which is felted and layered into a prefabricated filling, ready for use. The raw material is unspun cotton waste or cotton linters, removed at the ginning process during textile manufacture. Rolls of

white cotton felt are 24in (610mm) and 27in (685mm) wide, by 20m long and approximately 1in (25mm) thick. Two qualities are available, 2½oz per sq ft and 4oz per sq ft, the latter being a rather thicker, heavier felt.

For production purposes cotton felt pads can be made to almost any thickness and ready cut to size. During use any waste pieces of felt can be collected and kept, and then later carded and used as a loose cotton filling. Layered felts of this type have been in use for around fifty years in bedding and upholstery manufacture. Felted fillings are produced on a garnett machine which produces successive layers of fine cotton, to form thick pads of a predetermined thickness.

Its principal use is as a protective layer between fibre or hair and calico coverings. It has a smooth soft surface and tends to deaden any noise from first stuffings. Although felts have largely been superseded by a variety of upholstery foams, they are still produced in large quantities and used in reupholstery, restoration work, and are much in evidence in all types of bedding production. Flame-retardant cotton felts are available for special applications.

Wool felt or black felt
A soft and resilient top stuffing, made partly or wholly from a variety of woollen fibres. The raw materials for these fillings are mostly animal fibre which may originate from any of the following: sheep, lamb, camel, angora goat, cashmere goat, llama, vicuña and angora rabbit. These can be virgin materials or may be produced from recovered and reclaimed, spun, woven or knitted materials. The animal fibre content is not normally less than 85 per cent as defined in British Standard BS 2005.

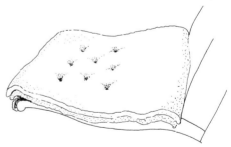

Two layers of cotton felt over curled hair provide a good basis for deep buttoning this chair back

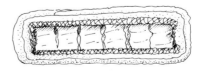

Layers of wool felt over coir-fibre pad provide the wrap on a spring cushion

Fig 6.15

Wool felts are manufactured in the same way as cotton felts by garnetting and layering to produce 20m rolls of three widths , 20in, 24in and 27in (510, 610 and 685mm). Weights are 2½oz per sq ft and 4oz per sq ft. Wool felts are easily recognised by their blue-grey colour with a mixture of many other colours in the form of yarns and reclaimed wools. They have a slightly softer, warmer feel than cotton felt, and by nature have a better tensile strength. Carpet underfelts are produced in a similar way from the same materials.

A modification of wool felt is Feltex, which is made by compressing the felt and needling it on to paper. This produces a dense, firm pad ideal for use as an insulator directly over frames, spring units and flexolator units. Another adaptation of wool felt is woollen mixture felts, which can have an animal fibre content as low as 60 per cent.

Upholsterers who prefer to work with loose fillings will buy wool felts and tease them out by hand for the building and shaping of stuffover work, particularly deep buttoning. A layer of curled hair followed by teased wool felt makes an excellent medium for shaped work in the traditional manner. (BS 1425 refers to cotton felts, BS 1762 refers to wool felts.)

Waddings

Traditionally a cotton filling, which is now only available as skin wadding, with a sprayed surface of cellulose. A 20m roll is 18in (450mm) wide and weighs 32oz (900g). Waddings are folded from a 36in (900mm) width down to 18in (450mm) and can be used single or left double. It will often be necessary to use more than one layer of unfolded wadding, depending on the work being done.

The sprayed skin surface provides a barrier when wadding is used as a top stuffing over curled hair; however, more than one layer is necessary to keep the hair from creeping through scrim and calico linings. Skin waddings are made from carded cotton, or carded rayon fibre, and the rayon type appears more white and silky than raw cotton. Wadding is a very useful smooth, soft, fine padding, which fills a variety of needs in upholstery and soft furnishing.

Flock fillings

Washed flock is a general term which describes a composition of new and old materials and textiles, which have been shredded and carded into a mass of clean fibre and prepared for use as loose fillings. The filling must be free fom any rubbish, grit or dust, and will conform to a standard of cleanliness as laid down by law in the 'Rag Flock Act'. The quality of washed flock is generally very good today, and contains a good proportion of pure wool rags, which gives the filling resilience and bulk, without too much weight.

An example of washed flock will show a mixture of textile fibres as follows: spun, woven or knitted

materials old or new, thread waste, card waste, jute waddings, cotton flocks or cotton mixture felts, together with proportions of wool waste, wool felts and synthetic yarns. The wool content will vary from 85 down to 50 per cent, depending on quality. Washed flocks are recognised by their grey blue colour with some other colours mixed in. In loose form flocks are sold in 56lb (25kg) sacks, or in smaller amounts by arrangement.

Woollen flock

This is a better quality flock filling, which does not contain less than 70 per cent wool fibres. It is similar in colour to washed flock but the large percentage of woollens present gives the filling much better resilience and bulk, with less weight. Wool flocks are governed by the same standards of cleanliness, and are sold by the kilogramme or pound.

Both the above fillings are basically top stuffings which may be used on their own or over fibre and hair first stuffings. Flocks are not produced as prefabricated pads like felts, and so can only be used as loose stuffings for application by hand in traditional work.

Flock fillings have been used since early times for upholstery and bedding, as stuffings for cushions and mattresses, etc. The term flock simply means to reduce textile fibres to fragments by cutting, tearing and grinding.

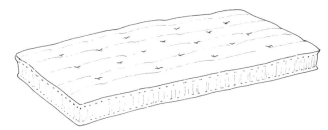

Fig 6.16 A stitched and tufted mattress, filled with washed flock and often covered with striped cotton ticking.

Kapok

A soft, fluffy upholstery filling used in seat and back cushions, and prefabricated cases. Kapok is also used as a mattress and pillow filling but is recommended generally for lightweight applications.

It is a light, silky vegetable down which adheres to the seeds in the seed pod of a tree known as *Ceiba pentandra*. This large tree grows best in Java which has the right soil and climatic conditions. After the seeds are removed, the soft fibres are tightly compressed by machinery into bales. The bales measuring 2ft × 2ft (610mm × 610mm) may often weigh as much as 85kg, or approximately 200lb.

When bales are opened for processing the kapok is converted into a usable filling. The machine used for this purpose is called a picking box, inside which huge wooden arms revolve on a steel axis at speeds up to 500rpm. The kapok emerges creamy white, soft and springy, and all seed particles, rubbish, etc., are caught in trays and removed from the base of the machine. The filling may be single processed or run through a second time to produce an improved quality filling called superfine.

By nature kapok is oily, water resistant, and so has a low absorbency rate. It was once used a great deal for cushions and mattresses on ships and boats, and is still used as a buoyancy aid in life jackets. Articles are filled by blowing the fibre into made-up cases, directly from storage hoppers. This eliminates handling and direct contact with the very fine kapok fibres.

As an upholstery filling, kapok should be used in a similar way to feathers and down. It should be contained in a proofed case, and movement restricted by sectioning or tufting whenever possible. Fig 6.17 shows two examples.

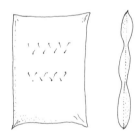

A front and side view of a tufted pillow, suitable for a chair back

A shaped kapok-filled cushion, which has three separately filled areas

Fig 6.17

Feather and down fillings
One of the few natural fillings which has been in use for several hundred years, and has not been superseded by modern fillings. There are no doubt many reasons for this: it is still available in quantity at a reasonable price, being a by-product of the food industry, and the feel, warmth and aesthetics of a good feather/down cushion cannot be easily copied or simulated.

Feather and down fillings are available in many different blends and qualities, and their resilience and support properties depend largely on their origin, type and the composition of the blends. Various types of feather, and small amounts of down are carefully mixed to suit particular purposes in bedding, upholstery, soft furnishing and also the clothing industry.

Down
Down is the covering of young birds and the under-covering of adult birds. It is found next to the skin on older birds, under the main feathers. Down grows especially thick on water fowl such as geese and ducks. Down has practically no quill, and the threadlike fibres radiate from a core centre in the form of a quill point.

Pure down is relatively expensive as only about 20 per cent of the entire covering obtained from a fowl is down. Owing to the difficulties of complete separation during processing, the inclusion of up to 35 per cent by weight of small, fine, fluffy feather is usually permissible in fillings which are labelled and accepted as pure down. This definition is given in BS 2005 Glossary of Terms for Fillings.

Eiderdown
This rare and expensive filling is the under-coating from the breast of the eider duck. It is lighter and warmer than any other known downs. The eider is a species of sea duck which lives in sub-Arctic regions.

The term 'eiderdown' is often used to describe an overlay or quilt for a bed. However, it is more correct to describe such an article as a down quilt, unless it contains 100 per cent pure eiderdown. The best quality downs used today are duck or goose down, which are mostly imported from Far Eastern countries such as China and Japan.

Goose feathers
The next in line for quality and value is goose feathers. It is a springy and buoyant filling due to the curved or cup-shaped contour of the quills. A mass of long, slender fibre grows from the curved quill of the goose feather, providing an excellent light filling with good resilience and loft.

Duck feathers
Not quite so valuable in filling terms as goose, as they do not have the abundance of fibre or the natural strength. However, they do have curved quills and provide a good grade filling at reasonable cost.

Poultry – chicken, turkey and others
These feathers have a relatively low buoyancy, due to their straight contour quills and lower compression resistance under weight. Poultry feathers should not be used where good resilience is required.

Feathers from these birds are often processed to improve their grading by either stripping and blowing the fibres from the feathers to produce a low-grade down, called featherdown, or alternatively the feathers are chopped into small, short pieces to produce a filling described as chopped feather. Both methods make use of the whole covering and may be used as lower grade fillings or blended in small quantities with other grades.

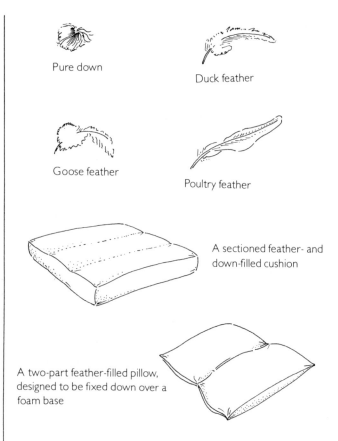

Pure down

Duck feather

Goose feather

Poultry feather

A sectioned feather- and down-filled cushion

A two-part feather-filled pillow, designed to be fixed down over a foam base

Fig 6.18

Cleanliness

Cleaning and sterilisation are, of course, important with any natural filling. Downs and feathers standards are laid down in BS 1425 Cleanliness of Fillings.

Blending and specifications

For cushions and quilts in furniture manufacture, pure down is not suitable as a 100 per cent filling, since curled feathers have much better bulk and resilience. Mixtures and gradings are given below.

> Pure down – with permissible 35 per cent fine feather
> Feather/down – a minimum of 51 per cent feathers mixed with down
> Down/feathers – a minimum of 51 per cent down mixed with feathers
> Feather – goose, duck or poultry 100 per cent or mixed, as labelled
> Featherdown – stripped feather fibre
> Chopped feathers – usually poultry

Polyester fibre fillings

It is probably true to say that a very large percentage of modern upholstery made today will contain some polyester fibre in one form or another. Over the last two decades the words Dacron and Terylene have become common terms in the trade. The development and use of these fibres has changed the look and feel of

modern chairs; they were in fact used commercially as early as 1955.

Polyester fibre is a soft synthetic filament, available in different deniers (thicknesses), and produced as waddings, battings and bonded insulators. It is a very clean white, versatile fibre filling, which is easily handled, and can be cut sewn or glued, to produce clean soft lines in modern and traditional work. Polyester fibre is produced basically as a top stuffing, or as a wrap, in many different weights and densities. It blends extremely well with all types of foam and makes a good overlay in the finishing of traditional upholstery.

There are basically two types of fibre, solid and hollow, and these are shaped to give varying degrees of resilience and feel. The fibre is produced in short staple length, or as continuous filament. All these basic physical characteristics are used to provide a variety of fillings for different uses.

Fibre structure and formation

Any man-made fibre can be manufactured to suit its end use by making it long or short, thick or thin, straight or shaped. Fig 6.19 illustrates the two types, solid polyester fibre, and hollow fibre. These are then shaped or curled by mechanically crimping in one of three ways, to give bulk and resilience. Finally the fibre is cut into short staple lengths, or left as continuous filament.

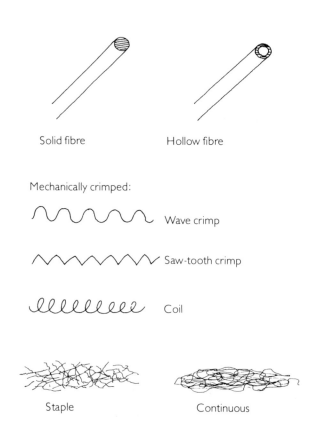

Solid fibre

Hollow fibre

Mechanically crimped:

Wave crimp

Saw-tooth crimp

Coil

Staple

Continuous

Fig 6.19 Polyester filling fibres for furniture and furnshings.

Processing

The newly formed fibres can now be processed into waddings, battings and compressed fibre pads. This is done by carding the fibres into a fine web. The webs are laid one upon another by cross lapping to form a given thickness. To provide stability and reduce fibre movement, and also maintain the physical properties of the filling, the battings are then bonded. Bonding is achieved in any of three ways: surface bonding, centre bonding or through bonding.

At different stages in the processing, resins are applied by spraying and then dried by hot air and cured while passing through an oven. The resin hardens while drying and bonds the surface fibres together, producing a material which is easy to cut and handle. Some battings are bonded in the centre as well as on the surface, to give better load support characteristics. Through bonding a batting is produced whereby the fibres are bonded to each other where they touch throughout the whole filling. This process eliminates the need for surface and centre bonding, and produces a filling evenly stable throughout, but with rather different characteristics. The upholsterer or manufacturer must choose the type of polyester filling that suits his purpose best (Fig 6.20).

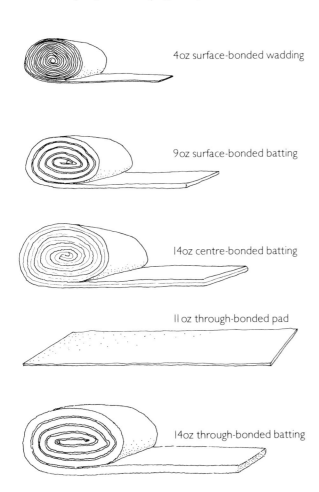

4oz surface-bonded wadding

9oz surface-bonded batting

14oz centre-bonded batting

11oz through-bonded pad

14oz through-bonded batting

Fig 6.20

Specifications using polyester fibre fillings

Wadding	27in × 2½oz/sq yd	50m rolls
	27in × 4oz/sq yd	40m rolls
	36in × 4oz/sq yd	40m rolls
	27in × 5oz/sq yd	30m rolls
Batting	24in × 9oz/sq yd	20m rolls
	54in × 14oz/sq yd	10m rolls

Insulator pad   11oz and 14oz through-bonded polyester wadding, in rolls and cut pads

Loose carded polyester   Standard quality cushion filling, 14lb bags

Hollofil fibre cushion filling, 20lb bags

Long fibre, very soft for quilts

Recommended filling and using techniques

Polyester filling as 100 per cent filling in cushions, recommended minimum densities:

Seat cushions, 3.15oz/sq ft/per 1in of border
Back cushions, 2.8oz/sq ft/per 1in of border

Polyester as a wrap-over foam core:

1   Cut the core to the finished size of the cushion
2   Height of the core should be equal to border height
3   Wrap one layer of 14oz/sq yd around a core of foam
4   Sew around sides for stability and neat appearance

Polyester fibre as a criss-cross wrap:

1   Cut two lengths of 14oz/sq yd batting
2   Wrap first length around cushion side to side and sew
3   Wrap second length around cushion front to back and sew at back

Polyester fibre as a glue-on pad to foam:

1   Cut two pads ¾in (19mm) less than plan size of core
2   Spray adhesive on edge of fibre, and exposed edge of foam
3   Pinch edges together and repeat on other side

Polystyrene beads

These are not an upholstery filling in the strict sense, but they have been used since the 1960s to fill large, shaped bags to make a type of fun furniture. A strong fabric bag or cushion, two thirds filled with polystyrene beads, makes an interesting and useful occasional form of seating.

The beads used are the white, soft pre-expanded styrene, made from petro-chemicals which are more often seen as moulded sheet or tiles for house insulation. With safety in mind, it is wise to buy the flame-retardant type, which are sold in labelled bags containing 10lb (4½kg). Polystyrene beads are not difficult to handle if they are funnelled through a large tube directly into a prepared calico case. The case can then be closed by machine, and put into a tailored cover, which is usually zipped across its base.

All fillings for use in upholstered furniture are now produced combustion modified (CM), which makes them flame retardant to the standards laid down in the Furniture and Furnishings (Fire) (Safety) Regulations 1988 (British Standards BS 5752 parts 1 and 2).

Cut and layered 100 per cent fibre filling

Folded 100 per cent fibre filling

Rolled 100 per cent fibre filling

14oz single-layer around a foam core

Two pieces of 14oz sewn around a slim foam core

Two pieces of 14oz batting cut and glued to a foam core

Fig 6.21 Uses of polyester filling.

Polystyrene beads pre-expanded by steam heat

A cylinder-shaped floor cushion filled with beads and pulled in at the centre

Fig 6.22

TRIMMINGS AND FINISHES

It is not possible to list all the different trimings that are available, as the variety is enormous and will vary from one manufacturer to another. The main types are illustrated (Figs 6.23–33). From the early seventeenth century, decoration has been added to upholstery and house furnishings in order to hide fixings and enhance and finish fabric work. Such trimmings were heavy and elaborate during certain periods, or were almost non-existent during others. Fashion, as it still does, tended to dictate the degree to which a particular style was decorated and trimmed.

The upholsterer will select and use the trimmings available, to obtain a pleasing and interesting effect. Selection should be based either on tradition or a customer's requirements, or simply as a functional method of closing and finishing. Woven trimmings were traditionally made from silk, wool or cotton, with sometimes the addition of fancy yarns or threads in gold, silver and other metals. Today, the majority of trimmings are woven from synthetic yarns, particularly acetate and viscose rayons.

Gimp and braid

Both these trimmings can be described as narrow woven fabrics produced on trimming machinery. The term gimp, however, is the method of making a fancy yarn by wrapping a group of threads with a number of other threads in a fine spiral. This forms a very narrow cord, and it is from this that gimp and braid trimmings are woven (Fig 6.23). Braids and gimps vary in width from ⅜in to 1in (10mm–25mm).

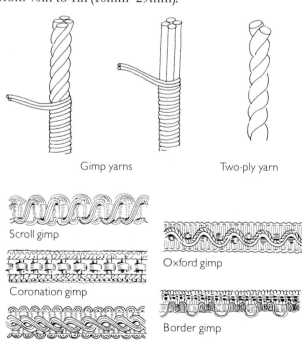

Gimp yarns   Two-ply yarn

Scroll gimp

Oxford gimp

Coronation gimp

Border gimp

Argyle gimp

Fig 6.23

Trimming cord

A decorative silk cord, made up from different fancy yarns, some of which are gimp yarns, and others which are two- and three-ply twisted yarns. By combining these some very interesting effects are achieved, particularly when different colours are used. Upholstery cords vary in thickness from $\frac{3}{16}$in to $\frac{3}{8}$in (5mm–10mm) in diameter (Fig 6.24).

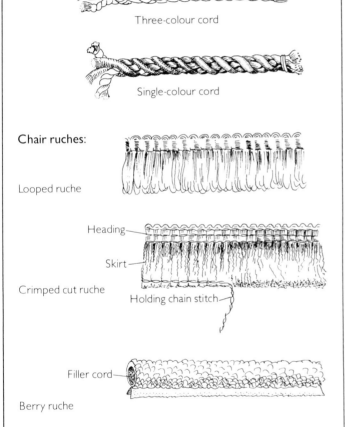

Three-colour cord

Single-colour cord

Chair ruches:

Looped ruche

Heading

Skirt

Crimped cut ruche

Holding chain stitch

Filler cord

Berry ruche

Fig 6.24 Furnishing cords.

Ruche

A narrow woven or knitted fabric, which has a heavy multiple weft to form a ruche edge, rather like a miniature fringe. There are three types, looped ruche, cut ruche and berry ruche, and they are all flanged to provide an edge for fixing or sewing into a seam (Fig 6.24).

Fringe

Another narrow woven fabric, which has cut or looped weft threads. These hang or extend beyond the warps to form a decorative edge. The weft threads forming the fringe are sometimes bunched or knotted together to produce different effects. Fringe is made up of a

heading and a skirt, and may also have tassels and balls added for effect and decoration.

Fringes are used as an edging which may be glued, pinned or sewn, mainly to chair bases. Carpets, pelmets and bed covers are all fringed when traditional effects are required. There is a wide range of types and sizes from small 1in (25mm) fringes to heavy furniture weights hanging to a depth of 8in (200mm).

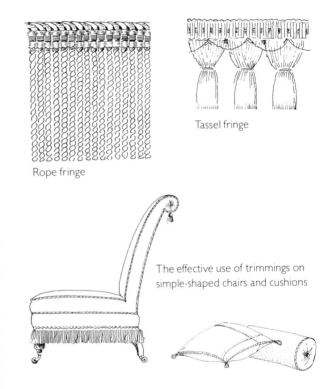

Rope fringe

Tassel fringe

The effective use of trimmings on simple-shaped chairs and cushions

Fig 6.25 Fringes.

Non-woven trimmings and finishes

Banding

A narrow strip of leather or plastic-coated fabric is folded and glued into a flat band of about $\frac{1}{2}$in (13mm) width. Bandings are designed to be fixed with studs or upholstery nails, around edges, facings, etc., and are mostly used in leather work, or with vinyl-coated fabrics.

Bandings may be purchased by the metre and in a variety of colours. Leather bandings can be bought by the roll, or made up especially for a particular job. The waste or offcuts can be sent to a banding maker, who will cut and skive the short lengths together and make up several metres for the job in hand. After cutting and joining the banding is formed by gluing, folding and tooling through a tooling roller. Alternatively, when only a few metres of banding is needed in leather it is reasonably simple to cut narrow strips with a good knife, about the width of the nail heads being used, and put the joints under the nail heads, at the end of each piece. This is a little more difficult with vinyls as both edges will have to be turned in.

Split banding or hidem banding
A relatively modern banding, made up from vinyl-coated fabric. The narrow strips are folded and machine-sewn to form a centre split around two small cords. This trimming is bought in 50m rolls in all colours, and is designed for fixing with staples or pinned with gimp pins.

The banding is opened at its centre for fixing and then closed to hide the fixing method. Ideal for the finishing of vinyl and leather coverings on modern upholstered chairs.

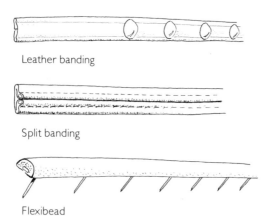

Leather banding

Split banding

Flexibead

Fig 6.26 Non-woven trimmings.

Flexibead
A flexible, half-round leather or vinyl-covered beading, which has been used as the traditional alternative to decorative nailing for many years. It was originally made with a lead core which was covered in leather and stitched by hand. Nails are inset at intervals along the bead for hammering into upholstered edges. Coach trimmers used flexibead made from solid brass, or leather-covered, for their vehicle interiors during the nineteenth century. The updated version used today has a flat wire core, with inset nails and compressed paper surrounding the wire which is coated in a bonded vinyl or leather covering. Flexibead can be bought in a range of colours in 100m reels (Fig 6.26).

FIXINGS AND FITTINGS

Tacks
Cut-steel, blued tacks are made in four sizes and produced in two grades, fine and improved. Fine tacks are the standard types used for most upholstery fixing work. Sizes are given as the overall length and are ¼in, ⅜in, ½in and ⅝in (6mm, 10mm, 13mm and 16mm).

This range will serve for most purposes, except when a very loose woven material is to be fixed or, when a substantial fixing is needed through several heavy layers. The improved range of sizes are slightly heavier gauge, and have larger heads. Many upholsterers make a habit of using improved tacks for webbing and hessian work and keep fine tacks for scrims, covers and general fixings. ¼in (6mm) sizes need only be kept in very small amounts, as they are useful only for very fine work, or on thin plywood panels.

For the occasions when a very long fixing is needed then fine tacks are available at ¾in and 1in (19mm and 25mm). All sizes are available in small 500g and large 10kg boxes.

Copper tacks are used in upholstery and furnishing in ships and boats or where furniture is to be exported to tropical countries.

Gimp pins
The gimp pin is a fine-cut steel pin which is coloured, and used traditionally for the fixing of gimps, braids and fringes. It is, however, very useful as a fine fixing in many areas of upholstery, particularly for finishing, and as a first fixing before bandings or nails are applied. Gimping pin sizes are ⅜in and ½in (10mm and 13mm) and pins are available in the following colours, white, black, fawn, grey, yellow, red, green, blue and brown. A 500g box of each will normally last a very long time.

Staples

Wire staples
Bright steel or galvanised steel ⅝in (15mm) wire staples are used in upholstery for spring work. Mostly for the holding of springs on to timber frames, and for edge wires, and the occasional fixing of lightweight tension springs.

Upholstery staples
An efficient, fast and very clean industrial fastener, which has taken over from the tack in the factory situation. The upholstery staple has a crown width of approximately ⅜in (10mm) and is made in four leg lengths: ⅛in, ¼in, ⅜in, and ½in (3mm, 6mm, 10mm and 13mm). They are produced for use in staple guns which may be manual, electric or pneumatic. An average box contains 10,000 staples in pre-formed magazine lengths. The standard size staple is available in a silver colour or with the crown surface painted black.

Gimp staples
These staples are narrow crown staples about 4mm wide, and when fired into fabrics are almost hidden. They are available in several different painted colours, and are used as final fixings on cover and trimmings. Because of the narrow crown width, a special gun is needed to fire this type of staple.

Loose Seat for a Dining Chair

3 The webbing is completely covered with a medium weight hessian, which is tacked and turned back at the edges. The hessian is pulled hand tight (see Fig 13.4).

I The loose seat frame rests in a rebate, with a gap of about ³/₁₆in (2.5mm or the thickness of a ten pence piece) all round to allow for the thickness of calico and covering.

2 English webbing is tightly strained and interwoven with spaces of about 1½in (38mm) between webs. ½in fine or improved tacks are ideal for fixing (see Fig 13.2).

4 Stuffing ties hold the curled hair filling in place, which is evenly teased to a good thickness of approximately 1½in (38mm). Alternative fillings of wool flock or firm grade seating foam may be used (see Figs 13.6 and 13.7).

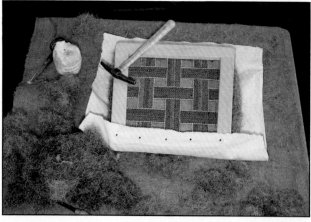

5 Cotton calico is cut oversize and set on by temporary tacking along the back edge of the seat frame. Pulling down tightly in calico continues until all the edges are fixed and the corners pleated (see Fig 13.8).

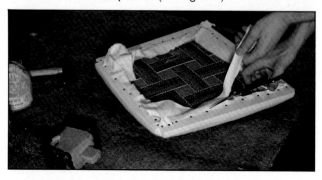

6 Adjustments can be made while the tacking is temporary. All tacks can then be driven home and excess calico trimmed off.

7 Second stuffing consists of two layers of skin wadding. No fillings should be allowed to run over the top outer edge of the frame.

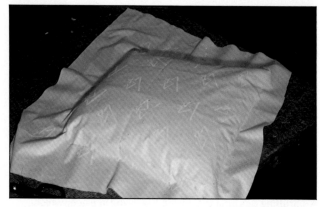

8 The top covering is laid over the seat and the grain of the cloth and the pattern are carefully lined up and centred (see page 113).

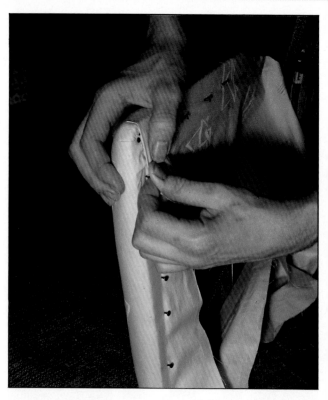

9 The covering technique and sequence of working is as for the calico. Corners must be smooth and tight with small folds or pleats.

10 After trimming, the seat is pushed down into the chair to check for a snug fit before an underlining of hessian or black cotton is tacked on to finish (see Figs 15.1 and 15.2).

Piped Scatter Cushion

1 To make a scatter cushion of average size, two pieces of fabric are cut 17in (425mm) square, and contrast or self piping strips 1½in (38mm) wide are cut and joined (see page 184, Fig 13.37).

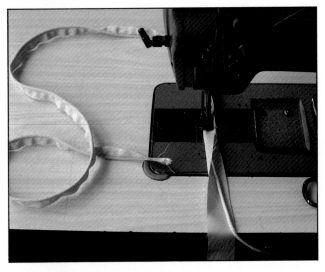

2 The piping is made up into a continuous strip using cotton twist piping cord (see page 124, Fig 9.24).

3 By laying all the cut edges together the strip is over sewn around the face edge of the fabric square.

4 The second fabric square is sewn face down over the first piece by over sewing along the same piping seam. A gap of about 8in (200mm) is left along one side for filling.

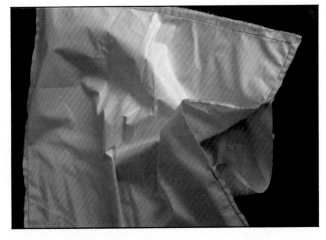

5 The cushion interior is made up from down-proof cotton cambric. Two pieces 17in (425mm) square are sewn together so that when turned the shiny surfaces are inside (see pages 187 and 67).

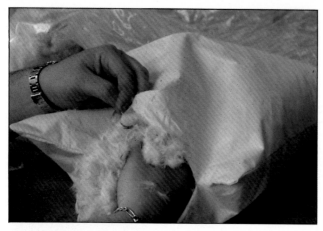

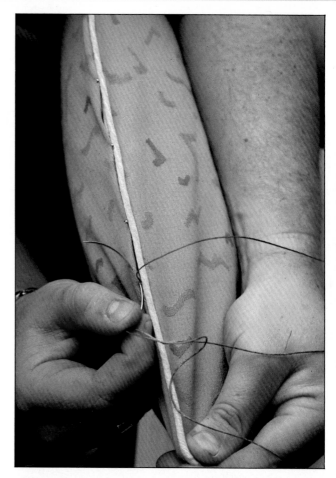

6 About 1lb (0.45kg) of mixed feather filling is needed to ensure that the case is well filled. The opening is turned in and closed by machine sewing (see page 187, Fig 13.44).

7 After cleaning, the feather interior is squeezed into the cushion cover and the corners pushed into place.

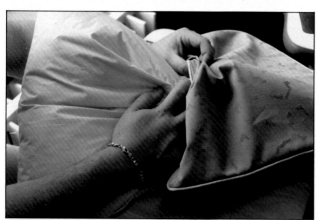

8 A small circular needle and some waxed thread are used to slip stitch and close the cover along the under edge of the piping (see page 120, Fig 9.17).

9 The completed cushion (see page 273, Fig 19.11).

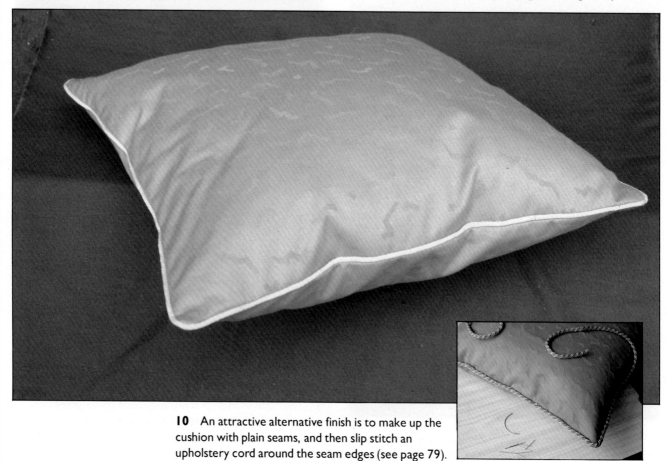

10 An attractive alternative finish is to make up the cushion with plain seams, and then slip stitch an upholstery cord around the seam edges (see page 79).

William and Mary Stool
c. 1690–1700

Made in walnut with crossed serpentine stretchers. This large stool was part of a suite or an extension to a chair.

Upholstery The work is carefully executed to match the framework. Strong linen cloth supports its fillings of wool and hair.

Coverings Embroidered velvet or wool tapestry has been trimmed with border fringes and tassels.

Framing staples
Heavy-duty stapling is now common in assembly of chair frames, and for the fixing of springs and spring units. These jobs call for staples of a heavy gauge with leg lengths up to 2in (50mm). Refer to Chapter 4.

Nails

Clout nails
These nails are bright steel wire nails with a large head, and are made in three leg-length sizes, ¾in, 1in and 1¼in (19mm, 25mm and 32mm). They are a universally useful nail, but their main function is in the fixing of springs and spring units. The clout nail is extremely strong and its large head provides a good sound fixing.

Bright steel jagged nails
A smaller slimmer version of the clout nail, but with a jagged leg design, which gives good holding in timber frames. Jagged nails are ¾in (19mm) long and are used particularly in the areas of spring fixing where movement of components can cause the loosening of fixing nails. A good example of this is the spring clips used to hold sinuous wire (zig-zag) springs.

Serrated clout tacks
The clout tack is a blued steel heavy tack, with a very large head and a jagged or serrated leg. These are designed as an alternative to the clout nail and they have very good holding properties similar to the jagged nail. Uses are in the springing area of upholstery production, and the length is 1in (25mm).

Upholstery nails
This is a range of decorative nails which is special to upholstery. They have a long and interesting history,

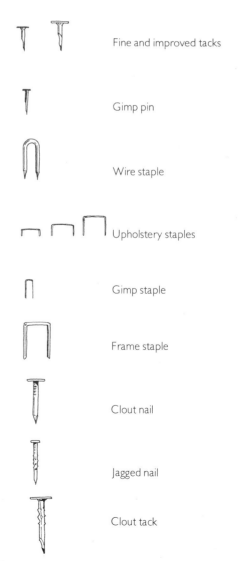

Fine and improved tacks

Gimp pin

Wire staple

Upholstery staples

Gimp staple

Frame staple

Clout nail

Jagged nail

Clout tack

Fig 6.27

and have been used by the upholsterer for well over 250 years. The early upholstery of leather-covered oak chairs had large raised head nails to fix and hold the leather in place and decorate chair edges. Brass nailing became particularly fashionable during the mid-eighteenth century and was specified by many designers of that period. Today, fixings are more sophisticated and the upholstery nail is only used as a decoration and finish in traditional and reproduction work. The range and design of nail heads is very wide, and selection must be made with care, as with all trimmings (Fig 6.28).

Standard size nails are about ⅜in (10mm) diameter with a ¾in (19mm) leg length. Surface treatment of the domed heads can vary from plain brass to intricate design, embossed pattern and enamelled paint finishes. British and French nails are particularly good, having a steel leg and a fancy raised head. A range of examples is listed below, and the nails can be bought singly or in boxes of 1000.

⅜in (10mm) antique on steel, polished brass, antique brass, antique on brass, electro brassed, Oxford hammered, speckled old gold, French natural, bronze renaissance, honeycomb, daisy, ¾in (19mm) antique on steel, ⅞in (22mm) antique on steel, ¼in (6mm) nickel-plated or brassed, ⅜in (9mm) enamelled, all colours.

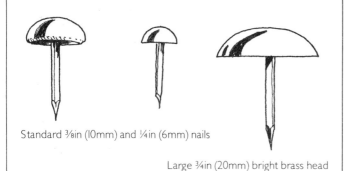

Standard ⅜in (10mm) and ¼in (6mm) nails

Large ¾in (20mm) bright brass head

Nail head designs

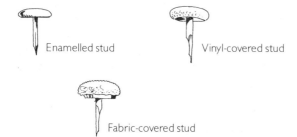

Enamelled stud

Vinyl-covered stud

Fabric-covered stud

Fig 6.28 Upholstery nails.

Press studs

There are several different methods of fixing upholstery covers down, and holding them in place, while at the same time allowing for easy removal at a later date. The press stud is universally used for this purpose. It is easily applied and can be used in a variety of ways. For example, fabric to fabric, fabric to wood or metal, and fabrics or straps to lightweight board materials.

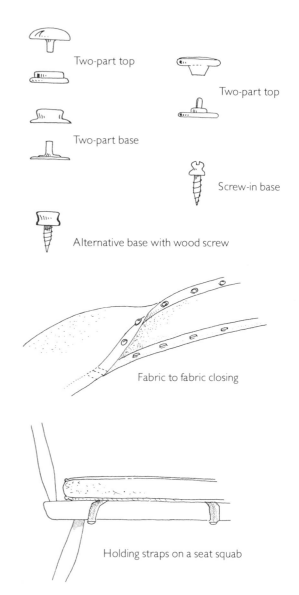

Two-part top

Two-part top

Two-part base

Screw-in base

Alternative base with wood screw

Fabric to fabric closing

Holding straps on a seat squab

Fig 6.29

The component parts are located and hammered together, producing male and female locations. The female base components can be screwed or bolted to timber or metal frames. The resulting joint is strong and holds well in the majority of upholstery situations. The strength of the joint produced depends largely on the number of press studs used in a small area.

The average upholstery covering is fairly heavy, but should this method be used on some lightweight cloths then reinforcement will probably be necessary. This can easily be done by using an edge which is folded several times or putting in a stiffener, such as canvas, scrim or a non-woven lining, before the studs are fitted. Most upholsterers use the standard silver chrome or nickel-plated press stud, but various types can be bought in enamelled colours. With thought and preplanning, press stud fixings can be located so that they are not visible, and are there simply to hold a component or an edge in place (Fig 6.29). Tooling for fixing press studs is shown in Chapter 4.

Ventilators and clips

The ventilator is used in cushion making and mattress borders to allow a flow of air into and out of a confined space. In all upholstered furniture the movement and flow of air is important. When coverings are used in cushion making which do not have the ability to breathe easily the vents should be fitted to allow easy air flow. Ventilators are always fitted to mattresses whatever the coverings may be. In upholstery a good example of the need for vents is when hides or vinyls are used as covers. Vents should be fitted at the backs or along borders of cushions where they will not be too obvious.

There are two types generally available, the brass ventilator, which requires tooling to fit it to a fabric, and the plastic vent, which can be simply fixed into a pre-cut hole by hand; ¾in (19mm) diameter is an average size (Fig 6.30).

Eyelets

A fitting which tends to be used in modern upholstery. Eyelets may often be needed in leather and canvas work and can also be used for ventilation. The eyelet is made in many different sizes from the small lace-hole

Brass ventilator and base

Plastic vent   Press-on clip

The assembled vent

Fig 6.30

type up to a 1in (25mm) diameter size. The tools needed to press eyelets into a fabric are fairly simple and are usually supplied with a pack of eyelet parts. An eyelet is made up from two parts, a top and a base ring, and these are fitted together with the fabric in between and hammered together. Once made, the fixing is permanent, so care should be taken to ensure correct positioning before a hole is cut.

Eyelets can be fitted where a permanent hole is

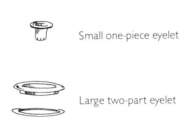

Small one-piece eyelet

Large two-part eyelet

Fig 6.31

needed, as a means of taking card, elastic or lace through a cover. They can also be used effectively as rivets to finish or strengthen a joint or at the end of a heavy seam (Fig 6.31).

SUNDRIES

Twines

Flax, jute, hemp and ramie have all traditionally been used to manufacture upholstery twines. They are all strong and durable vegetable fibres, each with its own particular character and properties. Upholstery twines are relatively fine and are graded sizes 1 to 4, size No. 1 being the finest. Best quality flax twines are widely accepted as being stronger and more durable than those heavier twines made from other fibres. A good grade twine is manufactured from good grade fibre, with a tight twist formation. Upholstery mattress twines are all a drab, brown colour. Twines may be strengthened and made more durable by the addition of oils and waxes. Many upholsterers who do a lot of stitch work, keep a lump of beeswax, through which a length of twine is drawn before use. This improves its natural strength and allows a certain amount of grip on other materials. A non-slip twine makes for good tight stitching, which holds shape well.

Size No.4 is a heavy twine used principally for tying in springs and for some lightweight lashing work and for buttoning. Size No. 2 is a good weight for stitching and the forming of edges. Size No. 1 is very fine but strong and can be kept for use on very small fine stitch work and hand sewing.

When an exceptionally strong twine is needed for tufting, buttoning or lashing down then a yellow nylon twine can be used. This has excellent resistance to rubbing and abrasion, and so is recommended when movement is likely on a buttoned chair seat or back. Twines are bought in 250g balls or cops (approx ½lb), and there are six balls to a pack. Large 1kg cops are also available.

Slipping thread

A heavy sewing thread which is made in several colours; however, the most used colours are the drab browns which will blend well with most coverings.

Slipping threads, which are made especially for slip stitching and hand finishing, are made from linen (flax) and sold as 50g skeins, or 500g cops. These threads are usually wax treated during manufacture. Skeins of thread need to be cut at one end to produce short lengths for sewing, and plaited for ease of handling and storage (Fig 6.32).

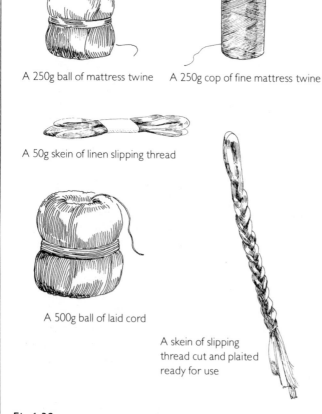

A 250g ball of mattress twine   A 250g cop of fine mattress twine

A 50g skein of linen slipping thread

A 500g ball of laid cord

A skein of slipping thread cut and plaited ready for use

Fig 6.32

CORDS

Laid cord

This is a heavy lashing cord, used to position and hold any form of springing, both traditional and hand built modern units. Laid cord is made from hemp, or flax and some jute. It is produced by laying the fibres together with a very small amount of twist, and takes its name from its laid construction. By making the cord in this way, very little stretch or give is experienced, and the cord will not slacken after use. Thus a tightly lashed seat will remain so for much of its life.

A heavy strong cord of this type has many uses in the upholstery workshop. Laid cord is produced in 600g balls, with six balls to a pack. 190m weighs approximately 1kg. Large 2½kg cops are made for bulk buying.

Cable cord

A lighter-weight cord made by twisting two or three plys together, and usually made from blended hemp and flax. It is equally as robust as laid cord and will give a little in use, however it is reasonably stable and very strong. 320m weighs 1kg, balls are 500g each.

Piping cords

These cords are made especially for use in upholstery and the sewing trade. The cord may be a filler or core folded inside a fabric strip which is then sewn into a seam or fixed to frame edges. Piping provides a reinforcement, or a decorative edge or an outline in a piece of furniture. They are available in many different sizes and materials, but generally fall in the three categories of fine, medium and heavy.

Natural cotton twist is the conventional material used for pipings and still remains superior to most others. Cotton is produced as standard or preshrunk pipings and bought in 1kg cops (approx 2lb). Some grades and types are given below:

Cotton twist – natural
Cotton twist – bleached, preshrunk
Jute twist – medium only
Braided washable cord, 4mm and 5mm
Paper twist – fine only
Braided paper cord, 4mm up to 25mm
Hollow soft plastic cord, 3mm up to 8mm
Foamed polyethylene – 3mm to 5mm diameter
Foamed PVC – with nylon core, smooth
Very soft hollow plastic, 6mm to 12mm
Jumbo supersoft, 6mm to 15mm
Flanged piping cords in a range of coloured plastics

For fixed upholstery, the selection of a cord depends on personal choice and cost, but for detachable and washable covers then paper cords should not be used (Fig 6.33).

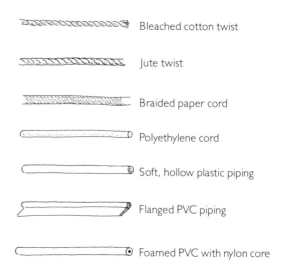

Bleached cotton twist

Jute twist

Braided paper cord

Polyethylene cord

Soft, hollow plastic piping

Flanged PVC piping

Foamed PVC with nylon core

Fig 6.33 Piping cords.

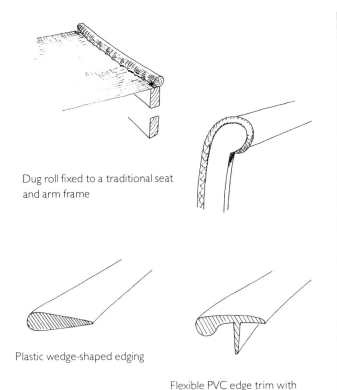

Dug roll fixed to a traditional seat
and arm frame

Plastic wedge-shaped edging

Flexible PVC edge trim with
right-angle flange for secure fixing

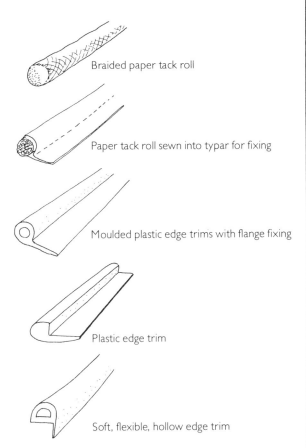

Braided paper tack roll

Paper tack roll sewn into typar for fixing

Moulded plastic edge trims with flange fixing

Plastic edge trim

Soft, flexible, hollow edge trim

Fig 6.34

Dug-roll or tack-roll edging

A large range of edge rolls and trims is available, made
from foams, compressed paper and soft plastics. These
have mostly superseded the traditional handmade dug
roll, which the upholsterer built on to frame edges. The
purpose of a dug roll is to provide a protective lip at seat
fronts, and around arm facings, etc. This simply
consisted of a hessian strip into which firm fillings,
such as coir fibre and cotton, were tightly compressed
and rolled, then fixed down along timber-frame edges.
For modern production purposes particularly, the
moulded or extruded ready-made edgings are clean,
easy to fix and consistent in shape. Little skill is needed
to produce a firm edge over which foams and upper
fillings are laid and fixed. Though material costs are
higher, the application is labour-saving, and consistent
with good-quality work.

Overall sizes vary with each type, but generally most
fall within the range of 13mm diameter up to 25mm
diameter. Some examples are given below (and see
Fig 6.34):

> Profile tack roll – foam, in 100m reels
> Typar covered supersoft roll – compressed paper
> Braided paper tack roll – 20mm and 25mm
> Plastic edge trims flat, round and flanged 9 to 21mm thick

SPECIFYING MATERIALS

A knowledge of materials and the way in which they
can be bought and used is essential to the upholsterer
if he or she is to create good, well-made articles of
furniture which can be sold for the comfort and
pleasure of others.

A chair, for instance, will probably contain at least
twenty different materials and fittings. Every one of
these items must be selected and bought and then
prepared and assembled into the finished design. Each
item has a special function and the failure of one may
affect many others in the way they perform in use.

The upholsterer is responsible for the cutting,
joining and fixing of foam, linings and covers, and must
be able to visualise the whole job even during the
earliest stages. In the factory situation the upholsterer
is not involved in the decision-making, designing or
buying but is merely there to assemble the components
which someone else has prepared. However, every
craftsman, or would-be craftsman, should make every
effort to be an all-rounder, so that his or her experience
and knowledge of the craft is as broad as possible.

The following is a list of materials which are required
for a small chair which has a seat and back to be
upholstered. List A is for a modern treatment of the
chair, and List B is for a traditional method of
upholstery. (The figure in the 'Amount' column
depends on the chair in question.)

List A

Back (inside)

		Unit	Amount
1	2in (50mm) rubber webbing, standard	*metre*	
2	10oz hessian × 36in (915mm) wide	*metre*	
3	Polyurethane foam 1⅝in (40mm) thick, soft sheet (CM)	*m sq*	
4	Polyester wadding, 5oz, 27in (685mm) wide	*metre*	

Back (outside)

| 5 | 10oz hessian × 36in (915mm) wide | *metre* | |
| 6 | Polyurethane foam, ¼in (6mm) thick, soft sheet (CM) | *m sq* | |

Seat

7	Zig-zag springs 9swg	*metre*	
8	12oz hessian × 36in (915mm) wide	*metre*	
9	Polyurethane chip foam, 1in (25mm) thick, 5lb (80kg) sheet	*m sq*	
10	HR Polyurethane foam, 2in (50 mm) thick medium sheet (CM)	*m sq*	
11	Polyester wadding 5oz × 27in (685mm) wide	*metre*	
12	Black under-lining 35in (890mm) wide	*metre*	

Sundries

13	Staples ⅜in (10mm)	*box*	
14	Gimp pins ⅜in (10mm)	*box*	
15	Adhesive (contact for foam)	*5 litre tin*	
16	Tape 50m	*metre*	
17	Spring clips	*each*	
18	Sewing machine thread	*cop*	
19	Laid cord	*ball*	
20	Piping cord	*reel*	
21	Back tacking strip	*reel*	
22	Tack trim or plygrip tacking strip	*roll*	

List B

Back (inside)

		Unit	Amount
1	2in (50mm) jute webbing	*metre*	
2	10oz hessian × 36in (91cm) wide	*metre*	
3	7oz scrim × 72in (1.8m) wide	*metre*	
4	Curled hair	*lb/kg*	
5	Calico 72in (1.8m) wide	*metre*	
6	Cotton felt 2½oz × 27in (685mm) wide	*metre*	
7	10oz hessian × 36in (91cm) wide	*metre*	
8	Skin wadding 18in (46cm) wide	*metre*	

Seat

9	2in (50mm) black and white webbing	*metre*	
10	6in (150mm) × 9swg double cone springs	*each*	
11	12oz hessian × 36in (91cm) wide	*metre*	
12	Coir fibre (Curlifil)	*metre*	
13	Scrim 72in (1.8m) wide, 7oz	*metre*	
14	Curled hair	*lb/kg*	
15	Calico 72in (1.8m) wide	*metre*	
16	Skin wadding 18in (460mm)	*metre*	
17	Black under lining 36in (91cm)	*metre*	

Sundries

18	Mattress stitching twine No. 2	*ball*	
19	Dug roll or tack roll ¾in (19mm)	*reel*	
20	Laid cord	*ball*	
21	Spring twine No. 4	*ball*	
22	Tacks ⅜in (10mm), ½in (13mm), fine	*kg*	

23	Gimp pins ⅜in (10mm)	*lb/kg*	
24	Back tacking strip	*metre*	
25	Slipping thread	*metre*	
26	Piping cord	*metre*	
27	Machine sewing thread (Koban 36)	*%*	
28	Trimmings	*metre*	

Cover

| 2 metres of 51in (130cm) | *metre* | |

Sundries – a nominal cost

These lists show the wide range of materials required for a small chair. Amounts would only need to be filled in when an accurate costing is required. Local code numbers of colours can be listed when buying foams and covers from regular suppliers. Most of the sundry items should be grouped together and a nominal cost figure charged after assessing the whole job. It would be an interesting exercise to write a third specification for the same chair, using a completely different range of materials.

Chapter Seven

Fabrics and Covers

Fabric manufacture is a fascinating and highly complex business with a long history and tradition. This chapter outlines the principal areas of manufacture in textile-making, beginning with some of the raw materials and following through to the finished cloth.

The upholsterer is one of the many people who select and use fabric with which to create a finished product. Furnishing and upholstery fabrics tend to be in the medium- to heavy-weight class, and are made and chosen for their strength and durability. A knowledge of all the processes involved in producing an upholstery cover is invaluable. It provides the necessary background when dealing with the great variety of coverings which passes through the workshop.

There are many instances when a customer will ask for advice and help in choosing a fabric. It is therefore important to the customer, and to the satisfaction of the upholsterer, that the right choice is made. This applies equally to modern production or restoration of traditional pieces. Basically the cover should give good service in the situation for which it is chosen, and at the same time be pleasing and visually effective.

What are the considerations when a choice has to be made? Putting colour and design aside because they are a matter of preference, from the point of view of value for money, the following comprehensive list is a helpful guide. It is, of course, unlikely that any one fabric will have all these qualities.

Pleasant and comfortable to the touch
Good shape retention
Some resilience
Dimensionally stable
Good resistance to abrasion
Good resistance to fraying
Resistant to fading and colour loss by rubbing
A carefully balanced composition
Good tear resistance
Good seam strength
Fire resistant to minimum standards

TYPES OF UPHOLSTERY COVER

To simplify the recognition of the many different types, it is useful to group covers under the following headings. The headings relate mainly to the different methods of making a fabric. Some examples are given in each case.

Woven, plain	*repp, tweed, calico*
Woven, patterned	*brocade, damask, tapestry*
Printed	*cretonne, chintz, union*
Pile	*velour, velvet, corduroy*
Knitted	*jersey, laminated, stockinette*
Coated fabric	*PVC-coated materials (vinyls)*
Non-woven	*spun-bonded, stitch-bonded*
Animal skins	*hide, suede*

Almost all upholstery covers will fall into one of the eight groups, and there are some which cross over into two groups because of their composite make-up; for example, pile and coated fabrics are produced on knitted bases in some instances. Apart from hides and various animal skins, upholstery covers are made in piece lengths. These lengths will vary according to the type of cloth, but generally the heavier cloths are the shorter pieces, and the lighter cloths can be made longer. Lengths therefore will range from 35m up to around 100m. It is important that a roll or piece can be handled reasonably easily during processing. After manufacture a fabric must be handled and stored carefully. A pole or tube is inserted in the centre of the roll to keep it rigid and round. Rolls should not be stored on end as this causes rippled creasing at the edges. Many fabrics, particularly pile and coated types, are badly affected by any kind of pressure whether from inside the roll or from outside.

The majority of covers used for upholstery are piece goods of a standard width. In Fig 7.1 a typical fabric

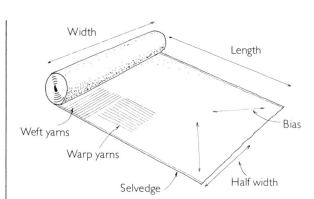

Fig 7.1 Roll or piece.

piece with trade terminology is shown. **Average width** – 120cm to 135cm. **Length** – along the roll (linear). **Weft** – cross yarns. **Warp** – lengthwise yarns. **Selvedge** – tightly woven edge strip. **Bias** – diagonal cut or line. **Half width** – used for estimating purposes.

Almost all fabrics, whether woven, knitted or coated, are made up from textile fibres. These fibres may be short, from 20mm up to ½m, and are called staple fibres, or may be continuous of any length. Continuous fibres are called filament fibres.

Textile fibres may be obtained from natural sources, i.e. animal, vegetable and mineral, or they may be man-made by regenerating organic substances such as cellulose, casein or proteins. In addition, there are those which are described as purely synthetic, which are derived by polymerisation of organic substances, for example coal and oil.

A family tree of textile fibres is given below, and classifies them in listed form under natural, man-made and synthetic types.

Natural textile fibres

Animal (protein based) staple
Wool – sheep
Hair – camel, goat, rabbit, alpaca, llama
Silk – filament, silkworm.

Vegetable (cellulose-based) staple
Seed – cotton, kapok
Bast – flax (linen), jute, hemp, ramie
Leaf – sisal
Fruit – coir, raffias.

Mineral
Rock – asbestos
Inorganic – glass fibre, filament.

Man-made

Natural polymer, filament or staple
Viscose rayon – cellulose, Evlan (wood pulp)
Acetate rayon – cellulose, ester, Dicel (cotton linters).

Synthetic

Synthetic polymer, filament or staple
Polyamide – nylon, Celon (coal)
Polyester – Terylene, Dacron (oil)
Acrylic – Courtelle, Dralon (oil, coal)
Polythene – Courlene (oil)
Polypropylene – Cournova, Meraklon (oil).

ORIGINS AND CHARACTERISTICS OF TEXTILE FIBRES

Wool

The major growers of wool staple are Australia, New Zealand and South Africa. Fibres are imported and blended with British wools. Processing of the wool into yarn is done in Britain. Britain has long been one of the leading producers of wool textiles.

Wool is the most important animal fibre. Hair from other animals can be processed on the same machinery, and these are camel hair, angora rabbit, cashmere and mohair from goats. Two types of yarn are produced from these wools – worsted yarn, which is long and fine, and woollen yarn, made from the shorter staples into a soft, more bulky product.

Physical properties
Fibres vary from fine and soft to coarse and very durable, with staple lengths from 3 to 15in (75–380mm). Wool strength is relatively low, but it has excellent bulk and resilience. Moisture absorption is high, which results in good affinity to stains and dyes.

Felting and matting can be a problem in wool fabrics,

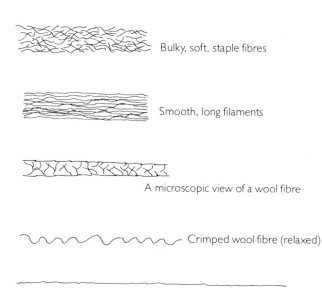

Bulky, soft, staple fibres

Smooth, long filaments

A microscopic view of a wool fibre

Crimped wool fibre (relaxed)

Wool fibre (stretched)

A microscopic view of a flax fibre (linen)

A flax plant stem showing fibre bundles below the bark

Fig 7.2

but this is largely overcome by processing and special finishes. Wool has good natural crimp or wave; the surface of a single fibre is scaled (Fig 7.2).

Uses
A good furnishing textile fibre used to produce: tweeds, moquettes, repp and wool pile fabrics.

Flax (linen)
A tough, bast fibre which grows annually in Russia, Belgium, Holland and Ireland. Flax may be grown for its fibre, or for its seed, from which linseed oil is produced. The best and longest fibres are called 'line', and the shorter fibres are 'tow'. Flax makes a strong, stiff and fairly durable fabric, and is often blended with cotton.

Physical properties
A strong fibre, which is very stable and non flexible. It is able to withstand laundering and cleaning, but is susceptible to creasing. It does not drape as well as most natural fibres, and is always cool to the feel. Linens do not have a great affinity to dyes and so are more often printed (Fig 7.3).

Uses
Traditionally used for loose covers and soft furnishings: union cloths, linen velvets, scrim and webbings, upholstery twines.

Silk
Raw silk is unwound from the cocoon of the silkworm. It is an extremely fine fibre and is the only natural fibre to be classified as filament. Between 1,500 and 2,000m can be unwound from one cocoon, which is about 2½in (6cm) long. Silk may be cultivated, or collected from the wild. The main production areas are China, India, Thailand and Europe. Italy and France are noted for their silk fabrics. Several cocoons are unwound together and carefully twisted to produce one fine yarn.

Physical properties
A relatively strong fibre, but silk does not have good resistance to abrasion. However, it has good elastic properties and an attractive sheen or lustre. As a fabric it is very springy and resistant to creasing.

Types of silk and uses
Traditionally large amounts of silk were used for furnishing, but because of its high cost it is only used in a limited way today. Denier, a measurement of silk or gauge, is still used today for synthetic fibres. The denier is the weight in grammes of 9,000m. Some traditional silk fabrics are brocade, damask and velvet.

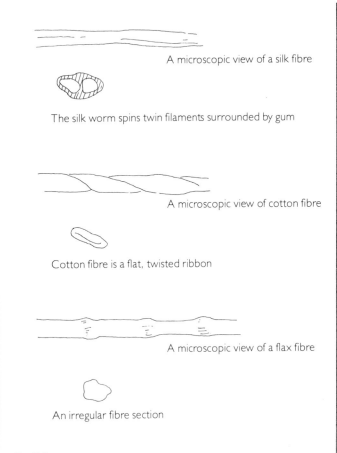

A microscopic view of a silk fibre

The silk worm spins twin filaments surrounded by gum

A microscopic view of cotton fibre

Cotton fibre is a flat, twisted ribbon

A microscopic view of a flax fibre

An irregular fibre section

Fig 7.3

Cotton
Large seed bolls are harvested from the cotton plant. USA, North Africa and India are the major growers, and processing is still largely done in the north of England. Cotton has been an important textile fibre for centuries and is still so today.

The quality of cotton varies enormously from one growing region to another.

Physical properties
Cotton has good strength and good spinning qualities, because of a natural twist in the fibre. Staple lengths range from ½in (13mm) up to 1½in (38mm). Fibres have good abrasion resistance, and hold colour well. The strength of cotton is increased when wet by about 25 per cent. If cotton is treated with caustic soda, a physical change occurs; this is used to produce mercerised cotton, and results in a very strong yarn. Cotton is usually bleached and preshrunk during processing.

Uses
Production of velours, denim, canvas, unions and linings (Fig 7.2). Mercerised cotton is used particularly for upholstery pile fabrics and in the manufacture of sewing threads.

Jute

It is obtained from the stem of the jute plant, which grows annually to a height of about 10ft (3m). Growing conditions are tropical, with high humidity and lots of heat. The growing areas are limited, and the main producers are India, Pakistan and Bangladesh. For a century or so Britain has been involved in the processing of jute; the main centre is Dundee in Scotland.

Physical properties

A tough and very durable fibre. Jute has very little elasticity, and can only be stretched about 2 per cent of its length before it will break. This quality makes it ideal for industrial applications. A stiff coarse fibre, which has good tensile strength, it is weakened by exposure to sunlight and so is not used where it will be affected in this way.

Uses

Hessians and tarpaulins, base cloths for linoleum, and backing yarns in carpet-making. Jute is also used in small percentages for upholstery fabrics. Other uses include wall coverings and wallpapers.

Hemp

Another tough bast fibre which has similar properties to flax. In fibre form it is rather heavier and more coarse. Its main use is in the making of twines and cords.

SYNTHETIC AND MAN-MADE FIBRE PRODUCTION

All these fibres are basically made in the same way, by forcing thick synthetic liquid through a series of small holes in a spinneret. A spinneret is very similar to the head on a water shower. The size of the hole determines the thickness and weight of the fibre (Fig 7.4). As the new filaments emerge they are set by

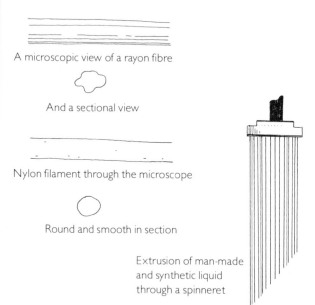

A microscopic view of a rayon fibre

And a sectional view

Nylon filament through the microscope

Round and smooth in section

Extrusion of man-made and synthetic liquid through a spinneret

Fig 7.4

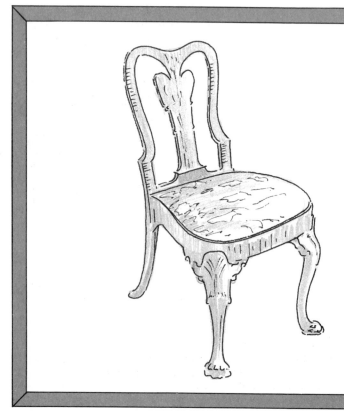

Queen Anne Side Chair
c.1715

A walnut side chair or small chair, typical of that period.

Upholstery On a framed loose seat or drop-in seat stuffed with animal hair and supported with strong linen cloth.

Coverings A variety of handmade needlework tapestries.

warm air or in mild acid baths. The processes are called dry or wet spinning, and in the case of wet spinning colour can be added to the baths to make coloured filaments. As the new filaments are set they are drawn or stretched, which adds to their strength. They can then be made into yarns in two different ways, by (a) twisting several filaments together to form a continuous smooth yarn or (b) crimping and cutting the filaments into short staple lengths (Fig 7.5). The resulting bulky fibre can then be spun on conventional machinery in the same way as cotton or wool (Fig 7.6), as follows.

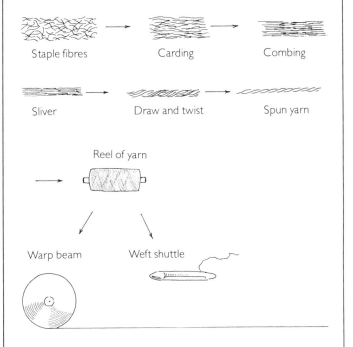

Fig 7.5 The production of yarn.

Fabric structure

Yarn

Yarns are made up in different ways and may be plain or fancy, depending on the type of fabric to be woven. Therefore, at the yarn-making stage the surface and texture of the fabric is planned. A selection of typical yarns is shown in Fig 7.7.

Weaving

Fabric is woven on a loom, using a series of warps, treads or yarns through which the weft threads are

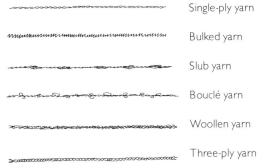

Fig 7.7 Conventional and fancy yarns.

passed, continuously from left to right and back. This method of making fabric has been used for many centuries. A side view of a simple loom is shown in Fig 7.8.

A full length of fabric which may be as long as 100m is called a piece. Any small part taken from a piece is a cut length. There are a great number of weave patterns which can be created using weft and warp yarns, these types of weave produce fabric with different

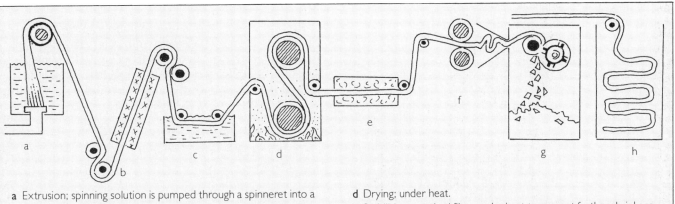

a Extrusion; spinning solution is pumped through a spinneret into a coagulating bath and drawn off as continuous filaments, which are collected together to form a continuous tow or rope of fibre. The bath removes the solvent from the spinning solution leaving solid acrylic filaments.
b Stretching; under heat to develop strength, i.e. the molecules are regularly lined up so that all the links in the chain are of equal length.
c Washing; to remove excess solvent.

d Drying; under heat.
e Stabilising; standard fibre under heat to prevent further shrinkage.
f Crimping; this helps when it is later spun into yarns, and adds resilience and improves handle.
g Cutting; to produce staple fibre which can be spun on cotton, worsted or other machinery.
h Collecting tow; collecting tow for use on special machinery which eliminates the need for conventional carding and combing.

Fig 7.6 Synthetic fibre (acrylic) production.

a Warp beam
b Warps
c Healds
d Reed
e Shed
f Shuttle
g Woven cloth
h Cloth beam

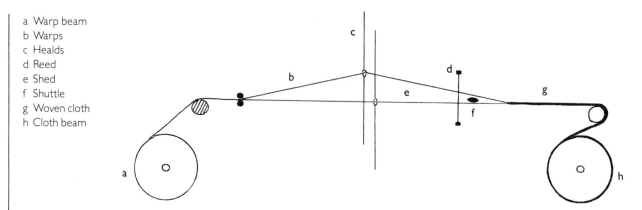

Fig 7.8 Parts of a simple loom.

characteristics and properties. Some examples of weave constructions are shown in Fig 7.9.

A standard simple loom can produce weaves such as plain, twill, satin and basket weave. A more advanced type called a Dobby loom can create small patterns repeated throughout the cloth. For the more complex longer patterns, a special loom fitted with a Jacquard system is needed. This works from a punched card system, which in turn controls the lifting and lowering of the warp threads during weaving.

The following is a list of fabrics which can be produced on the three types of loom:

Simple loom

Plain weave	Calico
	Cambric
	Duck
	Buckram
	Hessian
	Holland
	Repp
Twill weave	Ticking
	Tweed
	Denim
	Twill cloths
Sateen weave	Sateen linings
	Sateen-faced cloth
	Predominantly weft, faced
Dobby loom	All over pattern
	Fine cord
	Bedford cord
	Folk weaves
Jacquard loom	Brocade
	Damask
	Tapestry

Pile construction

Pile fabrics are particularly good furnishing fabrics, and their construction is very similar to that of carpets. There are three basic formations: weft pile, warp pile and terry weave. The three different constructions are shown in Fig 7.10.

Examples of weft pile types are: velveteen, corduroy and plush. Warp pile types are: velvet, figured velvet, moquette and velours.

Terry weaves are not normally used in furnishing and are mainly used for towel manufacture and clothing. Pile tufts can be U-shaped or W-shaped in warp pile velvets, and the face-to-face method is used a great deal to produce two pieces of cloth in one weaving process.

Knitted fabrics

The knitting of yarns together is an alternative method of making fabrics. There are two methods: weft knitting and warp knitting. Weft knitting can be done by hand with a pair of needles, or can be done on a machine. Warp knitting, however, is purely a machine process. Until recently knitted fabrics tended to be used for clothing more than anything else. Today knitted cloths are being introduced into furnishings more and more. By nature they are very stretchy fabrics, particularly weft-knitted types. One area in particular has shown an increased use of these fabrics, that is stretch covers, or loose detachable covers.

Knitted covers may be plain or highly patterned, or can be flat or pile. Their use in upholstery competes favourably with conventional woven types. In some cases the stretch characteristics are not required, and two fabrics are laminated together to produce a more

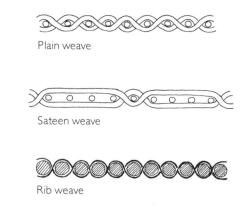

Plain weave

Sateen weave

Rib weave

Fig 7.9 Weaving.

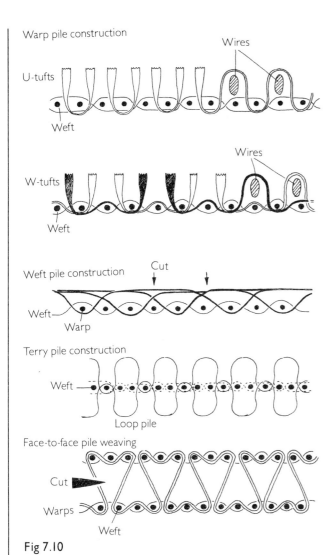

Warp pile construction

Wires

U-tufts

Weft

Wires

W-tufts

Weft

Weft pile construction

Cut

Weft

Warp

Terry pile construction

Weft

Loop pile

Face-to-face pile weaving

Cut

Warps

Weft

Fig 7.10

stable product. Thin veneers of foam are also used to back or sandwich two or more fabrics.

Purpose-built platform cloths are produced by laminating foams to warp knitted nylon fabrics. This produces a resilient, durable and stretchy cloth, which is ideal for use under cushioning, over some form of suspension. It is possible to vary the loop construction of a knitted fabric, to produce quite a heavy and non-stretch cover, and so the possibilities are enormous. However, the characteristics of covers made by knitting can never be quite the same as a woven cloth. This is noticeable as soon as a knitted type is cut and sewn, and applied as an upholstery covering. Providing the upholsterer is aware of the difference then any problems in application need only be small.

Fig 7.11 Interlocking loops form the construction in a knitted fabric.

Application of colour

Dyeing

There are an enormous number of dye types, either based on natural or synthetic substances. Selection of a dye or a number of dyes is done to suit the fabric type, and the fibes used to make it. It is important that penetration and affinity is good throughout the fabric, so that every yarn and its fibre is well coloured to a good depth. Dyeing may take place at different stages in fabric production. Generally, the earlier that the colouring takes place, the better the result will be.

Bulk dyeing is done at the fibre stage before spinning, this is expensive but ensures good deep colouring throughout. Yarn or skein dyeing takes place before weaving. Any multi-colour fabric with a woven design will have been yarn dyed.

Piece-dyed fabrics are those that are single colour, and colouring takes place after weaving. This is much the quickest and least expensive method of applying dye to a cloth. However, penetration may not always be as deep or permanent as with the other two methods.

When a fabric has been made up from two different raw materials then it is possible to cross dye, by using two different dye types. One of the colours will be accepted by a particular fibre and rejected by the other fibre. This produces an interesting colour sheen effect (Fig 7.12).

Printing

Printing is basically surface colouring applied to fabrics after weaving to give design and texture to the surface. A print design must be drawn up to suit the fabric being produced and must fit exactly into the cloth

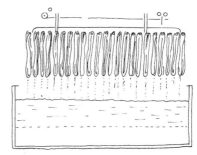

Hanks of woollen yarn being lifted from a large dye vat during yarn dyeing

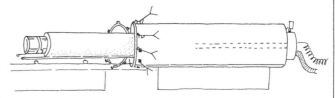

A roll of cloth being loaded on to a machine ready for piece dyeing under pressure

Fig 7.12

width. The length of the design is called the repeat, and this may well be up to a metre in size, before being repeated again.

There are a number of different ways in which a print can be applied to a fabric. Early printing was done with wooden blocks into which strips of copper were hammered to form the patterns. This method is slow and requires great skill by the printer. However, hand-block printed fabrics are still produced in small quantities.

Silk-screen printing is another traditional method using a fine silk fabric stretched over a wooden frame. This works like a stencil, with certain areas blocked out and the pattern left open to allow colour through on to the fabric. In both methods each block or screen represents one colour. Some designs have as many as fifteen different colours, but an average would be around seven.

Roller printing

Printing methods today are based on the same principles, but are fully mechanised to produce intricate, multi-coloured designs at high speeds. The engraved copper roller transfers colour paste from a small vat on to a woven fabric. The rollers are arranged in line, each one printing a different part of the design and a different colour. Once set up and rolling, this system is fast and efficient. Colours are finally fixed and the fabric finished and dried before rolling up into pieces.

Rotary screen printing

As the name suggests this is an advanced process, whereby the prepared screen, which is made from a perforated nickel mesh, is in cylinder form. The pattern design is applied using emulsions and works as a stencil. Colour is fed into the centre of the screen,

through a foam squeegee, in carefully controlled amounts. As fabric passes between the revolving screens and a conveyor, each screen makes its print on the surface before the cloth passes into a drying chamber. Fixing and washing complete the printing process.

In both mechanised processes fabrics may be printed on one or both sides at the same time.

Fabric finishing processes

Bleaching: a process of purifying and whitening a cloth to remove natural colouring with agents such as permanganates, or hydrogen peroxide.

Mercerisation: the treatment of yarn with solutions of caustic soda to give lustre and add strength. Used mainly on cottons and linens.

Shearing: a cutting process used to trim pile fabrics to produce a fine even surface on velvets and velours.

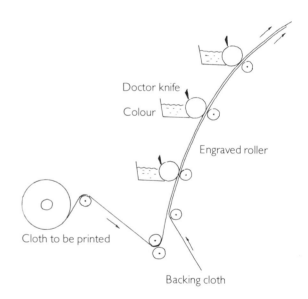

Fig 7.13 Diagram shows the principles used to roller print fabric.

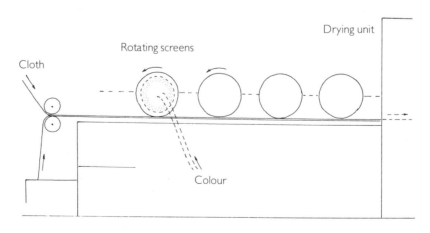

Part of a rotary screen-printing machine

Flameproofing

Most fabrics can be made flame resistant by treatment with chemicals. Some textiles and upholstery materials have a natural resistance to fire for example, PVC, wool, glass and hide. Chemicals used are mineral salts such as borax.

Calendering

A fabric is passed through a calendering machine to smooth and flatten it and to close gaps between the yarns. Heated or friction rollers may be used to give a glazed or semi-glazed surface to the cloth. A similar machine is used to emboss patterns or texture on to fabrics. Coated fabrics are given their grained surfaces in this way.

Plastic-coated fabrics

Although several different materials have been used to coat woven and knitted fabrics for upholstery, only one can be considered as outstanding, and has stood the test of time. This is PVC (polyvinyl chloride), which is a soft thermo-plastic.

Early coated fabrics called leather cloths were developed in the late Victorian period, and were produced by painting nitro-cellulose on to woven cotton. These were coloured and embossed or grained to simulate leather. The resulting coverings were rather stiff and unyielding and far more difficult to use than real leather. Although they were in use for a long time, with constant wear they became brittle and the coating was liable to cracking. These cloths and others such as American cloths and oil cloths have been long superseded by vinyl coatings. PVC-coated fabrics are made by calendering a vinyl paste with plasticisers on to a woven or knitted base (Fig 7.14). Three different types are produced: a solid vinyl layer on a woven cloth, an expanded vinyl layer on a woven cloth, and an expanded vinyl layer on a knitted cloth. Each of these types has different characteristics.

The most durable and most popular is the third type, which has a good top coating over an expanded core, fused to a flexible knitted backing. These coverings have good stretch properties, good resilience and a durable tough surface. Their use is mainly in the contract market of upholstery, public houses, hotels, vehicles and waiting rooms, etc.

Plastic-coated fabrics can now be made with surfaces which simulate a diverse range of different materials. They can be perforated, embossed, printed and coloured to give different properties to suit a variety of applications. Soft, smooth coatings in pastel shades may appeal for domestic use, or heavy, rugged, embossed surfaces can be used in cabinet work or even for external use.

Because of its thermo-plastic properties and low melting point, PVC supported and unsupported material can be shaped, moulded or welded on heat-forming machinery. One of its main benefits as an upholstery covering is that it can be easily maintained and cleaned. A wipe over with warm soapy water is all that is needed when soiling occurs.

Pattern in fabrics

A large percentage of upholstery covers have patterns woven or printed into them. There are generally three types: small all-over patterns, medium-sized designs, which are bold and clearly repeat regularly, and there are the very large designs, almost full-scale pictures, which take up most of the width of the fabric. Beside these there are those patterns which appear fairly small but in fact have a large repeat. There are also some patterns which are very complex, where the designer has cleverly covered the whole fabric and the repetition is not very obvious.

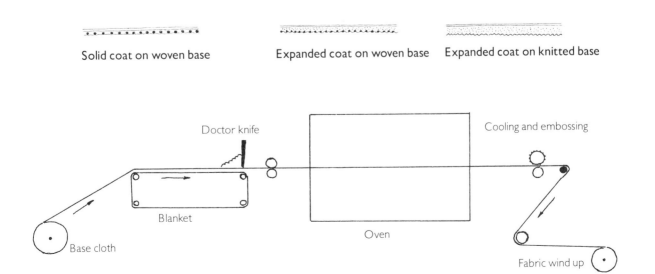

Solid coat on woven base   Expanded coat on woven base   Expanded coat on knitted base

Fig 7.14 Production of a PVC-coated fabric

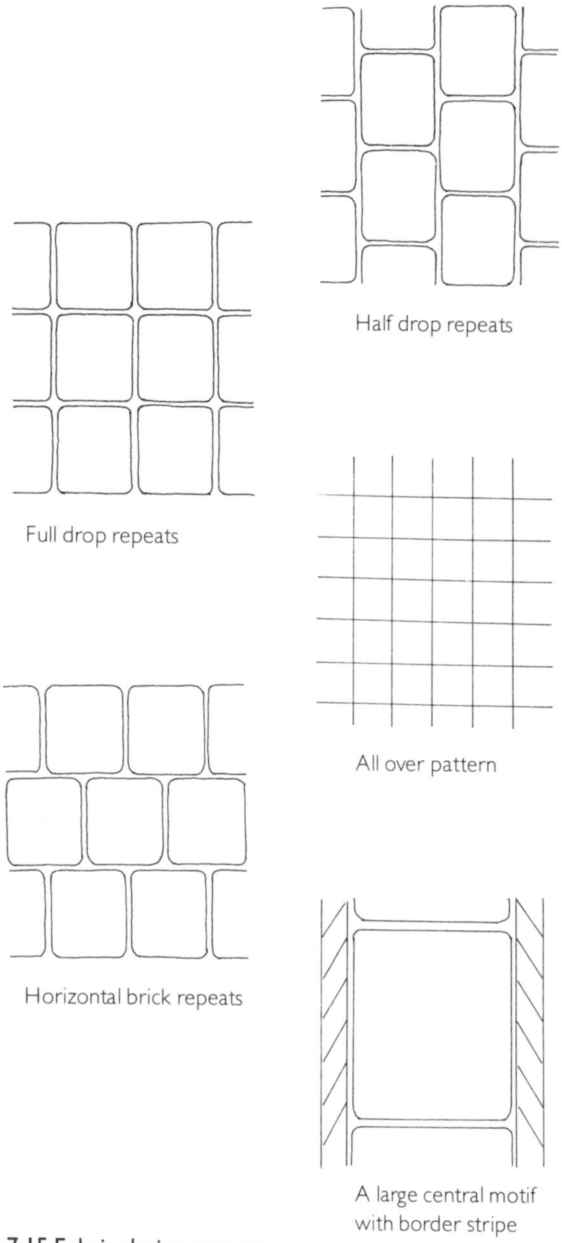

Half drop repeats

Full drop repeats

All over pattern

Horizontal brick repeats

A large central motif with border stripe

Fig 7.15 Fabric design repeats.

The upholsterer must appreciate these differences, and be aware of how the fabric designer lays out and spaces designs on to a cloth. Fig 7.15 illustrates five basic layouts. Handling and using these different formats provides valuable experience. The positioning of a patterned cover on to a piece of furniture, to show it at its best, is an important and interesting part of the upholsterer's work. Here, the upholsterer has some licence. Covers can be used to give interest to rather plain chairs or alternatively played down to create subtle effects. Pattern matching is another aspect, wherever possible the design should flow, both horizontally and vertically, with joins matched together and placed on to the upholstery so that they do not distract or interrupt the visual effect.

FABRIC NAMES AND DESCRIPTIONS
Flat woven
Baize
A heavy woollen cloth which has been felted, and the surface brushed and laid. Produced in plain colours, piece dyed. Commonly used as a lining cloth, and on card tables and screens.

Bedford cord
A strong plain or twill weave cloth, with cords or ribs running in the warp direction. Normally Bedford cords are plain colours with a warp-faced construction. Uses are in clothing and furnishing.

Buckram
A plain woven coarse cloth, made from jute or cotton. Sized with animal glues to produce a stiffened fabric. Used in upholstery and soft furnishing.

Bouclé
A warm thick cloth, with a rough surface produced by fancy yarns. Used for upholstery and clothing.

Calico
A general textile name used to describe plain-woven cotton cloths of different weights. May be sold bleached or unbleached in the loomstate. Used traditionally as an undercover or lining in upholstery.

Cambric
A lightweight, close-weave cloth made from cotton or linen. It may have as many as 90 yarns per inch. Often stiffened or proofed and used in furnishing for cushion cases.

Canvas
A tough cotton or linen fabric, plain woven and produced in a wide range of weights. Usually coloured plain or striped, it is suitable for internal and external use. Particular uses are deck chairs and support cloths in upholstery.

Denim
A yarn dyed, twill cloth, made from cotton. Denim is strong and durable, and used for clothing and furnishing.

Drill
Another durable, twill yarn cloth produced in cotton and rayon, and piece dyed. Very similar to denim and used mainly for clothing.

Duck
A name used to describe plain woven cotton or flax cloth similar to canvas. Heavy and durable and very stable. Used for belting, sailcloths and tents and makes a good support cloth in modern upholstery.

Hessian
A plain-woven jute fabric, usually undyed and produced in several weights. Warp and weft yarns are the same weight, but flat. Hessian is coarse but very strong and non-stretch. The heavy weights are called tarpaulin. Its uses are in sacking, upholstery, wall coverings and floor coverings.

Holland
A medium weight, plain woven cloth, heavily rolled and glazed. Produced plain or patterned and used mainly for window blinds.

Repp
A plain weave fabric with a very dominant rib running in the weft direction. Produced in good quality cotton or wool. A traditional furnishing fabric for curtains, loose covers and heavier weights for upholstery.

Scrim
A lightweight loosely woven, but strong fabric. Made from cotton or jute in a variety of low weights. Used as a foundation cloth in hats, soft furnishing and upholstery.

Ticking
A strong fine twill woven cloth, traditionally produced white with a black strip, but now made in plains or patterns. Used a great deal in bedding manufacture, to cover mattresses and pillows. Ticking makes good curtains and has some uses in upholstery.

Tweed
Generally a heavyweight, all-wool cloth produced in various weaves, plain, twill and chevron. Tweed is hard wearing and may have a smooth or rough surface. Harris tweed is well known for its durability. These cloths are usually single or two colour.

Printed covers

Chintz
A fine, plain woven cotton fabric, which is produced in plain colours, or more often with elaborate printed designs. Chintz is glazed or semi-glazed by friction calendering. Use in soft furnishing and as an upholstery cover.

Wing Armchair
c. 1730

A typical example of early Georgian upholstery, and probably made at the time when the architect William Kent began designing furniture for his houses and interiors. Beech frame supported on heavily carved Spanish mahogany legs.

Upholstery Well padded with wool and various grasses, with a removable wool or feather-filled cushion, supported on webbings.

Needlework produced from yarn or silk and wool mixed together, and embroidered into linen and silk foundations made durable and beautiful covers. The nailed-on type of upholstery was particularly fashionable, with loose squab cushions for seats.

Cretonne

A printed cotton cloth fabric slightly heavier than chintz and with no surface shine. Weft threads are usually dominant. A general purpose cloth often used in soft furnishing.

Union

A name used to describe furnishing fabrics which may be plain or printed, and made from a union of two main fibres, although others may be present in small quanitities. Printed unions of cotton and linen are traditional loose-cover fabrics. Unions may be plain or twill weave.

Jacquard weaves

Brocade

Using a variety of weaves, patterns are formed by the weft threads floating in the back of the fabric. Brocades are rich, colourful fabrics which were traditionally made from silk, and often hand embroidered. Today, rayons and synthetic yarns are used. Typical designs are small flower patterns blended with coloured stripes. Uses are soft furnishings and upholstery.

Brocatelle

A heavy figured cloth, with a relief pattern, in a sateen weave surrounded by a tightly woven background. Extra warps are introduced into good quality brocatelles. Uses are curtains and upholstery.

Damask

A single- or two-colour fabric which is figured by a warp-faced background with wefts forming the pattern. The pattern can be seen on both sides but is not reversible. Damask is produced in cotton, linen and rayons, but was originally a pure silk fabric. Patterns may be small or large. Used a great deal for curtains and upholstery.

Tapestry

A heavy closely woven patterned fabric with a compound structure. Early tapestries were handmade needlework fabrics, produced from cotton, linen and wool. There are different styles of tapestry cloths, many depict traditional scenes, or have geometric designs. The name tapestry is often used to describe any heavily patterned upholstery cover.

Pile weaves

Corduroy

A weft pile fabric, in which the weft yarns are cut to form grooves or cords running down the length of the fabric. Usually made from cotton in different weights, and may be yarn or piece dyed. Uses are clothing and furnishing.

Moquette

A weft warp-pile fabric which may have a cut or uncut pile, or a combination of both. Good moquettes have a wool pile and a cotton base. Moquettes may vary from loop pile, plain fibres, to cut pile types with several colours forming designs or stripes. Pile fibres may also be mohair or Dralon. A very durable upholstery fabric used in the contract and domestic market. Very popular in the 1940s and '50s and recently reintroduced.

Plush

A heavy long pile fabric, produced for upholstery and some clothing. The pile is less dense than in velvet, but can be long enough to simulate fur. Plush was very popular during the first half of the twentieth century as a durable wool or mohair pile cover with cotton or rayon as a base. It can be made with a warp or weft pile construction. Used in domestic and contract seating, particularly theatre and cinema seating.

Velours

A warp pile cloth with a good dense pile closely woven from cotton. Produced in several weights for curtaining and upholstery. Velours pile is laid in one direction, usually down the length of the roll, giving the surface a distinct shading. Uses are domestic upholstery and soft furnishing. The name is taken from the French word for velvet.

Velvet

A cut warp pile fabric which was traditionally silk on a cotton base. The pile may be formed over wires and subsequently cut, or two pieces woven face to face, and then cut to leave a pile on each (Fig 7.10). Velvet is a good furnishing fabric which has been used to cover furniture for some three centuries. Pile yarns in velvet today may be nylon, Dralon, linen or rayon. A versatile upholstery cover which can be used in most furnishing situations.

Velveteen

This is a weft pile fabric in which the pile is produced by cutting the weft floats after weaving. The base cloth may be plain or twill weave. Velveteen is a fine lightweight fabric made from cotton or rayon. It is not normally recommended for upholstery, but is very suitable for light use and curtaining.

Velvets and velveteens can be produced as figured cloths, in which the pile forms a design or pattern and the background is left flat. These make good furnishing cloths, and are particularly suited to traditional work.

SOME UNUSUAL UPHOLSTERY COVERS

Carpeting

A lightweight, hand- or machine-made patterned

carpeting, popular during the Victorian and Edwardian periods for upholstery. Pieces of carpet were applied and sewn into chair arms, backs and seats, bordered with plain cover.

Horsehair fabric

Another covering which was used largely during the early Victorian era. However, it is still made and used today in small quantities. A fabric made with pure horsehair wefts of selected colours, held together with cotton or rayon warp yarns. Surface designs are plain, striped or damask. A very tough and durable covering.

Tussah

A fine silk fabric made from spun, wild silks. It has an interesting rough textured surface, with a cool crisp feel. Colouring is usually natural – pale brown or stone.

Moiré fabrics

Very fine-ribbed fabrics, usually silk or cotton, which have been finished by calendering to produce a water mark on the surface. Colours are plain with the *moiré* lustre glinting to simulate water reflections.

Padded or quilted fabrics

These are printed covers which have lightweight wadding behind the surface and a calico backing. The printed designs are outlined by machine sewing to produce a shallow quilting, giving a three-dimensional effect. Fluted effects can be produced in the same way to give texture to plain covers.

Fig 7.16 shows some examples of a simple chair shape upholstered in a number of different fabric designs. Some designs may be more pleasing than others or more acceptable on larger pieces of furniture. Generally, large patterns or motifs will look better on larger pieces of upholstery, whereas small patterns can be equally effective on any size piece. Visualising the finished effect can often prove difficult. Keeping a portfolio of completed work will often help, or books and magazines can be kept for reference. A flat piece of fabric can appear very different when upholstered on to a three-dimensional shape.

CARE IN THE USE OF FABRICS

Manufacturers and wholesalers of fabrics for furnishing label their products to give information about each cloth. The amount of information given can vary, but generally labelling is good. The more detailed this is, the better from the upholsterer's point of view. Where a product is poorly labelled it is well worthwhile asking for more details, particularly before buying.

As an example a good label should indicate the fabric name and type, and a code number followed by a

Fig 7.16

colourway number, e.g. Salcome, TW 1092/4. This is usually followed by the fibre composition of the fabric, as a percentage of the whole content, e.g. 70 per cent wool, 30 per cent nylon, or in the case of a pile fabric, 69 per cent Dralon, 31 per cent rayon (100 per cent Dralon pile).

The current price of the fabric will often show a piece price, and a cut-length price per metre – this is normal practice. Two other important details are the cover width in centimetres, and the repeat length in the case of patterned fabrics. Most wholesalers are happy to indicate whether a fabric type is suitable, or is not recommended, for particular end uses.

Furnishing fabrics usually fall into different categories of use, i.e. curtain weights, upholstery fabrics or loose cover materials. Few fabrics fall into more than one of these. Textile manufacturers are conscious of the requirements of an upholstery cloth, and go to great lengths to see that their products meet these needs. Upholstery cloths are usually tested to determine how suitable they will be in use; this testing procedure can take place at one or all of the following points: after production by the manufacturer; at the distribution house; independently by a research association. Test results simply provide a guide for anyone buying and using a fabric.

Some of these results may be included on a label to indicate how a fabric stood up to simulated in-use conditions. It would be confusing to give all the test results obtained from a series of tests, but there are two or three recognised test results which are often issued on labels.

There is the rub test, for abrasion resistance; the fade test, for fastness of colour to light; and the fire test, for fire resistance to a particular source. Example results may read as follows:

1 Rub test, (martindale), 55,000 rubs
2 Colour fade test, Grade 5
3 Flammability to BS 5852 Part 1, ignition source 2.

Maintenance and after care is more important to the customer than to anyone else. The upholstery manufacturer and the retailer are often asked how a particular fabric should be cared for and cleaned. This applies especially to cushion covers and to loose covers. Fabric labels will usually state that a cover can be cleaned by standard cleaning methods, or it may detail suggested ways of removing stains, or simply state, for example, that a cover should be dry cleaned only. Methods of cleaning depend mainly on whether a cover is fixed or detachable.

Before you cut

The experienced upholsterer knows the value of making a routine check as soon as a new length of cover is received. While the textile manufacturer will make every effort to ensure product quality, it is the responsibility of the upholsterer to make a thorough inspection before a cover is cut. This will almost certainly save time, and keep irritating problems to the minimum.

Fabrics are the main source of complaint in any upholstery operation. The following therefore is a useful check list.

1 Is the fabric the one which was ordered?
2 Are the length and width as specified?
3 Is the colour correct and as per the sample?
4 Has it got damaged or dirty in transit?
5 Are there any faults or flaws in the fabric?

Some faults which often occur are bad creasing or crushing, yarns drifting and not square to the selvedge, large knots, missing yarns or broken yarns, distortion or bareness in pile fabrics, changes in density, and bad registration in printed covers. In many cases the manufacturer will have indicated that a flaw exists in the fabric by marking the fabric with a loop of coloured yarn tied in the selvedge. In such cases extra length will have been allowed in cutting. If the upholsterer finds that a fault is not acceptable and cannot be cut around, then an exchange length should be asked for.

BS specification 2543 specifies test methods, wear properties and care in use of upholstery fabrics. BS specification 5852 parts 1 and 2 gives test methods for flammability of furnishing fabrics and fillings.

FURNITURE AND FURNISHINGS (FIRE) (SAFETY) REGULATIONS 1988

The regulations took effect from 1 November 1988, 1 March 1989 and 1 March 1990. This simplified guide does not cover all aspects of the regulations, which can be obtained in full from HMSO. More information is also available from the TSO (Trading Standards Officer) for a particular area.

Fillings

Fillings must pass ignitability tests in Parts 1, 2 and 3 of Schedule 1, and parts 1 and 2 of Schedule 2. If old fillings are reteased and reused (for example non-foam fillings) they do not have to be replaced with new fillings which comply with the regulations. Replacement fillings must pass the relevant ignitability test.

Covers

All covers for upholstery must comply with the relevant ignitability test. The upholsterer must satisfy himself that the cover and barrier cloth used complies with the regulations.

Labelling

Furniture which has been stripped and reupholstered does not have to be labelled. However, if new or secondhand furniture is reupholstered and offered for retail sale it must comply with the relevant tests and labelling.

Trimmings

All braids and trimmings are not required to be resistant to ignition.

Cushions

Cushions which are an integral part of a piece of upholstered furniture must comply with the regulations applicable to that piece of furniture.

From 1 March 1993

All secondhand furniture for retail sale comes within the bounds of the regulations. **Exceptions:** Furniture manufactured before 1950; furniture for export.

Typical test ignition sources

Smouldering cigarette; burning match; butane flame; wood crib.

The old standards BS 3120/3121 have now been withdrawn from use.

Chapter Eight

Leather

Leather, probably in the form of raw hide, was certainly one of the first materials to be used by craftsmen to upholster chairs and seats. For centuries hide has had a special appeal, because of its versatility, strength and warmth.

No man-made material has yet equalled the feel and comfort experienced from new or well-worn leather. Architects, designers and manufacturers in many parts of the world specify leather for its variety, quality and reliability.

The natural skin or hide is porous, which allows it to breathe and gives it a high water permeability. These qualities are important in any upholstery covering, whether for domestic, contract or for vehicle upholstery. Leather is protective and insulates well against cold and heat, ensuring comfort with performance under most conditions. Although comparatively lightweight, leather is surprisingly strong and supple and is therefore suitable for moulding into quite complex shapes. This elasticity makes it the perfect material for upholstery and for clothing. Cow and ox hides are the most suitable skins for furniture application, mainly because of their natural properties and large economical size. Other skins such as horse, pig and calf are occasionally used and all have their own special characteristics.

Hides and skins are by-products of the food trade. Animals are bred for their meat, milk and wool and not for the value of their skins. Availability therefore fluctuates, and, as a result, prices of raw hide waver during the year. The number of cattle reared in Britain is far too small to satisfy the demands of the leather trade, and so large numbers of skins are imported from Denmark, Sweden and South America.

STRUCTURE

Raw hide has a three-tier structure; the top layer is called the corium minor. This shallow layer has the epidermis or outer surface, through which the hair grows, and various glands and muscles. The middle

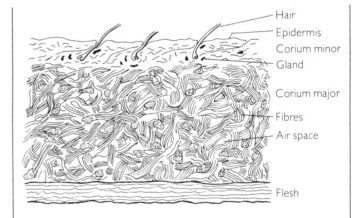

Fig 8.1 A microscopic sectional view of cow hide.

layer, which is the main part of the skin, is called the corium major. This is made up of millions of tiny fibrils, and these form the fibre bundles matted together with still air trapped between them. It is this strong, resilient layer that gives hide much of its outstanding properties. The third, lower layer is the flesh, which is mostly made up of fats and will be removed in the early preparation process. The terms grain side and flesh side are used to describe the upper and lower surfaces as the raw hide is processed into leather (Fig 8.2).

PROCESSING

Preparation
Pelts or raw skins contain large amounts of salt. To begin preparation the salts, flesh, fat and hair are removed to leave the grain and the corium. This is done by an alkaline treatment, which includes lime and various chemicals. The surplus parts that are removed

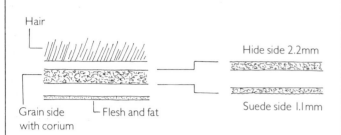

Fig 8.2 Separation of raw hide.

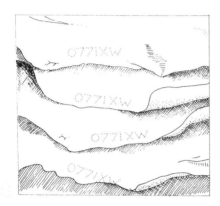

Batch control numbers stamped on to the hides

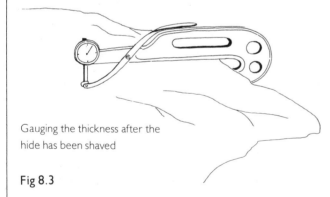

Gauging the thickness after the
hide has been shaved

Fig 8.3

are not wasted; the flesh and fat go into glue making,
while others are transformed into gelatines.

The clean hides are then trimmed and stamped with
a number which gives some control of their quality and
allows each hide to be identified later. It is at this stage
that the hides are split. They pass through a band knife
machine which separates them into two different
thicknesses. The upper split which contains the grain
is used for upholstery leathers, while the flesh split goes
into the making of fashion garments, linings and
accessories. The grain side which now measures about
2½mm in thickness is washed again to ensure a clean,
even surface for dyeing. To complete the preparation
work the hide is softened, to make it more relaxed and
supple, and then pickled in preservatives until tanning
can take place.

Tanning

Vegetable
Tanning is a process which preserves and textures the
hide and gives it the characteristic odour of fresh
leather. Traditionally, tanning liquors were made from
ground oak and sumac bark, but today mimosa tanning
is more common. The hides turn slowly in huge drums
absorbing the tanning liquids.

Mineral
In recent years, chrome tanning has largely taken over
from wholly vegetable tanning processes. The
mineral-tanning substances are chromium salts
(tri-valent chromium), which soften the hide and
colour it pale blue.

Combination tanning, using both vegetable and
mineral techniques, is quite common. This takes from
eight to twelve hours to complete, and the whole
tanning process about fourteen days. Modern
processing techniques can now produce good quality
leathers in two weeks, which by traditional methods
took up to six months.

However, as with any good natural material, speed of
processing is not the only consideration and for certain
types of hide, a slower, more natural tanning process
can produce a better quality and longer lasting
product. A combination of vacuum-pressure
techniques, combination tanning and careful curing
has proved to be the most suited to the making of
upholstery leather.

Tanning materials
Vegetable
Mimosa – The bark of the South and East African
wattle tree
Valonia – The acorn of a Turkish oak tree
Sumac – The ground bark of the sumac tree
Quebracho – Wood from the quebracho tree
Myrobalan – An Indian nut

Mineral
Chrome salts and basic chromium sulphate, a mineral
salt which has rapid penetration, contain tannic acid
which is applied in varying degrees, to swell, strengthen
and preserve hides.

Dressing
The hides are squeeze dried and stretched on
rectangular frames, to allow the tanning process to
continue for up to seven days. During this time the
hides are thoroughly examined for imperfections and
any small defects caused during tanning and
processing. Every hide is entered in a stock book, and a
batch card is issued, to follow the skin through all of
the remaining processes.

The hides are then soaked to rehydrate all the fibres

Walnut and Mahogany Side Chairs c. 1715–30

Upholstered chairs made with low backs and wide seats accommodated the hooped dresses and wide coats fashionable at the time.

Upholstery Rather lean and certainly not over-stuffed. Covers were tightly pulled down over rail edges, which were packed and stitched using grass or tow wrapped in linen cloth and webbing.

Coverings These were of great beauty and rich with colour, red being very predominant.

Imported velvets, silk damask and gros point needlework were all popular, but pictorial records indicate that for these types of chairs, geometrical designs and French pictorial motifs were embroidered a great deal as furniture coverings.

before being shaved to exact predetermined thicknesses – 1.3mm for the motor trade, 1.1mm for upholstery leather and 0.8mm for the fashion trade.

The shaved hides are oiled and dyed in huge drums, with carefully controlled acidity and temperature. Creases and excess water are removed before travelling into drying ovens.

The hides are now in a 'russet' state and are again inspected for surface faults such as scratches, barbed-wire marks, scars, and holes bored by insects. This is a convenient point for sorting and grading, and an encoded number is stamped on to the hides to show their level of quality, before finishing processes begin.

Colouring

To give a good surface for dyeing, some leathers are lightly sanded and air-blasted to remove dust. Staining can then take place with pure aniline dyes, and an application of synthetic sealer. Resin emulsions, polyurethane lacquers and epoxy resins are also employed to enhance and finish the leather surface.

Graining and finishing

The variations in grain and skin tone which occur in any animal hide can be corrected to a certain degree by embossing a natural grain on to the surface. Many grains and patterns may be specially applied in this way to give a variety of different effects, including the appearance of the skin from another mammal or

reptile. A suede finish can also be produced by buffing up the flesh side of the skin.

The very finest leathers can be simply aniline dyed to leave their attractive natural markings visible. This is often an acceptable part of the genuine nature of a hide. Some other decorative effects can be applied to customer requirements, such as antiquing, waterproofing, etc.

The finished hides are then measured to give the exact surface area in square feet or square metres. This is done on a pinwheel measuring machine, which calculates the area of a skin including all the irregular outer edges.

New hides are stored by draping several together over a 'horse' which is a high leather-covered bench, similar to a horse used in a gymnasium. Alternatively they may be rolled up individually or in twos on to wood poles ready for despatch to customers.

Special finishes and treatment

Antiquing

Most hides are of uniform colour throughout, but for some special uses in upholstery leather is produced with a contrasting grain. This finish gives the leather the appearance of age and tends to make it look used and subdued in tone. Many furniture makers who specialise in reproduction work favour this leather finish for their products. The darker inlay in the grain

Contrast coloured grain for antique effect

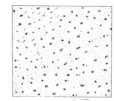
Pig skin

Printed grain

Printed buffalo grain

Fig 8.4 Effects of natural and applied grain.

pattern is produced by applying a contrast colour all over, and then removing most of it by washing the contrast colour from the high points of the grain pattern. Protective lacquers are then applied, leaving an interesting antique effect.

Rub-off finishes are also used to produce antique or used-hide effects. Rub-off is a process whereby the antiqued hide can be upholstered on to furniture and then colour removed from edges and high spots to give a worn or faded appearance. A wash-off liquid is used and the leather must then be resealed with a sealer. Hides can also be antiqued by hand by the furniture manufacturer. A chair, for example, can be fully upholstered using a russet hide. It is then passed on to a skilled polisher who antiques the leather to suit each particular piece. Basically, the open grain of the leather is filled with fine powder components which immediately give the leather an aged effect. The whole chair is then stained carefully with the required colour, and the polisher uses his stain to produce light and dark effects on the chair, almost as if a picture were being painted. Finally sealers and lacquers are used to complete the work.

Tooling
Leather has the capability and depth suitable for heavy embossing and tooling. The surface can be impressed with finely etched rollers and tools which are usually heated. The patterns embossed in this way are permanent. Tooled leathers are used for decorative purposes, pictures and leather inlays in cabinet work.

Gold-foil tooling is a skilled craft used to great effect on leather inlays for desks and table tops. This decorative work clearly demonstrates the great versatility of leather as a furniture material.

Some standard leather finishes
Chrome re-tan Very flexible leather can be made by first lightly chrome tanning, and then completing the tannage with vegetable tans.

Chrome re-tanned, antique rub-off finish Leathers which are combination tanned and completed with a rub-off finish which is used with wash-off liquids and sealer.

Chrome re-tanned – printed grain Upholstery leather which has been given an improved artificial grain after combination tanning.

Full chrome tanned – natural russet Leather which has received a full mineral tan, but was left at the russet stage, and coloured pale cream on the grain side only.

Full chrome tanned, aniline A soft, supple, chrome-tanned leather which has been aniline dyed through.

Full-grain hide A leather which has not been grain corrected, but retains its natural grain intact.

Suede
Suede surface is produced on the flesh side, and has a smooth, velvet-like feel. Usually tanned with a mixture of chromium and aluminium tanning salts, giving fine suede properties. The surface is buffed with fast-revolving emery-covered rollers, which cut the leather fibres down to an even suede nap. Suede is usually finished with silicone sprays which are anti-soiling and water repellant.

PROPERTIES OF LEATHER

Listed below are some of the physical properties which make upholstery leather an attractive and unique covering material.

Good tensile strength
Good resistance to tearing, due to its interlaced fibre structure
Resistance to puncture
Good strength-for-weight ratio
Good resistance to fatigue by flexing
Can be made dimensionally stable, or very flexible, to suit different purposes
Has good heat insulation
Excellent permeability to water vapours
Absorbs and disperses water well
Warm in winter and cool in summer
Good resistance to water and can be made waterproof
Good resistance to fire, and does not support flame easily
Mouldability is good; this helps in the work of upholstery, shoe making, etc.
Good resistance to rot or fungi attack

For upholstery purposes many of the properties and special qualities of leather are ideal. Its warmth, feel and attractive texture make it very appealing. However, the extensibility of full chrome hides must be carefully controlled, or they are likely to bag and crease when used to cover large areas on softly filled seats and backs and large cushions or overlays.

The selection of hides for different types of work is therefore important. For large areas of covering, softness is required but without too much stretch. However, where a design is to be fluted or buttoned a degree of flexibility is ideal, and will be contained by the upholstery technique. The companies producing leather for upholstery are continually developing and revising their processing techniques in order to provide the upholsterer with the ideal leather covering to suit every situation.

SOME FACTS ABOUT UPHOLSTERY AND PANELLING LEATHERS

Furniture leather is produced from carefully selected hides, as free from scars and defects as is possible. They are generally through-dyed for maximum scuff resistance and have enamelled or lacquered surfaces for maximum light fastness and abrasion resistance.

Special matching and colourings are always available from the leather companies. Natural aniline-dyed leather and suede are luxury materials which must be treated with care, and not used in conditions where excessive dirt or grease may result in permanent staining. Suede should not be subjected to direct sunlight.

Shape and dimensions

The shape and size of a typical hide are illustrated in Fig 8.5. This gives a guide to the larger panel sizes that are obtainable. Half hides would be cut from A to B, and the range of dimensions should be calculated at between 40 sq ft (3.7 sq m) and 55 sq ft (5 sq m) per hide. An average size would be 47 sq ft (4.3 sq m). Approximate measurements of the average hide would be:

> A to B – 7'6" (228cm)
> c to d – 4'3" (129cm)
> e to f – 5'9" (175cm)
> g to h – 6'3" (190cm)
> i to j – 6'9" (205cm)
> k to l – 5'6" (168cm)

Approximately eleven to thirteen dining chair loose seats can be cut from one hide of the average size shown, or seven top-stuffed or stuffover dining chair seats, one average size easy chair would use about one and a half hides. As a useful comparison, 1m of woven soft cover 120cm wide is equal to just over 12 sq ft (1.1 sq m) of hide.

UPHOLSTERY TECHNIQUES WITH LEATHER

Before the development of very soft chrome-tanned and retanned upholstery leathers, the business of

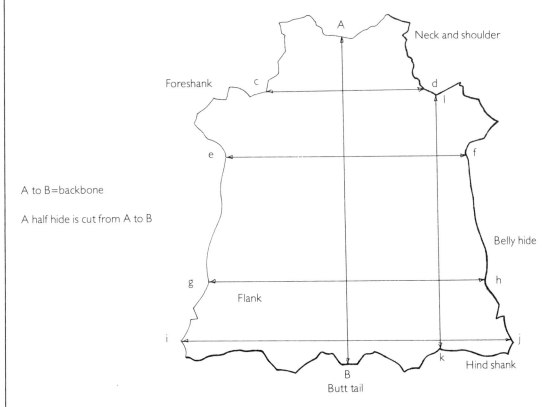

A to B=backbone

A half hide is cut from A to B

Fig 8.5 A full-size upholstery cow hide measuring approximately 48sq ft (4.4592sq m).

covering a fully upholstered piece of furniture in hide was rather specialised and involved much hard work. The hides used were of very good quality but were thick and rather stiff, and lacked the suppleness of modern leathers. Upholsterers who were good hide workers tended to specialise, and were a rather élite group.

In factory production, leather work was separated from soft cover work, and more time was allowed for a piece to be leather covered, often an increase of 50 per cent or more was normal. The nature of hide demanded much greater care, and finishing techniques, which are very different from those used for cloth, took longer. This careful treatment and the extra time required were also extended to the cutting and sewing processes, where the hide is prepared for the upholsterer. It was not unusual to see pieces of leather being warmed up over a stove or radiator, to make them more supple and easier to handle. In some cases, particularly if a hide was to be deep buttoned, it was damped with water and stretched, and then buttoned in while still damp. This is no longer necessary with modern leathers, but at the same time the technique of using leather is still very different from that of woven cloth.

Because hide has no directional bias as fabrics do, it reacts very differently to being pulled and fixed on to frames. For conventional covering, it is best temporarily fixed, and then eased out in all directions, until a smooth tight fit is produced. It may often be necessary to adjust the fixings several times. Once it is warmed by the hands, corners can be set in and pleated; its moulding properties help here a great deal. Provided that fillings are strong enough it is fairly easy to clean out a corner, leaving it almost free of pleats, then small amounts of surplus can be pulled back away from the corner, and eased out over the sides. There is no substitute for practical experience when dealing with leather. The best way to understand how this beautiful material can be used is to do it yourself, beginning with a small rectangular frame, and then going on to curved work. Modern upholstery techniques are rather different, covers are not required to be pulled drum tight, and fillings are generally much softer.

Cutting away excess and trimming off with scissors and a very sharp knife is very important in leather work. Thicknesses can build up, especially at corners and where seams are pulled over edges. If a sharp knife is used leather can be easily trimmed, and very clean cuts made to produce flat, even fixings. Leather is non-fray and is much more accurately trimmed with a knife than with scissors. Another feature of leather is that it can be permanently creased or pleated with finger pressure, or gentle hammering. This is a useful technique and can be used when it is known that a fold or pleat is needed in a set position. Traditionally, when rather heavy hides were used for deep buttoning, it was common practice to mark out button positions and then fold and hammer the pleats in, before commencing the button work. This practice can be used in any similar situations.

Taking care of the surface of leather is another important aspect, and is part of the handling technique. Pins and skewers cannot be used for holding purposes on visible surfaces, and tools generally must not become rough or burred where they come into contact with hide. For working in folds and tuck aways, a wooden dolly stick is preferred to a steel regulator. This is kinder to the surface and less likely to cause scratching. These are some of the basic practical considerations in the craft of working at the bench with hide.

MEASURING, MARKING OUT AND CUTTING

A new hide is a very irregular shape and no two skins are ever the same. It is therefore necessary to deal with each skin individually when marking out and cutting. There is a set routine for the checking and marking out of an upholstery hide. Careful inspection is absolutely vital, or expensive errors will almost certainly occur.

What to expect and what to check

First the usual checks should be made. Is the colour and type the one that was ordered, and as per sample? What is the area of the hide, is this exactly the right amount or is there some to spare? This will affect the marking out.

Then it is necessary to inspect the surface of the skin very closely. Some of the natural and processing

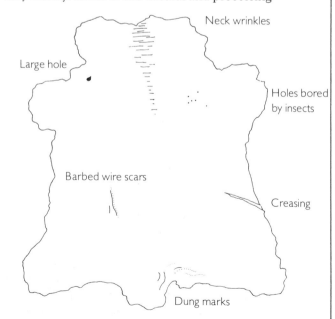

Fig 8.6 Some surface defects which may occur in a whole hide.

defects will almost certainly be evident. When any faults are located they should be lightly marked with a chalk ring round them. At the same time check the depth of wrinkling along the backbone, particularly along the neck end. Look at the marks from several different angles, as light can often play tricks, especially on dark colours. It can now be decided which of the defects must be completely avoided, and which will be acceptable for use on some of the less important cuts, e.g. outside arms, outside backs or hidden parts on the chair. With a clear picture of the skin in front of you, the larger parts can be marked out, bearing in mind that the many smaller parts will have to be fitted in around these.

A soft pencil or a stick of white chalk are good marking-out tools. All the waste strips should be kept if piping or bandings are needed, unless their surfaces are too rough, or their colour is not consistent with the main area. Having marked out the hide, each part can be initialled in a corner with chalk, this saves confusion once cutting is done. It also served as a check that no part needed for the job has been overlooked. If fly pieces are to be sewn on to any of the main parts, then at these points a chalk line should be drawn to show the full length of the fly position. It is wise to complete all the marking out before cutting commences (Fig 8.7).

The leather should be cut with a good pair of scissors, or small electric cloth cutters. In a factory situation, hides are dealt with in the same way, each one individually treated, it is only the cutting process which may be speeded up by the use of press cutting dies, or large electric cutters. Marking out is also aided with ready-made jigs or patterns, in perspex, cardboard or plywood.

SEWING

The joining of pieces of hide together is very much a machine process today, and this has almost entirely removed the need for hand stitching. Leather is, in fact, a difficult material to hand sew, and a great deal of skill and patience is needed to produce hand-made products. Some items in the field of sports equipment, saddle making and leather accessories are hand sewn. However, in most cases, there is a sewing machine which has been developed to deal with most joining operations. For upholstery purposes, standard industrial sewing machines and accessories are quite adequate for leather work. An industrial lock-stitch machine is capable of sewing six plies of modern leather together. Feed mechanisms and needles are important in the efficient sewing of hides. To feed leather plies through a machine, a standard drop feed is limited, though still used by many upholsterers. A better, more efficient work-feed system is compound feed where the needle rotates in unison with the feed dog. This system can be made even more effective if

The layout shown is a typical example, and is only approximately to scale for a chair of this type. Another half hide would have to be cut into to obtain two outside arms and some more piping to complete the job; alternatively, a larger skin of over 50sq ft would be needed. The layout also assumes that no major defects are present, except for some wrinkling along the back bone, which will show up on the extreme ends of the main parts and on the top platform piece, most of which is hidden under the cushion. This may not be acceptable in all cases.

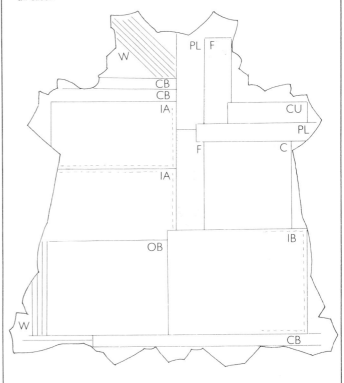

Key to parts:
W – welt or piping
PL – platform
F – facings
IA – inside arms
CU – underside of cushion
OB – outside back
IB – inside back
CB – cushion borders
C – cushion panel or top.

Fig 8.7 The cover parts for a small arm chair are marked out on to an average size hide.

the presser foot is of the alternating type, commonly called a walking foot. This combination produces very sound, even feeding at low or high speeds.

Needles and seams
Leather can be machine sewn very satisfactorily with a standard round cloth point needle. These needles pierce a clean round hole for the thread to be pulled into, and will produce a seam which will take strain well

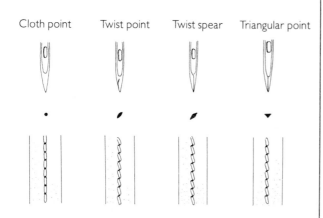

Fig 8.8 Seams produced in leather.

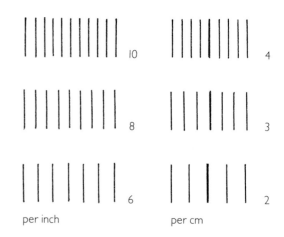

Fig 8.10 Recommended stitch lengths for hide work.

provided that thread tension and stitch lengths are correct.

Machine needles which are specially produced for leather work have different point designs. These are spear and chisel shapes, which have a cutting action as they pass through the leather. They are often referred to as leather points. These types are ideal for very heavy work on thick hide, and for top stitching and decorative stitching over a variety of seams.

Selecting needles is therefore dependent on the type of leather being used, and the complexity of the seams. The cutting action made by leather point needles tends to produce a large needle hole, and the stitches have a slanting, or zig-zag appearance, better suited to decorative work than for standard plain-sewn joints. Thread tension should be checked regularly, especially if hide thicknesses are varying. A good seam with correct tension can be tested in the same way as it would be for cloth. A small sample strip is sewn using two plies, and then strained by hand to see if the seam remains tight, and if there is any evidence of bursting, caused by needle holes tearing or lack of tension. A good seam in leather will show surface thread sitting down tightly between the holes, and on the suede side the thread will be almost invisible.

Stitch lengths should never be too small for leather work, or seams will be weakened by perforation. Ten stitches per inch (or 2.4mm) is the normal minimum. Eight or nine stitches per inch (or 3mm) is a good average setting. On decorative seams, then, much larger stitch lengths may be used and are very effective.

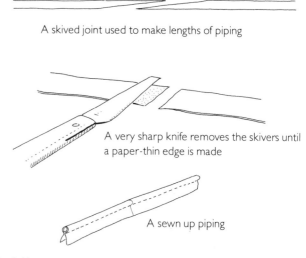

Fig 8.11

BUYING HIDE

Hide is sold in whole or half hides, on a pence per square foot basis, with minimum orders being half a hide, approximately 23.7 sq ft (2.2 sq m). Allowance must always be made for wastage which ranges from 25 per cent for soft upholstery to 50 per cent for panelling and large desk tops. Leather is usually supplied to the nearest hide or half hide over the quantity ordered. When furniture manufacturers order regularly, samples are taken from every order and retained at the tannery to facilitate accurate colour matching in the future.

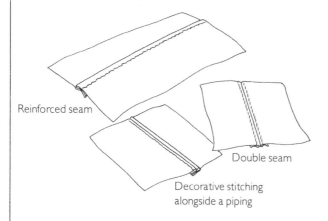

Fig 8.9 Using leather point needles.

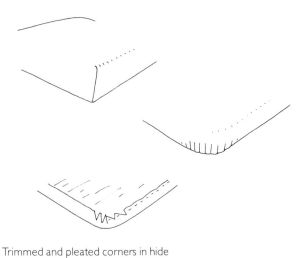

Trimmed and pleated corners in hide

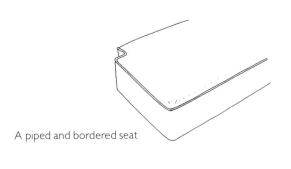

A piped and bordered seat

Border pieces can be cut slightly curved, which removes fullness
when the sewn cover is pulled on

Fig 8.12

Estimating amounts

A job can be measured for as if it were to be covered in
soft cover. When an estimated figure is arrived at, this
can easily be converted into square metres or square
feet. It is then necessary to add the allowance for waste
on to this figure and the total, which should always be
rounded up, is the amount of hide to be ordered. A
supplier will send the hide, or hides, as near in area to
the amount ordered as is possible from stock at the
time.

Example estimate

A chair requires 3m of 127cm-wide cover (3¼ yds of
51in-cover). This is converted into square metres,
approximately 3.85 sq m (42½ sq ft). A wastage
percentage of 25 per cent is added to this, giving a total
of 4.8 sq m (approx 53 sq ft). It will therefore be
necessary to buy one very large hide or one and a half
hides of a smaller size.

MAINTENANCE

Cleaning

Grain leather should be cleaned with a light, circular
motion, using a mild toilet soap and a damp cloth. This
should then be repeated using clean water only, taking
great care not to soak the leather. After cleaning, a
leather conditioner should be used, but only those
recommended by the manufacturers. A conditioner or
a hide food should never be used unless the hide has
been cleaned first, or there is a danger that surface dirt
will be rubbed into the grain and will act as an abrasive.

It is good policy to inform the upholstery buyer or
customer of which type of leather has been used, so
that future cleaning methods will suit the particular
type. Modern easy-care leathers do not need regular
feeding or cleaning, unless soiling is unusually heavy.
The soft soap method described is all that should be
needed under normal conditions, about once a year or
every two years. The mature patina which
accompanies well-used leather is desirable and gives
leather-covered furniture a distinctive appeal.
Discoloration does not affect the wearing properties of
leather. Various hide foods, which are recommended
by leather manufacturers, are designed to restore the
original surface and the feel of leather after gentle
cleaning. Wax polishes, spray polishes and saddle soaps
are not recommended for use on upholstery leathers.

Chapter Nine

Preparation of Materials

Careful assessment of the extent of the work and the materials required is an essential preliminary before attempting any practical work. A thorough and well-informed approach will save wasting time and materials later, and helps avoid the risk of costly mistakes.

REQUIREMENTS

The requirements of a piece of upholstery can be enormously varied, and will depend on the type, style and size of a piece. Traditional hand-built upholstery can usually be separated from modern work as the materials and approach to the job will be very different. Much of the upholstered furniture produced during or just after the World War II may be described as in between traditional and modern.

This was a time when upholstery construction and the materials available to do the job were changing drastically. The changes were influenced by the availability of spring units, filling materials and covers, and the development of new materials, mostly synthetic. Powered tools and the machinery used for upholstery were also changing – new and semi-automatic pieces of equipment were being developed and introduced so that labour-intensive processes could be updated.

The introduction of the staple gun during the mid-1950s had an influence on the way the upholsterer worked. Synthetic foams were introduced as replacements for rubberised hair, latex foams and cotton felts. Another change was the way in which work was being done, 'made-through' upholstery, where a whole piece was completed and finished by a single upholsterer was slowly being changed for group working methods. This type of production called for the various upholstery processes in a chair to be shared among a team or group of craftsmen, each one completing a part of the job and then passing it on to someone else.

For the upholsterer today, whose work is mainly restoring and reupholstery, the three distinct methods of construction demand a very flexible approach. Early styles built almost entirely by hand were sprung or unsprung, and had first and second stuffings in various natural fibre fillings. The middle or wartime-period styles contained machine-made spring units, fibre pads and fillings of cotton or wool felts. Modern upholstery contains large amounts of synthetic foam, on rubber or steel suspension, with soft fibre filling wraps. As the modern styles and methods have developed, more and more of the covering fabrics are tailored and machine-sewn.

Armed with this background knowledge it is the upholsterer's job to restore, renovate or change the particular pieces that pass through a workshop. In many cases simply changing a covering will alter the whole effect of a chair, while with others it may be necessary to alter completely the upholstery construction, particularly if a poor attempt has previously been made to reupholster. Each upholstery job should be assessed at the very beginning, and the requirements noted down in a job notebook. When several pieces of work are being dealt with at the same time, then details of each cannot be left to memory. Making careful notes of all that is agreed with a customer, and at the same time noting the type of work and any special requirements, is essential. These special requirements will include the general condition of the frame and any obvious faults that will need correcting.

The work should be measured for the new cover as soon as possible. This must be recorded and any changes in the construction allowed for. At this stage details of the new cover are also needed, as this may well affect the length of fabric required. It is necessary to know the cover type, its width and details of any pattern repeats. Trimmings, finish and decoration should also be agreed. Having collected as much information as possible about the work, and a thorough

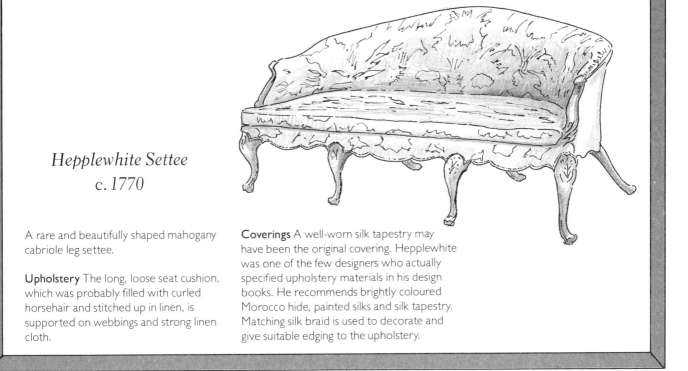

Hepplewhite Settee
c. 1770

A rare and beautifully shaped mahogany cabriole leg settee.

Upholstery The long, loose seat cushion, which was probably filled with curled horsehair and stitched up in linen, is supported on webbings and strong linen cloth.

Coverings A well-worn silk tapestry may have been the original covering. Hepplewhite was one of the few designers who actually specified upholstery materials in his design books. He recommends brightly coloured Morocco hide, painted silks and silk tapestry. Matching silk braid is used to decorate and give suitable edging to the upholstery.

inspection made, then an estimate of the cost of the whole job can be recorded and kept for reference.

For costing purposes a reupholstery job can usually be broken down into separate areas:

The frame
Note the condition of the frame and any repairs to the joints, the polished surfaces, the fittings, e.g. the castors, actions, etc., and the conditions of carvings and cane work. If necessary, some or all of the work may have to be carried out by a specialist, and an estimate for this obtained and recorded.

The covering and trimmings
At the time of ordering an up-to-date cost of the new cover will be quoted by the supplier. This is often a very large part of the overall cost of the job, and should therefore be noted in the job book. Timing is also important. If the cover being ordered is not in stock then find out how long it will take to arrive. As soon as this is known preparation or repair work can be started, and a date set for reupholstery and covering.

Trimmings can be chosen and matched from samples and, if necessary, ordered at the same time. A long delay caused by one small item can be very frustrating.

The upholstery
After careful assessment of the condition of a piece it can be decided how much of the work needs complete replacement and how much can be reused and kept

intact. The seat areas of chairs and settees suffer most wear, whereas the arms and backs often remain in good condition. The age of materials will often give a good guide and if condition is suspect then replacement is always best.

List the new materials that are needed, with their amounts, and then total the cost from a current price catalogue. Extras and unforeseen items should always be allowed for. Until a job is stripped down, there is always uncertainty about the condition of some items. The three separate costing areas of frame, coverings and upholstery can then be totalled to give an overall cost. It then remains to add a cost for each of the following:

1. Sundry items; tacks, staples, twines and cords, etc.
2. A percentage on all materials, to cover handling, transport, etc.
3. Labour costs; hours spent on each job
4. Delivery and collection as applicable
5. Overheads; the cost of running and maintaining a workshop.

It is not always necessary to deal with all these items separately. The percentage on materials can be permanently included in the materials prices. An hourly rate can also be set to cover labour and overheads together, and then reviewed every six months. The list would then read more simply:

1. Materials cost
2. Sundry items percentage
3. Labour cost per hour
4. Collection and delivery

A list of all the requirements for most types of work would read as follows:

1 Frame, repairs and restoration
2 Cover and trimmings
3 Upholstery materials
4 Sundries
5 Labour cost per hour
6 Collection and delivery

Figs 9.1 and 9.2 show a typical job sheet, or may represent a page or two in a record book.

Fig 9.1

Customer	Date	
Job		Costing
The frame Condition Repairs Restoration		
	Estimate	
The cover Type Design Width Length Repeat		
Upholstery Condition Replace	Materials	
Trimmings	Amounts	

Fig 9.2

Job		Cover		Cutting plan
Cut parts		Length	Width	
Inside back	IB			
Outside back	OB			
Inside arms	IA			
Outside arms	OA			
Seat	S			
Platform	PL			
Cushion	C			
Cushion borders	CB			
Inside wings	IW			
Outside wings	OW			
Arm facings	AF			
Back facings	BF			
Piping	P			
Others				

MEASURING FOR COVER

This is a job which must be done carefully and accurately, and kept as a record. Measurements for a cover can be taken from a bare frame or, in the case of new work, from a full-size drawing or a made-up prototype. In the case of reupholstery, the measuring for cover can be done directly from the existing upholstery, with any allowances made for changes in shape or upholstery design. If possible the type of covering should be known, so that sewn joints can be placed or matched correctly, or avoided. The direction and lay of a cover on to a piece of seating is important, and there are several unwritten rules which generally apply to most situations, and can safely be followed. For some plain coverings, however, the cover is often placed in such a way as to be as economical as possible. This tends to apply to those covers with little or no texture, or surface grain. The same treatment applies when using leather because this has no directional preference, and can be laid on to the work in the most economical way.

The general rule, however, is that the weft yarns in a woven fabric are kept parallel to the floor as far as possible. This means that the opposite warp yarns will run up and down or vertically to the floor. In the majority of woven covers the warp yarns are the stronger and therefore the more stable, and the covers will wear and drape better if laid on in this direction. On this basis measurements can be made and the 'lay' of the cover kept in mind along with the cover width.

The measurements taken first are for the largest pieces, the length being those that will run up the roll and the widths those that run across a roll of cover. If the width of the cover being used is 140cm, then the half-width measurement will be 70cm. This dimension should not include the selvedge. As the measurements are taken they can be recorded and where possible fitted into the half width and paired with the opposite half width. This can usually be done with inside arm

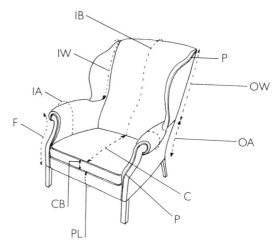

Taking length measurements from a wing chair

Taking width measurements, most of which can be paired on the cutting plan

Fig 9.4

covers, outside arm covers, wing parts, cushion panels, etc.

Finally, when all the parts have been measured and notes made, the length measurements are added together, excluding those that are paired, and a total length calculated down one side of the cutting plan.

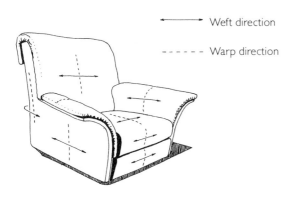

→ Weft direction

- - - - - Warp direction

Fig 9.3 The lay of cover on an easy chair.

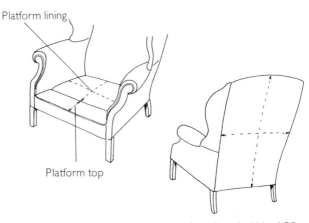

Platform lining

Platform top

Fig 9.5

Length and width of OB

COVER-CUTTING PLANS

The calculated length required for a job, which has been taken from a list of measurements, is only an estimate. Such an estimate can be used to provide approximate cover length or costings, but is not accurate enough for the purpose of actually marking out a cover, or cutting it. The need for more detailed dimensions depends rather on the type of work being done.

In traditional upholstery a measured estimate may well be good enough, as very little of the covering is tailored or machined. Pieces of fabric cut slightly oversize for each part of the job are adequate, and any shaping or trimming is done during upholstery, and then hand finished.

For new work or for reupholstery of modern seating a cutting plan is more accurate, and gives a clean

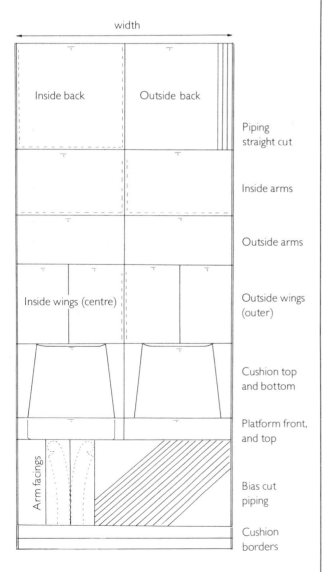

Fig 9.6 The parts on a chair or settee which can be paired or mirrored.

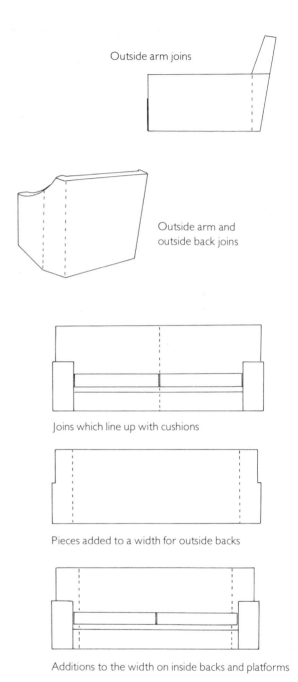

Fig 9.7 Joins that are acceptable for economy of fabric, by extending the whole width and the half width.

indication of all the parts and their shapes. Location marks can be drawn in where sewing occurs, and patterns, if any, can be more carefully considered and matched. Fig 9.8 shows two plans for the same chair.

In the factory situation where models are continually repeated in batches, then cover-cutting plans will exist from the production planning stage. These are then converted into full-size layouts from which patterns and jigs are made. A set of these is kept for each model or suite, for use in the cutting shop. Modified layouts are often made for the cutting of printed and patterned covers.

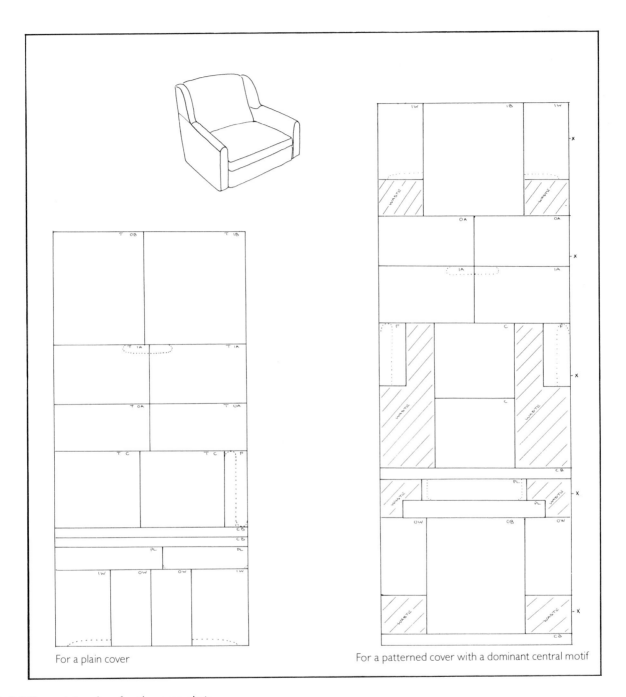

For a plain cover

For a patterned cover with a dominant central motif

Fig 9.8 Two cutting plans for the same chair.

Marking out

One of the simplest methods of marking out covers repeatedly and accurately is by chalking round moulds or patterns made from plywood, hardboard or sheet plastic (Fig 9.9). Marking out tools are white stick chalk, tailor's crayon or one of the more specialised chalks; wax chalks, which produce permanent marks on fabric; vanishing chalks, effective up to several days, after which the markings will disappear; fluorescent chalk, which shows up quite strongly under ultra-violet light only.

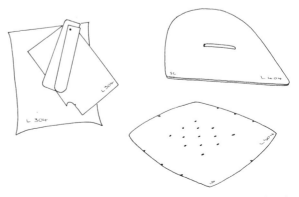

Fig 9.9 Cover-cutting patterns made up from plywood and plastic sheet, in sets.

Perforated patterns

Another very effective but basically simple marking-out system is by means of a large full-size stencil. This is made up from Kraft paper, and the outline of the cover parts is drawn on to the paper and then perforated with ⅛in (3mm) holes at about ½in (13mm) intervals. Cutting the holes can be done manually with a small punch or mechanically with an electric punching tool or a heated spike wheel. Once made, the pattern can be used repeatedly for up to a year or longer.

The stencil pattern, which is the same width as the cover being marked, is clamped down over a lay of cover and fine powder chalk contained in a muslin bag is dusted over to produce a dotted outline on to the top layer of cover. When removed the lay can be cut using small or large electric cloth cutters, depending on the number of cloth layers. Producing a Kraft pattern of this type is relatively simple, costs very little and is very accurate and quick to use. For small- and medium-size batch production this method is one of the most popular (Fig 9.10). In the areas of large-scale mass production of cut cover parts, more sophisticated systems can be considered. These generally do away with the business of marking out and as cover parts can be cut directly after laying up.

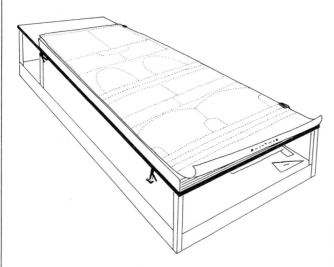

Fig 9.10 A perforated Kraft paper pattern being clamped over a cover lay prior to dusting with lay chalk.

Tramline jigs

A large board, usually plywood, is grooved or routed to the outlines of the parts, and forms the surface of the cutting table. The cover or cover layers are carefully laid up and clamped over the board. With a steel peg or pin fitted to the base of a vertical blade cloth cutter, in line with the blade, cutting can be done by steering the machine along the grooves, following all the outlines. This method is ideal where layouts are not too complex, but does rely on the skill and the memory of

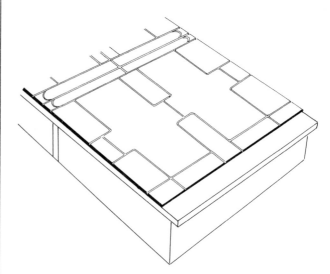

Fig 9.11 A grooved tramline jig mounted on to a cutting table designed to cut a pair of T-shaped cushions, with side borders and back border.

the operator. The whole operation is fairly fast and covers can be bulk cut without the need for marking out (Fig 9.11).

Press cutting

A cover cutting system whereby pre-formed dies are used to stamp out the cover parts under a large hydraulic press. The cutting operation can be either from above the fabrics or below. Where large numbers of repeated cuts are made every day then such systems are viable.

A good example of this kind of repetition is in the production of cushions or squabs made in batches of twenty or thirty several times per day. Systems of this kind are used in clothing production and for vehicle upholstery (Fig 9.12).

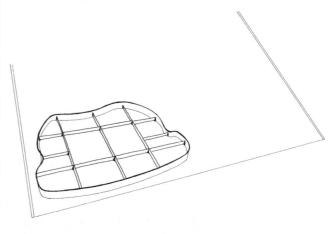

Fig 9.12 A toughened steel-press cutting die used under a hydraulic press to cut out fabric and hide.

CUTTING

In the average small workshop the upholsterer does all the cutting that is necessary as each job proceeds. A large cutting bench or table with some storage underneath is all that is required. The table surface should be kept clear and clean, and good lighting provided. If power cutting is used then overhead electrical points make working safer and easier. The size of the table should be as large as can be accommodated, but at least 10ft (3m) long and 5ft (1½m) wide. The width is important and ideally should be just over the dimensions of most of the cover widths used, i.e. 145cm. It is useful to be able to walk round the table on at least three sides to avoid having to disturb fabrics during marking and cutting. Tools for this work can be long and cumbersome, and so should be hung or shelved conveniently close to the table. T squares, set squares, straightedges and measuring sticks, plus large compasses, are all that are required.

Bulk cutting

The cutting of covers in bulk is usually referred to as multi-lay cutting. Several layers of upholstery cover are laid up on to a cutting surface to be marked out and cut in one operation. Multi-lay cutting tends to be more difficult when dealing with pile fabrics and fabrics with large patterns, but providing each layer is of an identical type then problems of movement or pattern matching can be overcome.

For this kind of factory operation, cutting tables may well be several metres in length, and the length calculated to allow for complete chairs or suites to be cut from each single layer. Thus, if a settee requires 11m of 130cm cover then the table should accommodate the piece in one lay, where possible. In such bulk production situations, cutting of the covers is powered by rotary and vertical blade cutters, which are skilfully used by male and female cutting specialists. After many repetitions, the different cutting layouts are memorised by the operators, resulting in very efficient and fast production.

Figure 9.13. Bulk cutting of a large cover lay. Notching and drilling takes place after cutting, sorting, labelling and bundling before transferring to the sewing area.

JOINING

By machine and by hand

The principal method of joining materials and fabrics in upholstery is by machine sewing. Hand stitching is used only when a machine is not available or when a join is to be made at the bench. In traditional work most of the joints are produced by hand if the type of work warrants such treatment, particularly in the areas of finishing and trimming.

In modern upholstery production the industrial sewing machine plays an ever-increasing role, and it is in this side of the trade that automation has advanced very rapidly during recent years. There are fringe areas where gluing and welding play their part, but this is mainly in the pre-forming and fabrication of components, prior to being sewn in by machine. Examples of these techniques are mainly decorative panels, which can be fluted or quilted by using thin sheets of PVC foam, over which coverings are welded or heat sealed.

Stitch types
Machine lock stitch

The lock stitch has been used for sewing fabric plies together for as long as the sewing machine has been in existence. It is the strongest seam stitch that can be produced and uses two threads which lock together at each stitch. The lock-stitch machine uses a needle thread and a bobbin thread, and interlocking takes place in the centre of the joint. Fine adjustments are necessary to obtain a well balanced stitch; tension on both threads should be set so that locking takes place inside the plies and not on the surface of either. At the same time the stitch-length control is adjusted to suit a particular fabric or material. The size of machine needles and the thread being used must be compatible, and selected to suit the materials being sewn. Generally, the heavier and thicker the plies, the heavier should be the needle and the thread.

Machine chain stitch

Chain-stitch formation is very different from a lock stitch, and tends to be most suited to lighter-weight applications. Chain stitch is not interlocking but is better described as interlooping.

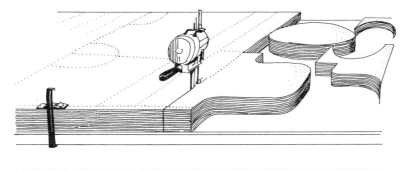

A chain-stitch seam can be produced at very high speeds and works with threads at lower tension. The stitch is formed by a single-needle thread, and does not require a bobbin. More complex and stronger seams are produced with two- and three-thread stitch formations, all of which are applied by needles and loopers. Although the stitch produced is not as strong or as durable as a lock-stitch seam, it does have some advantages, and is being used increasingly in furnishing and upholstery for preparation work, for example in the making of pipings, zip insertion and other pre-sewing operations. Fast continuous sewing, with very little stopping, makes chain-stitch seaming very attractive for modern upholstery manufacture. Three- and four-thread chain stitch overlocking machines are used to join and seal fabrics, particularly in loose cover and detachable cover making. Fig 9.14 illustrates the variety of seamed joints which can be produced and used on upholstery covers.

A seam should be selected for its quality, strength or decorative appeal. This often depends on the cover type being used. There are, for instance, some pile fabrics on which a top-stitched seam will have very little effect, and are therefore best left plain sewn. However, the same seam used on a piece of leather or plain linen looks extremely attractive.

Piped and welted seams are very strong and tend to make attractive joints on almost any furnishing fabric, and are therefore used a great deal. Reinforced seams may be used purely for their strengthening function or applied simply to enhance an edge or joint.

The careful use of colour can also add interest to a seam, welts and pipings made up in contrasting or complementing colours are used to give clear outlines and accentuate design shapes. Single and double rows of brightly coloured machine thread can be used in the same way (Fig 9.15).

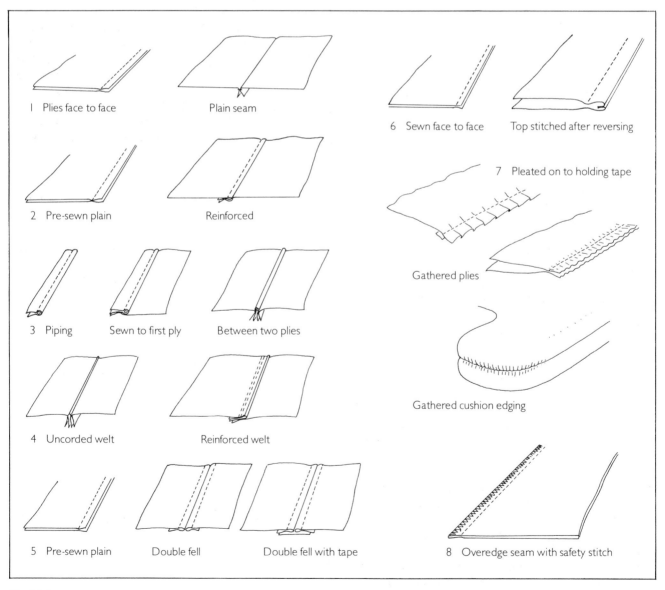

1   Plies face to face   Plain seam

2   Pre-sewn plain   Reinforced

3   Piping   Sewn to first ply   Between two plies

4   Uncorded welt   Reinforced welt

5   Pre-sewn plain   Double fell   Double fell with tape

6   Sewn face to face   Top stitched after reversing

7   Pleated on to holding tape

Gathered plies

Gathered cushion edging

8   Overedge seam with safety stitch

Fig 9.14

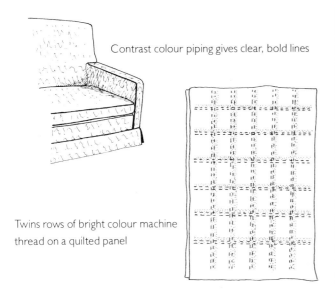

Contrast colour piping gives clear, bold lines

Twins rows of bright colour machine thread on a quilted panel

Fig 9.15.

Some seam types and their applications:

1 **Plain seam:** single or double sewn; produces a strong face-to-face joint.
  Uses: the main jointing method for all covers.

2 **Reinforced seam:** plain sewn and then top stitched to produce a very strong seam.
  Uses: not used a great deal on pile fabrics, but looks best on plain woven flat cloths, coated fabrics and hide.

3 **Piped or welted seams:** a plain seam with piping inserted between the plies, the piping may be corded or uncorded; produces a strong joint.
  Uses: a good general seam, which produces a bold and strong joint on most upholstery covers. Used a great deal on conventional loose covers and boxed cushions.

4 **Double fell seam:** a plain seam which is top-stitched on a twin-needle machine. This produces a decorative joint.
  Uses: used to decorate and flatten a plain seam on most covers. Looks best on coated fabrics and hides, and flat plain woven covers.

5 **Reinforced fell seam taped:** a twin-needled plain seam, with a reinforcing tape laid under. Produces a strong and decorative seam.
  Uses: mainly where strength is needed on flat areas and around curved foam covered edges. Has little decorative effect on pile covers such as velvet, velours and corduroy.

6 **Top-stitched edge seam:** a plain sewn edge seam which is over stitched after reversing. Produces a heavy bold edge.
  Uses: used to support and decorate edges on soft covers and soft hides.

7 **Gathered seam:** a plain seam which may be taped or untaped. Forms gathering at different densities as a decorative effect, or as a functional seam along edges and around cushions. May be produced by hand or on a machine with a gathering function. It is possible to make all the seams on a lock-stitch and a chain-stitch machine but this is unlikely in practice. Overedge seams, however, can only be made on three- and four-thread overlockers or overedge machines.

8 **Over-edge seam with safety stitch:** a complex four-thread chain formation which oversews the edge of the fabric plies and produces a safety seam parallel alongside the overlocking.
  Uses: seals raw edges on all soft woven covers and is very flexible. It is ideal on knitted or stretch fabrics. Used a great deal on loose covers, bed covers and washable cushion covers.

Hand-sewn joints

Lock stitch

Using a 5in or 6in (125mm or 150mm) circular needle and a strong waxed linen slipping thread or mattress twine, a lock stitch is used to sew hessian, scrim and lining materials together. Making these joins is part of the upholstery process at the bench. The two pieces to be joined are trimmed and turned in, and then skewered to hold them in place. Stitches are simply formed by catching each ply, drawing them together and locking with a single or double knot about every half inch (13mm) (Fig 9.16).

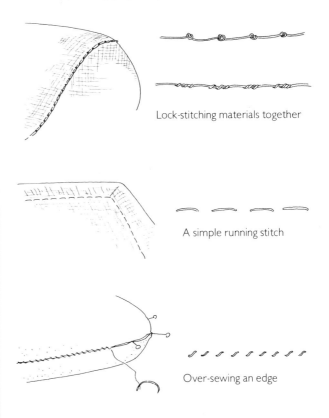

Lock-stitching materials together

A simple running stitch

Over-sewing an edge

Fig 9.16 Joining by hand stitching.

Running stitch

A simple but effective means of holding materials in place, temporarily or permanently using twine and straight or circular needles. It is formed by runninig the needle in and out of the plies to be fixed together. No knotting or locking is used except to commence and finish the seam. This method is often used as a pre-sewing aid before a piece of work is machine sewn and is also used to ruche or gather fabrics (Fig 9.16).

Oversewing

A simple method of binding two edges together with a curved needle and twine or thread, by oversewing closely and drawing up tight. No knots are used except to begin and finish work. Used in any situation where the quick binding of fillings, linings or hessians is needed (Fig 9.16).

Slip stitch

An extremely effective and strong stitch which invisibly joins fabric plies together. It is used a great deal in upholstery for finishing, closing and locating cords, piping and covers. Using a small 2½in or 3in (63mm or 75mm) circular needle and a waxed linen slipping thread, cover edges can be drawn together.

While in modern work the stitch has largely been superseded by various metal and plastic tacking strips, in traditional work the slip stitch is still used a great deal, and is an extremely effective stitching method. If the slip stitches are kept small and close the join produced can be equally as neat as a machine-sewn seam. A slip stitch is effectively a closing seam and so is used where two turned in edges come together, the edges may be butted or overlapped (Fig 9.17).

SEWING-MACHINE PRACTICE

Requirements

To be an all-rounder the upholsterer should have a good knowledge of machine-sewing practice, and be reasonably skilled in sewing techniques. It is most likely, however, that generally the bulk of sewing work is done for the upholsterer by a skilled machinist who specialises in making up sewn covers of all types in every kind of covering. Much of the skilled work which was traditionally done by the upholsterer at the bench has now passed into the hands of the sewing machinist. This is certainly the case in the production of modern new work, particularly in the factory situation. It has been the trend during recent years to design upholstery with a bias towards tailored sewn-up covers, which can easily be located and fixed into chair frames over sprung foam-filled foundations (Fig 9.18).

This technique has tended to de-skill many of the upholstery operations which were traditionally labour intensive. Sewing-machine practice is therefore a very important part of any modern upholstery production

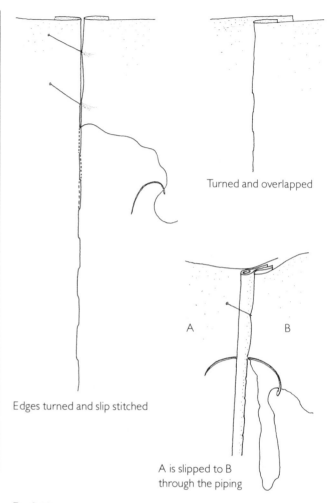

Turned and overlapped

A   B

Edges turned and slip stitched

A is slipped to B
through the piping

Fig 9.17

process. At the same time the methods used to make up upholstery covers have also been subjected to rationalisation by using breakdown techniques. Rather than have a machinist make up the whole of a sewn job from start to finish, as much of the preparation and pre-sewing work as possible is done separately, allowing

Fig 9.18 A tailored and machined cover held in place entirely by zips and clips.

the machinist more time to make up and assemble the prepared parts.

Zips, for example, can be inserted into borders or edges and then given to the machinist as a ready-made component. Top sewing or twin-needle operations can be done before or after the main assembly. Piping can be ready made, or ruching put around panels or facings. By adopting these methods of production the machines themselves can be operated with specialist types run separately away from the main area.

Making up of a complete cover becomes less complex and production generally smoother and faster. However, experience has shown that the final making-up operations are better left to individual machinists to complete right through. Besides allowing better job satisfaction, no two machinists work in exactly the same way and the problems associated with breakdown methods are less likely. At the other end of the scale there is still a large number of medium- to small-size companies who prefer to work in the conventional way, by allowing the machinist to complete the whole of the work, from cut cover parts through to the finished made-up covers.

The design and development of new, more sophisticated machines has made the task of making up covers easier and more efficient. The combination of compound feeding, alternating presser feet, makes smoother and more positive sewing. Needle positioners and underbed thread trimmers have removed some of the more tedious aspects of machining. Improved needle design also assists smooth production, and aids seam quality.

In the reupholstery business a sewing machine is always needed and will always be part of the workshop equipment. The sewing work can either be done on the premises by a specialist, or taken to an out worker, who will relieve the upholsterer of most of the sewing on a weekly basis. All other sewing work can be done by the upholsterer. In the area of traditional upholstery the bulk of the machining required will be in cushion making; this can regularly be cut and prepared and then left to the machinist for making up.

When any piece of upholstery work is completed, it is the upholsterer's responsibility to see that the whole job, including the sewing, is to a high standard. It is therefore essential to have a sound understanding of the machinist's work, and of sewing-machine practices as well as machine maintenance.

Stitch types
No matter how sophisticated or well developed an industrial sewing machine appears to be, the basic forming of a stitch remains the same.

The basic stitches used in the furniture industry are:

1 Lock stitch
2 Single-thread chain stitch
3 Two-thread chain stitch
4 Overedge chain stitch
5 Overedge with safety stitch

Most sewing machine work produced for upholstery uses the lock stitch.

Sewing machine threads
Threads are produced from cotton and some synthetics, or blends of both. Cotton machine threads are made in three types: soft, glaced and mercerised.

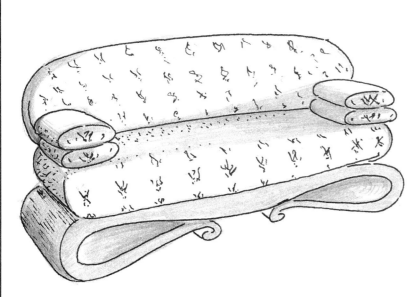

Danhauser Sofa, Vienna
c. 1820

The stuffed seat rests on an interesting pre-formed plywood base with hardwood facings.

Upholstery Heavy wooden frames, the webbings and curled hair fillings lined with calico. The arm bolsters and stitched shapes were wrapped in cotton waddings, with main stuffings of tow or grass.

Coverings Machine woven in lightweight tapestry with symmetrical overall patterns.

Soft are the standard threads with no special treatments. Glaced threads have a polished surface, which gives them extra strength and resistance to abrasion. The mercerised types have more lustre, and resemble silk. They have good tensile strength. There are two synthetics mainly used for machine threads, polyester and nylon. These are produced as continuous filament, spun staple yarn, or monofilament (Fig 9.19).

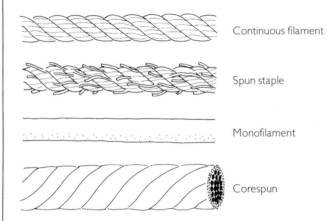

Fig 9.19 The construction of synthetic machine thread.

Blends
A blend of cotton and synthetic fibre gives a thread combination of good strength, and the feel, handle and friction resistance associated with cotton. The synthetic content is usually higher than the cotton content. An example of a blended fibre is corespun, in which the core of the thread is polyester, and the outer casing is cotton (Fig 9.19). Corespun machine threads are particularly suitable for high speed sewing operations, and are very durable in most situations.

Monofilament
These threads are extruded as a single, solid filament of nylon. They are produced as clear or coloured, but have a tendency to shrink. Monofilament tends to produce harsh, stiff seams, and so is used only for specialised applications.

Fig 9.20 illustrates the construction of a variety of machine threads. Thread twist is very important. Most threads have a left or Z twist to suit the sewing machines used today.

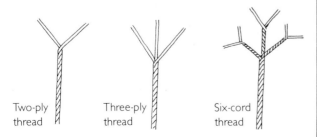

Fig 9.20 Machine thread made from cotton yarns.

Thread sizes
There are two size gradings for sewing machine threads, one for cotton and a separate range for synthetics and blends. In both, the higher the size number then the finer is the thread. A range of sizes and their recommended application is given below:

Cotton	Synthetic	Needle size		Application
Cotton	Metric	Singer	Metric	
3/14	20, 25	19–22	120–140	Heavy
3/20	36	18–21	110–130	Medium
3/24–3/30	40, 50	17–19	100–120	Light

Needles
Needle sizes are also given above. It is important to relate thread size to needle size. In successful stitching much depends on finding a proper balance between the two. No matter how suitable a thread may be for an application, if the needle being used is too small, the thread cannot pass freely through the eye, or down the long groove. This may result in fraying and weak seams. Too large a needle produces poor loop formation and causes missed stitches. It is always advisable to keep needle sizes as fine as possible, yet ensuring a free flow of needle thread. This helps to reduce damage to the fabric, and the likelihood of puckering. The sizes shown are a general guide only and manufacturers will advise and recommend in the use of particular products.

Fig 9.21 shows the thread path through a needle and details of needle construction. The range of needle sizes for use in upholstery sewing is generally from size 17 up to size 23. The approximate metric equivalents are size 100 up to 150. The higher size numbers are the heavier needles.

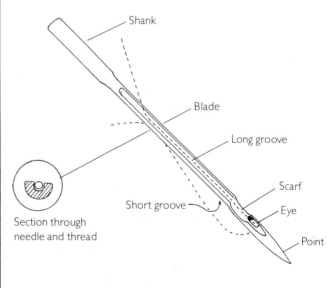

Fig 9.21 An industrial sewing machine needle with the thread path dotted in.

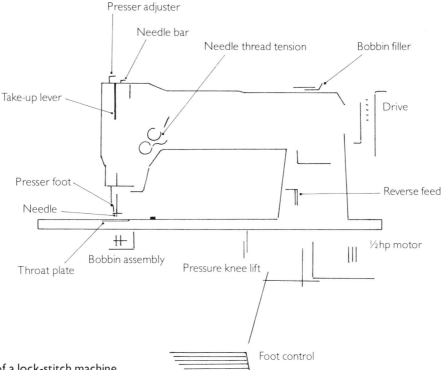

Fig 9.22 The main features of a lock-stitch machine.

THE INDUSTRIAL MACHINE

A general view of the lock-stitch machine is shown in Fig 9.22, and the main features are indicated. The lock-stitch machine uses two separate threads: (a) the needle thread and (b) the bobbin thread. Both threads are fed under tension, with the tension mechanisms set to ensure balanced stitch forming. To form the stitch the threaded needle goes down into the fabric to a set depth and as it is withdrawn a loop of thread is formed on the opposite side of the long needle groove. A rotating hook is timed to revolve and pick up the looped thread, which is then passed completely around the bobbin and its case. As the needle emerges from the fabric it pulls the stitch into place and the take-up lever tightens the needle thread. This take-up action is necessary because several inches of thread are needed to travel around the bobbin, but only a small amount is actually used to form one stitch.

The bobbin

Bobbin capacity is the limit to which a lock-stitch machine will run, after which a fresh bobbin must be inserted before sewing can restart. Improved bobbin sizes will allow extra stitching time, but this is not very long when machines are used at high speeds. A machinist ensures that stopping time is reduced to the minimum by making sure that fresh bobbins are being refilled during sewing. Prewound bobbins can be purchased in quantity which can save the machinists time. They are manufactured to suit all types of lock-stitch machines.

Work-feed mechanism

Fabric plies are fed through a sewing machine at the rate set by the stitch length control. Feeding is achieved by the feed dog passing through the throat plate and rotating in time with stitching. The plies are held down on to the feed dog by the presser foot. The pressure of the presser foot on to the fabric should be just enough to ensure positive feeding. Drop-feed systems are the standard type fitted to conventional machines and most domestic machines. For improved feeding of fabrics of the heavier type upholstery weights, compound feeding systems were introduced some years ago, commonly called needle feeding. This system includes a needle-rotating action which moves back and forward with the feed dog. Upper plies are therefore more evenly fed, and drag from the presser is reduced (Fig 9.23).

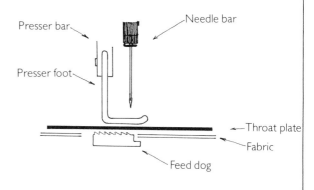

Fig 9.23 A typical work-feed mechanism.

Presser feet

Presser feet design is based on the seam types required. There are many variations and combinations to suit all types of work. For the machining of upholstery covers, the basic designs are:

a Plain foot
b Hinged plain foot
c Piping foot fixed and hinged
d Alternating plain foot
e Alternating piping foot
f Plough foot, twin needle
g Plough foot, single needle
h Zipper foot, adjustable

Except for types **d** and **e**, those listed are all easily detachable and interchangeable. The alternating presser types are a more permanent fixture and are not designed to be interchanged. To achieve the best seam results plain feet should be used for all flat seams and top-stitched joints, and piping feet used for piping and

a Plain presser foot, usually fitted as standard. A detachable accessory which is adequate for plain seams and flat sewing of several plies. May be successfully used to insert zips.

b A plain hinged foot used for most flat-seam operations. It adjusts itself well over uneven plies and joins.

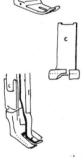

c Piping foot, specially designed and very sturdy. It is available in several sizes for the making of corded piping and piped seams.

d Alternating presser, ideal for heavy seaming over varying thicknesses. Particularly suitable for upholstery work and the sewing of hide.

e An alternating presser foot with piping function. May be interchanged with d. Very sturdy and ideal for heavy work at speed. The foot gives very positive feeding of plies and piping to several thicknesses.

f Plough foot designed specifically for use on a twin-needle machine, for the production of top-stitched seams.

g Single needle plough which is hinged and sprung and, usually is adjustable for left- and right-hand top stitching on reinforced seams.

h A standard zipper foot which is adjustable for left- and right-hand insertion of zip fasteners. May also be used to produce piping in small amounts if a piping foot is not available.

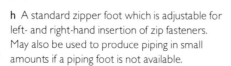

Fig 9.24 Presser feet used on the lock-stitch machine.

welting. However, in practice, where only one machine is available to do a variety of heavy upholstery work a standard presser with interchangeable feet is probably the best choice.

Machine sewing techniques

Getting to know a sewing machine well and becoming familiar with a particular type can take several hours, but it is the starting point of a machinist's training. All sewing machines tend to have characteristics which are peculiar to each and these have to be recognised. Some straight sewing on a length of fabric is a basic way of commencing with emphasis on the starting and stopping procedures. These must be learned by repetition and are essential to achieve good results. The machinist must be aware of what the machine is doing and how it is working, so that when a small problem occurs it can be corrected immediately. Machine control is another aspect which gradually grows with practice. After several hours' exercise in stopping, adjusting, turning and slow controlled sewing, speed can be increased and the sewing made more complex. Lines drawn on cloth or paper can be accurately followed, beginning slowly and working up to good speeds.

As control and routine corrections become familiar, fabric types can be experimented with so that many different kinds are used. Eventually, exercises which relate more closely to upholstery sewing can be attempted. These will include seams using the whole range of stitch lengths, various plain, reinforced and piped seams all produced in different covers. Fabrics should vary from fine lightweight cottons to heavy velvets and tweeds. After thorough familiarisation the same joints in vinyl and leather should be tried. The machinist must be aware of the physical differences in the construction of fabrics during the making-up process. For example, a glazed cotton chintz has very little elasticity or give, and will easily crease under the machine foot, whereas an all-wool tweed, though much heavier is very pliable and has some resilience in all directions. These two covers are very different from velvet, which is a heavy-pile fabric and prone to movement during machining. The difference in sewing-up and manipulating the three types soon becomes very obvious, each one requiring very different treatment and handling.

A cover should be selected that is found easy to work with, and some making-up exercises completed. These can be in the form of box, cylindrical and pyramid shapes or any three-dimensional design which needs thought and care in the way it is assembled. When the stage is reached where all types of cover and a large number of exercises have been completed, the speed of working should be increased. Although demand for different styles inevitably changes with fashion, the plain seam and the piped seam will always be the two basic joints.

— Chapter Ten —

Foams

Latex or rubber foam was the first type of upholstery foam produced, and was used commercially for the first time in 1932. Until then the fillings in upholstered seating were all natural fibre materials such as animal hair, coconut fibre, cotton and feathers.

Latex

The liquid latex was mechanically whisked in huge containers to aerate the mixture into a cellular foam. The foamed liquid was mixed with a gelling agent and then poured into moulds which were sealed and heated in giant ovens. This produced vulcanised and cured soft rubber components, which finally had to be washed, squeezed through rollers and then gently dried.

The feel and hardness of the foam components was adjusted in two different ways, either by whisking more or less air into the liquid latex, or by varying the mould designs so that the cavities in the cured foam were larger or smaller. In latex foams the density or weight of a given piece was expressed in pounds per cubic foot, and this figure related very closely to the feel and hardness of the foam. Therefore a high-density foam was generally heavier and firmer than a low-density foam.

Plastic, polyether and polyester

When plastic foams were developed and then used generally for upholstery in the early 1950s, the terms density and hardness were not related in the same way. The new materials were generally much lighter in weight and the way in which they reacted to pressure was rather different. For a time the two different types of foam competed with each other for the seating market. This led to a great deal of confusion, because the new polyethers were being assessed and specified in the same way as latex foam.

It was soon realised that plastic foams had great potential in upholstery, particularly the polyether types, while polyester foams were best suited as packing materials and as textile laminates (Fig 10.2).

The development of foams for upholstery and bedding had a tremendous effect on seating and bedding design, and eventually led to totally different methods of upholstery being used. Deep springing and suspension were no longer necessary to provide comfortable chairs and sofas. The work became cleaner and simpler, as cut foam components were produced ready to glue or staple into chair backs and seats. Suspension systems became slim and lightweight using latex-tension types rather than deep-compression springing. Latex foams and polyether foam were rarely used together but tended to compete for different levels of the market.

When pincore latex blocks were developed with different cavity structure, foam cutting and fabrication became possible during the 1960s. The moulded blocks were relatively small but the fine pin-hole cavity construction enabled furniture manufacturers to cut and hand-build in foam, which had not been possible before. The upholsterer running a small business was then able to buy foam which could be easily carved and

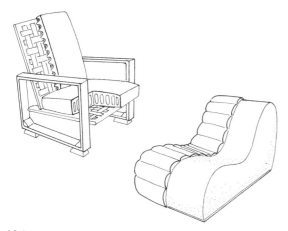

Fig 10.1

Cavity latex-foam mattress interior

Moulded latex-foam sheet

A two-part moulded cushion

Moulded cavity sheet

Pincore moulded block

Conventional polyurethane foam

Compression-cut polyurethane

A moulded polyurethane cushion

A moulded HR seat foam

Cut HR foam

Reconstituted chip foam

CM HR foam

Fig 10.2 Foam types and their development.

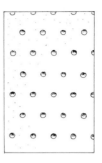

Staggered-cavity type used for mattresses

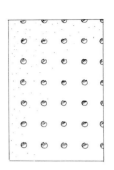

Square-cavity type used for furniture which allows for cleaner cutting

Fig 10.3 Pincore latex foams.

fabricated in small batches to suit various jobs. Lamination of different densities was also possible for the first time (Fig 10.3).

It was during the 1970s that latex foams were completely superseded by polyethers, having enjoyed a lifespan of some thirty years or so. At the same time a new breed of plastic foams entered the market, called high-resilience (HR) polyurethane foams. They are formed of basically the same oil-based family of materials but with a different chemical balance and different processing methods. These new foams, although more expensive to produce, were widely accepted for use in good-quality cushioning, particularly in seats. Other differences are the use of more rubbery and elastic polymers, and a cell structure which is much more irregular, both of which improve the resilience and breathing properties.

A combination of the conventional polyurethanes and HR foams then provided the upholstery manufacturer and the upholsterer with two excellent filling materials which became universally used and accepted for a wide variety of modern and reproduction work.

It was also during the 1970s that foam cutting and conversion machinery became sophisticated and capable of producing two- and three-dimensional shapes which previously could be made only by expensive moulding techniques. Photoelectric profile machines introduced to this country are now capable of cutting and copying quite complex shapes directly from drawings and templates.

MAKING FOAM

Today's upholstery foams are lightweight, flexible, open-cell materials made from polyurethane plastics, which originate from oil-based chemicals. The chemicals used have to be carefully handled and very accurately metered from storage tanks to a mixing head at the point where the foam is to be made. The ingredients for foam making include: toluene-di-isocyanate (TDI), polyols, which are polyether glycol

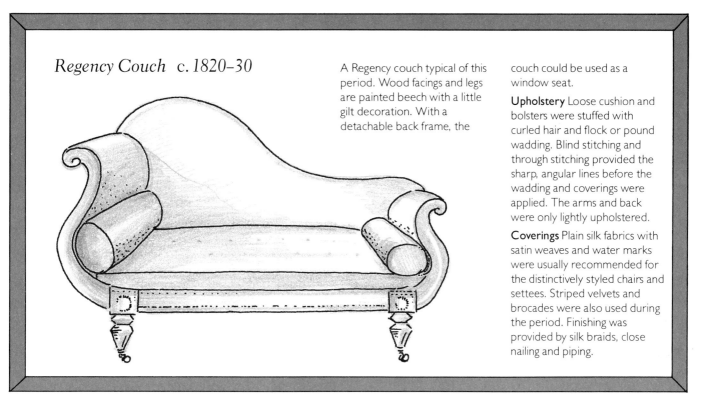

Regency Couch c. 1820–30

A Regency couch typical of this period. Wood facings and legs are painted beech with a little gilt decoration. With a detachable back frame, the couch could be used as a window seat.

Upholstery Loose cushion and bolsters were stuffed with curled hair and flock or pound wadding. Blind stitching and through stitching provided the sharp, angular lines before the wadding and coverings were applied. The arms and back were only lightly upholstered.

Coverings Plain silk fabrics with satin weaves and water marks were usually recommended for the distinctively styled chairs and settees. Striped velvets and brocades were also used during the period. Finishing was provided by silk braids, close nailing and piping.

---

resins, blowing agents, water, fillers and pigments for colouring. Graphite and melamine are now added to modify combustion.

At the mixing head the ingredients come together and are dispensed into a slow-moving paper trough. The trough is, in fact, a three-sided conveyor which travels a distance of about sixty metres. It is during the time that it takes the ingredients to travel this distance that the foam is formed into a long continuous block or loaf. Immediately the chemicals are evenly dispensed into the trough, chemical reaction takes place and the liquids swell and rise, filling the trough as it travels along the moving conveyor (Fig 10.4).

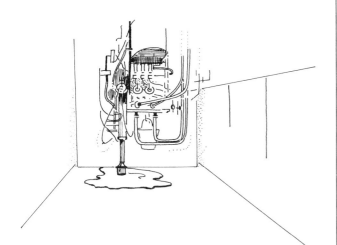

Fig 10.4 The polyurethane mixing head dispenses liquid chemicals into a moving paper trough.

The block of foam being formed is about two metres wide and rises to approximately one metre high. As the chemical reaction occurs, heat is generated inside the foam and with the help of a setting agent the foam is self curing. The top surface of the foam block is controlled and kept flat by a grid and rollers so that it does not rise or dome. This ensures that a compact rectangular shaped block is formed and waste is kept to a minimum during trimming and conversion (Fig 10.5).

At the end of the sixty-metre run, the now-stable block of new foam is cross cut at 2½-metre intervals and the blocks which are free from the paper trough continue their travels on an open conveyor to a storage area where they are stood on end for a day or two, to age and become completely stable (Fig 10.6).

Each block of new foam is stamped and numbered with its appropriate batch number and type. The whole process of making foams in this way is very automated and carefully controlled. Samples are taken regularly from the new blocks to check that densities are correct and quality generally is good. An electronic scanner may also be employed to control quality. Foams can also be produced on vertical production systems, which reduce the size of the plant and produce different-shaped blocks.

Reconstituted foam or chipfoam

Chipfoam is made from reconstituted waste foam. The waste cuttings which come from the conversion and fabrication processes are cut into crumb-size pieces and mixed with liquid chemicals similar to those used to make the original foams. The consolidated mixture

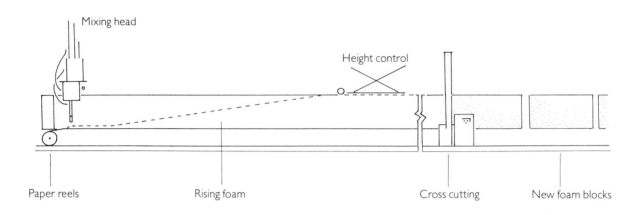

Fig 10.5

is compressed into blocks to different densities and can then be dealt with and cut in exactly the same way as blocks of standard foam.

Most foam-producing companies make about six different grades of chipfoam. These are generally much heavier and more dense than standard foams, and are used for heavy load-bearing applications.

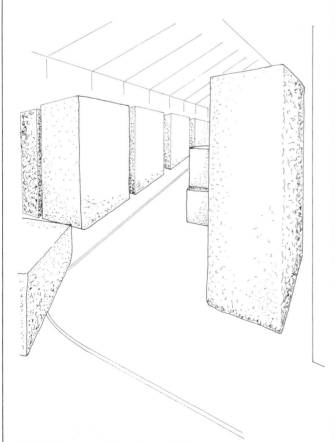

Fig 10.6 Storage of new foam blocks.

MOULDING

Polyurethane foams can be moulded in individual moulds to produce ready-shaped components for a variety of trade uses. To make this method of production economically viable, long runs of the same components are required. This relates rather well to vehicle seating production and to contract furniture

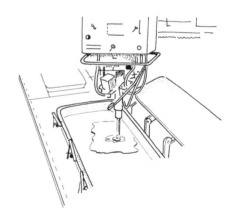

Fig 10.7 Filling a small mould with liquid polyurethane.

upholstery rather than the domestic market. The method of production is similar to that used to produce latex foam. A quantity of liquid urethane is metered into shaped metal moulds which do not have cavity formers.

There are two methods used, known as hot cure and cold cure. In the former the moulds are over-heated after being filled to cure the foam. In cold-cure production the chemical mixture is similar to that for standard foam making, where the foaming reaction is self-curing and external heat is not needed. Cold-cure moulded foams have a high degree of resilience and are ideal for contact and heavy-use applications.

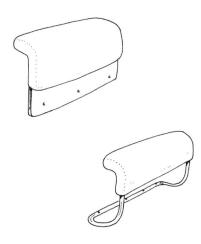

Fig 10.8 Polyurethane foam moulded directly on to chair arm components.

The foam-moulding process is used to create ready-to-cover components for chairs and seating. Frame parts, such as arm assemblies, plywood laminates and metal frames can be fitted into moulds and foam is moulded round them. This creates almost instantly upholstered parts which are ready to cover and bolt into main frames (Fig 10.8).

FOAM CONVERSION AND FABRICATION

The outer surfaces of a new foam block have a rough heavy skin which is formed against the waxed paper during the foaming process. Before the block can be converted and cut into sheet of varying thicknesses, the top and bottom surface skins are removed. A large horizontal blade foam splitter is used to slice off the skins and then convert the block into sheet.

The horizontal blade remains stationary but is adjustable vertically to produce the different depths of cut, while the foam block moves on a conveyor forwards and back as each cut is made. The blades on these machines are smooth band knife blades and may be single or double edged. To reduce friction and assist smooth cutting of the foam the blades can be lubricated. Each block can be cut in standard thickness sheets or in varying thicknesses depending on the cutting programme selected, and the batch requirements. As demand varies, a block may be only partly converted and then stored for later use (Fig 10.9).

A more sophisticated conversion machine which uses a carousel conveyor system is capable of cutting several new blocks at one pass, if demand is sufficient.

Cutting machines

Vertical band knife machines
Vertical band knife machines are the most versatile and

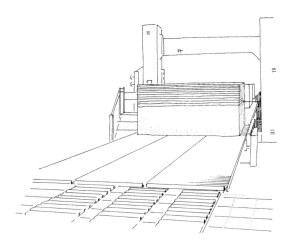

Fig 10.9 A new foam block being converted into sheet on a horizontal band knife machine.

most used machines for the cutting of foam parts. These have mobile tables, adjustable fences and blade-angle adjustments when needed. The throat or maximum cutting height can be as much as one metre on the larger versions. Sheet and small blocks can be cut and dimensioned to almost any shape. Plywood moulds and patterns are used to cut shaped work, and the adjustable fence can be set for straight cuts at a predetermined distance from the blade. With a throat height of up to one metre it is possible to shape several layers of foam pieces at one time. These machines are operated manually by skilled cutters who are able to produce quantites of parts at high speeds (Fig 10.10).

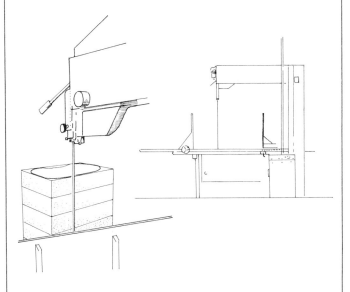

Fig 10.10 Two views of vertical band-knife cutters showing blades, tables and adjustable fences.

Nosing machines

Nosing machines are more specialised and are designed to produce radius cuts usually around the edges of thick foam parts, for example on seat and back cushions where gently curving edges are preferred to square sections. The machine has a very fast vibrating blade which is adjustable and interchangeable. The blade operates a set distance from a back fence and trims the foam edge as it is pushed through the machine (Fig 10.11).

A more sophisticated nosing or radiusing machine preferred by many converters is the horizontal band knife type. In this machine the complete blade and cutting mechanism moves in an arc to produce a nosing cut, while the foam component remains stationary. These machines work faster and are probably safer to use. The machines are simple and easy to use with press-button control.

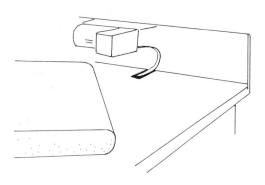

Fig 10.11 A cushion-nosing machine produces radiused edges in a variety of sizes.

Compression cutting

Foams can be cut while they are under compression or distorted and this method is used to produce three dimensional shapes from foam parts. The machine used is an adaptation of the vertical or horizontal band knife, so that the cut made is in fact straight, but because the foam is held and distorted when it is released after cutting a profile shape is produced. A good example of this cutting method is the domed seat squab, which is produced by compressing the flat foam with a male and female mould. Another example is the profile scalloped cutting used for lightweight mattresses. In this instance a roller fitted with rows of protruding nodes compresses the foam and an adjacent blade cuts through the centre of the foam as the roller returns. Compression cutting is an interesting and useful method of foam cutting, and no doubt will continue to be developed and used to advantage in the future (Fig 10.12).

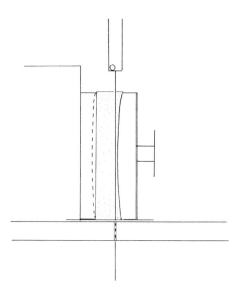

Fig 10.12 A seat squab being compression cut to produce a domed surface.

Profile cutting machines

An automatic profiler is capable of cutting large numbers of shaped pieces of foam directly from a large block. The mobile horizontal blade makes a very fine cut in all directions and is guided by an electronic eye which follows a set template or drawing. Smaller, less sophisticated machines are used for small batches which may be automatic or manually operated. Ideal for production of numbers of cylinder or wedge-shaped components (Fig 10.13).

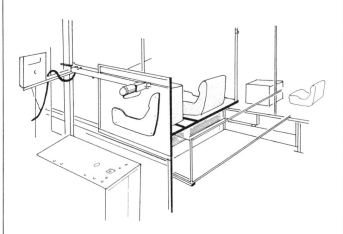

Fig 10.13 An automatic profile-cutting machine which will follow any template mounted on the copying board.

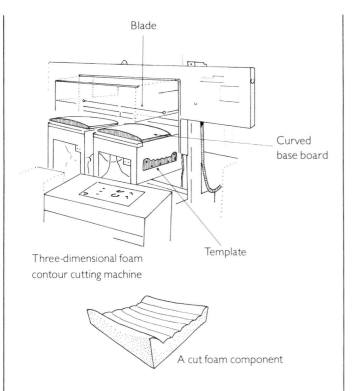

Blade

Curved
base board

Template

Three-dimensional foam
contour cutting machine

A cut foam component

Fig 10.14

Fig 10.15 Polyurethane or polyester foam on a peeling
machine. A large moulded cylinder of foam is peeled to
produce thin sheet down to 1.8mm thickness.

Contour cutting machines

These are fully automated foam-cutting machines
which produce high quality contour cut components
in three dimensions. They are fitted with scanning
heads to follow drawings and cut at a rate of five to ten
metres per minute. The cutting blades are horizontal
and cut in all directions, carefully following the set
drawings. The cutting action is a combination of
distortion cutting and profile cutting, together
producing three-dimensional shapes. Each component
to be cut, usually in twos, is slightly distorted or angled
on a base board, the blade then profile cuts the foam,
to a template or drawing in the opposing direction.
When released from the base the foam resumes its
original form and cut waste is removed.

Foam peeling

The cutting of foam by peeling is effectively used to
produce very thin sheets, which is quite difficult to do
on any of the other cutting machines. A separately
moulded block is produced to a cylindrical shape and
this is mounted on to a foam-peeling machine. In
principle this works in the same way as some wood
veneers are produced when a log is rotary cut. As the
foam rotates, a thin continuous sheet is produced by a
very sharp moving blade set closely to an edge guide.
Hundreds of metres of thin foam sheet can be obtained
from one block using this method. Although some thin
foams are used in upholstery, most are used in fabric
manufacture and quilted panels for bedding (Fig 10.15).

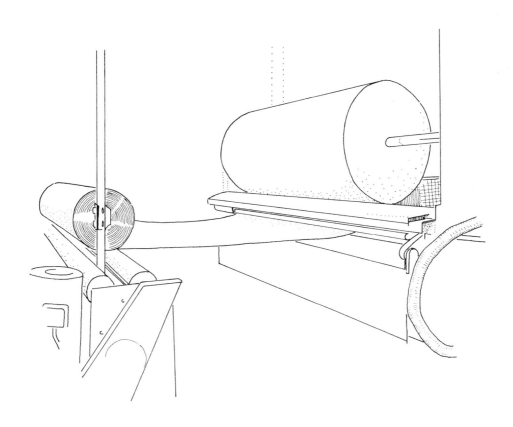

FABRICATION

Contact adhesives are applied by scraper, aerosol or spray gun to assemble foam parts. Most polyurethane foams have good stretch properties and good tensile strength, which make shaping and fabrication reasonably easy. Edges can be folded and glued; thin wraps can be easily compressed to produce complex forms and clean curves. It is essential to keep gluing to the minimum, and not to over spray so that adhesive gets on to the wrong surfaces. Good fabrication relies on clean joints and accurately cut parts. When working with flexible materials there is often a temptation to be less accurate than with more solid materials. This is because foams can be adjusted easily or stretched if necessary, but it is important to know when to stretch and when not to stretch. Unnecessary tensioning in

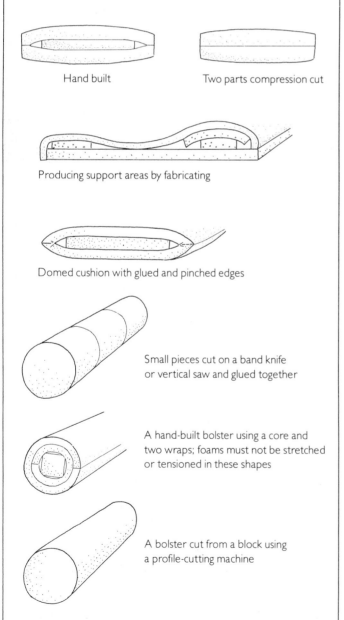

Hand built   Two parts compression cut

Producing support areas by fabricating

Domed cushion with glued and pinched edges

Small pieces cut on a band knife or vertical saw and glued together

A hand-built bolster using a core and two wraps; foams must not be stretched or tensioned in these shapes

A bolster cut from a block using a profile-cutting machine

Fig 10.16 Cutting and fabricating domes and cylinder shapes.

the wrong place nearly always leads to distortion, and the application of too much glue will usually produce rippled or distorted surfaces. Any uneven surfaces or poorly fitting joints in foam will eventually be transmitted through the coverings. It is therefore essential to work as accurately and as cleanly as possible, treating the foam parts as if they were timber or metal. The technique of fabricating with foams is soon learned, if cutting is accurate and joining is done cleanly and carefully.

It is often the case with some complex foam components that during fabrication some of the parts need to be bent or distorted to produce concave or convex shapes. This is done by using firm and soft foams laminated together, or by gluing strips of tape or calico and putting the foam in tension, before wrapping with softer top layers. These techniques are now used a great deal in foam fabrication (Fig 10.18).

In modern foam work, polyester fibre of different weights is used as a wrapping or topping to finish a fabricated component. The two materials, polyurethane foam and polyester fibre are universally used together in almost all modern and reproduction work. There are two reasons why this combination has become so successful. A fibre wrap produces a very soft, smooth finish which is ideal for modern upholstery and would be difficult to create with foam alone. Secondly, the fibre makes a very good protective layer between cover and foam, reducing the possibility of friction and abrasion which can result in fabric wear on the underside. Foam surfaces can be very coarse and abrasive, causing pile loss in velvets, and unnecessary wear in most fabrics. Where a fibre wrap is not being used it is normal practice to cover the fabricated foam in a thin stockinette sock. This makes for easier handling, upholstering and machine filling, particularly in cushion making, and allows covers to move freely in use.

Three-dimensional shapes can be produced by careful cutting and building of foam parts. Back supports, lumbar supports and headrests are typical applications. Edges can be kept square, or made rounded or pinched to a point by gluing. Quick-setting contact glues are ideal for this type of work. Three methods of producing cylindrical bolster shapes are shown in Fig 10.16.

a   Cutting short length parts to a template and gluing these together
b   Hand building by wrapping around a centre core
c   Profile cutting directly from a block.

Nosed edges can be made by direct cutting on nosing machines or by hand fabricating in the following ways. A length of foam can be simply folded and glued to form a nose at one end. One or more edges can be glued and pinched to produce a radius. Good glue is needed for this method and is usually more effective with the softer grades of foam.

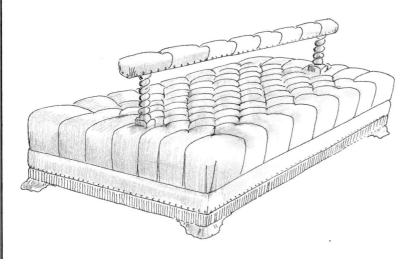

William IV Library Seat
c. 1835

A handsome and well-upholstered low library seat with centre back rest on twist turned supports. Such examples were long, heavyweight bench style seats, designed for use in the private libraries of large houses. They provided versatile occasional seating arrangements in the centre of large rooms.

Upholstery Although sprung upholstery was slowly emerging as a new medium, firm hair-filled top-stuffed seats remained popular for some years. Tufted and buttoned surfaces exhibited the best handwork skills of the early Victorian upholsterer. Stuffings of hair and wool provided comfort and softness on firm webbed and stitched foundations.

Coverings Cow hides and softer Morocco goat skins combined well with oak wood, which was fluted and carved along the base to reflect an earlier rustic style.

Leather work was trimmed and decorated with brass nails, set close or spaced to finish the green and brown colourings of the period. Alternative coverings were plain wool cloths and hair cloths, all functional and hard wearing.

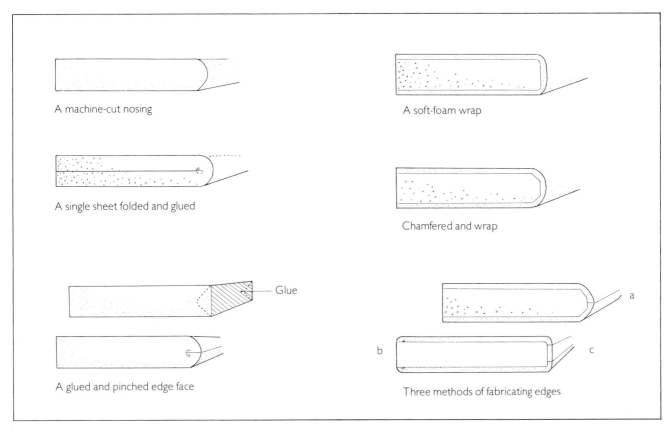

A machine-cut nosing

A single sheet folded and glued

Glue

A glued and pinched edge face

A soft-foam wrap

Chamfered and wrap

a

b

c

Three methods of fabricating edges

Fig 10.17 Nosed and radiused edges.

Soft wraps around firmer cores is another good method. The core edges may be chamfered or left square depending on the nose shape required. Where the wrap is to be taken over on several sides of a core then separate top and bottom layers are glued to the core and the edges are pinched together.

Using cotton tape or strips of calico, foam components can be fixed and shaped in various ways. The technique of distorting and bending of foams to produce curved and fitted upholstery is now widely used. Work of this kind should be done with care and some experimenting will be necessary with various grades. The foam is held in curve using a former and the tape is glued on and fitted to hold the shape. There will be some loss of shape initially, but this can be allowed for.

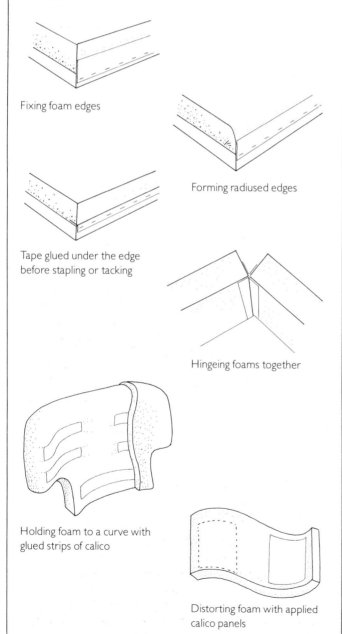

Fixing foam edges

Forming radiused edges

Tape glued under the edge before stapling or tacking

Hingeing foams together

Holding foam to a curve with glued strips of calico

Distorting foam with applied calico panels

Fig 10.18 Using tape and calico strips.

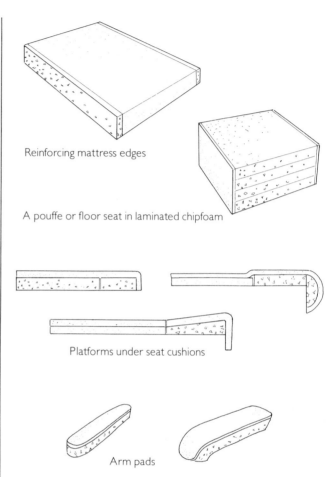

Reinforcing mattress edges

A pouffe or floor seat in laminated chipfoam

Platforms under seat cushions

Arm pads

Fig 10.19 Using chipfoam.

By nature polyurethane foams are mostly soft, resilient materials. A much firmer product is often needed as a buffer or an insulator and chipfoam makes an ideal edging and support in this way.

Foam pieces can be drilled and slit to accommodate various features in upholstery. Fly pieces can then be hooked or zipped to form pull-ins through slits in the foam. Buttoning is often more effective and more precise if holes are drilled before covering.

Where small protruding shapes occur, such as in T-shape cushions, it is more economical to cut the main part and add on the shaping pieces by gluing. Whenever possible, glue joints should be covered by wrapping and not exposed directly to covers.

Foam parts of all types are almost always cut larger by about 5 per cent over the finished size. The increase should be in all directions and ensures good fit and well-tensioned coverings. This extra allowance also takes care of initial height loss which occurs to some degree in all foams when they are first used and compressed. The example in Fig 10.21 has a little extra foam at each corner which will be compressed when it is covered. This extra ensures that the corners are well filled and the cover is tight. The addition of a fibre wrap will produce the same effect.

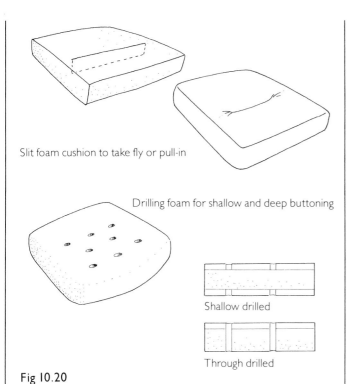

Slit foam cushion to take fly or pull-in

Drilling foam for shallow and deep buttoning

Shallow drilled

Through drilled

Fig 10.20

Chamfering

Using straight edges and templates and a cutting table, foam can be chamfered to produce trimmed and angled edges. After chamfering to any angle, the cut surface where possible should be inverted, leaving a smooth surface to the cover. Doming of small cushions is also possible by chamfering and lamination.

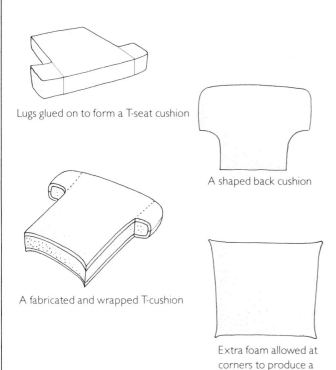

Lugs glued on to form a T-seat cushion

A shaped back cushion

A fabricated and wrapped T-cushion

Extra foam allowed at corners to produce a well-filled cushion

Fig 10.21

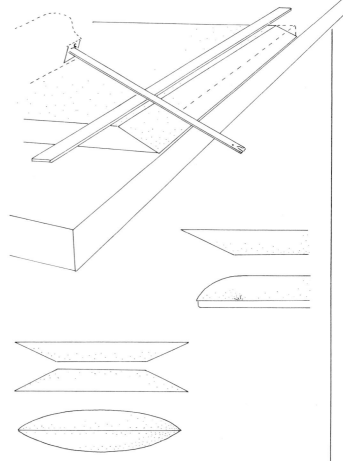

Fig 10.22 Chamfering.

Cutting oversize

Foams should always be cut oversize. Cushions and mattresses particularly should be made up 5 per cent larger than the intended finished size. Foams of all types have a tendency to be weakest at their edges and so, where possible, this should be allowed for. When foam is being used in conventional fixed upholstery edges can be stiffened by cutting the foam 10 to 15 per cent oversize, or by adding inserts on to the base layers. Chipfoams are ideal for this purpose and should certainly be used when covering in hides and very heavy fabrics.

SPECIFYING FOAMS

Making the choice

It is to the mutual benefit of the upholsterer or upholstery designer and the foam manufacturer that foams are correctly selected and specified. It is not absolutely essential for the maker of upholstered furniture to have a deep knowledge of foam manufacture. It is, however, important that the supplier and the purchaser have a working relationship and agree that the foams specified for particular jobs are the most suitable. The suitability of a foam will depend on several important factors: how the foam is to be supported or suspended; what kind of job it will be doing when in use; and how long the foam is expected to last and go on doing its job.

In practice the upholsterer will ask how well a foam will behave during fabrication and fixing. For example, not all foams have good tensile strength and cannot therefore be stretched or stapled into a job. These foams are better suited as cushion interiors, or perhaps as cut parts that are glued in place and then wrapped and covered.

All these points must be considered as well as the basic properties of the foam. Together the foam supplier and the purchaser should assess the design and the upholstery work involved and then draw up a short list of selected grades. To help users of polyurethane foams, the industry has agreed a selection procedure which is based on BS 3379, 1975, and an amendment to this added in 1978. By carrying out different tests of long periods with many different samples, a set of samples has been agreed and most foam manufacturers produce foam-specification lists for their own products all based on the same standards.

It is possible to study a foam supplier's brochure and make a selection of foam for a particular end use. However, it should be noticed that in each category of use there may be several options and the buyer will then need to know what the difference is between these. It is at this point that the foam manufacturer's advice must be sought, so that the choice can be narrowed down to one or perhaps two foams.

Usually the difference between two similar foams which fall into the same category of use is the cost. Both foams will be suitable for a similar application, but one will have a higher density than the other, and will therefore cost more. If a foam is being purchased for reupholstery work and only small amounts are needed, then it is wise to buy the best in all cases. However, for quantity production the choice may be influenced by cost, and the ability to keep the end product competitive at a certain market level. Assuming that two different foams will both do the same job adequately, then the lower-priced foam may well be chosen.

CLASS OF FOAM

The class of a foam is related to its performance in use; it is in this area that recommended applications are given. By subjecting a number of foam samples to a series of very strenuous pounding tests, it can be shown how a foam will respond to constant use. The class of a foam is also related to its density or weight and hence to its eventual cost. Several foam samples are subjected to 80,000 poundings by a heavy indentor which exerts a force of 168½lb (76.5kg). After the tests the samples are measured and the loss of thickness and hardness is

evaluated. The hardness loss can be given as a percentage of the foam's original hardness.

A class of performance is then determined and expressed as five different areas, with recommended applications for each. The list of classes is as follows:

Class of performance	Type of service	Recommended application
X	Extremely severe	Heavy duty, seating
V	Very severe	Seats, public, contract and vehicle
S	Severe	Vehicle seats, domestic furniture seats, backs and arm rests for theatre and transport
A	Average	Domestic furniture backs/arm rests, private vehicle backs/arm rests
L	Light	Padding, scatter cushions, pillows

Density

The actual density of a piece of foam will depend on its chemical make-up and the amount of polyurethane and additives present in the foam. The density of foam is measured in weight by volume, the volume being a cubic metre and the weight in kilogrammes. This is normally written in technical literature and manufacturers' lists as kg/m^3. The density of foam is closely related to its likely performance and also to its cost. The choice of density should be generally based on customer requirements, the application, and an agreement with the foam manufacturer.

Using the British Standard guide

All foam produced for home use in load-bearing applications, such as seating and general upholstery, can be specified under the following headings, type, grade and class.

Type of foam

This describes the different types of foam that are made, and each type has a prefix letter.

Type B   – block or slabstock conventional polyether.
Type CB – block or slabstock HR high resilience.
Type M   – moulded conventional polyether.
Type CM – moulded HR high resilience.
Type RE – reconstituted foam or chipfoam.
Now under review following the new regulations, 1 November 1988.

When looking through a supplier's lists, the prefix letter will indicate the type of foam being offered. All foams are CM/HR types – combustion modified, high resilience.

Grade of foam

The grade of a foam relates to its hardness or feel. The figures used are given in kilogrammes weight (kg) and in

Newtons of force (N). The feel or hardness of a polyurethane foam is not related to its density. Density figures are therefore given separately by foam manufacturers.

To arrive at a grade of hardness for a foam, a sample is depressed using a flat circular indentor, creating an indentation of 40 per cent. The weight or force required to do this is the recorded degree of hardness. Those foams with low hardness figures are therefore the softer foams.

Most foam manufacturers will give two sets of figures: **a** hardness in kgs and N, which have a tolerance or range for each foam, and **b** grade, which is a round figure taken from the range in Newtons. For example:

Hardness		Grade
N	kg	
61–85	8–12	70
86–110	14–18	100

The following is an example of two foams chosen for two different applications. The type of foam is decided first and then the grade selected, based on its feel. Using the recommended application list, the class of the foam is chosen, and then finally the density can be established.

1
Type	CM/HR
Grade	100
Class	A

Application: a domestic chair headrest.
Density: could be 20kg/m^3.

2
Type	CM/HR
Grade	150
Class	S

Application: a domestic chair seat cushion.
Density: could be approximately 35kg/m^3.

Foam manufacturers usually give other helpful pieces of information and lists of figures as a guide to their foam products. These can all be used to help in the selection of foams for use in upholstery. Elongation figures, for example, will give a good indication of the stretch properties of a foam. The feel or hardness of a foam may also be expressed in words, for example, firm, medium, very soft, feather soft. The minimum tear strength is also often specified in Newtons per 25mm and this will usually indicate if a foam can be fixed with staples. Resistance to ignition is also given, for example, resistance to ignition source 5(9) Pass.

Reconstituted chipfoam
This range of foams is usually specified by density and type only, as their class of use is not comparable with other types of foam. They are all generally in the very heavy and high-density ranges and are also combustion modified.

Incorrect use of foams

The result of using foams for upholstery which have been wrongly specified is the general discomfort to the user and shabby appearance of the upholstery. Performance is the main consideration and therefore the class of use has to be correct. Selecting the wrong grade will equally cause problems, where a foam is too hard or much too soft for its application.

Bottoming is a common fault where a foam does not support well enough and is squashed completely in use. This leads to eventual collapse and loss of shape. Bad frame design can also contribute to rails and suspension feeling through the foam. The vulnerable areas on most designs of chair and settee are seat fronts, inside-back lumbar supports, and the upper parts of inside arms.

As a general rule good performance can be reasonably assured if a minimum density of 28kg/m^3 is kept to for all seating applications. Obtaining the right feel will then depend on thickness of the foam, its grade and the surrounding materials, such as fibre wraps, suspension and cover.

The new fire safety regulations

Polyurethane foams for use in upholstery and bedding are now the subject of stringent testing and new government legislation. All foams produced for seating must be CM/HR types (combustion modified, high resilience). Standards have been set for their resistance to ignition and burning for the safety of the consumer. These standards are continually being monitored and reviewed. Similar legislation for upholstery fabrics and barrier cloths is also laid down in the Furniture and Furnishings (Fire) (Safety) Regulations 1988.

For testing purposes fillings are split into five categories:

1 Slab polyurethane foam
2 Crumb polyurethane foam
3 Latex rubber foam
4 Fillings other than 1, 2, and 3, but single fillings
5 Fillings consisting of more than one filling as a composite

Information is available from the Department of Trade and Industry, or the Furniture Industry Research Association, or any supplier of foams, fillings and fabrics will help.

Chapter Eleven

Frames and Structures

With a few exceptions upholstery is built on a frame or structure. This is the skeleton of a piece of upholstered furniture, and may be a box, a frame or simply a board. In British upholstered furniture, timber has always been the predominant material and is still the most used material today.

Throughout the history of the chair, metals have played a significant part in frame construction and today compete successfully in many areas. Where a frame is part of the visible design fashion tends to dictate the material and its finished surface. But in fully upholstered furniture, metals, timbers or plastics are used and are combined to produce a structure which is strong and functional.

The requirements of an upholstered frame are an ability to withstand many different kinds of pressure, while remaining strong and supportive with some flexibility. Frame design is an important part of seating manufacture and several factors must be considered before making can begin.

A frame must be able to withstand the pulling and straining forces imposed by webbings, suspension materials and springing systems. The process of upholstery can put strain on a frame as the upholstery is being built and fixed. Timbers particularly must have good holding properties for screwing, stapling and nailing. The machinability of timber is also important, so that accurate, well-fitted joints can be produced. When assembled, a frame must be dimensionally stable, and be able to cope with the weights, pressures and forces that are exerted in normal and excessive use. Dimensions and proportions are other considerations which are closely linked with good design.

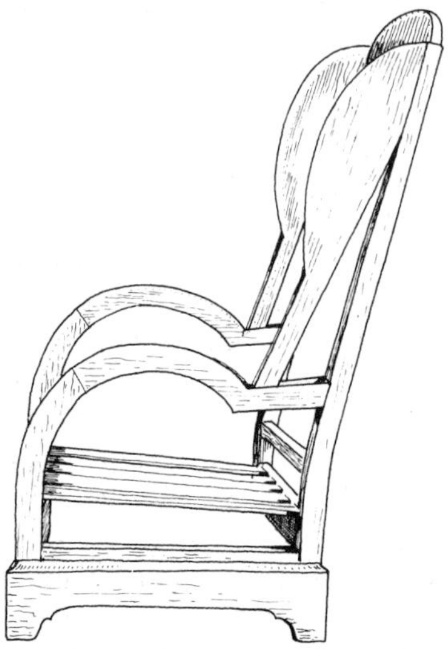

While comfort means different things to different people, and aesthetics are important, in practice chairs and seating are basically functional items which have a job to do and should therefore be fit for their purpose. An upholstery frame cannot be designed or made in isolation, and the upholstery layout and arrangement must be considered at the same time. Rails, supports and fixings have to be positioned and related closely to the whole of the upholstery and its covering.

MATERIALS

Timbers for chair frames

Beech, birch, ash and mahogany are the main woods used for frame making. Ramin and sapele are two other hard woods which have the required qualities. All the timbers used should be free from defects, wild grain or irregular surfaces, and not prone to softness, lifting grain or splitting. Suitable timbers are air- and kiln-dried to controlled moisture contents in the range of 9 to 12 per cent. This provides a timber that is reasonably stable and suitable for working, and for its eventual use in domestic and contract situations. All the above timbers have good properties at a reasonable cost and

Fig 11.1

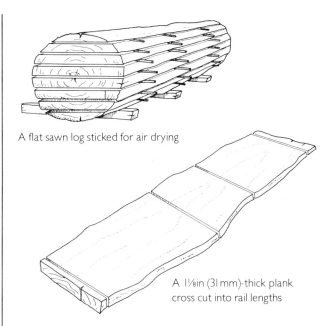

A flat sawn log sticked for air drying

A 1⅛in (31 mm)-thick plank cross cut into rail lengths

Fig 11.2 Upholstery frame timber.

primarily work, joint and glue well, and have excellent holding properties.

Traditionally, softwoods have not been used for the making of frames that are upholstered in the conventional way. However, in Scandinavian countries, where good softwoods are readily available, they are used for upholstery framing. Providing that fixings are generally heavier and the methods of upholstery are not dependent on conventional tacking and stapling, then designers can utilise softwoods in a way not practised in Britain.

Beech and birch
Both of these are good chair-frame materials and are considered the best of the hardwoods for upholstered frame working. Their properties of strength and holding are exceptionally good. They work well with moderate ease for most hand and machine operations. Both timbers can be successfully turned to fine dimensions, and they clean up well to produce very smooth surfaces.

Beech has a close, straight-grained structure which lends itself well to steam bending. Its stiffness and bending strength is superior to most other timbers. The bending process is used to advantage for frame components where design demands curved sections. Although insect attack may occur in the timber, its durability means that this causes few problems.

Timber derivatives
Board materials of various kinds, produced from timber, now make up a large percentage of the content of modern frames. These may be sheet materials converted into piece parts or pre-formed laminations where shaping is required. Basically, most frame

structures are box formations, and board materials lend themselves well as main structures or as linings and stiffeners. Generally they are used in combination with solid timber rails and with some metals. There are four board materials that are widely used for upholstery frames: plywood, hardboard, millboard, chipboard.

These all have very different characteristics. They are chosen carefully for particular uses and incorporated into timber frames. Although the most expensive, plywood is probably the most versatile and strongest of the boards used. It is available in a wide range of types and thicknesses from 1mm to 20mm. The thinner sheets can be easily bent or formed to provide large curved surfaces. Plywood is also used for stiffening and reinforcing frames, as gussets, corner blocks and linings.

Hardboard and millboard are generally used to line and infill on upholstery framing. They are both used particularly on back rests, inside arms and platform fronts. Thicknesses vary from 6mm down to very thin millboards at 1.5mm. Both boards are lightweight and flexible and make good supports and stiffeners, for wood and metal structures. They are both very dense materials and have good staple- and nail-holding properties. Layers of hardboard and millboard can be laminated together to produce shaped components.

Medium-density fibreboard (MDF)
Chipboards and MDF boards are, by nature, generally much thicker and heavier than the other types. Their use in upholstery frames has increased, though they are primarily cabinet-making and building materials, and if used in large amounts in a frame there is a noticeable increase in weight. However, where a strong board of good thickness and strength is required these can be successfully used. Wings, arms and seat fronts are often produced in good quality boards. Thicknesses range from 6mm to 30mm for use in furniture.

All board materials should be used with the recommended jointing and fixing techniques so that they improve and strengthen rather than cheapen the frame-making process.

Metals
Steel in the form of rod, bar and tube is welded and bolted to produce upholstery frames. Angle iron, U-bar and steel lath are also used to some extent. It is sometimes simpler and less costly to produce a frame in metal than in timber, particularly if compound shapes and curves are involved in the design. During the mid-Victorian era, craftsmen produced chairs and sofas using rod and lath construction. Many examples of these are still being restored and reupholstered today (Fig 11.4) Frames of this type had a strength and flexibility that the heavier timber frames did not have.

Square and round section tube are the most common sections used for frame making. Their

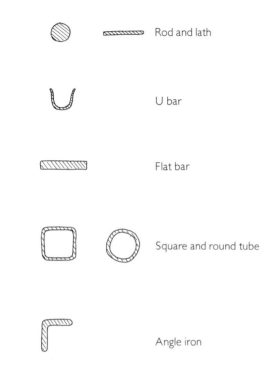

Rod and lath

U bar

Flat bar

Square and round tube

Angle iron

Fig 11.3 Metal sections.

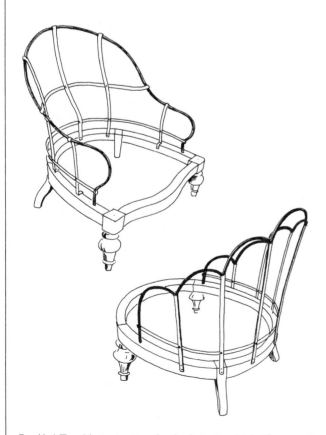

Fig 11.4 Two Victorian iron-back chairs in which 10mm rod and 20mm lath are combined to produce strong, flexible frames with interesting curving lines.

excellent strength/weight ratio makes them ideal framing materials. Where necessary, timber base frames or boards can be added to provide easy fixing for the upholstery. Metal frames require a different approach to the upholstery design and application. Clips and adhesives are used as fixings, and tailored jacket covers can be clipped or zipped to hold them in place.

Plastics
There are three plastic materials used in the manufacture of upholstered seating. All these are rigid plastics and have to be moulded to produce frames or frame components. Plastics are suited to low- or high-volume production but are seldom used for bespoke or one-off pieces of upholstery. The mass production of plastic structures is mainly in the area of

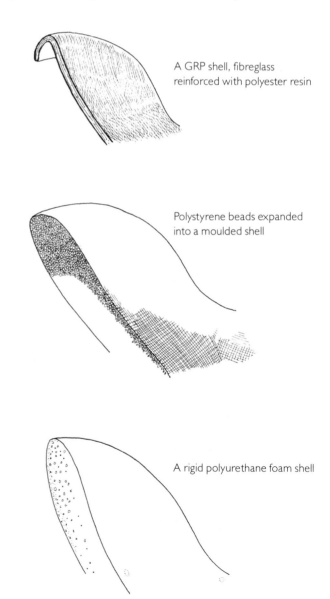

A GRP shell, fibreglass reinforced with polyester resin

Polystyrene beads expanded into a moulded shell

A rigid polyurethane foam shell

Fig 11.5

Fig 11.6 Conventional chair frame construction using solid timber.

Fig 11.7 An alternative construction using lightweight rails and plywood stiffeners.

Fig 11.8 Bent steel tube framing, supporting pre-formed plywood seat and back boards.

contract seating for public buildings etc. However, some moulded components are made and then bolted into timber frames particularly where the component would be expensive to produce in wood. This technique is used a great deal in domestic upholstery design.

The three plastics chiefly used are: GRP, (glass-reinforced polyester resin), expanded polystyrene and rigid polyurethane foam. Of the three, expanded polystyrene is generally the most popular choice. Small white beads of polystyrene are dispersed into aluminium moulds, which are then heated in steam ovens. The beads expand and link together filling the mould under pressure. The resulting component is a white lightweight structure. Fillets and boards of plywood are usually incorporated into the mould to provide stapling and fixing points. Where necessary extra strength can be provided by reinforcement with layers of hessian bonded on to the face of the moulded part (Fig 11.9). A number of other plastic materials have been used successfully to produce seating of various kinds. These are: perspex (acrylic), polyethelene, ABS (acrylonitrile butadiene styrene), toughened polystyrene, and PVC (polyvinyl chloride).

Fig 11.9 A typical polystyrene chair shell with a seat board moulded in and reinforced with hessian.

Prie-dieu Chair
c. 1840–60

A mid-Victorian upholstered single chair, with high, straight back and low seat. The back curved out to a broad top to provide an arm rest while praying. Also popular with ladies wearing large bulky dresses.

Upholstery Firm and unsprung and stuffed with curled animal hair over a mixture of seaweed and grasses. Well-stitched edges gave a good foundation for the heavy fabrics. Coverings of needlework, tapestry and velvets were neatly decorated with silk cord and gimp.

DESIGN AND CONSTRUCTION

A chair structure or frame has two distinct areas which are referred to as the outsides and the insides. The line and form of the outsides is produced by the frame materials and rails, and is generally rigid with light padding to protect the edges and corners and the coverings. Visually, the outsides give a chair its main form and shape; this can be made to appear angular and sharp or soft and sculptured, depending on the shaping of rails and the amount of padding applied to the outsides (Fig 11.10).

The insides and their shape and line are produced by the upholstery, using various fillings, foams and suspensions. The shape of the insides is important and is basically functional, providing soft and firm areas to cradle and support the sitter. A comfortable chair has four basic components, a seat, a back and two arms. Each of these is linked and related to produce varying degrees of comfort. Proportions and dimensions of the insides are variable within certain ranges, beyond which the chair ceases to function well. Historically, seating dimensions have changed from a generally upright sitting position to the lounging position. The easy chair or lounge chair is now dual purpose or even adjustable to provide different sitting angles. The day bed or couch is no longer produced in quantity to provide an alternative to the upright chair.

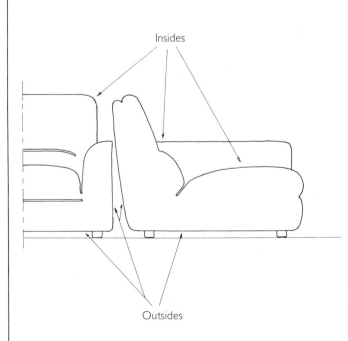

Fig 11.10 Outsides are produced by the frame line (firm). Insides are produced with the upholstery materials (soft).

Dimensions of seat, back and arms can be varied to provide seating for different functions, i.e. dining, writing, resting, lounging, etc. At the same time, the insides of a chair are angled or raked so that the sitter is supported and made to feel secure. There are no strict rules regarding the dimensioning of a chair or setting of the angles of seat and back. Most people are aware of the extremes, for instance a bench seat placed by a wall giving a 90° angle can be tolerated for only a short time. A canvas deck chair can be tolerated for much longer, but the effect of the hard front rail and the short seat depth and unsupported back make it limited as a good seating medium.

A more ideal easy sitting position is somewhere between these two, and a study of existing upholstery of different kinds will provide a historical background and a record for the upholsterer and the upholstery designer.

Several other factors can influence the feel and support of a piece of upholstery:

1   The thickness of fillings and foams
2   The strength and resilience of fillings
3   The flexing and support of suspension systems
4   The height of a seat above the floor
5   The height of an arm rest above the seat
6   The height of a back rest above seat level
7   The width of a seat
8   The provision of flat, domed or concave surfaces
9   The provision of wings or lugs on a chair back
10   The provision of loose cushions or bolsters.

Fig 11.11 gives some typical seating variations and approximate dimensions. These range from low level to high, and from deep to shallow, but are all acceptable sitting variations.

Upholstered chairs are produced for many different sitting purposes, but basically they can be arranged into four groups:

● resting and lounging
● dining and writing or working
● use in transport
● occasional use only

In the first group the upholstery content is very important and is expected to be at a maximum, both in depth and in comfort. The second group requires only minimal depth and softness, but design and support are critical. In the third group the upholstery and filling depths are perhaps a compromise. Research will show that foam and filling thicknesses are in the medium range of 1in to 3in (50 to 75mm), and shape and support are equally as important as for the second group. Group four is variable and generally less specific. Upholstery in this case may be at an absolute minimum, with filling thicknesses basically unimportant.

Dimensions and proportion in chairs are linked to filling thicknesses and their degree of hardness and support. The upholstery designer has to be aware of all the combinations, and these include springing and suspension. A chair has to be suitably comfortable and supportive when in use and when the materials and fillings are in a compressed state. Most forms of upholstered seating have a seat and a back rest, and the angle between these should be in the range 100°–110°

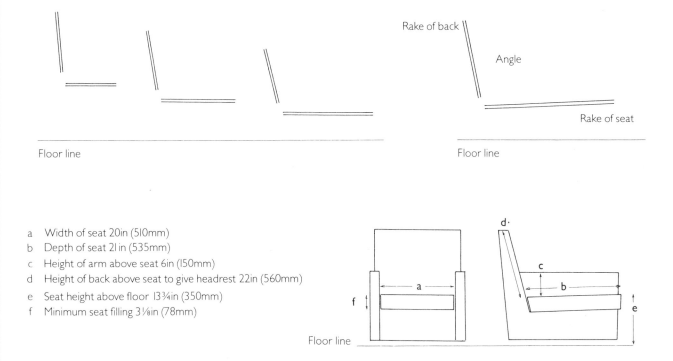

a   Width of seat 20in (510mm)
b   Depth of seat 21in (535mm)
c   Height of arm above seat 6in (150mm)
d   Height of back above seat to give headrest 22in (560mm)
e   Seat height above floor 13¾in (350mm)
f   Minimum seat filling 3⅛in (78mm)

Fig 11.11 Dimensions and proportions for seating.

(Fig 11.11). Any increase in the seat rake or slope causes the sitter to be pushed back more firmly into the back rest. Rake or slope in a seat can be created by adjusting suspension or varying the thicknesses and support of fillings. This technique applies equally to back rest design. Lumbar support which is essential is often created by an increase in the strength of suspension or alternatively the thickness or hardness of the filling materials. However, for production purposes it is often better to create the correct angles in the frame design, rather than have to produce variations and shapes with fillings.

There are three basic upholstered chair frame constructions: fixed mono frames, KD (knock down) frames and unit frames. The mono frame is a complete free-standing structure, made and assembled and finished ready for upholstery. It is made up from machined timber and board piece parts and may have elements of metal and plastic. A KD frame is a frame that is manufactured in sections, and assembly takes place after the sections have been upholstered. KD fittings of various kinds are used to hold the sections together. This method of making is designed principally for mass production and involves repetition work on a larger scale. Although basic materials costs may be higher, speed and uniformity of production result from the breaking down of the product into small sections.

This production method is also used to some extent for the home assembly market. A chair, for example, can be bought as a flat pack and assembled for use later. Kitchen and bedroom furniture is also made and sold in this way. The unit frame is based on the principle of versatile seating, which can be arranged to suit different room situations. The units are usually of two types, standard seats and corner seats, with a facility for arm supports to be added. The individual units may be simply free standing or bolted together for different seating arrangements. Since the 1960s, when modular seating became popular, it has tended to become used more in hotels, shops and waiting rooms than in domestic situations.

Joints

The mortise and tenon joint and the dowel joint are the two traditional timber frame joints suitable for all types of frame structure. Often both joints are used in the same frame, the dowel joint being used to peg the opposing tenon. However, frame manufacturers today tend to equip themselves to produce one or the other joint, so that production is based on drilling machinery for dowelling or on mortising and tenoning machines.

The two joints are often compared for their strength and durability, and exhaustive tests have shown that in a range of types and sizes there is very little difference in performance between the two. A tenon thickness of 10mm and a dowel diameter of 10mm are about

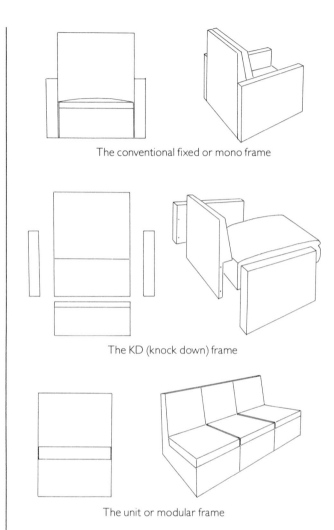

The conventional fixed or mono frame

The KD (knock down) frame

The unit or modular frame

Fig 11.12 Three basic frame types.

average for most main joints. Lengths of tenon or dowel will vary depending on rail dimensions. Dowel joints may have one, two or three dowels in each, again depending on rail size. Main structure rails should all have three dowels where possible.

Where it is important to stop a rail from twisting in use, for example a stuffing rail, then joints are housed as well as dowelled (Fig 11.13). The lap joint and the finger joint are both used extensively to lengthen rails and as corner joints. They are both good machine-made joints and lend themselves well to modern frame production.

Stapled and glued butt joints are an effective alternative to the other more conventional joints, particularly if gussets and stiffeners are used as braces. These relatively modern jointing techniques have also been subjected to stress testing and results compare favourably with all other jointing methods. The two surfaces to be joined are glued and stapled together, with staples up to 2½in (63mm) long. The joints are then braced with plywood gussets, glued and stapled to the outer surfaces (Fig 11.14). Figs 11.15 to 11.25 illustrate some alternative structures.

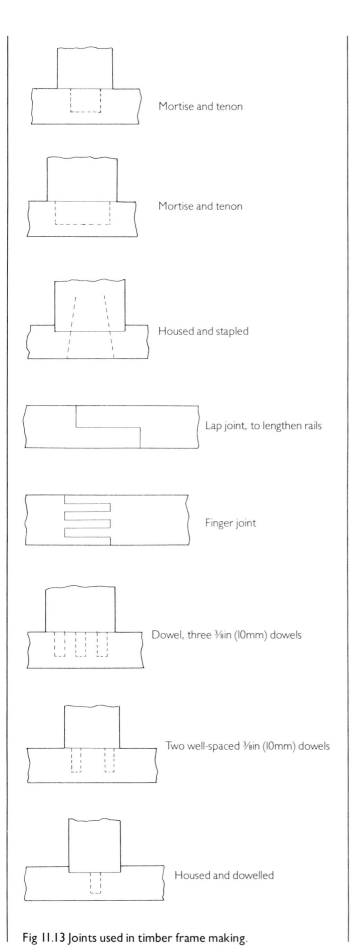

Mortise and tenon

Mortise and tenon

Housed and stapled

Lap joint, to lengthen rails

Finger joint

Dowel, three ⅜in (10mm) dowels

Two well-spaced ⅜in (10mm) dowels

Housed and dowelled

Fig 11.13 Joints used in timber frame making.

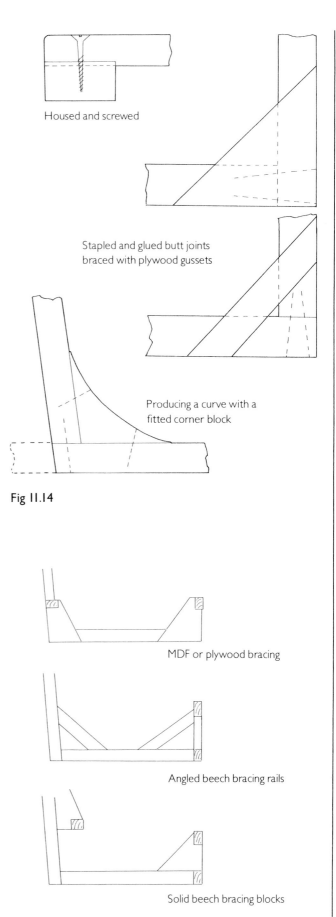

Housed and screwed

Stapled and glued butt joints braced with plywood gussets

Producing a curve with a fitted corner block

Fig 11.14

MDF or plywood bracing

Angled beech bracing rails

Solid beech bracing blocks

Fig 11.15 Alternative seat structures.

Walnut Ladies' Chair
c. 1860

A Victorian chair which was usually made as part of a suite. Certainly one of the better designs of the Victorian era, and has been reproduced in large numbers during the last twenty years.

Upholstery The buttoning was pulled deeply into a well, filled with horsehair and wadding. The wide, sprung seat provided ample sitting room, since the chair was used a great deal for nursing, sewing and conversation.

Coverings Appear to have been varied, but velvets and damask were the most usual. Linen chenille and hides were occasionally used where interiors demanded something out of the ordinary.

   Trimmings used were woven gimp, silk cord and brass nails.

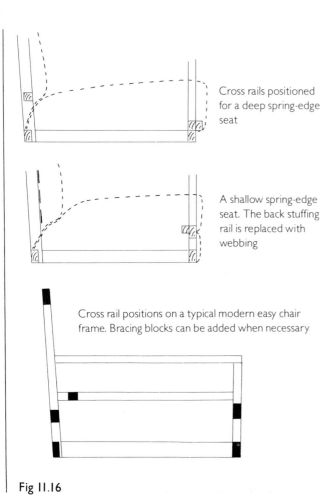

Cross rails positioned for a deep spring-edge seat

A shallow spring-edge seat. The back stuffing rail is replaced with webbing

Cross rail positions on a typical modern easy chair frame. Bracing blocks can be added when necessary

Fig 11.16

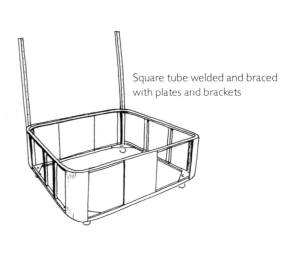

Square tube welded and braced with plates and brackets

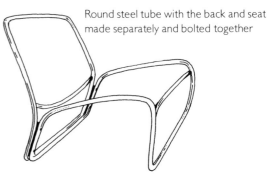

Round steel tube with the back and seat made separately and bolted together

Fig 11.17 Single mono frames: two modern metal chair frames.

Fig 11.18 Unit frame: a timber chair frame, lined and stiffened with plywood and millboard

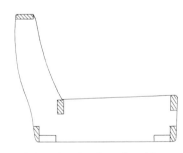

An end elevation showing rail positions

End boards are from ¾in (19mm) plywood or MDF, cross rails are from 1⅛in (30mm) beech

Fig 11.19 A unit frame constructed from end boards or end assemblies and cross rails.

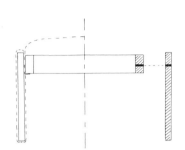

Knock-down construction of a small stool using a beech seat frame and plywood ends

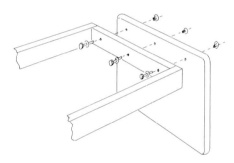

Bolts, washers and T nuts are used to join the components

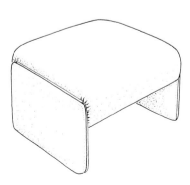

Fig 11.20 KD construction stool.

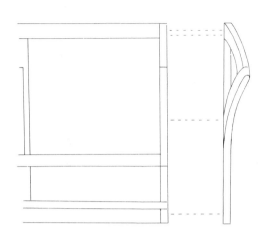

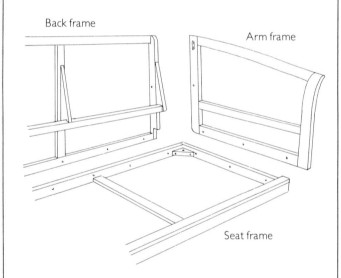

Back frame

Arm frame

Seat frame

Fig 11.21 A settee frame made up from four separate components.

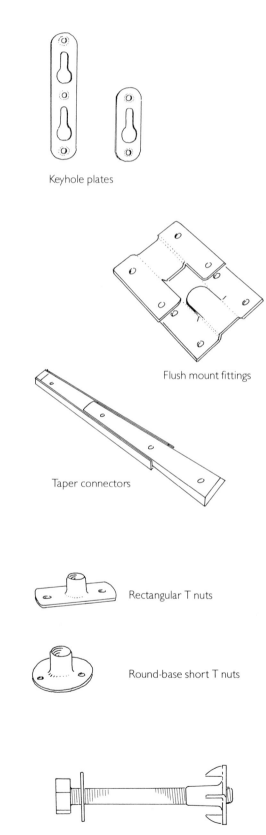

Keyhole plates

Flush mount fittings

Taper connectors

Rectangular T nuts

Round-base short T nuts

Hexagon head bolt, washer and pronged-base long T nut

Fig 11.22 KD fittings used to join upholstered chair parts.

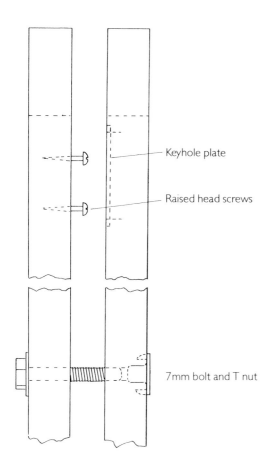

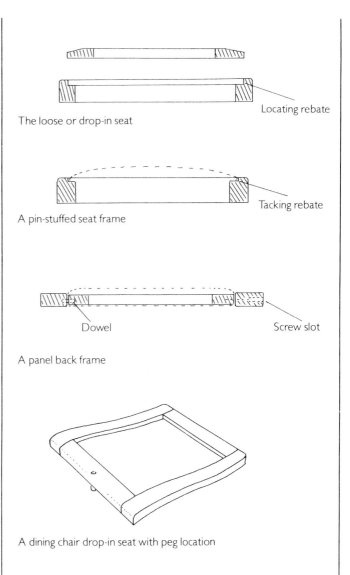

The loose or drop-in seat

Locating rebate

A pin-stuffed seat frame

Tacking rebate

Dowel

Screw slot

A panel back frame

A dining chair drop-in seat with peg location

Keyhole plate

Raised head screws

7mm bolt and T nut

Fig 11.23 Beech rails prepared for assembly with KD fittings positioned.

Fig 11.24 Small traditional seat and back frames for dining, desk and reading chairs.

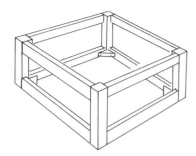

The corner blocks serve as braces to keep the frame square and as fixing points for castors; they must therefore be of a good thickness and well fixed

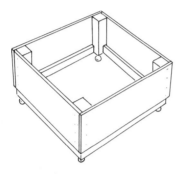

Plywood, MDF or chipboard may be used for a carcass of this type

Fig 11.25 Two modern stools illustrating frame-up construction and box construction

— Chapter Twelve —

Springs and Suspension Systems

Early support materials for chairs and seating had little resilience or spring in them, but simply cradled the upholstery stuffings and cushions. The full weight of the sitter was absorbed by the seat webbings, strips of leather or strong canvas.

The fillings used at that time, such as hair, feathers and rags, would have soon compressed under these conditions and so had to be continually shaken and turned to keep the upholstery lively and comfortable. It was not until the middle of the nineteenth century that the metal coil spring was produced in quantity for use in upholstery. These early springs were made from heavy gauge wire, with a large number of coils (Fig 12.1).

Sprung upholstery soon became very popular and fully upholstered chairs and sofas often had sprung arms, backs and seats. Chairs and sofas became larger and more cumbersome to facilitate the use of large numbers of springs. The development of the spring interior mattress and the spring cushion followed on from this, all

hand built, providing a great deal of work for the upholsterer (Fig 12.2).

The same double-cone-shaped compression spring is still produced and used today for hand-built upholstery and in mattress making, and has changed very little in its shape and the way that it works. The steel wire used is now very much stronger and the number of coils per spring is fewer. The wire ends are machine knotted rather than bound or clipped, but basically the spring remains the same.

The first half of the twentieth century saw many different developments in spring and suspension design, from large machine-made double spring units to lightweight moulded rubber diaphragms. During this

Fig 12.1 An early hourglass, double-cone spring made from heavy gauge wire and a large number of coils; the ends are wire bound.

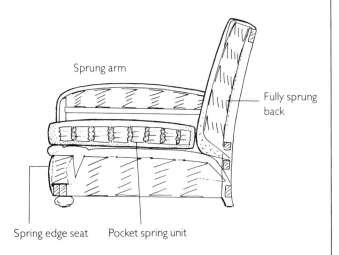

Sprung arm

Fully sprung back

Spring edge seat   Pocket spring unit

Fig 12.2 A traditional fully sprung stuffover easy chair containing a large number of compression springs. Chairs of this type were large and heavy and were hand built in the early years of the twentieth century.

period almost all upholstered seats had some kind of springing as a foundation. Even small drop-in seats for dining chairs were sprung with metal compression or tension springs.

Gradually, the need for sprung upholstery has lessened and seating design has turned full circle. High-quality resilient foam fillings have made suspension unnecessary in dining chairs, desk furniture and occasional seating. The strength and resilience of foam as a filling has enabled the upholsterer to produce comfortable chairs with platforms of webbing and boards. In lounge furniture, however, a variety of suspension systems still forms the basis of seat and back upholstery. These are generally in the form of ready-made units using compression and tension springs or a combination of both. The use of rubber and elastic webbings has increased to the point where the market is equally shared by the two materials, metal and rubber.

METAL SPRINGS

Spring steel wire is the basic material for metal spring making. The higher the carbon content in a wire, the stiffer and more resistant it becomes as a spring. Generally, the wires with a high carbon content and good tensile strength were used to produce tension springs, and standard spring steel wire was used for the making of cone-shaped springs and the barrel types used in mattress interiors.

Wire drawing

Wire is produced by taking a high-carbon wire rod, and after suitable heat treatment and cleaning, drawing it through a series of tungsten carbide dies to reduce its cross sectional area by 70 to 80 per cent. The cold working from the drawing process increases the tensile strength by about 40 per cent. Direct cooling is necessary during drawing to stop the wire overheating, and after stabilising, the new wire is wound on to reels or coils for use by the spring maker. Before and after the rods are drawn microscopic and electronic checks are carried out to ensure consistent quality.

Modern high-speed, wire-forming machines on which upholstery springs are made demand a higher quality and more consistent wire than at any time in the past. The tensile strength of modern spring wire may be as high as 110 tons per sq in and the carbon content in the range of 0.5 to 0.7 per cent. After forming, the steel springs are squashed by hand or machine for a few seconds to restore the elastic properties which may have been affected by cold working.

Gauges and sizes

Steel spring wires are produced in SWG (standard wire-gauge) thicknesses, from 7swg down to the very thin wires at 22swg. A range of typical compression spring sizes and wire gauges follows:

Height	by	gauge
3in (75mm)	×	10swg and 12swg,
4in (100mm)	×	9swg, 10swg and 12swg,
5in (125mm)	×	9swg, 10swg, and 12swg,
6in (150mm)	×	9swg, 10swg and 12swg,
7in (175mm)	×	9swg, 10swg and 12swg,
8in (200mm)	×	8½swg and 9swg,
9in (230mm)	×	8½swg and 9swg,
10in (255mm)	×	8swg and 9swg,
12in (305mm)	×	8swg and 9swg.

Bundles of these springs are made up and sold in quantities of 50 and 100. Fig 12.3 shows the double-cone, open-coil spring traditionally used for hand-built upholstery, together with the single-cone spring and the barrel type. These are manufactured on an automatic machine called a coiler and knotter, and are produced at a rate of several hundred per hour. The double-cone spring is also known as the hourglass or waisted spring.

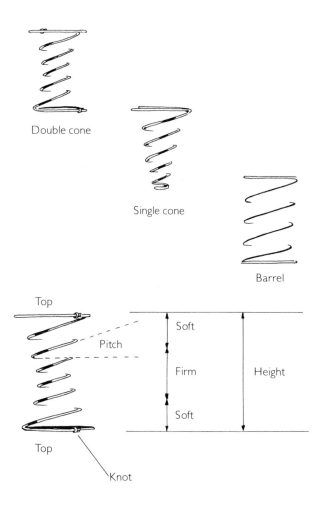

Fig 12.3 The double-cone spring is reversible and knotted at each end. The pitch of each coil is set by the coiling machine and is variable for different springs. As the diameter of the coils becomes narrower, a firm area is produced at the centre of the spring. A single cone-spring is firmest at its base.

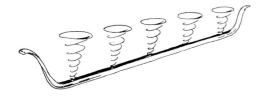

Fig 12.4 Single-cone springs mounted on a U bar for use in a bed base.

Single-cone types are made specifically for use in spring units and are rivetted on to steel lathes and covered with a mesh stop. They are also used in bed bases and supported on metal U-bars (Fig 12.4).

Barrel springs, which are made from the finer gauge wires, are straight sided and are designed for use in mattress making. Although much softer to feel and lighter in weight, they are grouped close together into pocket spring units. As many as 300 may be used in one double mattress interior. Each spring is pocketed in cotton calico, separated by a sewn seam and the single rows of pocketed springs are clipped together to form a large mattress unit. The unit is completed with a metal edge strip or wire clipped to the outer springs (Fig 12.5).

Spring units
A spring unit is basically a number of springs assembled and linked together. Units are factory made and supplied ready for use to upholstery and bedding manufacturers. There are several different types, and may be reversible or non-reversible, made up from compression and tension springs. Generally reversible

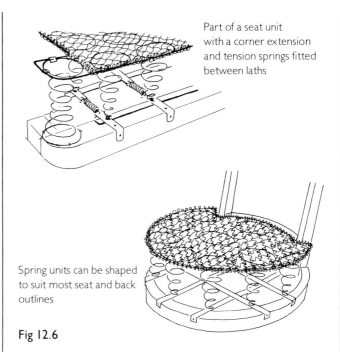

Part of a seat unit with a corner extension and tension springs fitted between laths

Spring units can be shaped to suit most seat and back outlines

Fig 12.6

units are used for mattresses and cushions, and the non-reversible units are fixed into seating with laths and wires. Figs 12.6–12.10 show the following main types of unit and their construction:

1 Mesh top unit
2 Clip top unit
3 Open spring unit
4 Pocket spring unit
5 Double spring unit
6 Box spring unit

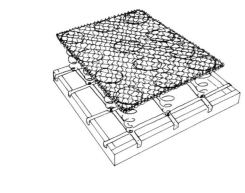

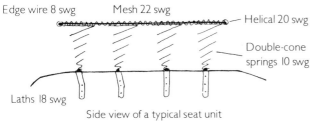

Edge wire 8 swg Mesh 22 swg Helical 20 swg Double-cone springs 10 swg Laths 18 swg

Side view of a typical seat unit

Fig 12.5 A mesh-top spring unit

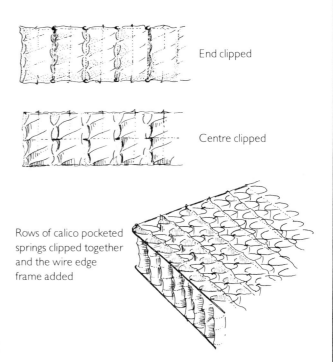

End clipped

Centre clipped

Rows of calico pocketed springs clipped together and the wire edge frame added

Fig 12.7 Pocket spring units.

Tension springs

Tension springing is designed as a lateral suspension system and works by being tensioned across a seat area. This type of springing takes up far less space in a chair frame and is generally a more lightweight form of support. The close-coiled tension spring was the first of its kind to be used in upholstery. Sometimes called a cable spring, it is fixed and suspended under tension across a timber or metal frame, and equally spaced at approximately 2½in (65mm) centres. The two sizes normally produced for upholstery are ½in (13mm) diameter by 14swg and ⁵/₁₆in (7mm) diameter by 18swg. The two sizes can be made to any length up to a maximum of 22in (550mm) long, and the larger diameter used in seats and the smaller 7mm springs used in back rests.

In stuffover upholstery work where the springs are not seen, no surface finish is needed on the springs, but

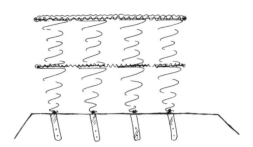

Double-cone and single-cone compression rings mounted on 18 swg steel laths

Fig 12.9 A double seat spring unit.

where an open platform is produced for cushioning they are usually braided or plastic covered. A braided tension spring has a woven rayon sock over its surface, which acts as a protective coating. Alternatively, a narrow PVC sleeve is inflated and the springs inserted into the sleeve. When deflated the sleeve shrinks to form a tight fitting protective cover (Figs 12.11 and 12.12). Close-coil tension springs are normally stretched 3 to 5 per cent of their length.

Serpentine or zig-zag springs

These are tension-type springs, but of a completely different wire formation. High-carbon steel wire is formed into a sinuous strip of various widths and from diffrent wire gauge sizes. As the serpentine formation is produced the continuous strips may be arced, semi arced or flat formed. The automatic machines can be set to produce continuous 100ft rolls, or cut lengths in batches or nests of any number.

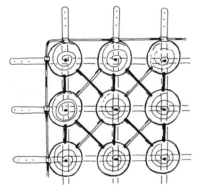

A simplified spring unit with long clips used in place of mesh

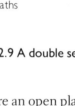

Helical wire 17 swg

Steel strip
³⁄₈in × ¹⁄₃₂in
(10mm × 1.4mm)

Spring wire 15 swg

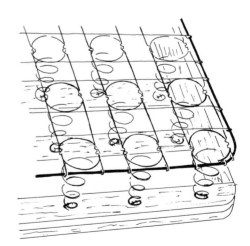

Interlocking crimped wires hold the unit together and the springs are stapled down to the base frame.

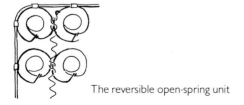

The reversible open-spring unit

Fig 12.8

Fig 12.10 A box spring.

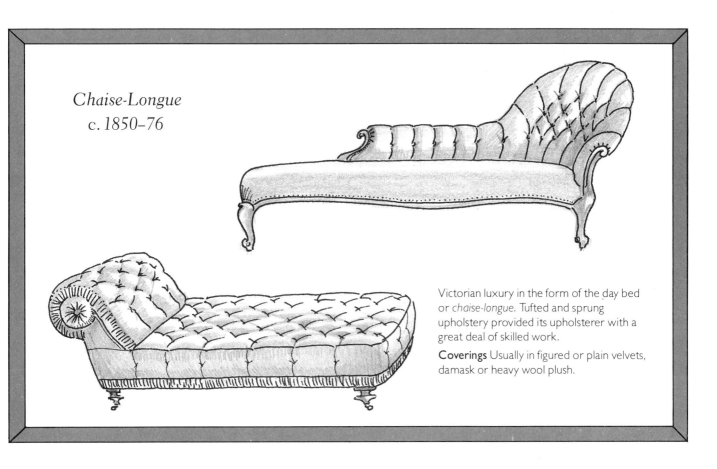

Chaise-Longue
c. 1850–76

Victorian luxury in the form of the day bed or *chaise-longue*. Tufted and sprung upholstery provided its upholsterer with a great deal of skilled work.

Coverings Usually in figured or plain velvets, damask or heavy wool plush.

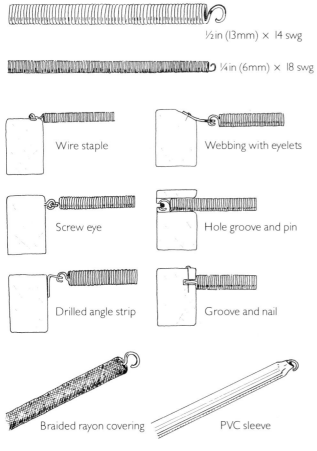

½in (13mm) × 14 swg

¼in (6mm) × 18 swg

Wire staple

Webbing with eyelets

Screw eye

Hole groove and pin

Drilled angle strip

Groove and nail

Braided rayon covering

PVC sleeve

Fig 12.11 Close-coil tension springs.

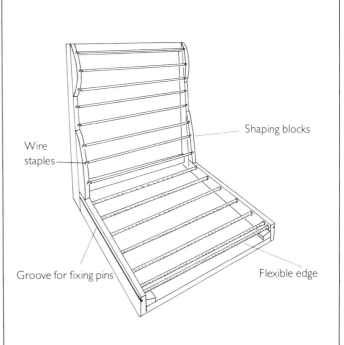

Wire staples

Shaping blocks

Groove for fixing pins

Flexible edge

Fig 12.12 Close-coil tension springs provide the suspension in this occasional chair, at reasonable cost.

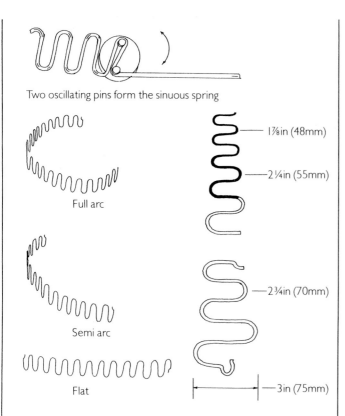

Two oscillating pins form the sinuous spring

Full arc

Semi arc

Flat

1⅞in (48mm)

2¼in (55mm)

2¾in (70mm)

3in (75mm)

Fig 12.13 Serpentine or zig-zag springs can be produced in various formations: arcs and end configurations, 1⅞in (48mm) standard zig-zag loop, 2¼in (55mm) medium loop, 3in (76mm) large loop.

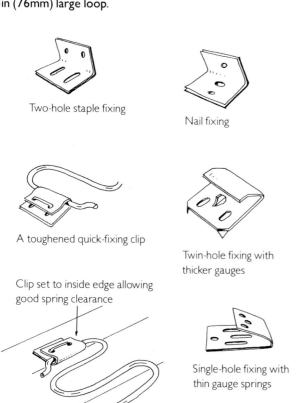

Two-hole staple fixing

Nail fixing

A toughened quick-fixing clip

Twin-hole fixing with thicker gauges

Clip set to inside edge allowing good spring clearance

Single-hole fixing with thin gauge springs

Fig 12.14 Serpentine spring clips.

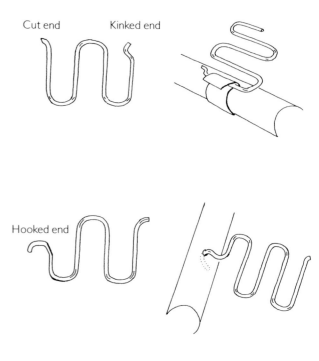

Cut end   Kinked end

Hooked end

Fig 12.15 Fixings into tube frames.

Fig 12.13 illustrates the various types and the different formations available. The ends of cut strips are kinked to provide a non-slip fixing in the clip. A hooked end can also be formed, where springs are to be directly located into holes in metal chair frames.

The standard wire gauges used for serpentine springing generally range from 9swg to 12swg, 9 and 10 gauge for seat springs and 11 and 12 gauge for back springs. By nature the high-carbon wire used for the springing is very tough and can only be cut using heavy bolt croppers or a bench-mounted cutter designed specifically for wire cutting (Fig 12.16).

Selecting and measuring
To obtain an accurate length measurement of a serpentine spring, one end of a spring should be balanced on a metre stick and the spring flattened out until the distance between the extreme outside ends can be taken. The length of the strip as measured will be less than the distance to be spanned. Springs should not be measured with a tape around a curved spring. In most cases the direction of springing is normally from top to bottom on back, and from back to front in seats. Where frames are of an irregular shape it can be an advantage to fix from side to side. The following tables give a guide to gauges, sizes and spacing for seats and backs:

Gauges and sizes for seats					
Inside seat dimension	gauge	Height and lengths 1⅛in (30mm)	1½in (38mm)	1¾in (45mm)	2in (50mm)
18in (460mm)	9½	16¾in (425mm)	17¼in (436mm)	17⅝in (445mm)	
19in (485mm)	9	17⅞in (452mm)	18in (460mm)	18⅜in (470mm)	
20in (510mm)	9	18⅝in (475mm)	19in (485mm)	19⅜in (495mm)	19⅝in (500mm)
21in (535mm)	9	19⅝in (500mm)	20in (510mm)	20⅜in (520mm)	20⅝in (525mm)
22in (560mm)	9	20⅝in (525mm)	21in (535mm)	21⅜in (545mm)	21⅝in (550mm)
23in (585mm)	8½	21⅝in (550mm)	22in (560mm)	22⅜in (570mm)	23⅝in (600mm)

Gauges and sizes for backs

Inside dimension top to bottom	gauge
16¾–21⅝in (425–550mm)	11½–12
21⅝–23⅝in (550–600mm)	11–11½
24⅝–27⅝in (625–700mm)	10½–11

Lengths should be found by fixing a spring at the bottom rail and pulling to the top rail, locating into the clip and adjusting until the suitable curve is found. This will give the length of the springs to be cut.

Spacing of serpentine springs should fall between 4in (100mm) and 5in (125mm) centre to centre and clips fixed at these centres. Link sizes will then be between 2½in (63mm) and 3⅜in (85mm).

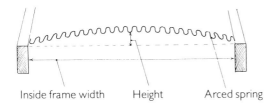

Inside frame width   Height   Arced spring

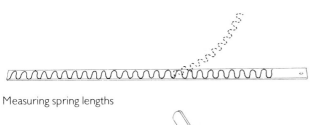

Measuring spring lengths

A resilience spring cutter

Fig 12.16 Measuring and cutting.

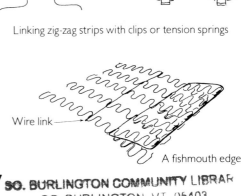

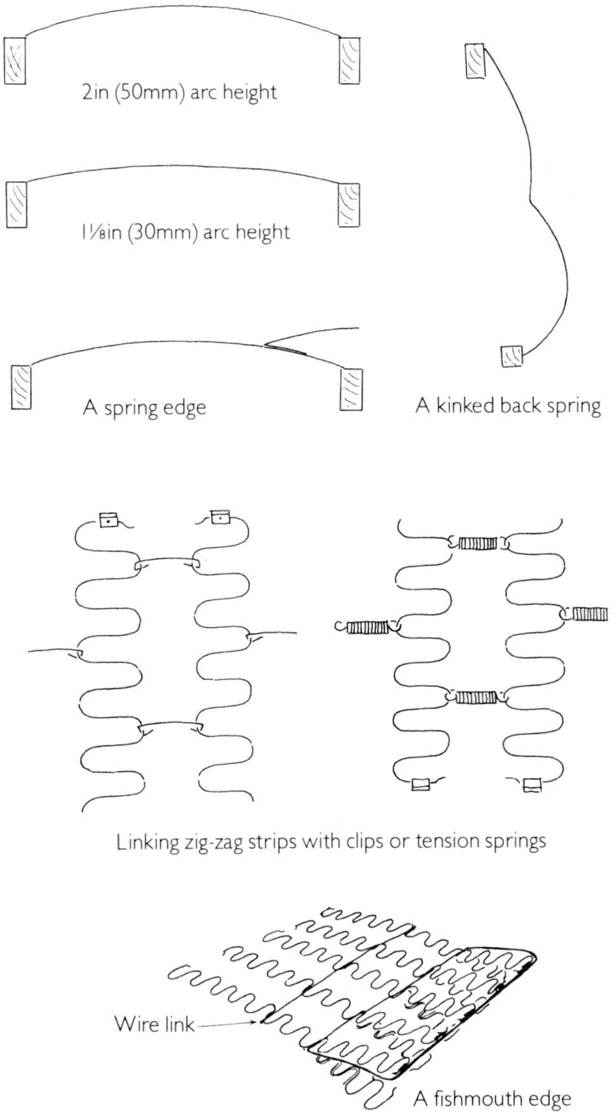

2in (50mm) arc height

1⅛in (30mm) arc height

A spring edge

A kinked back spring

Linking zig-zag strips with clips or tension springs

Wire link

A fishmouth edge

Fig 12.17

Arcs

Full round 8in (200mm) arcs may be used for backs and seats with varying wire gauges. The 12in (305mm) arcs are mostly used in seats, and give a lower dome to the upholstery. Flat arc springs make a firm platform and are used particularly with reversible cushions in seats (Fig 12.17).

The fishmouth spring edge

A spring edge can be produced for seat fronts by applying and clipping formed strips on to the normal seat lengths. An edge wire is then shaped and clipped on to the front edge of the strips, and returned at the ends. The edge wire is of a heavy gauge and normally follows the frame outline (Fig 12.17).

Pullmaflex suspension systems

This springing system is basically a tension-spring type, consisting of a flat grid made up from flexible tempered wires linked together with heavy gauge paper-covered wires and paper centre cords. The grids, which can be of different designs and strengths, are located into timber or metal frames with staples, clips and tension springs. The fixing methods used and the strength of the springs determine the degree of comfort and support of the unit. Pullmaflex systems are suitable for bed bases, chair seats and backs, and are used in vehicle seating. The system is very lightweight and can quickly be located and fixed, using staples or clips.

Fig 12.18 shows some typical Pullmaflex units and

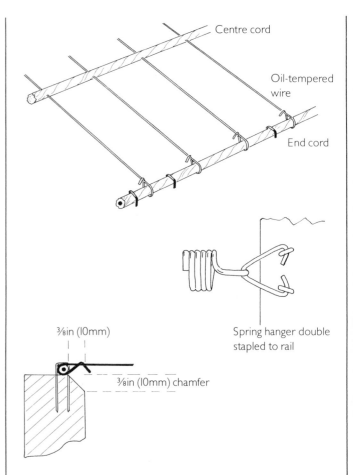

Fig 12.19

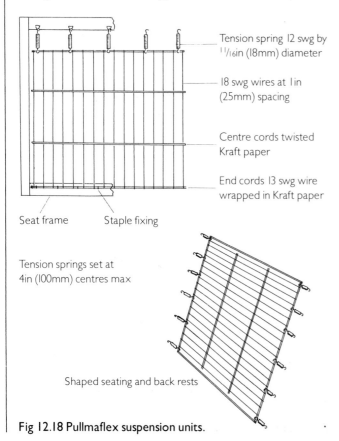

Fig 12.18 Pullmaflex suspension units.

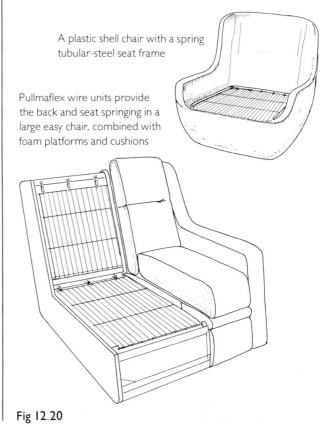

Fig 12.20

fixing techniques. The combination of high-carbon tempered steel wires and twisted Kraft paper produces a tough and resilient platform, which is well suited to today's modern upholstery production, particularly with polyurethane foams and foam cushioning. Vertically and horizontally fixed units, with or without tension springs, provide a versatile range of upholstery design specifications (Figs 12.19 and 12.20). Grids can be made up to specified sizes and clipped into tubular steel frames, ready to drop into shell chairs, and for use in knockdown seating.

Applications

Generally, seats are sprung from back to front and chair backs from top to bottom. However, where frames are contoured, then side-to-side suspension provides a sprung support which follows the frame shape. A Pullmaflex wire grid can also be used as an unsprung platform for foams and cushioning. In this case the outer cords are stapled directly to timber rails and the centre cords fixed to stuffing rails (Fig 12.21).

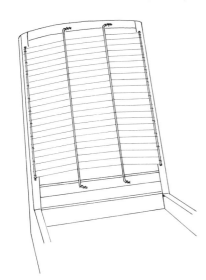

Fig 12.21

As a guide to grid sizes, the pad width is always 3in (75mm) less than the inside frame measurements, rail to rail. The pad length is generally calculated at 1in (25mm) less than the inside frame measurement of the other two rails. Fixings are vitally important and should be to the following minimum sizes: nails, 14swg by 1in (25mm) length; staples, ⅜in (10mm) crown by 1in (25mm) leg length, or ⁵/₁₆in (8mm) pointed crown by 1in (25mm) long. Ideally nails and staples should have serrated or self-glued legs. The pull or tension of Pullmaflex units for normal applications is a maximum of ⅜in (10mm). Seat units will give maximum comfort and service with ¼in (6mm) tension.

RUBBER SUSPENSION

As an alternative to metal springing, resilient rubber suspension was developed during the mid-1950s. It was

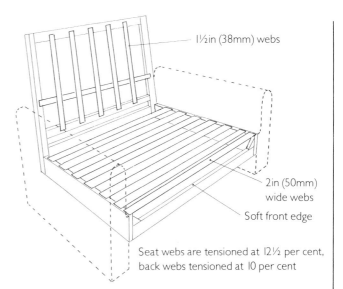

Fig 12.22 Resilient webbing fitted to the carcass of a large easy chair.

produced as webbings and in sheet form and has largely replaced the close-coil tension spring but works in a similar way. Using a variety of different fixings the webbings are stretched and fixed across metal and timber frames, either in one direction only or interlaced in two directions. The structure is basically a synthetic rubber sheet which is reinforced with synthetic textile cords laminated into the rubber. The cords are laid and sandwiched into the rubber in a single or double layer. The fabric cords provide a reinforcing core, and limit the stretch of the webbing. The resulting product is a strong but resilient material capable of supporting heavy weights and producing a feeling of buoyancy associated with comfort.

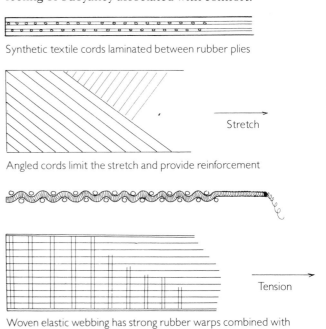

Fig 12.23 Rubber and elastic webbings.

Another more recent development is woven elastic webbing which has an entirely different construction. Elastic webbing is made up on a loom by weaving braided rubber cords and synthetic yarn to produce a strong resilient webbing in widths of 1in (25mm) up to 2¼in (57mm). The different constructions are shown in Fig 12.22. Both types are manufactured in a number of grades suitable for use in chair seats and chair backs. Resilient webbings can be made up to order in specified widths and lengths, or purchased in rolls of 50 and 100m.

Structure

Pirelli resilient webbing is a flat rubber spring made from rubber and cord. The rubber provides resilience, the cord controls the degree of elasticity and provides reinforcement. The cords are visible at the edge of the webbing in two layers which run diagonally across the webbing in opposite directions. As the webbing is stretched the cords in each layer turn towards the direction of pull. The rubber progressively resists the forces until the non-stretch cords embedded in the rubber prevent further deflection. This type of resilient webbing is made in standard, super and superflex grades and in widths from ¾in (19mm) to 2¼in (57mm) (Fig 12.24).

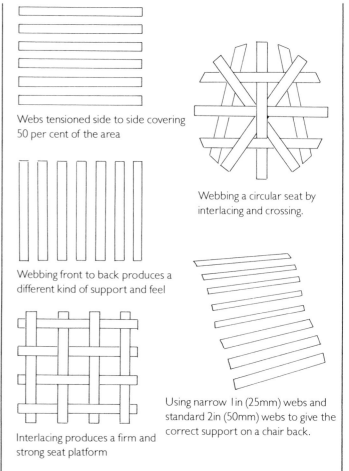

Webs tensioned side to side covering 50 per cent of the area

Webbing a circular seat by interlacing and crossing.

Webbing front to back produces a different kind of support and feel

Interlacing produces a firm and strong seat platform

Using narrow 1in (25mm) webs and standard 2in (50mm) webs to give the correct support on a chair back.

Fig 12.25 Design of resilient webbed supports with webbing patterns.

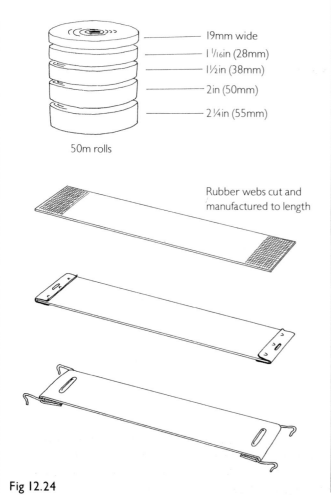

19mm wide
1¹/₁₆in (28mm)
1½in (38mm)
2in (50mm)
2¼in (55mm)

50m rolls

Rubber webs cut and manufactured to length

Fig 12.24

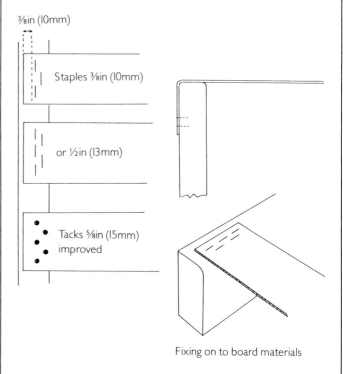

⅜in (10mm)

Staples ⅜in (10mm)

or ½in (13mm)

Tacks ⅝in (15mm) improved

Fixing on to board materials

Fig 12.26 Fixing with staples and tacks.

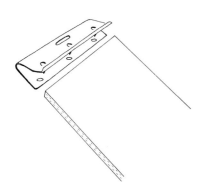

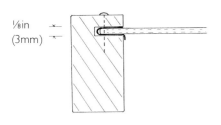

¹⁄₈in
(3mm)

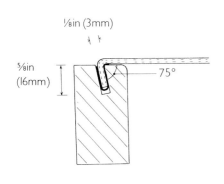

¹⁄₈in (3mm)

⁵⁄₈in
(16mm)

75°

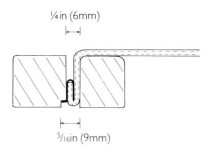

¹⁄₄in (6mm)

⁵⁄₁₆in (9mm)

Fig 12.27 The steel webbing clip.

Elastic webbings have rather a different structure which is basically woven. Warps of rubber cord which are over wound or gimped with synthetic yarn, are woven together with polypropylene weft yarns to form a heavy weight elastic webbing. Stretch characteristics can be varied by the yarn making and weaving process. Resistance is built in by the overwinding of the rubber warps and as these are stretched and the spiral yarns surrounding the rubber are elongated, they compress the rubber.

Application

All types of rubber and elastic webbing can be tacked or stapled to timber rails. Care should be taken to see that fixings are adequate and as recommended. Timber rails must be well rounded where webbings are located. Plates, clips and hooks are easily fitted to webbing ends for easier and faster fixings and for application to metal frames. See Figs 12.26–12.30.

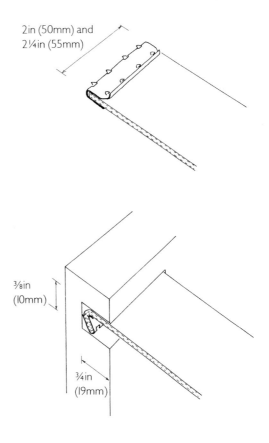

2in (50mm) and
2¼in (55mm)

³⁄₈in
(10mm)

³⁄₄in
(19mm)

Fig 12.28 The steel mortise clip. The clip allows a neat invisible fixing below the edge of timber rails. The 19mm deep mortises can be sloped or angled in the rail to give rake and shape where needed.

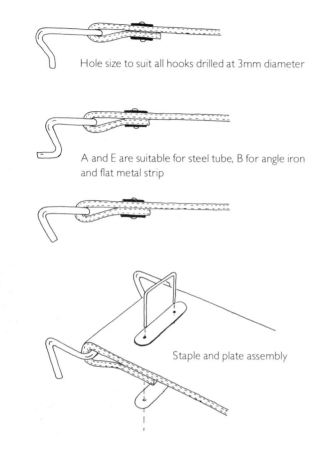

Hole size to suit all hooks drilled at 3mm diameter

A and E are suitable for steel tube, B for angle iron and flat metal strip

Staple and plate assembly

Fig 12.29 Hook fixings into metal frames.

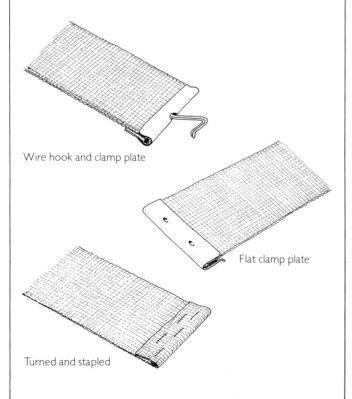

Wire hook and clamp plate

Flat clamp plate

Turned and stapled

Fig 12.30 Elastic woven webbings.

Tensioning

All resilient webbings are designed to be fixed under tension. The amount of tension can vary enormously ranging from 7 per cent to 100 per cent in some cases. Generally it will be found that elastic types require more stretch than do the laminated rubber webbings.

Some typical specifications for both types are given below:

Laminated rubber webbing
colours – beige, black and brown.
Width 2in (50mm)
Cut lengths or 50m rolls
Composition: natural and synthetic rubber, with fabric component, multi-filament
Rayon or nylon and cotton
Thickness approximately 2mm
Fabric cord, angle 43°

Woven elastic webbing
colours – brown, black or white.
Width 1⅛in (30mm) and 2in (50mm)
Composition: synthetic rubber warps

Polypropylene fibre weft
Thickness approximately 1.5mm.

Resilient webbing suspension is a simple and very versatile method of springing a chair seat or back. It is easily cut, stretched and fixed, and needs no special or expensive equipment. Webbing manufacturers recommend that attention is paid to the various fixings and that the best method of fixing is chosen to suit each different job or application. This type of upholstery suspension depends entirely for its success on secure and strong fixings and adequate numbers of webs spaced and tensioned correctly to suit the surrounding upholstery and its function.

Chair and settee seats, for example, take a tremendous pounding during an average life span. Approximately 80 per cent of a sitter's weight is placed on to a seat and a small percentage on to the chair back and arms. As a person sits down in a lounge chair, the force put on to the suspension can be as much as double the sitter's weight. As a good general guide not less than 50 per cent of a seat area should be covered by the webbing. Therefore spaces between webs should be equal to the width of the webbing being used.

In almost all cases the failure of resilient webbing suspension is caused by bad application of the webs and not by any weakness in the webbing itself. Likely causes of failure are:

1   Poor frame design, and the use of rails not strong enough to take the strain imparted by the suspension
2   Frame rails that are rough and do not have their inside edges removed
3   Fixings that are inadequate and poorly applied
4   Webbing densities too low, putting too much strain on too few webs
5   Underfilled upholstery, which results in feel-through and not enough spread of the load.

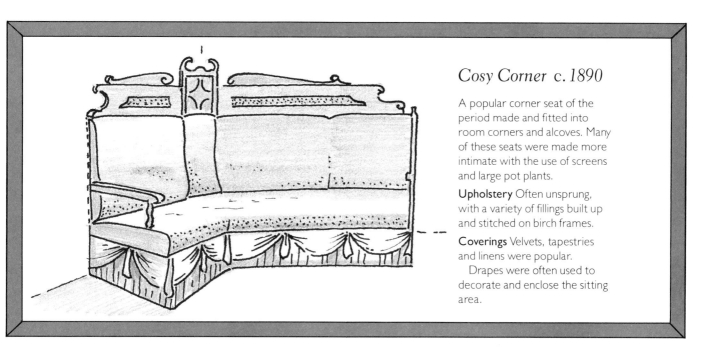

Cosy Corner c. 1890

A popular corner seat of the period made and fitted into room corners and alcoves. Many of these seats were made more intimate with the use of screens and large pot plants.

Upholstery Often unsprung, with a variety of fillings built up and stitched on birch frames.

Coverings Velvets, tapestries and linens were popular.

Drapes were often used to decorate and enclose the sitting area.

Selection of resilient webbing

To help the upholsterer and the upholstery designer select and use resilient webbings it is useful to know how this type of suspension behaves under different conditions and at different tensions.

Deflection

Deflection is the distance by which the underside of a cushion lowers when a seat is being used. The amount of deflection is determined by the initial tension at which the webbing is stretched on to a frame, the density of webbing in the seat area (which should not be less than 50 per cent), and the web pattern employed (see Fig 12.25). The width of the webbing selected and its type can also have some bearing on seat behaviour. Standard, superflex and elastic webs all have different characteristics, and the wide 2¼in (57mm) webs are much less elastic than the 1½in (38mm) widths, for example. Another factor which may affect the seat or back design is the span of the frame. Longer spans tend to produce greater deflections than shorter spans at specified tensions.

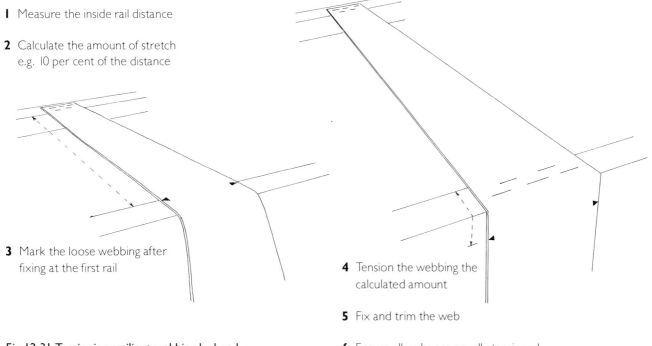

1 Measure the inside rail distance

2 Calculate the amount of stretch e.g. 10 per cent of the distance

3 Mark the loose webbing after fixing at the first rail

4 Tension the webbing the calculated amount

5 Fix and trim the web

6 Ensure all webs are equally tensioned

Fig 12.31 Tensioning resilient webbing by hand.

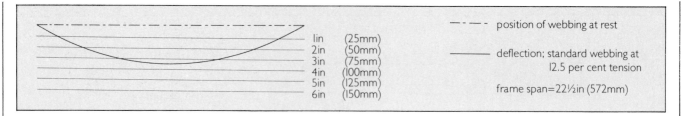

Fig 12.32 The chart shows standard Vitastretch webbing deflected by average weight and the area required below a typical seat span.

Methods of application

Webs applied from the front to the back of a seat have the advantage that the width and the weight of the sitter is distributed across all the straps by the cushion, so that the greatest load falls upon a large number of straps. Also, the cushion is free to rise and fall between the chair rails. A disadvantage is that a soft front edge cannot be treated using this method.

Webbing tensioned from side to side has the advantage that the chair can be given a soft front edge, and that the area of heaviest load occupies the rear half of the seat, where webs should be closer together and given more initial tension. Webs should be interlaced with overspans, which are very large or very small, and where very firm areas of support are needed. Generally, webbings for chair backs can be of the narrower type because loads are much less than in seats.

When webbing is placed from side to side in backs it is possible to create support in the lumbar region by the use of webs at slightly higher tensions or at higher density, while still allowing softness behind the shoulders.

It is usually recommended that where seat and back areas span more than 24in (610mm) that the interlacing method is used wherever possible. The chart in Fig 12.32 shows a typical deflection result using standard Vitastretch webbing tensioned at 12½ per cent over a frame span of 22½in (572mm).

Platforms and diaphragms

Flat, resilient platforms made from rubber and compositions of rubber and woven fabric are another form of chair suspension. These methods of springing are well suited to lightweight unit frames and for use on tubular steel structures. The smooth, flat area created by a diaphragm or platform works well in combination with foam units and foam cushions. The examples illustrated show corner-fixing methods, front to back fixings and side-fixing types ideal for use on curved and shaped framing. The fixings are four point, three point and two point, using special studs for diaphragms, and wire clips or staples for the fabric platforms.

Tensioning is generally much lower than for individual webbings because of their overall strength. Jigs and special tools are needed where large numbers are being fitted on a regular basis.

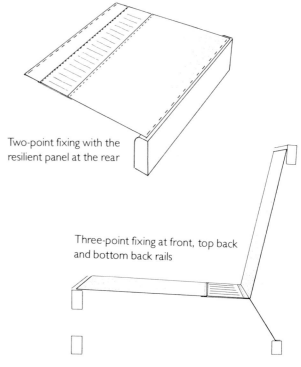

Two-point fixing with the resilient panel at the rear

Three-point fixing at front, top back and bottom back rails

Fig 12.34 Two versions of the Pirelli Fabweb platform.

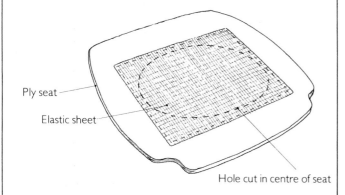

Fig 12.33 A simple woven elastic platform stretched and stapled over a plywood seat. The seat is upholstered and screwed down into a timber or metal chair frame.

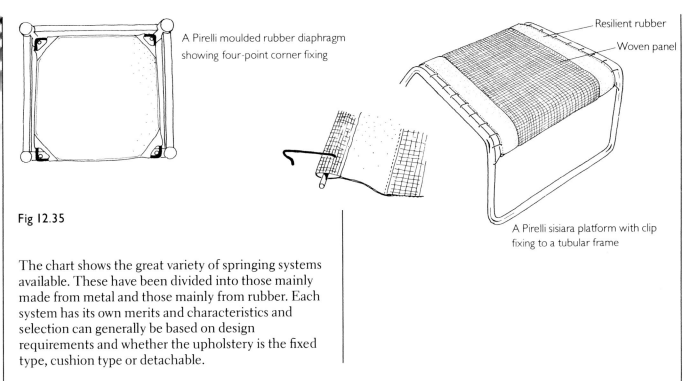

A Pirelli moulded rubber diaphragm showing four-point corner fixing

Resilient rubber

Woven panel

Fig 12.35

A Pirelli sisiara platform with clip fixing to a tubular frame

The chart shows the great variety of springing systems available. These have been divided into those mainly made from metal and those mainly from rubber. Each system has its own merits and characteristics and selection can generally be based on design requirements and whether the upholstery is the fixed type, cushion type or detachable.

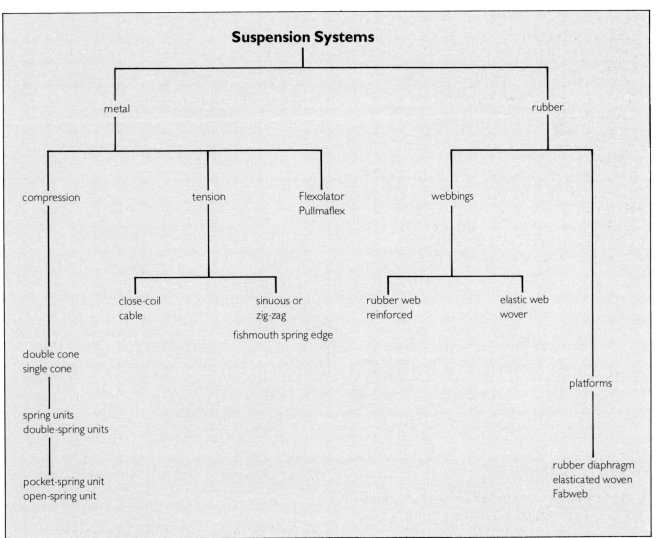

Suspension Systems

- metal
  - compression
    - double cone
    - single cone
    - spring units
    - double-spring units
    - pocket-spring unit
    - open-spring unit
  - tension
    - close-coil cable
    - sinuous or zig-zag
    - fishmouth spring edge
  - Flexolator Pullmaflex
- rubber
  - webbings
    - rubber web reinforced
    - elastic web wover
  - platforms
    - rubber diaphragm
    - elasticated woven
    - Fabweb

— *Chapter Thirteen* —
Traditional Techniques

From the middle of the seventeenth century the upholstery of chairs and seating took on a more structured form. The building and filling of padded areas slowly developed into the craft of traditional upholstery as we know it.

From the middle of the seventeenth century the upholstery of chairs and seating took on a more structured form. The building and filling of padded areas slowly developed into the craft of traditional upholstery as we know it. Contributions from European craftsmen influenced the way in which various natural materials and fillings were used and shaped to produce what is now widely known as the stitch up, or stitched-edge upholstery. Upholsterers used and developed these techniques to build and shape loose fillings to make up fixed pads, loose squabs, cushions and mattresses.

As in all craft work the basic skills and techniques must first be learnt and then practised until they can be done quickly and well. The results of repeated and steady practice are very rewarding as a series of skills is built up and knowledge is stored and remembered. This chapter can be used as a reference and a useful reminder. Watching an upholsterer at work is another valuable way in which the basic skills can be appreciated, while at the same time keeping a log book and filling it with sketches and notes.

A great deal can also be learned by stripping old pieces of upholstered furniture, providing that it is done carefully and in the correct sequence, and that the various methods and materials are noted down. Upholstery is one of the few crafts in which a piece of work can easily be dismantled to discover how it was built in the first place by a craftsman of another era.

BASIC TECHNIQUES

Webbing a frame
English and jute webbings are the traditional materials used to support most types of upholstery. These are

Fig 13.1 A traditional scroll-end sofa with bolster and seat cushion, all hand built and stitched up in scrim.

fixed and interlaced using a web strainer to produce a well-tensioned base. It is better to use too much webbing than not enough, and spacing of the webbing should be at least adequate for the job that it will perform.

A good general formula which will suit most types of work is to fix webs at 5in (125mm) centres, or in the case of seats, where most strain is likely, fix the webbing with spaces equal to the width of the webbing, for example 2in (50mm). Other than in very lightweight work, a minimum size tack of ½in (13mm) fine or improved should be used. Where stapling is preferred then ½in and ⅜in (13mm and 10mm) should be used for fixing, the longer staple used for frames where the timber is old and already full of tack holes (Figs 13.2 and 13.3.).

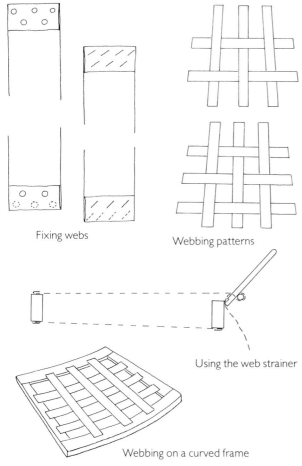

Fixing webs

Webbing patterns

Using the web strainer

Webbing on a curved frame

Fig 13.2

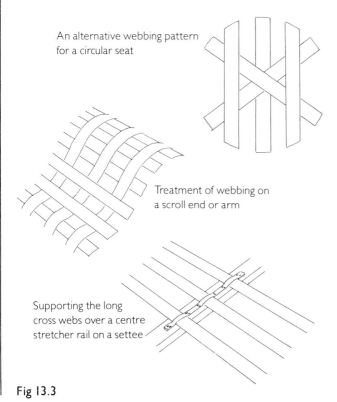

An alternative webbing pattern for a circular seat

Treatment of webbing on a scroll end or arm

Supporting the long cross webs over a centre stretcher rail on a settee

Fig 13.3

Lining up in hessian

Hessian is the first covering over webbing where a piece of work is simply top-stuffed and is unsprung. The hessian used is 10oz or 12oz weight, and is strained tightly in all directions. ½in (13mm) fine tacks or ⅜in (10mm) staples are used in most cases. Loose seats, top stuffed seats and inside arms are lined up in this way (Fig 13.4).

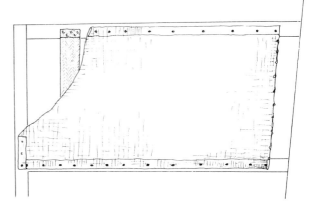

An inside arm lined with 10oz hessian: this should be pulled tight by hand and the edges turned and tacked

Fig 13.4 Lining up in hessian.

Knots

The slip knot and the half hitch
These two knots are used most often by the upholsterer, and should be practised until they can be done by feel, or literally with closed eyes. There are many occasions when the knots have to be tied quickly under a seat or inside the back of a chair where visibility is very restricted. The slip knot, which is very similar to the hangman's knot, is used at the beginning of most stitching and tying operations. It is the perfect starting point and not only fixes the twine or thread but also draws together the materials being sewn. In buttoning work the slip knot is used to fix and draw a button into place and hold it temporarily. As work proceeds the button can then be tightened or loosened on the slip knot as required.

The half hitch is used a great deal to lock-stitch a material and to finish off a row of stitching or sewing. Two half hitches together will seal and finish a job before the loose end is trimmed. These two knots are constantly used to start off and finish most stitching and tying operations (Fig 13.5).

Stuffing ties and stuffings

All loose stuffings in upholstery work are tied in with ties of twine. The ties are worked into the hessian with a 5in (125mm) curved needle or a springing needle. Where stuffings are applied directly on to timber then

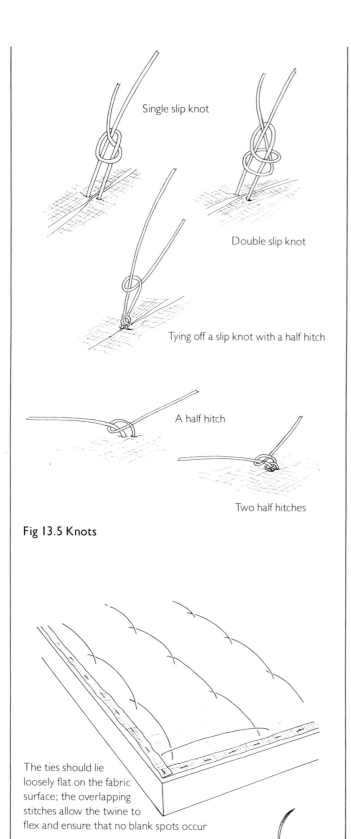

Single slip knot

Double slip knot

Tying off a slip knot with a half hitch

A half hitch

Two half hitches

Fig 13.5 Knots

The ties should lie loosely flat on the fabric surface; the overlapping stitches allow the twine to flex and ensure that no blank spots occur

Stuffing ties formed by back stitching at about 5in (125mm) spaces

Fig 13.6 Stuffing ties.

the ties are tacked down and left as raised loops. For example, on arm tops and arm pads (Fig 13.6).

Loose fillings such as curled hair, flocks and coir fibre are pushed under the ties in small handfuls to build an even, resilient padding. As the filling thickens it must be teased out with the fingers to make it even and free

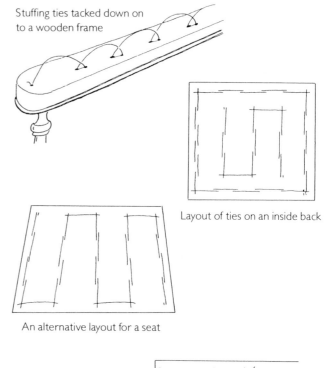

Stuffing ties tacked down on to a wooden frame

Layout of ties on an inside back

An alternative layout for a seat

Layout of ties on a border

Fig 13.7

from any lumps. Applying fillings to a large area can be tiring work, but creating an even layer is essential; the more the stuffing is worked and teased, the better will be the finished results. It is good policy to run stuffing ties vertically on chair arms and inside backs as this will lessen the likelihood of the fillings slipping down at some time in the future (Fig 13.7).

Temporary tacking
This is the method used to hold down linings and covers temporarily at intermediate stages during upholstery. Temporary tacks can be applied quickly, and removed easily when adjustments are necessary until a piece of work is ready for final tacking. Temporary stapling is much more difficult and rather slow in comparison. In traditional upholstery temporary tacks are used continuously throughout a job, particularly at corners during pleating, around facings and in hide work or any other difficult coverings (Fig 13.8).

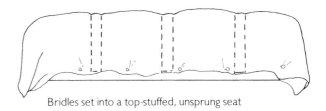

Bridles set into a top-stuffed, unsprung seat

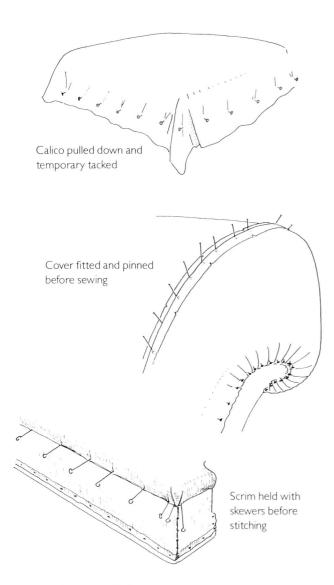

Calico pulled down and
temporary tacked

Cover fitted and pinned
before sewing

Scrim held with
skewers before
stitching

Fig 13.8 Temporary fixings.

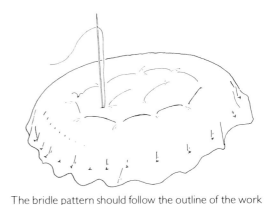

The bridle pattern should follow the outline of the work

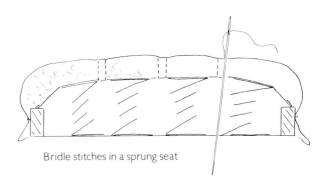

Bridle stitches in a sprung seat

Fig 13.9 Bridle stitching.

Skewering

Upholsterers' skewers and long pins are used in the same way as temporary tacks. There are many occasions when it is necessary to hold scrims, linings and fabrics in place while they are adjusted, checked or matched before fixing by stitching or tacking. This is good practice and allows for the work to be constantly checked and adjusted before permanent fixing. Pins and skewers are also used to hold covers while they are matched or fitted around edges or to shapes prior to sewing by hand or machine. Pleats, folds and turnings can also be temporarily held in the same way. This helps in the forming of good shaped work and the aligning of joints and folds (Fig 13.8).

Bridle stitching

As the name implies, bridle stitches are put into traditional work to hold and stabilise stuffing and scrims. Once the bridle stitches are in place edge building can continue. Temporary tacks or skewers can

be safely removed, and the bridled scrim will remain square and tightly in place. Bridle stitches are formed with a long running stitch, using a two-point needle and a medium-grade twine. The stitch begins and ends on the top surface of the scrim, starting with a slip knot and finishing with half hitches (Fig 13.9). The pattern of the bridles should roughly follow the outline of the piece of work, the spacing of the rows is best kept at about 4in (100mm), or closer on small pieces of work.

After the bridling has been stitched in and before tying off, the stitch is tightened down by working along the ties, lightly compressing the fillings. When an even, flat surface has been created with the stitches all at the same depth then the last tie can be looped back and tied off. Some examples of bridle patterns are shown in Fig 13.10.

Where a seat or back is to have surface shape then the careful placing of the bridle stitches will help to maintain the shape required. The tightness and depth of the stitches can also be adjusted to produce shape.

On unsprung work, bridles run through to the webbed base, but on sprung areas the stitches stop at the hessian level and should not be taken through the springing or down to the webbings. If this is done then the bridles will simply slacken when the springs are eventually compressed in use (Fig 13.9).

Regulating

The regulator has many uses in traditional handwork, but its main purpose is for the moving and regulating of fillings. For example, as a stitched edge is being built the stuffing can be moved forward into the edge with the regulator before stitching progresses. This will help to strengthen and harden an edge. Continuous and careful regulating along an edge can often lessen the need for large amounts of stitching, particularly where a small roll-over edge is being made on an inside back.

At least two sizes of regulator should be kept, a heavy gauge and a medium size and, for very fine regulating through linings and covers, an old, broken, smooth-point needle or an upholstery skewer – both will do the job well. A regulator is also very useful as a holding tool while scrim or linings are being folded and pleated at corners and where access is difficult (Fig 13.11).

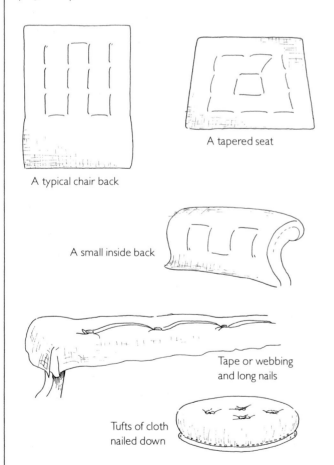

A typical chair back

A tapered seat

A small inside back

Tape or webbing and long nails

Tufts of cloth nailed down

Alternative methods are used when bridles cannot be sewn through

Fig 13.10 Bridling patterns.

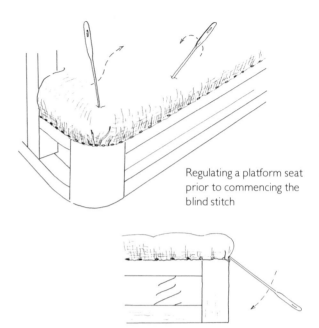

Regulating a platform seat prior to commencing the blind stitch

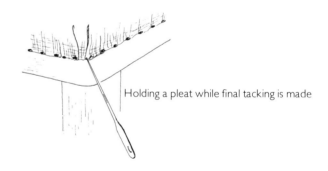

Using the regulator to firm an edge and produce a good shape

Holding a pleat while final tacking is made

Fig 13.11 Uses of the regulator.

The stitched edge

Stitched-edge upholstery was first developed and used by upholsterers in the eighteenth century. It began as a roll edge in which a small amount of loose filling was rolled in linen scrim, and tacked neatly around the frame edges on French and English chairs. The roll was held down and made firm by a series of stitches sewn in at an angle along the edge of a seat or back. This created an edge height above the timber rail and produced upholstery with a flatter surface and a border. Covers could then be pulled over or bordered to give a sharper and more angular appearance. The more rows of stitching added to the edge, the firmer and higher the seat above the rail (Fig 13.12).

From this technique developed the well seat, with a high edge all around the seat and a dish or well shape created in the centre. The well was then filled separately and created a soft comfortable area in a seat or a chair back. Often the centre was tufted or buttoned as a decoration and to hold the fillings in place.

Turkey or Turkish Chair
c. 1850

An interesting style introduced at the time when stuffover work was again becoming popular. The new coil springs were used to full avantage in seats and backs, and sometimes in the base of the chair behind the long fringes to provide a rocking action.

Coverings Heavy and usually in dark colours, for example wool plush cut moquette, chenille and machine-made tapestry panels.

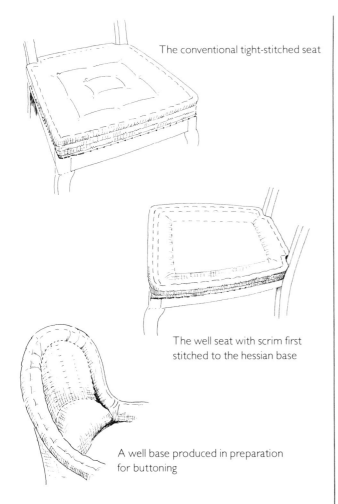

The conventional tight-stitched seat

The well seat with scrim first stitched to the hessian base

A well base produced in preparation for buttoning

Fig 13.12

A firmer, more compact seat was developed from this as an alternative in which the first stuffing was laid all over a seat, covered in scrim and then stitched around the edges. As the edges were turned in and stitched up, the scrim became stretched and taut. The top or second stuffing was then tied in over the scrim as a second or softer layer. Linings and covers could then be added. Today both methods are used in hand-built traditional upholstery.

The well-seat technique is mostly used only as a foundation for buttoning or to create a soft back rest, or a platform for a cushion. The firmer two-layer method is preferred for most other work. There are two basic stitches used to form an edge of this type, a blind stitch and a top stitch. The blind stitch is applied first and creates a firm foundation for the subsequent rows of top stitching. The blind stitch, so called because it only shows on the edge face of the upholstery and does not pierce the top of the scrim, pulls small amounts of stuffing outwards as the stitch is tightened. Two or more rows of blind stitching can be used, one above the other when a high or very firm edge is to be built.

Fine flax stitching twine and a straight two-point needle are needed for this type of work. The stuffing is first regulated with a steel regulator and the first tie put in with a slip knot. The blind stitch is then worked along the edge, beginning with a left-hand end and working to the right. A good firm pull is required after each stitch and a leather stitching glove can be used to protect the hand from the sharpness of the twine (Fig 13.13). When a blind stitch is completed the edge can be regulated again to improve its evenness.

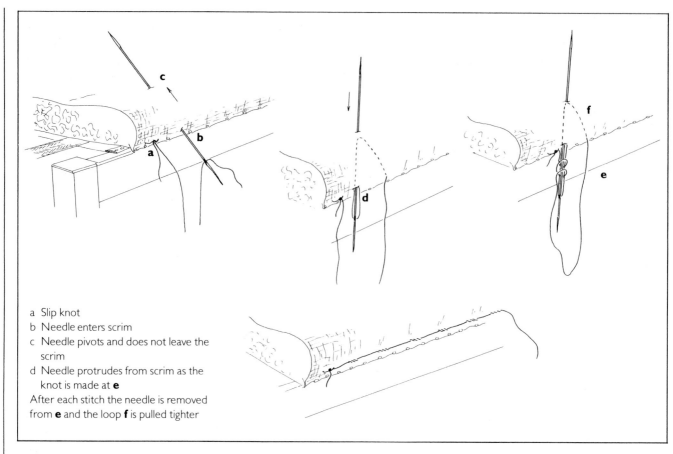

a Slip knot
b Needle enters scrim
c Needle pivots and does not leave the
   scrim
d Needle protrudes from scrim as the
   knot is made at **e**
After each stitch the needle is removed
from **e** and the loop **f** is pulled tighter

Fig 13.13 The blind stitch.

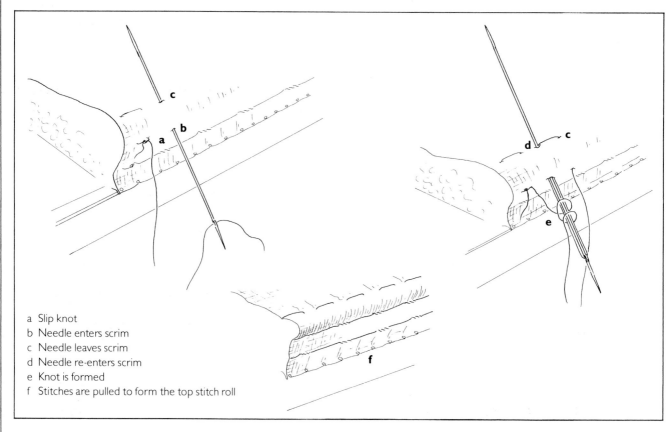

a Slip knot
b Needle enters scrim
c Needle leaves scrim
d Needle re-enters scrim
e Knot is formed
f Stitches are pulled to form the top stitch roll

Fig 13.14 The top stitch.

Top stitching follows the blind stitching and its function is to pinch and hold the upper part of an edge into a sharp, firm shape. The more rows of top stitching that are applied, usually the sharper the edge becomes. Two rows of top stitch are normal on an average edge, a third or fourth row would only be used on very large or high edges. A top stitch is formed in the same way as a blind stitch except that the stitches are closer together and the twine pierces through the scrim on the top of the edge and shows as an even dotted line on the surface (Fig 13.14). As it is tightened the stitch pinches the packed scrim into a neat sharp edge. The size of the roll is determined by the positioning of the needle and the amount of scrim taken in by the needle.

Edge types
Several different stitched edge types, and shapes are possible using the blind- and top-stitched technique.

Roll edge
A soft rolling edge can be built using one or two blind stitches only, and no top stitch. This kind of edge is suitable for use on chair arms, and backs where fillings are relatively thin. The stitches are used simply to firm the edge and leave a lightweight roll (Fig 13.15).

Similarly, a top stitch can be used on its own with no blind, providing the edge is regulated well to move the stuffing up to the edge; this is then captured and held by one row of top stitching. This treatment is ideal for thin-padded panels usually surrounded by show-wood.

A roll edge can also be created with one blind and one top row of stitching, by keeping the top stitch very large and taking in a good amount of scrim and filling. The surface row should be set well back from the edge and regulating is again necessary to produce an even, well-shaped roll.

Feather edge
This type of edge is exactly the opposite to a roll edge. It is intended to be very sharp and very firm so that facings and borders can be trimmed up to it. Such an edge will remain as a visible sharp line supporting the

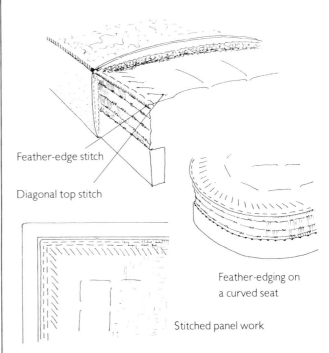

Feather-edge stitch

Diagonal top stitch

Feather-edging on a curved seat

Stitched panel work

Fig 13.16(a) Feather-edge stitching combined with diagonal top stitching.

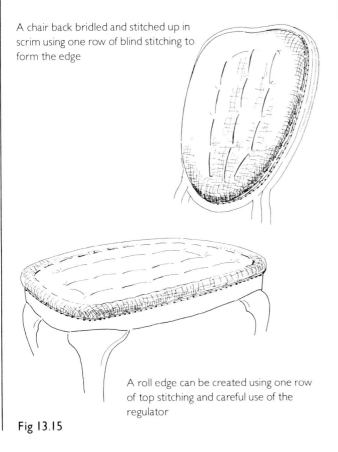

A chair back bridled and stitched up in scrim using one row of blind stitching to form the edge

A roll edge can be created using one row of top stitching and careful use of the regulator

Fig 13.15

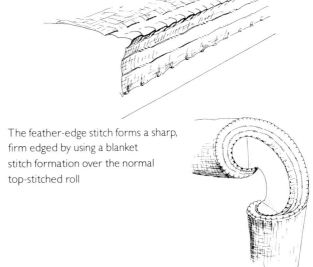

The feather-edge stitch forms a sharp, firm edged by using a blanket stitch formation over the normal top-stitched roll

Fig 13.16(b) Feather-edge stitching.

covering and trimmings. Typical applications are at arm fronts, seat fronts and cushion edges, where a permanent firm edge is needed. It is regularly used in leather work on club chairs, Chesterfield arms and leather-covered squabs.

The feather-edge stitch is worked around an edge after it has been built in the standard way, with two blind and two top rows of stitching. The small roll is created with a small, tight top stitch, or the second top-stitch row is pinched in half with an overedge blanket stitch or another small fine top stitch. Immediately the stitch is applied, the point of the edge becomes tight and firm; the closer the stitches, the tighter the feather edge is made. Stitches spaced ¾ in (19mm) apart give a standard feather edge, and when spaced at ⅜ in (10mm) the edge becomes very firm.

Creating a good feather edge depends very much on a sound, well-shaped standard edge being built in the first place. This type of edge requires some practice and should be tried out on small areas of work such as arm fronts and arm pads or small stuff-over dining-chair seats. If the top-stitched edge is weak or lacks filling then adding a feather edge stitch will not improve the line or shape (Fig 13.16).

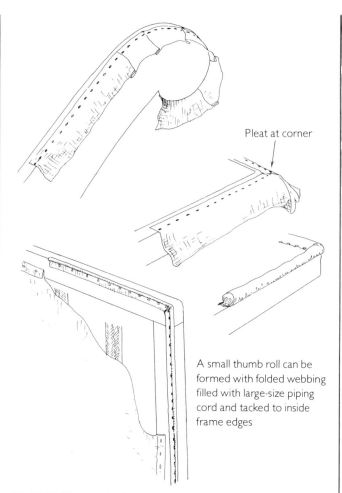

Pleat at corner

A small thumb roll can be formed with folded webbing filled with large-size piping cord and tacked to inside frame edges

Fig 13.18 Pleating the hessian is necessary when shaped and curved rails are dugged.

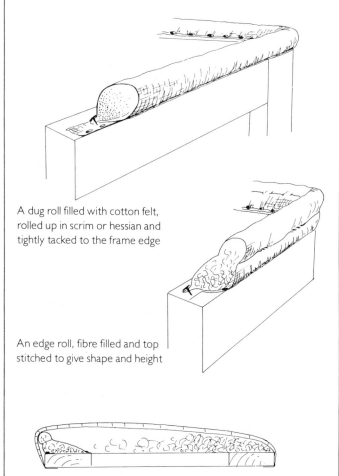

A dug roll filled with cotton felt, rolled up in scrim or hessian and tightly tacked to the frame edge

An edge roll, fibre filled and top stitched to give shape and height

A loose seat with edge roll built along the front

Fig 13.17 Dug rolls and edge rolls.

Dug roll and edge roll

A dug roll is a simplified version of the edge roll produced by upholsterers to make a relatively shallow edge on the inside edges of seats, arms and chair backs. The roll has no stitching and is created by rolling up small amounts of stuffing in hessian or scrim along a timber edge and then fixing with staples or tacks. A variety of edges can be built in this way using different materials and fillings. To form a sharp, upstanding edge, a row of top or through stitches can be added to form an edge roll (Fig 13.17). The stitches will add sharpness and height to the roll. Very small and firm dug rolls can be made by folding webbing in half and inserting fillings or piping cords, then tacking down along the edges of arms, wings and small seats (Fig 13.18).

Filling for the dug roll and the edge roll can be coir fibre, curled hair, felts or flocks, or any other loose filling available. Compressed paper is used in the ready-made dug rolls, which can be bought on the roll and cut to length ready for use as instant dug fillings. Sizes range from small-finger size to 1½ in (38mm) in diameter.

Buttoning

Deep buttoning and surface buttoning have been used by upholsterers since the Victorian era to fix and decorate fabrics into chair seats and backs. Much earlier work of this kind, particularly in shaped upholstery, had tufts and ties rather than buttons. The tufts were made from pieces of leather, gathered fabric or wound wool. Tufting and tying in was an essential part of traditional upholstery, particularly in cushion and mattress making. This ensured that loose fillings were held in place and would not distort or become lumpy. Tufted and buttoned upholstery was also associated with coach trimming. The seating in rail coaches, horse-drawn coaches and cars was trimmed and tufted on ash framing and later on to plywoods. Much of this work was in hide to withstand the rigours of extreme temperatures and rough use by travellers. During the second half of the nineteenth century buttoned upholstery flourished and Victorian craftsmen excelled in the buttoning and fluting of shaped work.

It was during the 1950s that the surface buttoning of upholstery again became fashionable, partly as a decorative feature and also as a method of holding fabrics into compound shaped work. Buttons also increased in size and shape, from the small Victorian buttons the size of a farthing to large machine-made buttons some 2in (50mm) across. In good reproduction work and the restoration of antique pieces, deep buttoning is still done by hand using small buttons (size 22–24) and a mixture of traditional and modern materials.

The buttoning process begins with the marking out of a prepared base. The base may be a well type, which is the method usually chosen for backs, or the tight-stitched foundation which gives a much firmer job. In both cases a centre line is drawn vertically on to the scrim, giving an accurate starting point from which all other measurements can be taken. The buttoning pattern is then worked out and temporarily marked by sticking tacks into the scrim and, at the same time, measuring the spaces until a suitable arrangement is found.

There are a few general rules which apply to most button layouts and will help to obtain good balanced results. The outer buttons on all sides of the pattern should not be placed too close to the edges. The distance usually depends on the size and shape of the piece of work. As a very general rule 2½ to 3½in (63mm to 90mm) is average spacing. On the other hand buttoning which is set too far in from the edges will look lost and unprofessional (Fig 13.19).

The shape of the layout should, as far as possible, conform to the general proportions and shape of the piece being buttoned. In the same way the size of the diamonds should be in keeping with the overall size of the area being buttoned. The following examples will

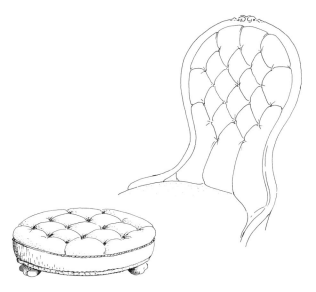

Fig 13.19 Deep-buttoned work which shows how the arrangement of buttons relates to the size and shape of the pieces.

give a useful guide: 4½in × 2½in (114mm × 63mm) and 5in × 3in (125mm × 75mm) are small diamonds and will suit dining chairs and sewing chairs. 6in × 4in (150mm × 100mm) diamonds are about medium sized and would be correct for larger seats and backs of lounge chairs, *chaises longues* and headboards for beds. Anything above these sizes, for example 7in × 5in (175mm × 125mm) or 8in × 6in (200mm × 150mm), would look well on sofas, settees and large wing chairs. Fig 13.20 shows how a diamond buttoning pattern is marked out on to a prepared base.

When a suitable pattern is set out with the tacks pushed into the scrim, permanent marks can be made with chalk or felt-tip pen. All the button position marks should then be transferred to the back of the upholstery where the button twines will eventually be tied. Where a tight-stitched base is being used, the scrim can then be cut at each mark. The cuts should be large enough for a hole to be made into the first stuffing of approximately 1in (25mm) across (Fig 13.20).

When all the cuts are made and the holes cleared in the first stuffing, the second stuffing is tied in over the scrim. This can be curled hair and cotton felt, loose wool flock or curled hair and wool felt. If possible and if time allows the new top stuffing should be left to settle and condense for a day before buttoning begins. Alternatively, a heavy weight may be laid over the area to be buttoned for an hour or two. If a well base is being used as a foundation, as is more often the case, the well should be filled to a good density and to a depth of about 3in (75mm). Cotton or wool felt makes a good soft topping before the cover (Fig 13.21).

The second part of the preparation work is to measure for and cut the upholstery fabric, and then

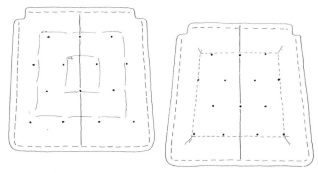

Two seats with the centre line drawn in tacks placed at the button positions

After marking out, the cuts are made into the scrim to produce deep holes in the first stuffing

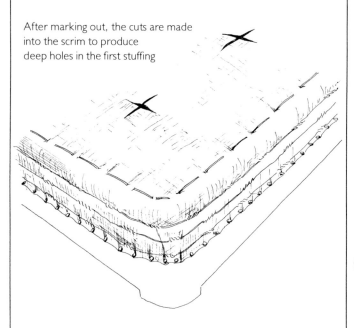

Fig 13.20 Marking out for deep buttoning.

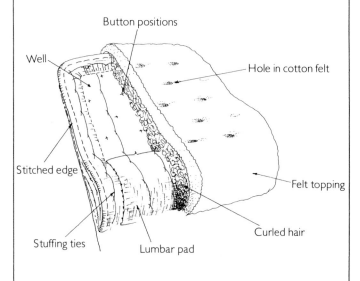

Button positions

Well

Hole in cotton felt

Stitched edge

Felt topping

Curled hair

Stuffing ties

Lumbar pad

Fig 13.21 A chair back prepared for deep buttoning

mark out the reverse side with the button pattern. There are two methods commonly used to take the measurements for the cover. Using a linen tape measure, the length and width of the cover required can be found by laying the tape across the prepared top stuffing from one tacking point to the other. The tape is then gently pushed down into each hole allowing a generous depth at each button position. The line of holes chosen for these measurements should be those with the most button positions, ensuring the maximum length required. The width measurement is taken in the same way. A little extra should be added to these measurements to allow for pulling and tacking down (Fig 13.22).

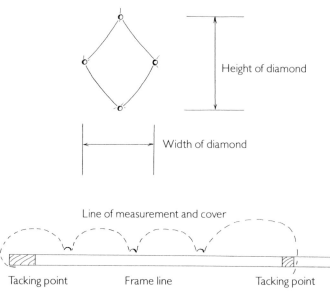

Height of diamond

Width of diamond

Line of measurement and cover

Tacking point   Frame line   Tacking point

Fig 13.22

The second method is to measure directly from one tacking point to the other and then add a buttoning allowance figure for every space between buttons along the line being measured. For example, 1¼in (32mm) is a typical average allowance and this should be added to the direct measurement once for every space between buttons (Fig 13.23).

The cover can then be cut out and laid face down ready for marking the button positions. A vertical centre line is drawn on the back of the cover, and this will match up exactly with the centre line previously drawn on the chair scrim. Before button positions can be marked the buttoning allowance must be made. This allowance is important and is made in order to give depth to the buttons and produce the pleats or folds which form the diamond pattern.

The amount of allowance made depends on the depth of buttoning required and the size of the individual diamond patterns. With experience and practice, buttoning allowances will become familiar and easily calculated. The allowances for deep

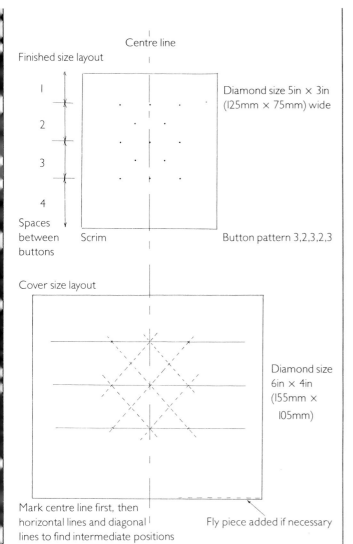

Centre line

Finished size layout

Diamond size 5in × 3in (125mm × 75mm) wide

Spaces between buttons

Scrim

Button pattern 3,2,3,2,3

Cover size layout

Diamond size 6in × 4in (155mm × 105mm)

Mark centre line first, then horizontal lines and diagonal lines to find intermediate positions

Fly piece added if necessary

Fig 13.23

first, and steadily work out from this point. Care must be taken not to disturb or break the wadding or felt topping, and to ease each button carefully into place to about half depth.

A slip knot is made in each twine to hold the buttons at their temporary depth. Fig 13.24 shows the method used to hold the slip knot at the back of the work. When all buttons are in place the diamond pleating can be adjusted and folded using the flat end of a regulator or dolly stick. Pleats should always be turned to face downwards on a chair back and forwards on a chair seat. Temporary tacks or skewers can now be used to set the cover to the frame, and the outer pleats held in place. This is followed by another pull on each button twine to tighten down the buttons just enough to ensure that each diamond appears smooth and full. Further adjustments will be necessary with the regulator and the fingers to line up all the pleating and complete the outer fixings before the final tacking off (Fig 13.25).

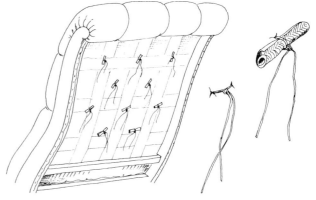

Fig 13.24 Holding the slip knot at the back of the work.

buttoning are simply the difference between the diamond size on the scrim and the diamond size measured over the stuffing and down into the holes. This extra is then added to the width and height of the diamonds when they are marked on to the reverse side of the cover.

The following gives some typical diamond sizes and their allowances:

Scrim size diamond	Allowance	Cover size diamond	Approx. depth of stuffing
4½in × 2½in (114mm × 63mm)	1in (25mm)	5½in × 3½in (140mm × 90mm)	1¾in (45mm)
5in × 3in (125mm × 75mm)	1¼in (32mm)	6¼in × 4¼in (160mm × 108mm)	2in (50mm)
6in × 4in (150mm × 100mm)	1½in (38mm)	7½in × 5½in (190mm × 140mm)	2½in (63mm)
7in × 5in (175mm × 125mm)	1¾in (45mm)	8¾in × 6¾in (222mm × 170mm)	3in (75mm)

When all the marking out is complete buttoning can begin. It is usual to put the buttons on the centre line

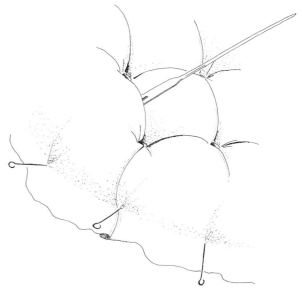

Fig 13.25 Completing the outer fixings.

Direct 'fingering-in' method

When the process of buttoning has become familiar, and the manipulating and folding of different fabrics can be worked with some confidence, then a more direct and much quicker method of buttoning can be used. Most experienced upholsterers are able to rely on their judgement and feel for fabric and filling, and for putting in deep buttoning on a prepared base. Almost all upholstery fabrics have a grain or a pattern surface which can be used to advantage to keep the work balanced, square and to an even depth.

The base or foundation is carefully prepared in the usual way, with button positions marked and holes produced in the top stuffing. The fabric is then measured for and cut, but not marked out except perhaps for a centre line. However, if a patterned cover is being used then a centre line is usually obvious and can be used to start off the first buttons. Preparation of the base for this method is very important so that the button holes can be found easily and quickly. The middle diamond is produced first by fingering in the fabric into the four holes. At the same time a check should be made that enough cover has been allowed to reach the tacking off points. When a satisfactory diamond shape has been created, the two vertical buttons and the two horizontal buttons can be tied in and pulled to half depth.

Pleating should begin immediately and then continue as the remaining buttons are fingered in and tied. The pattern should gradually build up from the centre by pleating, fingering the cover into the hole and then buttoning in. Some upholstery fabrics will fold and lay easily into place, while others may be difficult and will require more careful and consistent working.

When all the buttons have been adjusted to depth and tightened, the outer pleating can be skewered in place. It is often necessary, when using the direct method, to make adjustments at this stage. Any buttons which are out of line will have to be quickly removed and repositioned using fresh twine. Tacking off is normally completed before the button twines are finally knotted and trimmed.

Alternative buttoning patterns

Fig 13.26 shows three alternative layouts which can be used in chair backs to produce effective patterns:

1   The centre row of buttons is left out, to create short flutes
2   A row of half diamonds with long pleats radiating vertically
3   Diamonds which reduce in size to suit a waisted frame.

Vandyking

The jointing of leather by hand in a zig-zag line in buttoning work was traditionally called vandyking. But today the term is more generally used to describe the sewn joint used to widen any covering in buttoning

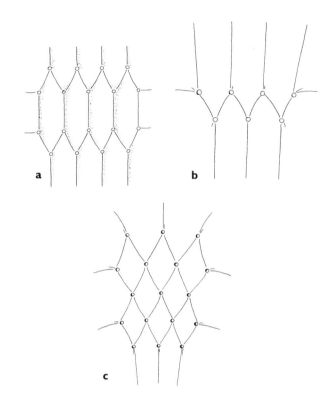

Fig 13.26 Diamond buttoning patterns.

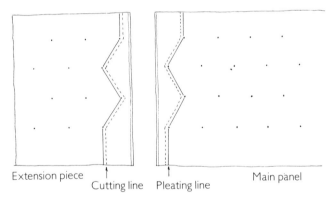

Extension piece   Cutting line   Pleating line   Main panel

The join should be hand sewn or machine sewn before buttoning begins

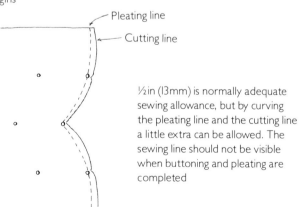

Pleating line

Cutting line

½in (13mm) is normally adequate sewing allowance, but by curving the pleating line and the cutting line a little extra can be allowed. The sewing line should not be visible when buttoning and pleating are completed

Fig 13.27 A vandyked joint is used to widen fabrics for deep buttoning.

work. The join follows the line of pleating between buttons, and once the buttoning is in place the joint line is no longer visible.

There are two methods commonly used to prepare the join. The main panel of covering is marked out alongside the extension piece, so that both relate to each other and line up. A chalk line is then drawn between buttons and extends up and down to the outer edges of the cloth. A second line is then drawn on the waste side of the first line to give the same allowance and the cutting line. When the waste is cut off the two pieces should marry together, and can be sewn up by hand or by machine (Fig 13.17). The second method gives more waste allowance and is used when the joint is being laid in by hand, and not sewn. This method relies on the tension of the buttoning to keep the join in place.

Fluting

Fluted upholstery is sometimes called channel work and describes separately filled sections. The sections are divided by hand- or machine-sewn seams. Each section of flute is separately filled to produce a strongly defined surface pattern. Fluted upholstery design can be used to interesting effect on chair backs, cushions and bed headboards (Fig 13.28).

A fluted panel is made up of a base cloth of hessian or calico, a layer of soft filling and a top cover. The panel can either be built directly on to a ready sprung or first-stuffed base, or machine-made then filled and applied as a pre-formed component.

The first method is basically a hand-built process. The prepared base is marked out to the fluted design using chalk or pen with strong clear lines. A row of stuffing ties is stitched in along the centre of each channel. The reverse side of the cover is then marked with the flute lines with the addition of a fullness allowance and a sewing allowance. An average fullness allowance is 1in (25mm) or ⅝in (16mm) if shallower flutes are preferred. A sewing allowance is also added and this is normally ⅜in to ½in (10mm to 13mm). Fig 13.29 shows the marking out method.

Fluted designs may be straight lines or a series of curved lines. The lines may run vertically, horizontally or in rare cases diagonally to produce effective panelling.

Sewing the cover in place should commence at the centre of the work by filling the centre flute and

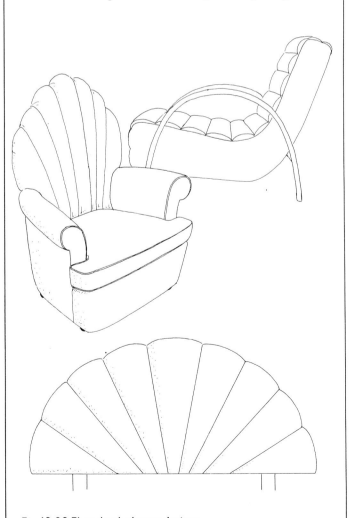

Fig 13.28 Fluted upholstery designs.

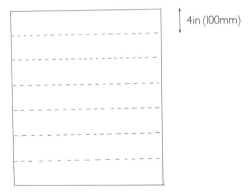

4in (100mm)

Flute lines drawn on a base

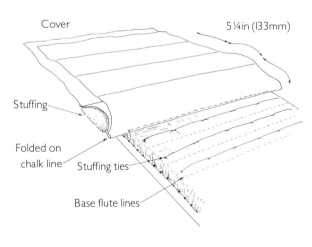

Cover

5¼in (133mm)

Stuffing

Folded on chalk line

Stuffing ties

Base flute lines

Fig 13.29 Marking out for fluted upholstery.

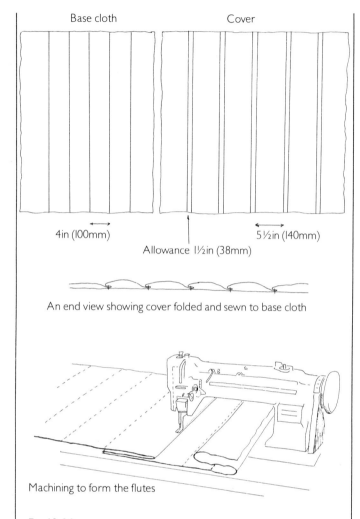

Base cloth   Cover

4in (100mm)   5½in (140mm)

Allowance 1½in (38mm)

An end view showing cover folded and sewn to base cloth

Machining to form the flutes

Fig 13.30

positioning the cover by folding on the flute lines and pinning in place. Both sides of the centre flute are sewn in using a small running stitch or a slip stitch. Working out from the middle, the other flutes can be filled and sewn. At the outer edge the last flutes are filled and tacked off to the required finish. The flute ends should be well filled and tightly strained to improve the crispness and line of the panel. Pulling should be concentrated along the seams to produce good results. If a pre-sewn and filled panel is to be made, it is produced off the job and then fitted and fixed into place over a first stuffing.

Making up the panel begins with a base cloth of reasonably stiff hessian or calico which is cut and accurately marked out with the flute lines. The cover is cut a little larger to include the allowances for fullness and sewing (Fig 13.30). The flute lines are marked out on the reverse side of the cover using white chalk or tailor's crayon. The spaces between the lines will be approximately 1in to 1½in (25mm to 38mm) wider than those marked on the base cloth, depending on the depth of fluting to be produced. Base cloth and cover

are then machine sewn together by folding on the lines and machining to the matching lines on the base (Fig 13.30). Sewing begins on the left hand end of the base cloth and continues across the panel until all the flutes are machined down.

Each individual flute is then filled with a ready-made strip of filling. The filling can be skin wadding rolled up to the required thickness, cotton felt cut into strips and layered, or polyester fibre, which is rolled or layered. These three are all fairly soft; if a more substantial filling is needed to give more depth and bulk then curled hair can be teased out and laid evenly between the two thicknesses of cotton or wool felt.

The various fillings are inserted into the flutes with fluting stick. This is simply a piece of ¼in (6mm) plywood cut ½in (13mm) narrower than the flute being filled and at least 6in (150mm) longer than the panel. (See Chapter 4, Fig 4.12.) When the panel is complete it can be stapled or tacked into place over a ready-made base. In fluting work the base should contain any springing required and be upholstered up to the first-stuffing stage. The fluted panel takes the place of a top stuffing or second stuffing.

Curved fluting

Where fluted areas remain in straight parallel lines, filling and making up is relatively easy. However, curved flute work can present problems, and will need more careful handling. In many cases sewing the cover down to its base will be worked along an inside curve and sometimes on the full bias of the cloth. Puckering and distortion may occur with some fabric types. Adjustment and varying the density of filling should correct this, but is much easier when hand building than on machine-sewn panels.

The filling of curved flutes may also be difficult on

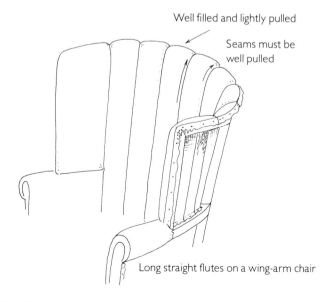

Well filled and lightly pulled

Seams must be well pulled

Long straight flutes on a wing-arm chair

Fig 13.31 Pulling and fixing the flutes.

pre-made fluting, particularly if the flutes narrow towards their base. It is possible to use a shaped fluting stick purpose-made for each job or alternatively each flute may be filled during the sewing operation. This will work reasonably well providing that the panel is not too big or if a long-arm sewing machine is available. Figs 13.31 and 13.32 show some of the alternative treatments used in flute work.

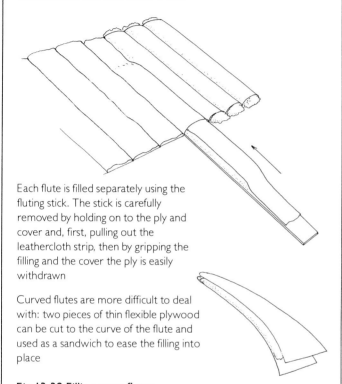

Each flute is filled separately using the fluting stick. The stick is carefully removed by holding on to the ply and cover and, first, pulling out the leathercloth strip, then by gripping the filling and the cover the ply is easily withdrawn

Curved flutes are more difficult to deal with: two pieces of thin flexible plywood can be cut to the curve of the flute and used as a sandwich to ease the filling into place

Fig 13.32 Filling sewn flutes.

ORDER OF WORKING

Each traditional piece of upholstery that is undertaken must be assessed and dealt with according to its particular design, shape and function. In the case of chair work the sequence in which the upholstery is built on to the frame is a very set process. It applies to most conventionally-shaped chairs and settees. The more recent the piece, the more likely there may be a change in the standard method of working.

The average armchair or wing chair should be dealt with by completing the inside first, then the outside:

1 Upholster and cover the inside of the wings and arms first
2 Put in the inside back and its covering
3 Build and upholster the seat
4 Apply trimmings such as piping or ruche to the edges if desired
5 Upholster the outside wings and arms
6 Cover the outside back
7 The outsides complete, turn the chair over and fix the bottom edges
8 Add a bottom lining of hessian or black cloth.

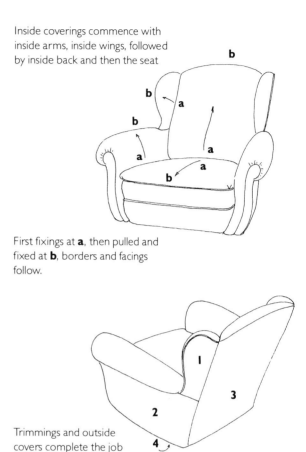

Inside coverings commence with inside arms, inside wings, followed by inside back and then the seat

First fixings at **a**, then pulled and fixed at **b**, borders and facings follow.

Trimmings and outside covers complete the job

Fig 13.33

This method of working is practised by most upholsterers and will be second nature to them. It allows the upholsterer to work easily and freely without being obstructed at tuckaways, and makes for easier and more accurate cutting. There is, of course, always the exception. It may sometimes be necessary to upholster a job completely in calico using the normal methods and then to cover the chair in its top cover, repeating the same sequence again. This would be normal practice when a chair is not being completely stripped but just recovered with perhaps a new top stuffing. Some traditional work may well be partly KD (knockdown), which simply means that an arm or a back rest is detachable. These have to be almost fully upholstered and then fixed to the main frame with bolts or dowels, before being trimmed and finished. Some examples of this type are ottomans with hinged lids, couches with detachable back rests, or adjustable armchairs – of which there are many different kinds.

Loose cushions in seats and backs are usually measured for, cut and made up as soon as the inside covering is completed. This allows for adjustments where necessary before outsides are fixed. However, if only reversible seat cushions are needed these can easily be dealt with last.

Cutting

The cutting and fitting of covers and linings on chairs and settees can be one of the most difficult areas of upholstery. All upholsterers will no doubt remember how they have had to learn by their mistakes or their near misses. In most instances, if a wrong cut is made, there is usually some way of overcoming the problem without actually having to replace an expensive piece of fabric.

With care and practice the art of cutting and manipulating fabrics is soon learnt. At the same time, the reaction of different types of cover to being cut and stretched is equally important. Leather, for example, works and cuts very differently to a piece of cotton chintz, and the difference has to be appreciated. Some fabrics fray very easily while some will tear with very little resistance. The whole range of upholstery coverings is very wide, but generally it can be said that providing a covering is recommended for use in

a The tongue
b The stuffing rail
c The arm front

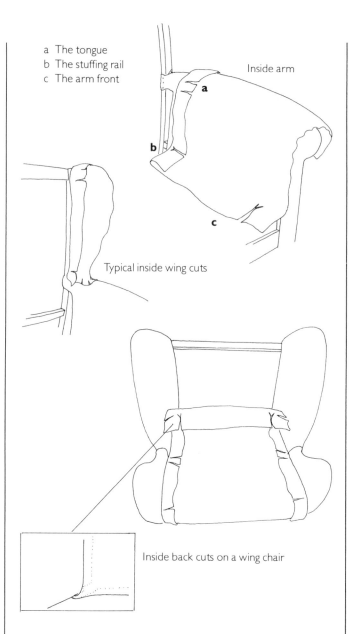

Typical inside wing cuts

Inside back cuts on a wing chair

Fig 13.35

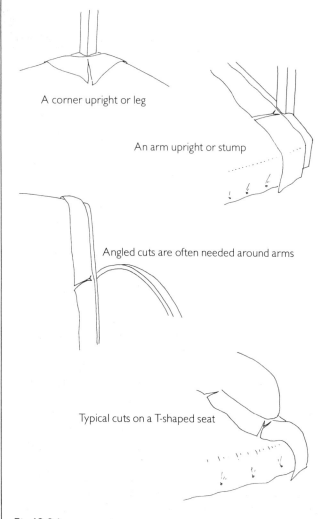

A corner upright or leg

An arm upright or stump

Angled cuts are often needed around arms

Typical cuts on a T-shaped seat

Fig 13.34

upholstery it will be reasonably durable and have good strength.

Most of the cutting required at the bench is in the shaping and trimming of covers so that they will fit the frame being upholstered. Trimming is also required at corners and over edges where pleats and folds are being made. Cutting positions have to be determined by assessing depth of filling and positioning cover parts so that the cut being made is in the right place and to the correct depth. Most cover parts can be partly cut and partly tucked away before a cut is made. This method is by far the safest and hence the more accurate.

By temporary tacking the piece in place, and using the fingers to tuck the fabric partly away, the depth and position of cut can easily be found. Careful snipping of the cover with the scissors will allow it to be pushed into place as a test for accuracy. Further snipping may then be necessary to complete a good fit. Figs 13.34,

Iron-Back Chairs c. 1860–90

Three interesting examples of mid-Victorian iron-back chairs. The iron frames were supported on beech or mahogany frame seats, with turned or cabriole legs.

Upholstery A good degree of comfort is provided by a fully sprung seat and a well-curved back filled with cotton waste, flock and curled hair. These types of chairs have good lumbar support, with wrap-around sloping backs which are deep buttoned or pulled in with a sewn fly.

Coverings Would be chosen to suit the particular surroundings, some in heavy wool plush or velvet; others were delicately covered in damask or plain satin.

13.35, and 13.36 explain how the different cuts are made which would suit the average armchair.

Cutting methods are often closely related to the way in which a piece of cover is first fixed and positioned. Positioning is important and must be reasonably good before any attempt to cut is made.

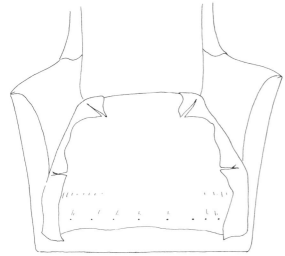

The back cuts take the cover around the two back legs. The front cuts allow the cover to tuck away and pass the arm uprights. The amount of tuck away or depth of filling must be gauged before cutting.

Fig 13.36 Cutting an armchair seat cover.

Working methods
The inside arms on a chair are normally temporary tacked at the stuffing rail, and then pulled upwards and over the arm. This is physically easy and gives the best result. Once the arm cover is temporary tacked at the top and bottom cutting can begin.

Inside wings are slightly different. These are normally temporary tacked along the inside of the chair back leg and then pulled over to the outside of the wing edge. The cover or lining can then be smoothed down to reach the arm where cuts are usually necessary. Finally, to complete the wing the cover is pulled upwards and over the outer-wing shape. The back leg tacks can then be released to make further cuts and pull out any more fullness.

Inside back covers are always fixed at the bottom first, by temporary tacking and cutting to reach the back tacking rail. The cover is then well pulled to the top and fixed, beginning at the centre and stretching to the outer corners. The edges at each side are then folded back and the cuts made at top, middle and bottom where rails appear. Providing the normal procedure is being followed, the seat cover can be cut and pushed into place at the seat back rail position. This is then pulled firmly forward to the front and fixed on the face of the rail or under as appropriate. Treatment is then similar to the inside back: the sides are half tucked away to give cutting positions.

Cushion making

Cushions for traditional upholstery generally fall into two categories, the unbordered pillow types, and the bordered or box constructions. Unbordered cushions are simply made up be sewing two identical pieces of cover together. An opening is left along one side for filling and this is later closed by hand slipping, by zip, or by machine sewing. The edges or seams may be trimmed during making up with piping or ruche. Alternatively, cording, gimp or fringe can be hand sewn on after the cushion is made. The outline and shape of an unbordered cushion is partly determined by the cutting plan and partly by the amount of filling used.

Flat squabs and pads are normally hair filled with wraps of cotton wadding, or cotton felt as outer fillings. Cushions of this type are often lined with ticking or calico, particularly if the cover is removable for cleaning. Fig 13.37 shows some examples of simple unbordered cushions and cutting plans. The depth of filling that is pushed into these cushions will change the shape. This shape can be compensated for during cutting or may be accentuated, depending on the result that is required.

Imaginative trimming can produce very effective results on simple cushions of this type. The three most commonly used trimmings are upholstery gimp, silk

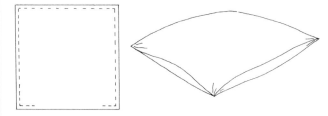

Two pieces of cover machine sewn together; the opening may be slip stitched or zipped

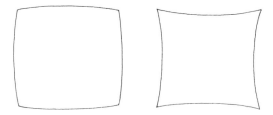

Two alternatively cut shapes to produce a straight-sided cover or inward-curving edges which are accentuated when the cushion is filled

Fig 13.37 Simple unbordered cushions.

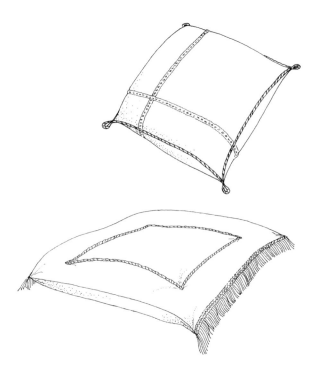

Fig 13.38 Simple feather-filled cushions trimmed by hand with cord, fringe and gimp.

cords and various fringes. These can all be applied by hand sewing both on the surface of the covers or along the edges. Fig 13.38 shows two interesting examples.

Envelope and overlay styles can be created by trimming and boxing the cushion corners. This technique is used to remove the pointed corners of the cushion and produce an envelope or boxed corner. The corners can be removed before or after making up, depending on the types of trimming required (Fig 13.39).

Boxed cushions

The boxed cushion is without doubt the most used conventional construction for all types of application. The cover parts required are basically the same for most types, a top piece, a bottom panel and border strips with joins at each corner or alternatively along each side (Fig 13.40).

The choice of seams and trimmings is the same as for the unbordered cushion, with some being applied during making up or sewn on after. The making up sequence is important, but will vary a little from one machinist to another.

1 Border strips are joined together
2 The rear border strip may be cut wider and a zip inserted if required
3 The rear border strip is joined to the other borders
4 The continuous border is then sewn around the top panel and closed off
5 If the borders are not corner joined notching is needed to locate the bottom panel accurately
6 The bottom panel is sewn in, and where required an opening left for filling at the rear end.

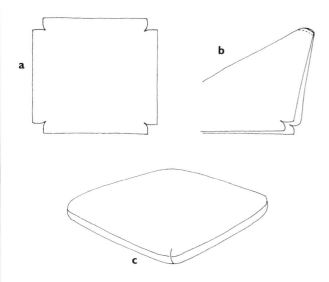

A development of the simple cushion; the corners are sewn across to produce a boxed-envelope style

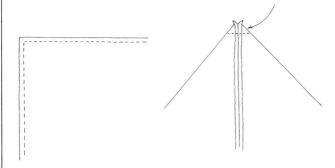

Fig 13.39 Unbordered envelope cushions.

Joints may be at sides or at corners to suit application

Cutting the pieces for bordered work

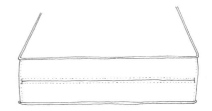

Seams may be plain, piped or trimmed

Fig 13.40 The boxed bordered cushion.

Where seams are to be piped or ruched this is done by sewing these to the top and bottom panels before the above sequence begins.

Pipings, particularly in cushion making, should be bias cut as this allows for some flexibility in the joint and works well around curves. This applies to all piped seams in upholstery but often economy dictates that straight-cut waste is used.

Bolster cushions

Bolsters are usually circular or oval in section and their construction is basically a single curved panel, hand or machine sewn to the end caps. The ends can be varied to produce a variety of different effects (Fig 13.42). The main panel should be notched at intervals along its edge to ensure that the two ends are in line and twisting does not occur, particularly when oval sections are being made.

Fig 13.41 A piped and bordered cushion set in a bay window seat.

Cushion interiors

Traditional cushion interiors can be made up with any of the following filling materials: carded cotton or wool felts, curled hair mixtures, or feathers and down. Each of these alternatives will produce a different feel and they have to be selected and used to suit the type or period of the work.

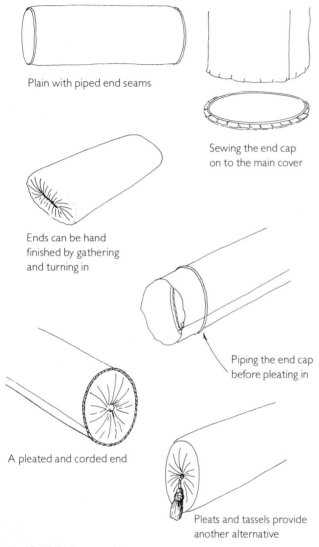

Fig 13.42 Bolster cushions.

Curled hair gives a resilient but firm interior, whereas wool and cotton felts bed down flat to make a warmer and slightly softer pad. Depending on the grade and quality of feather fillings, these will produce very soft, warm and resilient cushions which can be shaken up and turned to keep them fresh and lively. An 80 per cent feather–20 per cent down mixture makes the ideal cushion interior of this type.

One other cushion type which the upholsterer may be called upon to produce occasionally will be the spring-interior cushion. These were made in great quantity between 1930 and 1950, and if pieces of upholstered furniture of this period are to be restored to their original condition, new spring units can be bought and made up to any size required. The spring units used are either the open types or pocketed types, similar to those used in mattress production today. (See Chapter 12, Figs 12.7 and 12.8.)

Hair-filled cushions are made up in machine-sewn cases of ticking or good quality scrim. After filling and closing, the edges should be stitched to hold the fillings in place and create firm edges which will hold their shape. The simple squab types are top-stitched with a running stitch ¾ in (19mm) or so inside the edge. Heavier bordered cushions are blind stitched along the top and bottom edges to reinforce and hold the shape. A mattress stitch is used – this is a simplified version of the blind stitch used for chair work. It has no knots and is pulled tightly to draw the hair to cushion edges. A fine waxed linen mattress twine should be used. Cotton or wool felts can be used to complete the filling.

Feather and down interiors are made up from proofed ticking or waxed cambric. Both these are

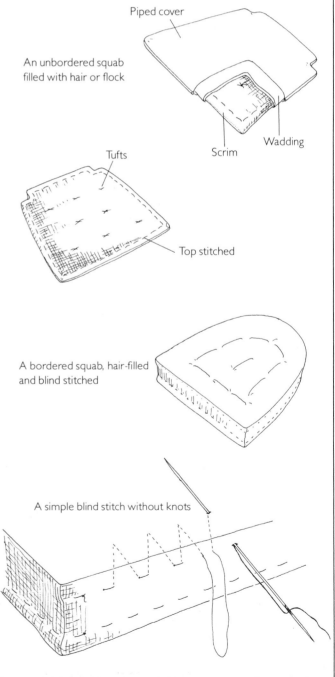

Fig 13.43 Cushion interiors.

cotton fabrics which are purpose made as pillow and cushion linings. The linings are machine made and machine closed. Most feather-filled cushions are sectioned to divide the filled areas into smaller compartments. This technique controls the movement of the filling and holds the feathers where they are needed most during use. An average-size seat or back cushion is divided into three sections with two strips of cambric cut 2½in (63mm) wider than the border widths. This extra height allows for the crown of the cushion to be higher than the outer edges. Fig 13.44 shows the basic construction.

The top panel is sewn in place using a closing seam, and an opening is left at the end of the case for filling purposes. The filling and closing of these cushions can be a very messy and dusty business and should therefore be done outside a building rather than inside a workshop. With the greatest care in the world, feather and down fibres will escape into the atmosphere and soon fill a room or work area. Most practising upholsterers will, if at all possible, have their cushions made up and filled for them by companies who specialise in this work. This avoids unnecessary labour time and keeps dust levels down. Most feather companies will do the work in a matter of a few days to agreed measurements or to a template, or alternatively will fill cases made by the upholsterer. The average size seat cushion for a lounge chair will require approximately 2½ to 3½lb (1.15 to 1.6kg) of filling.

Feather cushion interiors are normally made 3–4 per cent larger overall than the finished cover size.

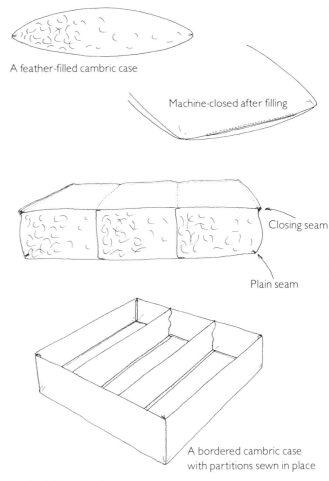

A feather-filled cambric case

Machine-closed after filling

Closing seam

Plain seam

A bordered cambric case with partitions sewn in place

Fig 13.44 Feather interiors

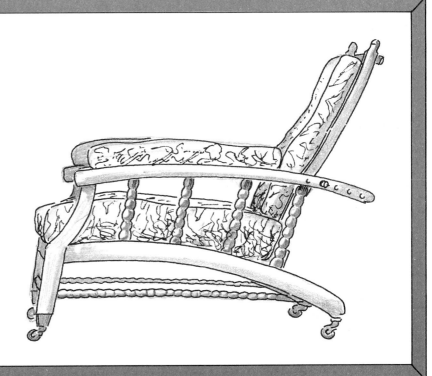

The Morris Chair
c. 1870

An adjustable chair made from ebonised oak and beech and designed by William Morris and Co. Originals were hand crafted, but later many factory-made copies were produced using a simpler construction in oak.

Upholstery Chairs of this type were simply upholstered with loose sprung cushions resting on cane-work or wood laths in the ladder-back style.

Morris specified and designed fabrics for his handmade furniture using Utrecht velvets and printed linens.

— *Chapter Fourteen* —
Modern Techniques

Modern upholstery design and the materials used have been influenced mainly by developments in the plastics industry. Basic techniques have changed to take advantge of the new materials, and to make the upholstering of furniture less labour-intensive.

Machines, of course, have also played a part in simplifying the upholsterer's work. However, there are still many upholstery operations which are difficult to mechanise, and in many areas the work is hand applied and assembled. The designer of a chair must consider the methods of construction and the techniques to be used as part of the design process. It is possible to produce a piece of upholstered seating almost completely by machine, but this basically demands simplification of the product and usually results in design for the machine's sake. Developments over the past few years have shown that machines are best used to produce components or piece parts which can then be assembled by the upholsterer. Suppliers to the industry now offer a wide range of ready-made components, and the upholstery manufacturer has the choice of buying in or making up. There is always someone somewhere who is willing to specialise and supply.

The modern chair is made up from the following main components:

1 Suspension; seat and back
2 Boards or linings
3 Insulating pads
4 Edgings and trims
5 Foams as base fillings and cushioning
6 Soft top fillings; polyester fibre, feathers and down, etc.
7 Linings; calico, stockinet
8 Covers; fixed and loose
9 Fittings – hooks, studs, zips, etc.

Fig 14.2 shows a section through a typical piece of upholstery made up from many of the materials listed. Good-quality modern upholstery relies on the careful selection of materials, and the precise and accurate cutting of foams and fabrics. The frame and its suspension are, of course, equally important and must both be adequate in terms of their strength and resilience in use.

The industrial sewing machine is almost certainly the major piece of equipment in the production process. The emphasis on fitted and sewn covers in jacket form has generally removed much of the responsibility from the upholsterer. Therefore seam quality and well-made sewn covers are vital to the success of much of today's modern upholstery work. Accurate assembly, fixing and finishing are the upholsterer's main contributions and, because covers differ so much in their weight and type, a wide range of skills is needed to produce good line and finish.

INSULATING AND LINING

Suspension systems in upholstery made from rubber products or steel springing require good insulation. Hessian and non-woven polypropylene cloths are used as first coverings, followed by pads of good density

Fig 14.1

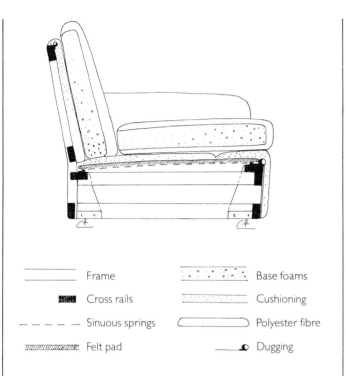

Frame

Cross rails

Sinuous springs

Felt pad

Base foams

Cushioning

Polyester fibre

Dugging

Fig 14.2 An armchair in section showing the upholstery layout.

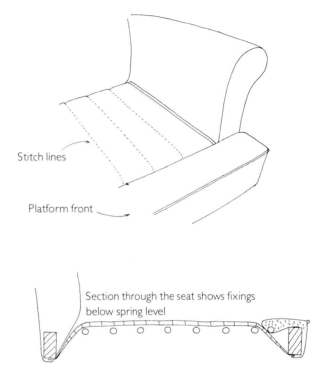

Stitch lines

Platform front

Section through the seat shows fixings below spring level

Fig 14.3 Insulating pads over tension springs or webbing.

designed for this purpose. Pads of this type are bonded polyester fibre, needled felts or bonded felts similar to carpet underfelts. Insulating pads are also produced using firm foams which may be chip foams or high-hardness polyurethane sheet. Lining cloths, such as 12oz hessian, are often bonded to the underside of the foams to form a resilient but dense barrier over the suspension. Where specially made up pads are not available, then cotton or wool felt fillings laid over hessian make excellent substitutes.

Lining pads over tension springs or rubber-webbed seats can be made up to suit different types of chair. These are the kind which are visible when the seat cushion is removed. Two pieces of strong, plain platform cloth are cut to the width of the seat and long enough to fix below the back and front seat rails. The two pieces are machine sewn along each side only, and then turned. To complete the pad a filling of firm ³⁄₈ in (10mm) thick foam or three layers of skin wadding is inserted into the platform cloth bag. Fixings for this kind of pad are important and must be well below the level of the suspension and at the front and back of the seat only so that the pad can flex easily during use (Fig 14.3). After the filling has been inserted rows of machine stitching can be added to stabilise the whole pad and keep the filling and its covering in place.

Insulating pads form the basis of upholstery work over all types of suspension. They do the same job as the first stuffings in traditional upholstery, providing a

firm but flexible foundation under the softer foams and fillings. Fig 14.4 shows how the pads are fitted over spring units and sinuous units.

Lining cloths are used to line up chairs and settees on all areas that are not boarded with hardboard or millboard panels. The choice available to the upholsterer is a range of hessians or non-woven polypropylene cloths. Both can be purchased in different weights and widths; generally the heavier the weight per square metre, the tougher and more durable

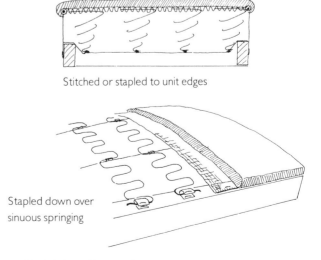

Stitched or stapled to unit edges

Stapled down over sinuous springing

Fig 14.4 Felt or fibre insulators over suspension units

the cloth will be in use. Hessians tend to be graded in ounces per square yard, for example 7½, 10 and 12oz, and polypropylene in grammes per square metre, 75g and 100g.

Linings and insulating pads are essential in good modern upholstery work and provide a durable foundation. Without such materials much more strain and wear is placed on the upper fillings and foams. Seat areas are generally the most important, simply because of the loads which will be applied to them in use. Arms and back supports should also be insulated but are less vulnerable.

The outside areas of chairs and settees should be lined and padded so that covers are well supported. This ensures that a piece of work looks well upholstered and will often save the outer covers from surface damage or puncture. The extra work and materials involved are well worthwhile and add up to a good finish, which is so important in a competitive market. A chair that is unlined on its outside frame areas soon takes on an undernourished appearance, losing its appeal as a piece of good craft work (Fig 14.5).

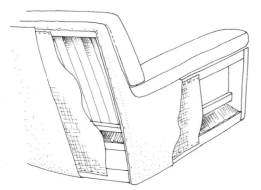

Hessian or polypropylene cloths fixed with no turnings to avoid raised edges; the linings should be tight and strong

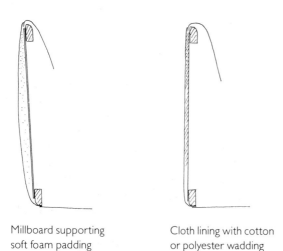

Millboard supporting soft foam padding

Cloth lining with cotton or polyester wadding

Fig 14.5 Linings on outside backs and arms.

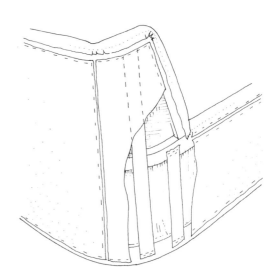

Fig 14.6 Using webs to support outside linings and covers on shaped framework.

Where frames are curved or shaped, the outer line can be maintained by adding a well tensioned webbing or two. The webbings will support the lining and so hold the cover out to its correct curve. Cardboards and millboards can also be used to give good support and shape on outside backs and outside arms (Fig 14.6).

EDGE TRIMS AND ROLLS

Stuff-over chair frames can be trimmed and upholstered with a variety of edge-support materials, Not all edges need such treatment, but those where shape and support are required should be trimmed with a firm edging before fillings are applied. The types used for modern upholstery are similar to the dug roll but are manufactured from compressed paper, plastics or moulded foams. Seat fronts in particular require trims of this type to reduce the sharpness of rails and to give support to foams and fillings. The use of ready-made edgings reduces foam thicknesses and produces a stuffover edge with shape and depth. Other edges best treated with a roll of some kind are arm fronts and inside arm and wing frames.

Where roll-over effects are to be produced a large edge trim is fixed to overhang the frame. Foams and cover can then be shaped around the trim (Fig 14.7).

Small edge trims are also used by stapling around outer frame edges so that a lip is formed. The lip is similar to a large piping and produces a convenient edge against which outside coverings can be closed and finished (Fig 14.8).

An edge roll can be fixed to overhang a seat or arm front. This extends the line of the upholstery and makes a ledge against which a border can be back tacked or so that a facing can be set in. If the placing of a roll or trim is planned before the upholstery is begun,

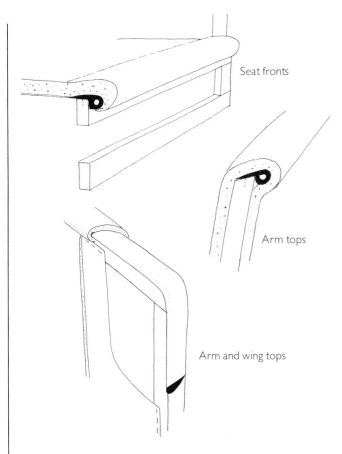

Seat fronts

Arm tops

Arm and wing tops

Fig 14.7 Plastic trims provide support and shape.

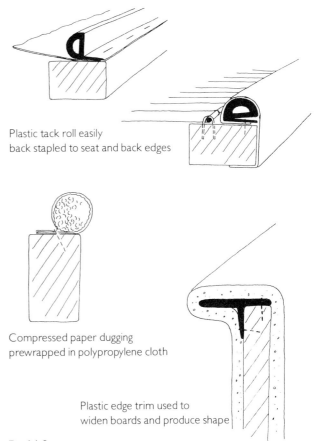

Plastic tack roll easily
back stapled to seat and back edges

Compressed paper dugging
prewrapped in polypropylene cloth

Plastic edge trim used to
widen boards and produce shape

Fig 14.9

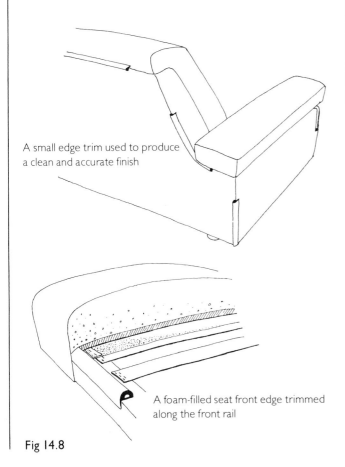

A small edge trim used to produce
a clean and accurate finish

A foam-filled seat front edge trimmed
along the front rail

Fig 14.8

the design and appearance of the finished work will be both interesting and pleasing.

Fig 14.9 shows how a tack roll is stapled to a seat or back rail edge to produce a neatly raised edge over which fillings for fixed or platform upholstery can be located. Compressed paper tack roll is used in the same way and may be located on top of a rail or fixed to hang over the edge. This treatment will either extend or raise the upholstery. A variety of flat or T-section trims can be used to widen and support frame edges made from plywood or chipboard.

PLATFORM SEATS

A platform is basically an upholstered support designed to have cushions resting upon it. The cushions may be the loose reversible type, or fixed in place either permanently or detachable for cleaning. The term 'platform' normally refers to a seat but may also refer to a chair back which will support cushions in the same way. A platform can be sprung edge or firm edge, depending on the particular design and its cost. Spring-edge seats cost more to produce in terms of content and time. Platforms need not be heavily upholstered providing that the suspension is adequately insulated and the edges are well built.

It is normal practice to give a platform a gutter which is set in a short distance from the edge. It is at this

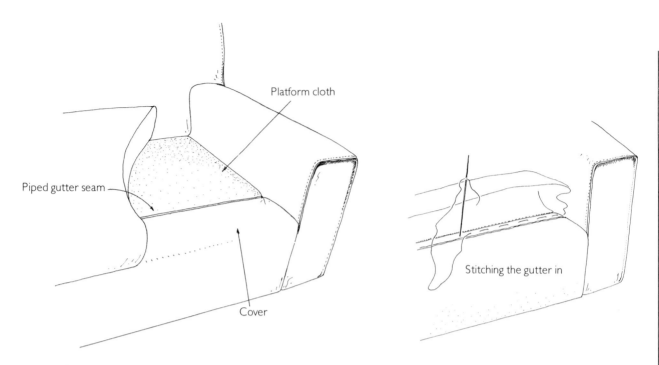

Fig 14.10

point that the gutter is formed and a strong platform cloth used to cover the remaining area of the seat or back. The gutter creates a shallow well in which a cushion can sit. This will hold the cushion in place and stop slipping or movement when the seat is in use (Fig 14.10). The use of a platform cloth saves on the cost of expensive cover, and in the case of pile fabrics gives a better surface on which the cushions rest. Where a platform seat is to be built the suspension must be as flat as possible. Selecting the best form of springing is therefore important. A platform with a

domed or raised surface will not allow the cushions to sit well into place and will lead to unnecessary movement and gaps under the cushion edges.

At the point where the platform cloth and the cover meet, the two are machine sewn together, using either a plain or a piped seam. A tape or webbing can also be incorporated into the seam, which will serve as a fly used to fix the gutter down. The tape can be either glued or hand stitched in place on to the foam base fillings (Fig 14.11).

If the tape or the webbing is not used a large seam

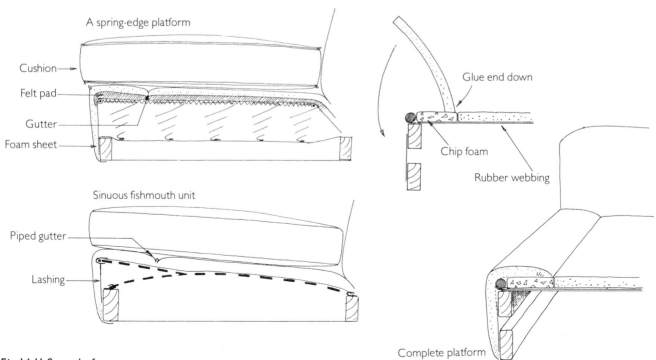

Fig 14.11 Seat platform.

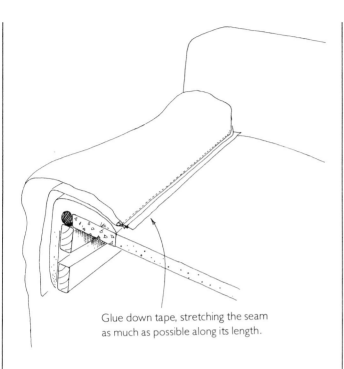

Glue down tape, stretching the seam
as much as possible along its length.

Fig 14.12(a)

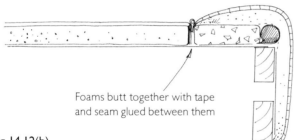

Foams butt together with tape
and seam glued between them

Fig 14.12(b)

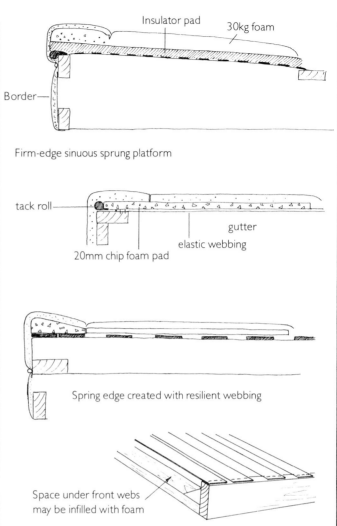

Firm-edge sinuous sprung platform

Spring edge created with resilient webbing

Space under front webs
may be infilled with foam

Fig 14.13 Seat platforms.

allowance should be made; this will be used for
stitching down to form the gutter. Figs 14.12(a) and (b)
show two methods of securing a tape by gluing. The
glue should be contact-foam adhesive and applied with
a scraper or by spray to all the surfaces to be joined.

In Fig 14.12(a) the foam remains continuous and the
tape is glued to the top surface, keeping the line of the
gutter straight or parallel to the seat front edge. In
Fig 14.12(b) the platform foams are cut or remain
separate so that the seam and tape can be glued and
sandwiched between them. Where possible the gutter
seam should be stretched end to end as it is glued
down.

   Before the cover is pulled over and finally fixed it is
good practice to apply a thin top stuffing to the front
edge. This can be polyester wadding, cotton wadding or
felt and will raise the front edge well above the main
seat area if needed.

   Forming gutters on spring edges and firm edges is
basically the same. It is only in traditional work that a
truly independent spring edge can be created (see
Chapter 16). A semi-soft front edge can be produced

with rubber webbing or close-coil tension springs if the
front top rail of a seat is laid down and fitted in flat.
This creates a space below the front two webs or
springs. The space may be left clear or infilled with
foam to help support the suspension (Fig 14.13).
Flexible edges of this kind on seat fronts can only be
built on chairs up to a maximum width of 26in
(650mm). Wider seats and settee seats cannot be
treated in the same way.

WORKING WITH FOAMS

There is a wide range of polyurethane upholstery
foams being produced. All of these fall into one of the
following categories or types: conventional polyether,
high-resilience polyurethane and reconstituted
chipfoams. To work with these modern fillings the
upholsterer needs to appreciate the basic differences
and to know something of the physical character of
each. Conventional foams are finely structured with
small even-sized air cells. Their stretch characteristics
are good, and they can be glued and stapled down on to
frames very successfully. Equally, because of their fine

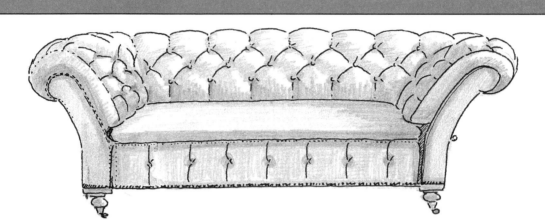

Chesterfield Settee c. 1880

A Victorian double-ended couch with drop-arm action at one end. The frame is made from birch or beech and the legs from mahogany.

Upholstery Deep buttoned with spring-edge seat produced in two-, three- and four-seat versions. Back and arms are fully sprung on a webbed base. Fillings were horsehair, grass fibre, wool flocks and cotton waddings.

Coverings Silk and worsted velvets, cut moquettes and hides were favoured by the Victorians. Some of these settees were covered in tapestry and not buttoned. Silk gimps and cording were stitched under edges and around facings to decorate and disguise hand-sewn joints.

The Chesterfield is a handsome and impressive piece of upholstery which may have taken its name from the Derbyshire town or from one of the Earls of Chesterfield.

structure they can be cut and trimmed reasonably accurately, leaving a smooth, even surface on to which covers can be laid. It is recommended, however, that, wherever possible, an interlining of fine stockinet or thin wadding is laid over the foam before covering. This will help in two ways. Firstly, it will allow the cover to move freely over the foam surface when the upholstery is being used, reducing abrasion. Secondly, the lining will assist the upholsterer and stop foam and fabric gripping each other; additionally any glued joints will be camouflaged and will not be telegraphed through the cover.

High-resilience foams should, wherever possible, be lined in the same way. Although HR foams have a superior feel and polyethers have resilience properties, the stretch characteristics of each are very different. Generally, they do not flex very well and so should not be tensioned or stapled over upholstery frames. They are easily recognised by a more open and random cell structure which gives them their excellent high-resilience qualities. These foams are therefore best cut to any shape by machine and then glued or taped on to frames. They are extensively used as cushion interiors to any required thickness, and preferably wrapped with waddings and linings before covering.

Chipfoams are, by nature, much heavier and coarser than the other two foams. They are produced specifically as robust first stuffings. They have a relatively rough-cut surface because they are made from granulated chips of the other two foams. Chipfoams should always be wrapped or topped with layers of softer foam. They can be successfully stapled or glued down, and because of their high built-in density they are unlikely to bottom under the heaviest of weights. This makes them ideal as edgings and base fillings on firm bases and frames. Most polyurethane foams can be successfully moulded, and where foam components are required regularly in large quantities the tooling and moulding costs are worthwhile. This method of production applies particularly to the vehicle seating industry and to some extent in contract furniture production. Chapter 10 should be referred to for more details of upholstery foam manufacture and the foams' physical properties.

To ensure good results from the use of foam fillings, great care must be taken in marking out and cutting. Foam-filled upholstery should display a feeling of generous proportions, good line and a professional finish. To help achieve this, the length and width dimensions should be a fraction larger than the finished sizes required. Cut edges for shaping should, where possible, be placed on the inside of a fabricated shape. The outer line or edge of a foam unit will inevitably feel weaker than the centre area. As covering is applied the edges will distort and become crushed. This can be compensated for by increasing the proportions of the foam and strengthening at the edges where possible (Figs 14.14 and 14.15).

It is good practice to make the foam and the framework combine to produce the shape required. Large, flat areas of foam filling should, where possible, be avoided. A gentle domed or raised surface area is always preferable and will hold and support the covering much better. This is because foam fillings generally lose height during the early stages of use. Initial height loss, as it is referred to, should be kept in mind and allowed for. The loss is likely to be only around 3 to 5 per cent, but this amount can cause upholstery covers to become baggy and loose on flat surfaces, particularly where foam sizes have been kept to a minimum.

Parts of a chair or a complete piece of seating are slowly built up, from the frame and suspension to the foaming-up process. Until the outline and shape of the work is built in foam, the cover cannot be measured for or cut and fitted. Where a piece of upholstery is being restored or recovered, the style and shape will already

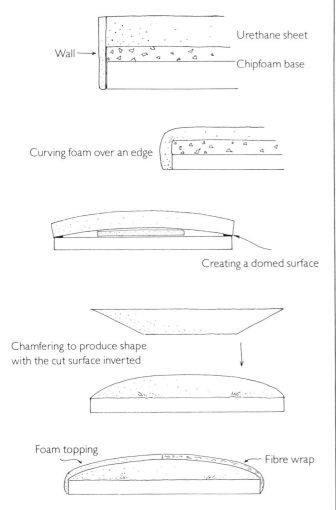

Fig 14.14 Working with foam.

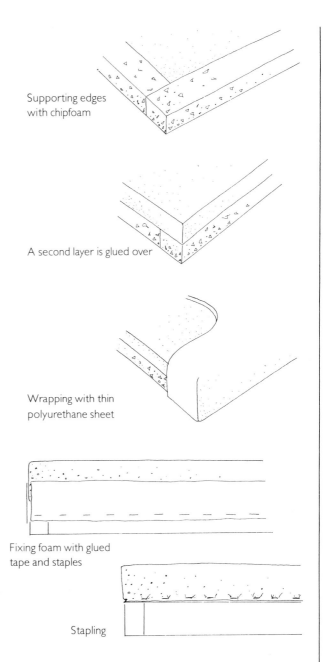

Fig 14.15

be known. However, when new work is being produced from drawings or sketches, some imagination and careful planning is needed. Each stage must be considered and some trial and error will be necessary before a good result is obtained. Where possible, the designer or the upholsterer should make a number of accurate sketches, showing several views of each area and also the whole piece. From these a pattern of work and the best approach can be determined.

Obtaining a good sitting position and the right degree of comfort can often prove difficult at first. Therefore, testing a particular foam and getting the right thickness can be done by using odd pieces and adapting them; in fact, this is usually the best solution. Using the techniques described to cut and fabricate the foam, a seat or back, for example, can then be cut and tried for shape and comfort. Adjustments and changes will be inevitable. It is often wise, initially, to cut and fabricate with very little glue being used. This gives the opportunity for a dry run and makes alterations much easier.

In most cases foam fabrication in seating is a sequence of cutting and fitting the base foams which are used to form the required shape. These basic shapes are then covered with a topping foam which overlays and smoothes the outline. The topping is then followed with a cloth or stockinet lining, or, if preferred, a skin of polyester wadding.

Figs 14.16 and 14.17 show two examples in which glue is used only around the perimeter edges. However, glue will also be needed to hold down foams in concave areas, and also in those places where fabric and fabric seams are to be held in position by gluing. Platform gutters are a good example. The pre-form chair in Fig 14.17 has an area where the seat meets the back which should be glued to hold the curve. Otherwise, generally, glue should be kept to the minimum.

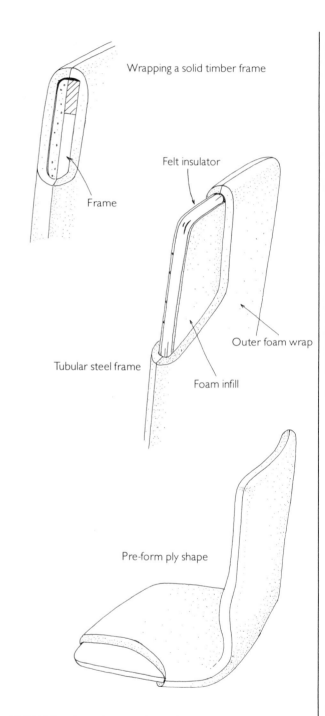

Fig 14.17 Using sheet foam with pinched and glued edges.

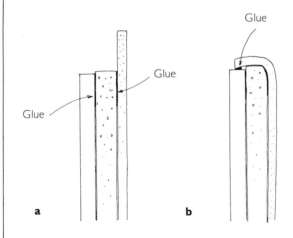

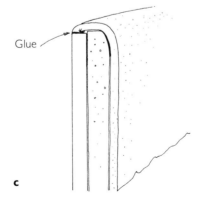

Fig 14.16 The gluing sequence for producing a nosed foam edge suitable for a small chair back or headboard.

To create large shapes in foam, such as wedge shapes or cylinders for application in chairs and settees, small power tools are very limited. If a band knife or a profile cutter is used then the job is relatively simple. All that will be needed is a template for the machine or its operator to follow. When these machines are not available it is possible to produce such shapes in small quantities by laminating several smaller cuts together. For example, the curved arm tops (Fig 14.18) could be produced by using a small jig to cut several half round lengths and then gluing these end to end. Fig 14.19 refers to this method.

Fixed upholstery covers and foam fillings are used in this standard easy chair

Reversible seat and back cushions and zip-on detachable arm rests make cleaning of the main parts easier

Fig 14.18 Two different chair designs which show fixed and cushion upholstery.

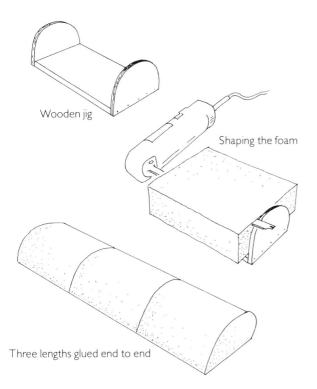

Wooden jig

Shaping the foam

Three lengths glued end to end

Fig 14.19 Cutting foams to produce large shapes.

BUTTONING

Surface buttoning and deep buttoning in modern upholstery are based on traditional techniques but are prepared for by using foam fillings and pre-sewn covers. The methods used require longer preparation time, but less time for upholstery and finishing.

Surface buttoning

Shallow or surface buttoning is used either to decorate or hold in a piece of upholstery cover. The cover is temporary tacked or skewered in place over the fillings, and the buttons tied in. The position of the buttons may be marked using a template or located on sewing lines which have already been determined. Some typical surface button patterns are shown in Fig 14.20.

When all the buttons are tied in position, the cover is pulled out, tightened and fixed. Sewing lines are often used to produce surface effects and buttons placed on the lines to create pull-ins, often where two lines of sewing meet or cross over.

Loose cushions and pads may be buttoned to stabilise fillings and hold covers in place. In modern upholstery this is only done if design or fashion demands such treatment. This would probably be the case if a chair made in the 1970s is being reupholstered, for example.

Feather, or feather and down cushions are never buttoned or tufted. This is because the thickness of filling is constantly changing and it is necessary to shake up a feather cushion to restore its shape after use.

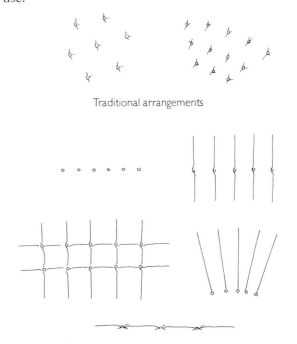

Traditional arrangements

Modern treatments using sewing lines and buttons for effect

Fig 14.20 Surface buttoning patterns.

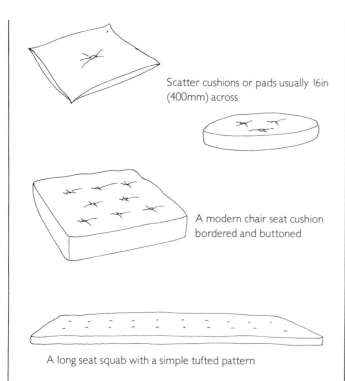

Scatter cushions or pads usually 16in (400mm) across

A modern chair seat cushion bordered and buttoned

A long seat squab with a simple tufted pattern

Fig 14.21 Buttoned and tufted cushions.

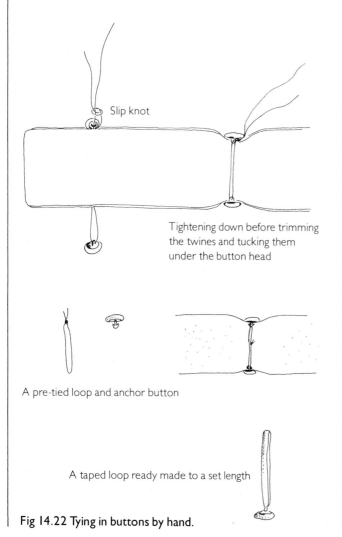

Slip knot

Tightening down before trimming the twines and tucking them under the button head

A pre-tied loop and anchor button

A taped loop ready made to a set length

Fig 14.22 Tying in buttons by hand.

When foam cushioning is to be buttoned, it is normally treated as reversible. The buttons are fixed in as a pair with one on each side of the cushion. The twines may be tied in by hand or a ready-made loop or tape used. Fig 14.22 shows the two methods.

Deep buttoning

The diagonal pleat lines in diamond button work are machine sewn to remove the fullness created by the depth of the buttons. In traditional work this fullness is folded under into neat diagonal pleats; by preparing the cover before buttoning begins, the need for any hand work is eliminated. Preparation work can begin when the cover has been cut to size. The button positions are marked on the reverse side and the diagonal lines drawn in (Fig 14.23). The amount of cover to be sewn is generally determined by the size of the diamonds and the depth to which the buttons will be pulled. The only accurate way to find this is to do a sample piece of buttoning by hand and mark the cover where the pleating occurs. The sample can then be removed and the cover laid out flat on a table. The button positions and the pleating will then be clear. A template or pattern can then be made from stiff card

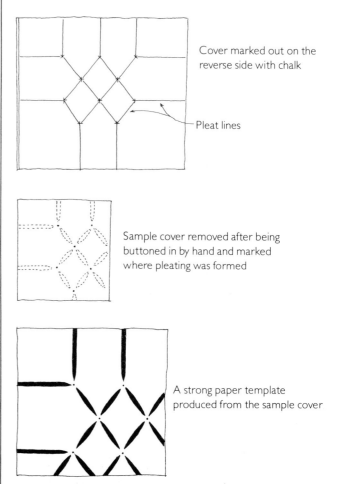

Cover marked out on the reverse side with chalk

Pleat lines

Sample cover removed after being buttoned in by hand and marked where pleating was formed

A strong paper template produced from the sample cover

Fig 14.23 Preparing covers for deep buttoning.

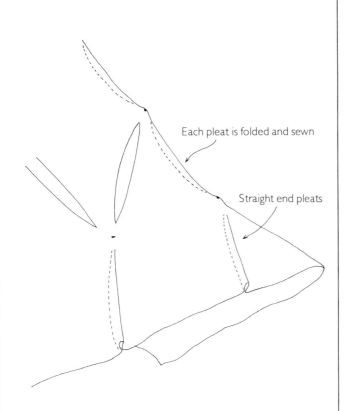

Fig 14.24 Sewing in the pleats.

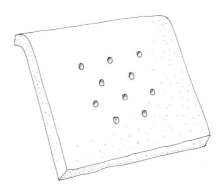

Hole cutters for use with an electric drill showing two methods of producing the cutting edge; a bent wire may be used to clear the tube

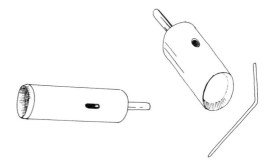

Fig 14.25 A piece of 2¾in (70mm)-thick foam with holes cut in preparation for deep buttoning.

or Kraft paper. The straight outer side pleats can also be sewn in or alternatively left unsewn to be put in by hand later (Fig 14.24).

Preparation of fillings for deep button work
The minimum depth of fillings for a deep button panel of this type is 2¾in (70mm). Most chair work of any size will need depths of around 2¾in to 3¼in (70 to 83mm) with a soft top stuffing laid over a medium-firm base foam. The choice of filling will depend on the type of work and individual preference. As well as polyurethane foams, latex foam or rubberised hair are both suitable. Soft top fillings may be wool felt, cotton felt or polyester fibre waddings .

Whichever base filling is being used it is first glued or stapled in place and the button positions marked clearly. Holes are then cut to accommodate each button, these must be large enough to take the button, the top cover and some of the top stuffing. A minimum size hole of 1in (25mm) in diameter will be needed for average size buttons. The holes are cut in the filling with a tubular steel cutter; if this is not available, a fairly neat hole can be cut with a good pair of scissors. The holes should be the full depth of the filling. When all the holes are cut the soft top filling is laid over the base and the holes located through this with the fingers.

The preparation work is completed by making the buttons and cutting the twines to length. The sewn cover is then carefully located in place and buttoned in by beginning at the centre and working out to the sides of the panel. Slip knots should be used on button twines so that button depths can be adjusted as work progresses.

Machine-sewn vandyked joints are made where necessary on large pieces of work where more than one width of cover is needed. Refer to Chapter 13, Fig 13.27. Once this method of buttoning has been used on several different size jobs, the templates or measurements should be kept and reused on future work. This will speed up the process of deep buttoning into foam.

Care should be taken not to sew too much of the cover into the diagonal pleats as this will tend to shorten the overall size of the cover in its width. As a result, the cover will be too tight and will appear strained across the buttoned area. If too little is sewn in down the diagonal pleat lines there is no problem – the folds will simply overlap the sewing. This will give the appearance of normal hand-pleating diamond buttoning. The straight end pleats can be either hand folded or machine sewn, either method allows for excess cover to be tucked in as the edges are pulled over and fixed.

FLUTING AND QUILTING

Fluted panels and quilting are very similar processes and are produced on the sewing machine for use in modern upholstery. The term fluting is generally used to describe a series of vertical or horizontal lines sewn into a surface. Quilted effects, however, tend to be more random and can be produced to any formal or informal design. The depth of stitching for both is created by machine sewing through a cover and a soft padding of foam or other filling. A good combination is foam and polyester fibre.

A sandwich of upholstery cover and filling and a lining cloth is cut and laid out, then pinned together. The pattern of the fluting or quilting is chalked in on to the surface of the cover. This is then carefully followed on the sewing machine, to produce a deep quilted or fluted effect. The depth of the work depends entirely on the type or thickness of the filling being used.

Producing this type of work on a standard lock stitch sewing machine is limited to small panels, simply because of the height of the presser foot above the throat plate, and the limited space to the right of the needle. Large fluted or quilted panels have to be made on long-arm sewing machines which are specially designed for this kind of work. Single-needle and multi-needle quilting machines are also purpose-made for work of this kind, and large quilters, capable of producing deep quilted panels to any size, were developed and used mainly in the bedding industry. These have been used for many years in mattress production.

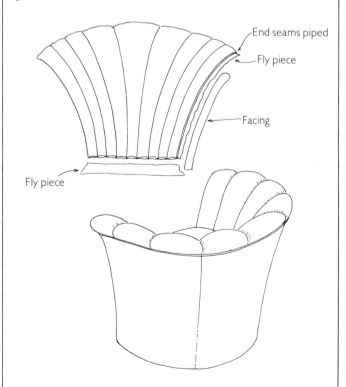

Fig 14.26 Fixed fluting in a lounge tub chair.

Narrow fluting could be produced on a multi-needle quilter

Fig 14.27 Horizontal flute lines used on a jacketed cover made up to fit an occasional club chair.

Both the long-arm machine and the quilter are of a heavy construction, with high-lift presser feet and heavy-gauge needles up to size 24. Such machines are capable of sewing through foam thicknesses of 2in (50mm) or curled hair pads, which can be quite dense. The making of soft quilts with soft fibre fillings is relatively easy. Where a large amount of this type of work is being produced special spoon-shaped or boat-shaped feet are used to help the feeding of the materials through the machine.

Fluted panels generally tend to be produced for fixing into upholstered chairs and are incorporated into the upholstery by sewing or stapling (Fig 14.27). Quilts for upholstery are mostly made up as complete separate components and then clipped or zipped in as overlays. Loose or detachable overlays or quilts will normally have covers which can easily be removed for cleaning or replacement. A chair or sofa may have one or more quilted components. Up to four or more small quilts may be arranged and fixed separately on arms, seats and backs.

One large quilt, if carefully shaped, can be laid over the inside area on a chair. Basically, a quilt is a very simple piece of upholstery, providing softness and warmth and visual appeal. The two main parts of a detachable upholstery quilt are the interior, made up from 14oz or 18oz polyester fibre wadding and a good quality lining, and the outer quilt cover which is tailored to suit the surrounding upholstery (Fig 14.28).

Divan Chair and Stool
c. 1885

A large lounge chair supported on turned legs and china castors. The deep, wide seat is said to be too large for one person and too small for two.

Upholstery The arms, seat and back are fully sprung on a birch frame. First and second stuffings of grass fibre, horsehair and pound wadding give good comfort and provide depth for buttoning.

Coverings Printed cottons often made into loose covers were put on to lounge chairs of this type for summer use. Examples in hide and American cloth were used in clubs and games rooms.

The interior should be constructed in the form of a large bag, and then filled and closed permanently. This can then be sewn through the surface to contain the filling and create fold or shape. Fig 14.29 shows one method of quilting the filling and the special presser feet that are available for this type of work. The feet allow good positive feeding of the materials and help to produce even, flat seams through heavy fillings and fabrics. This method of construction is the simplest of the three described. The quilting pattern can be of any suitable design, but the amount of sewing through should be kept to the minimum if the filling is to remain buoyant and soft. Too much sewing will stiffen the quilt and restrict its flexibility and resilience.

Two other construction techniques are shown in Fig 14.30. Double-layer quilts are made up as two separate halves. This allows for good depth of fillings in the finished product, but avoids the need to sew through the whole of the quilt depth. This construction is often used in bed quilts because it produces good depth with warm air trapped in the centre of the two layers. Each half is made up and sewn

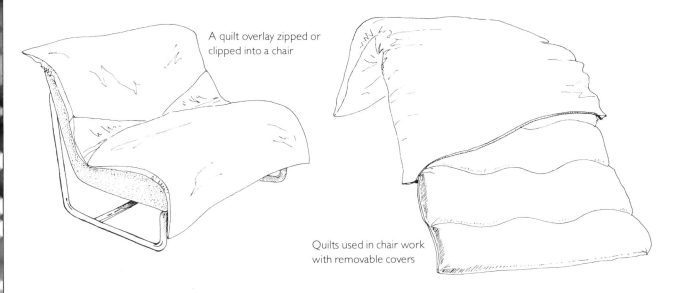

A quilt overlay zipped or clipped into a chair

Quilts used in chair work with removable covers

Fig 14.28

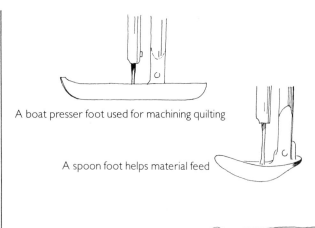

A boat presser foot used for machining quilting

A spoon foot helps material feed

Simple functional quilting used to hold fillings in place

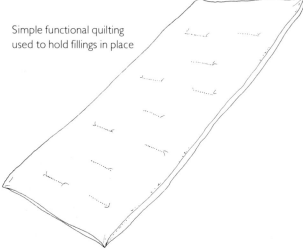

Fig 14.29 Special presser feet for quilting.

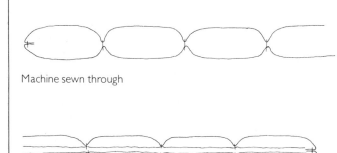

Machine sewn through

Double layer with two separately sewn through halves

Sectioned quilt producing a deeper product

Fig 14.30 Three quilt constructions.

through using a very fine soft lining on the underside. The two halves are then sewn together, either by overlocking the edges all round or by sewing up in a bag fashion, and reversing and closing in the usual way.

Fig 14.30 shows a view through a sectioned quilt produced as a made-up case, and then filled up and closed after. This method is similar to feather-filled cushion construction and again allows for a variety of fillngs to be used and to a good depth. However, making up is more time consuming and uses a little more lining cloth.

Quilt covers

Covers are normally made up some 3 per cent larger than the interior. This allows for a little movement of the inner and also for any shrinkage that may occur in

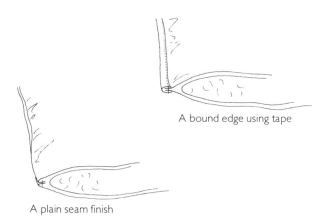

A piped or welted seam

A flat border inserted into the edge seam

A bound edge using tape

A plain seam finish

Fig 14.31 Alternative quilt cover edging.

cleaning. Basically, the simple two-piece construction is used, and the edges decorated or left plain sewn (Fig 14.31).

Flat border inserts are used for design effect and may be self-coloured or contrasted. Piped or welted seams with or without a piping cord are also used to give a quilt a positive line. Another type of edge closing is the taped centre edge, using a coloured bias tape. This technique lends itself well to the mass production of quilt covers and is used more in continental than British furniture.

Quilted panels

Fixed quilted surfaces have long been used in the upholstery of chairs and settees, partly as a functional technique and also as a way of introducing interest into chair inside backs and cushion surfaces. This technique generally uses relatively shallow sandwiches of filling or foam combined with a cover and a lining. The quilted panels are made up in the preparation of covers and sewn in before upholstery work beings. In Fig 14.32 a number of sewn panels is shown. The seam types are all lock stitch with a large stitch setting. Some interesting and pleasing effects can be created by using twin-needle sewing lines of zig-zag lines. It is also interesting to experiment with brightly coloured sewing threads to obtain contrasting surface seams, particularly on dark fabrics.

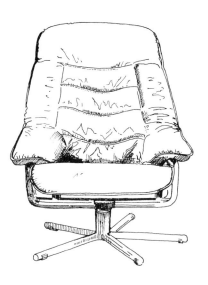

Fig 14.33 A good example of quilted leather used on the inside back and seat of this executive chair.

CUSHIONS AND INTERIORS

Most cushion interiors for modern upholstery are foam filled. The foams are either cut or moulded and are covered or wrapped with linings or soft synthetic fibre fillings. For very soft applications, such as back rests and head rests, loose or layered polyester fibre can be used on its own without foam. When long production runs of cushion interiors to a specified design are planned the moulding of foams is a good proposition. Various features can be moulded in, such as holes or dents for buttons or edge grooves to take heavy seams. This kind of detail helps with the production and speed up the fitting of covers. Many large manufacturers of upholstery provide an after-sales service and will sell components such as moulded cushions to anyone recovering or reupholstering their products.

Cut and fabricated interiors are generally made up by foam converters who specialise in this type of work. Sophisticated machinery is used to cut foam components which are assembled using adhesive spray equipment. The same techniques can be used by the upholsterer running a small business. It may be necessary to laminate two or more thicknesses together or alternatively purchase cushion thicknesses from an upholstery warehouse. These can easily be adapted or added to, to produce different shapes.

Rounded or nosed edges can be made by trimming and chamfering and then wrapping with polyester fibre. Shapes can be cut by using a hand-powered foam saw to any reasonable depth. Almost all foam interiors are finished by covering in stockinet cloth or by wrapping in polyester fibre. Polyester fibre waddings and batting should be cut to size with scissors and then glued or hand stitched in place over foam interiors. Fig 14.34 shows some examples of moulded and

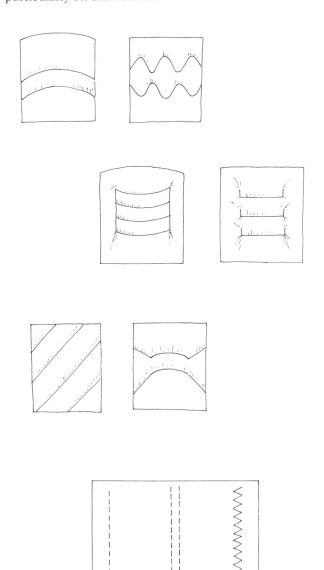

Three seam types which are suitable for quilting: single lock stitch, twin lock stitch and zig-zag lock stitch

Fig 14.32 Quilting designs for fixed covers in upholstery.

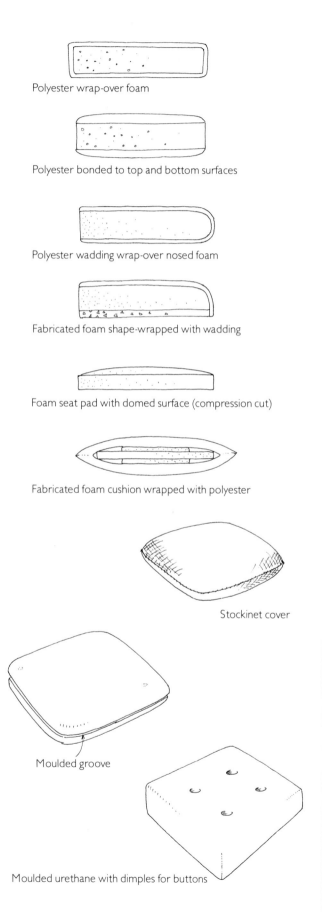

Polyester wrap-over foam

Polyester bonded to top and bottom surfaces

Polyester wadding wrap-over nosed foam

Fabricated foam shape-wrapped with wadding

Foam seat pad with domed surface (compression cut)

Fabricated foam cushion wrapped with polyester

Stockinet cover

Moulded groove

Moulded urethane with dimples for buttons

Fig 14.34 Cushion interiors.

fabricated interiors. It is a good general rule to make up all types of cushion interior 3 or 4 per cent larger than the finished cover size. This ensures a well-filled cover and allows for slight initial loss of height in fillings.

There are two types of polyester filling, loose fibre, which is suitable as a stuffing in sectioned cushions and is used in the same way as feather fillings, and layered batting or wadding. The layered types should be applied as layers and wraps and are not suitable as loose stuffings. They should not be cut up or recarded as problems will result from movement, which will cause lumping and unevenness (Fig 14.35).

Excellent alternatives to polyester fibre for soft applications are the traditional feather fillings. These, of course, are always contained in cambric cases. They make good fixed- or loose-cushion interiors and are widely available in several grades and mixtures. When

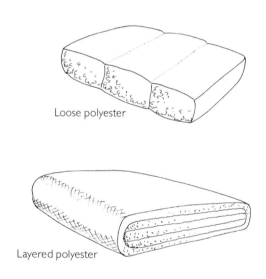

Loose polyester

Layered polyester

Fig 14.35 Using polyester fibre filling.

used as wraps over foam they are best fixed in place by stapling the edges of the cambric case around the perimeter of a seat or back, and they should be restricted by sectioning or with pull-ins, using fly pieces. These techniques help to contain the feathers in small areas (Fig 14.36).

Most feather-interior cushions are the loose type with an average thickness of 4 to 5in (100 to 125mm). They are not normally fixed but remain removable and reversible so that the filling can be plumped up and kept soft.

Cushion covers

Cushion covers will generally fall into three distinct types or constructions, depending on the design and general line required of the upholstery. These are bordered covers, unbordered covers and those which are a combination of the two. Covers are made up to fit into a particular space on a piece of upholstery. The

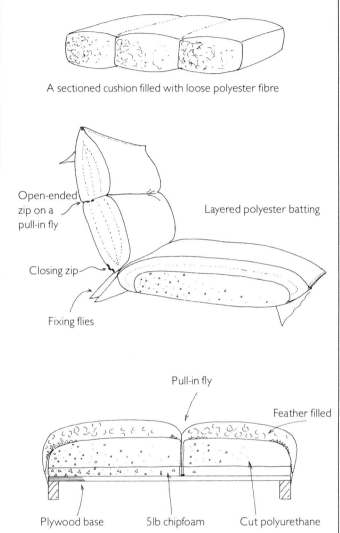

A sectioned cushion filled with loose polyester fibre

Open-ended zip on a pull-in fly

Layered polyester batting

Closing zip

Fixing flies

Pull-in fly

Feather filled

Plywood base   5lb chipfoam   Cut polyurethane

Fig 14.36

shape and size of the space should be measured and drawn, or an accurate template taken with the usual allowance of ⅜in (10mm) for sewing. It is often more accurate to make a template from a piece of calico or similar cloth, particularly on unbordered or partly unbordered shapes. Corners can be pinned into place as a check for shape, and the calico is then trimmed.

Location marks are also important and should be marked or snipped into the edges at intervals around the cover pieces. This is good practice with any fitted and sewn covering, as it makes machining more precise and ensures good fit. This is particularly so when a cushion cover is made up from a large number of small parts. Cushions with outlines which are mainly straight can be simply marked out from measurements directly on to the cover, and no template is necessary. However, where difficult shaping occurs, such as in a D-shape seat, a template is needed to reproduce an accurate cushion shape.

Fig 14.37 shows the cover parts for the seat cushion in the tub easy chair at the beginning of this chapter. This has two side borders, a zipped back border and the front edge is nosed. In Fig 14.37 the three types of construction are shown; bordered, unbordered and combination.

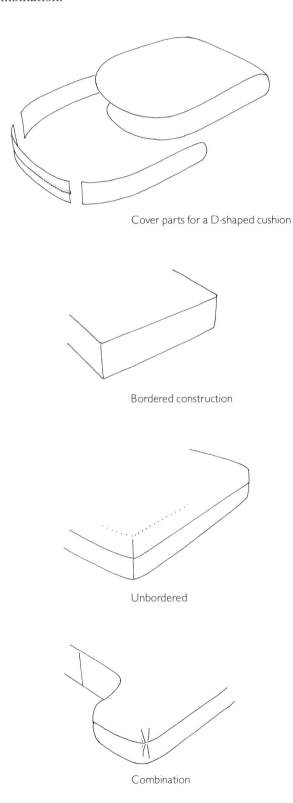

Cover parts for a D-shaped cushion

Bordered construction

Unbordered

Combination

Fig 14.37 Cushion constructions.

Baverstock Folding Chair
c. 1898

An upholstered chair with a difference, using strong canvas-based carpeting in the Axminister style. These chairs were very popular at the end of the nineteenth century and were made as singles or in suites. Knotted fringes provided some decoration, and fixings were made with brass raised-head nails into the turned cross nails.

Upholstery Arms and head rests were stuffed and stitched to give shape and depth.

Cushion seams

There is a wide choice of seam types for the making up of cushion covers. The seam chosen should reflect the style and design of the piece and should also be suitable for the cover being used. Generally, seams in modern upholstery are plain, reinforced or piped. Occasionally a more decorative joint is used by gathering or by sewing in a ruche or a fringe. Some examples are illustrated in Fig 14.38: (a) plain, (b) piped, (c) top stitched, (d) sewn through and (e) ruched.

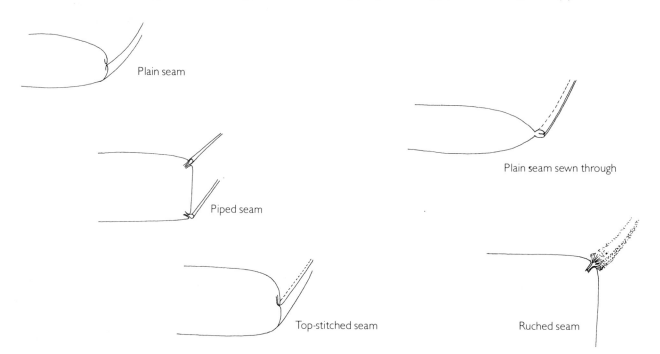

Fig 14.38 Cushion seams.

— Chapter Fifteen —

The Traditional Chair

There is no better way of learning about a craft than to study its history. The skills and techniques used by past craftsmen can provide a rich and useful background and give the upholsterer a depth of knowledge which will be invaluable.

Restoring and reproducing good pieces of upholstery is important. This kind of work is both worthwhile and fascinating to any lover of good furniture. Originals, where possible, can be carefully brought back to their original condition and copies faithfully reproduced.

In most traditional pieces of upholstery there are three principal areas of study. These are: frame design and construction, upholstery methods and materials, and covering fabrics and trimmings. These three combine to produce upholstered chairs which will give good service and, at the same time, are pleasing as pieces of craft work. Traditional upholstery is still alive and well, and demand for good work of this kind is increasing all the time.

The upholsterer is often called upon to recreate and

restore old chairs and sofas and, in fact, many specialise in this kind of work. For example, a set of chairs may be acquired for restoration and at the same time an extra one or two chairs made up and added to the set. This may be because some have been lost or simply to increase the number in the set.

This chapter sets out to show some of the more popular pieces of traditional upholstery and some have been included to illustrate particular techniques of upholstery construction. The principal dimensions are shown where possible, but these can vary enormously from one area of the country to another.

Notes and drawings are used to describe frames, the upholstery method and finishing techniques.

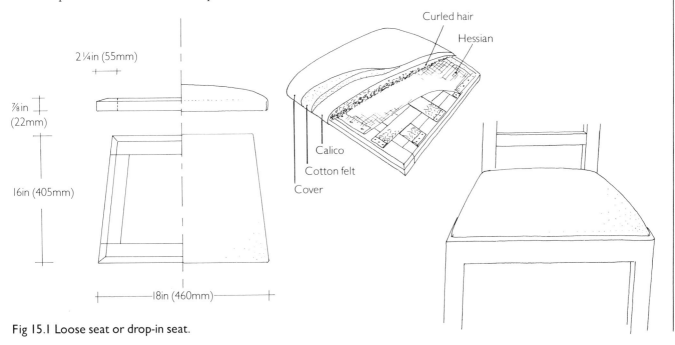

2¼in (55mm)

⅞in (22mm)

16in (405mm)

18in (460mm)

Curled hair

Hessian

Calico

Cotton felt

Cover

Fig 15.1 Loose seat or drop-in seat.

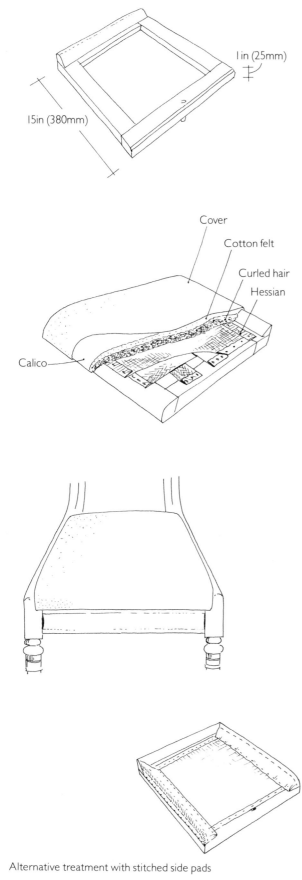

1in (25mm)

15in (380mm)

Cover

Cotton felt

Curled hair

Hessian

Calico

Alternative treatment with stitched side pads

Fig 15.2 Drop-in seat with dowel peg location.

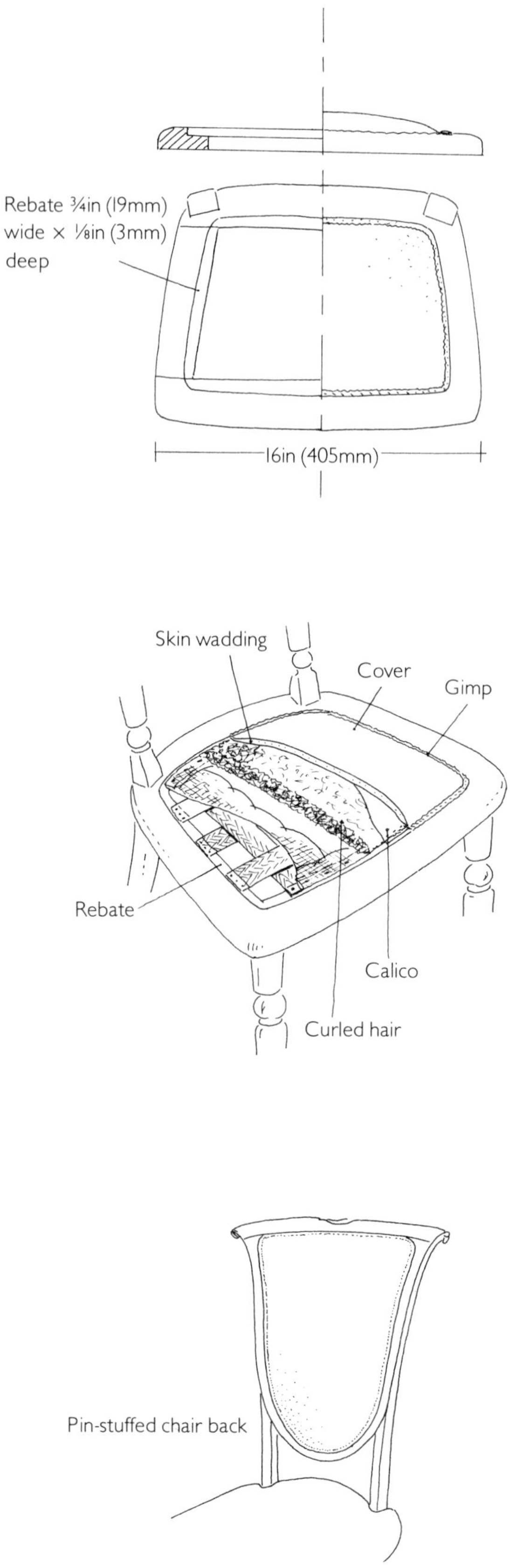

Rebate ¾in (19mm)
wide × ⅛in (3mm)
deep

16in (405mm)

Skin wadding

Cover

Gimp

Rebate

Calico

Curled hair

Pin-stuffed chair back

Fig 15.3(a) Pin-stuffed seats and backs.

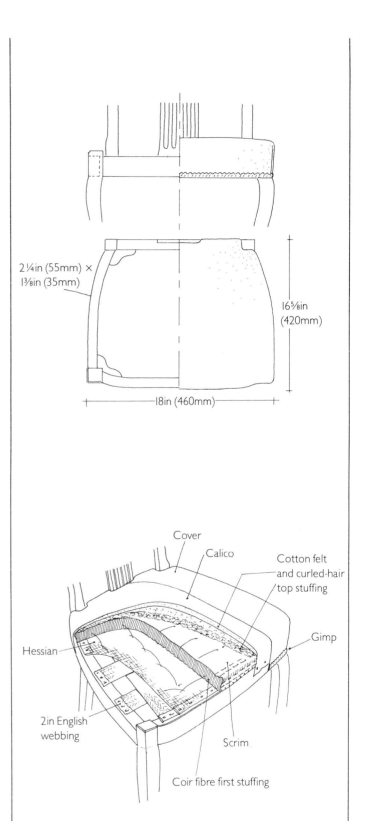

2¼in (55mm) × 1⅜in (35mm)

16⅝in (420mm)

18in (460mm)

1 OB
2 Skin wadding
3 Webbing and hessian
4 Curled hair
5 Wool or cotton felt
6 Calico
7 Cover
8 Gimp

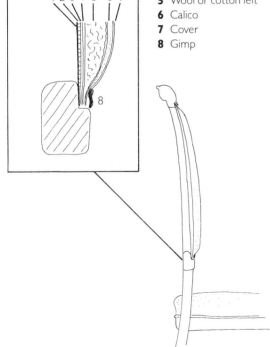

Fig 15.3(b) A pin-stuffed chair back set into a rebate. The upholstery begins with the outside back and the other work is built on to this.

Cover

Calico

Cotton felt and curled-hair top stuffing

Hessian

Gimp

2in English webbing

Scrim

Coir fibre first stuffing

Fig 15.4 Top stuffed unsprung stuffover seat.

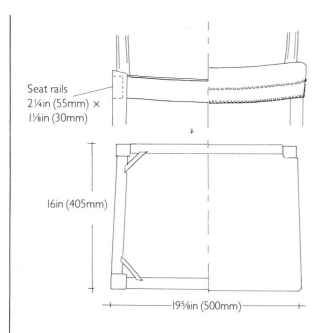

Seat rails
2¼in (55mm) ×
1⅛in (30mm)

16in (405mm)

19⅝in (500mm)

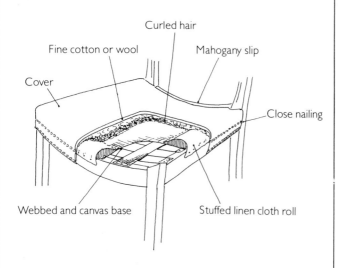

Fine cotton or wool

Curled hair

Mahogany slip

Cover

Close nailing

Webbed and canvas base

Stuffed linen cloth roll

Fig 15.5 An early form of overedge upholstery.

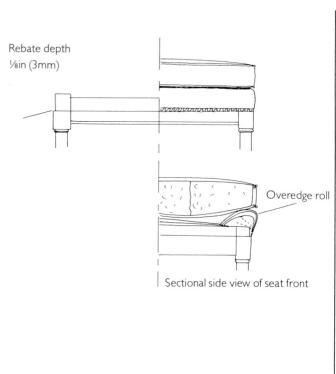

Rebate depth
⅛in (3mm)

Overedge roll

Sectional side view of seat front

Well

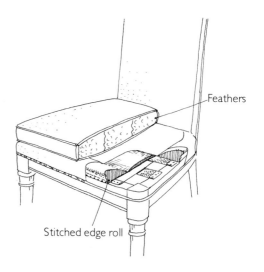

Feathers

Stitched edge roll

Fig 15.6 Bergère-style seat with loose cushion.

Three Pieces from an Edwardian Suite c. 1900

A simple, heavily stuffed *chaise-longue* on turned legs, with matching armchair. Often only the seats were sprung and the rest of the upholstery filled with a variety of poor-grade fillings.

The very upright version of a Chesterfield sofa which lacked the grace and generous lines of the Victorian pieces. Only a small amount of buttoning was evident in these suites.

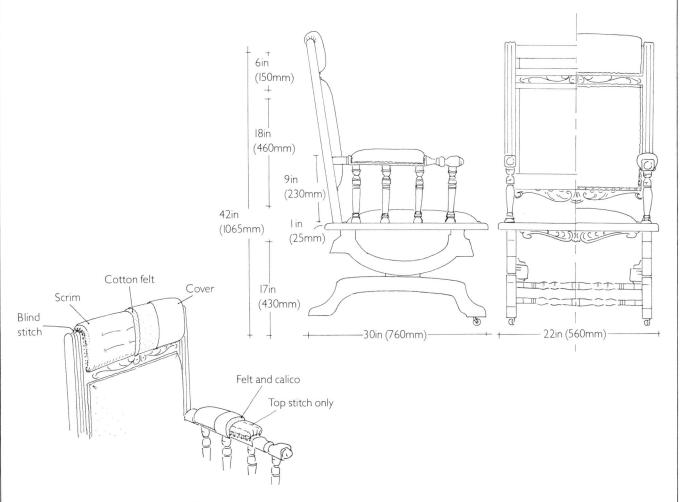

Fig 15.7 Rocking chair using pin-stuffed techniques.

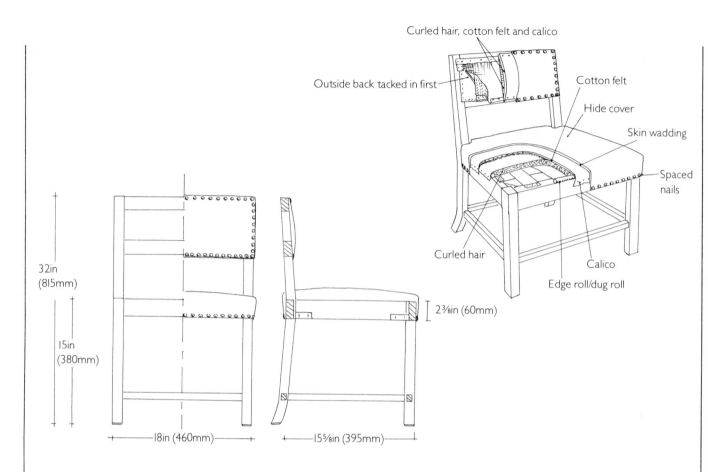

Curled hair, cotton felt and calico

Outside back tacked in first

Cotton felt

Hide cover

Skin wadding

Spaced nails

Curled hair

Calico

Edge roll/dug roll

32in (815mm)

15in (380mm)

2³⁄₈in (60mm)

18in (460mm)

15⁵⁄₈in (395mm)

Fig 15.8 Cromwellian-style dining chair in hide.

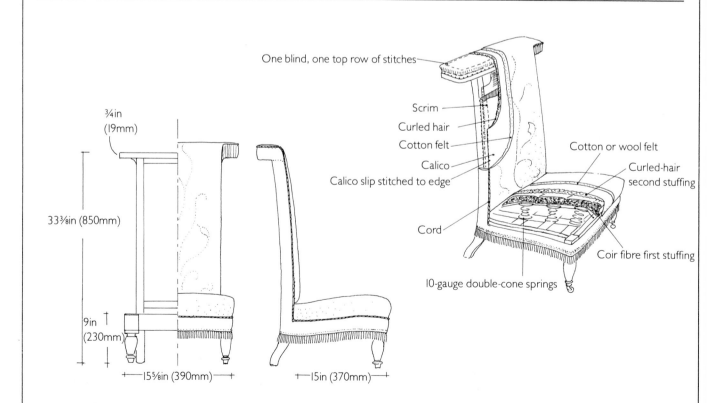

One blind, one top row of stitches

Scrim

Curled hair

Cotton felt

Calico

Calico slip stitched to edge

Cord

Cotton or wool felt

Curled-hair second stuffing

Coir fibre first stuffing

10-gauge double-cone springs

¾in (19mm)

33³⁄₈in (850mm)

9in (230mm)

15⁵⁄₈in (390mm)

15in (370mm)

Fig 15.9 Prie-dieu chair.

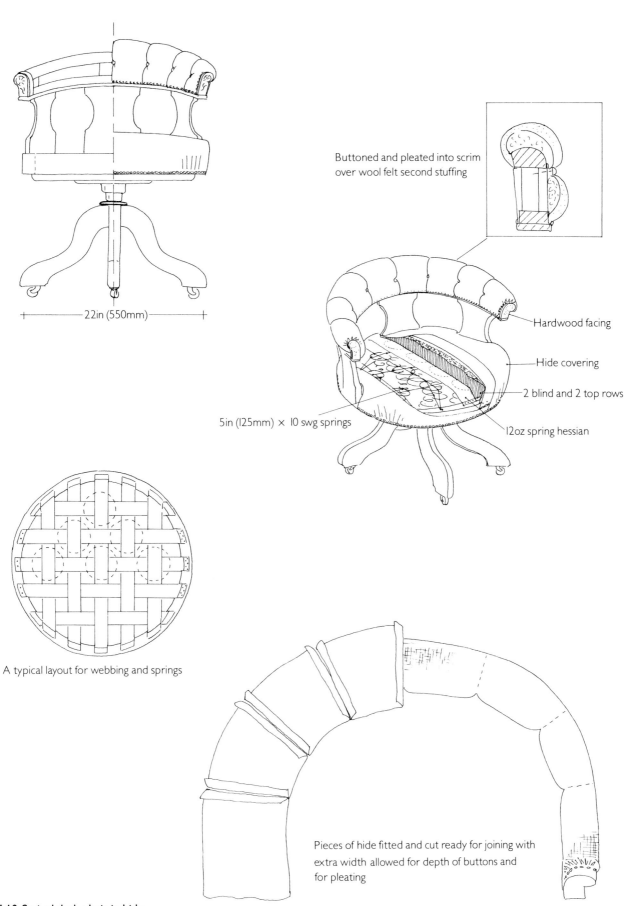

22in (550mm)

Buttoned and pleated into scrim over wool felt second stuffing

Hardwood facing

Hide covering

2 blind and 2 top rows

5in (125mm) × 10 swg springs

12oz spring hessian

A typical layout for webbing and springs

Pieces of hide fitted and cut ready for joining with extra width allowed for depth of buttons and for pleating

Fig 15.10 Swivel desk chair in hide.

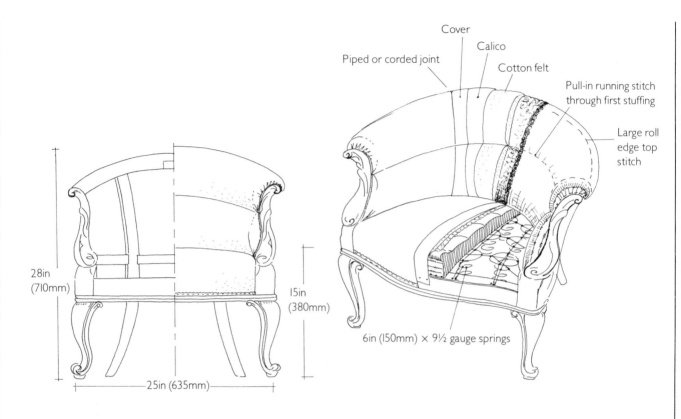

Fig 15.11 Large Victorian tub chair.

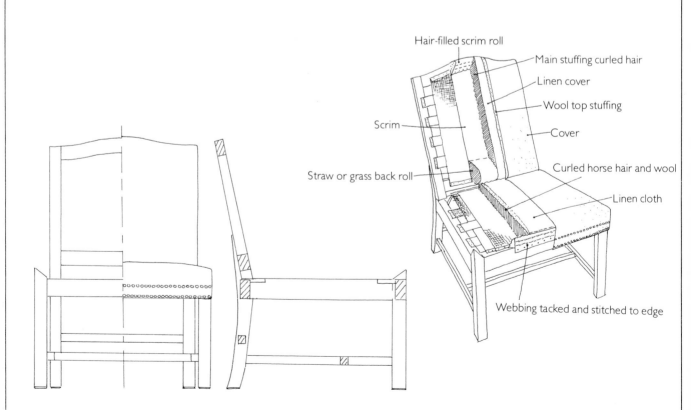

Fig 15.12 Eighteenth-century back stool with early stitched edge upholstery.

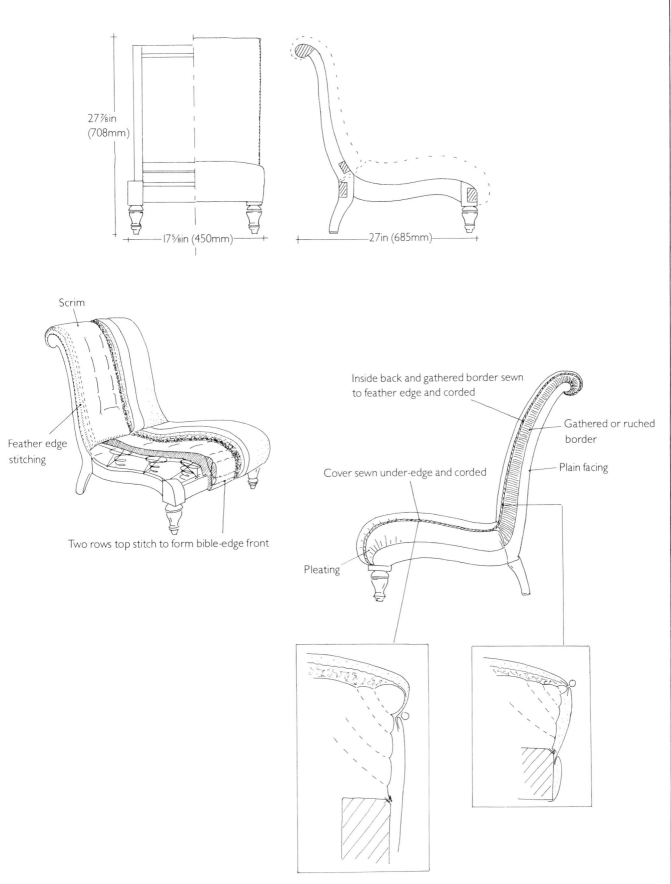

Scrim

Feather edge
stitching

Two rows top stitch to form bible-edge front

Inside back and gathered border sewn
to feather edge and corded

Gathered or ruched
border

Plain facing

Cover sewn under-edge and corded

Pleating

Fig 15.13 Victorian sewing chair with bible-edge front.

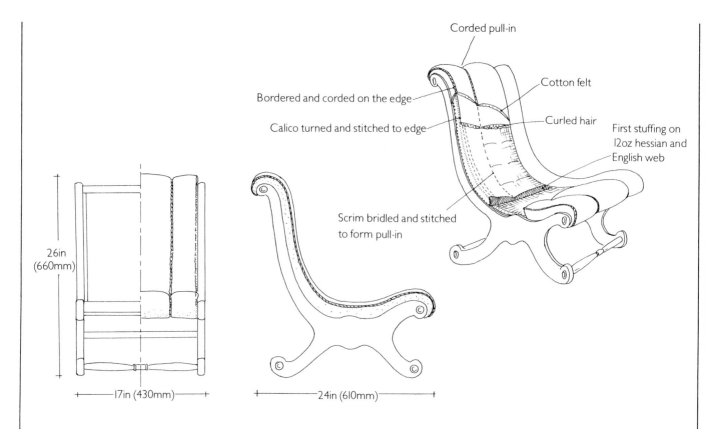

Corded pull-in

Bordered and corded on the edge

Cotton felt

Calico turned and stitched to edge

Curled hair

First stuffing on 12oz hessian and English web

Scrim bridled and stitched to form pull-in

26in (660mm)

17in (430mm)

24in (610mm)

Fig 15.14 Slipper chair.

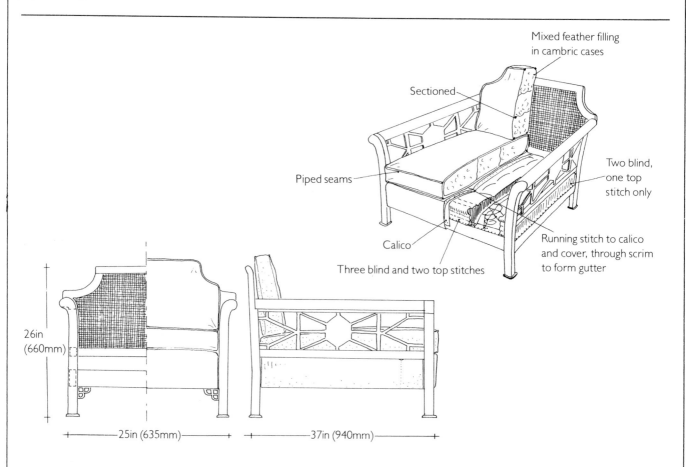

Mixed feather filling in cambric cases

Sectioned

Piped seams

Two blind, one top stitch only

Calico

Running stitch to calico and cover, through scrim to form gutter

Three blind and two top stitches

26in (660mm)

25in (635mm)

37in (940mm)

Fig 15.15 Bergère chair.

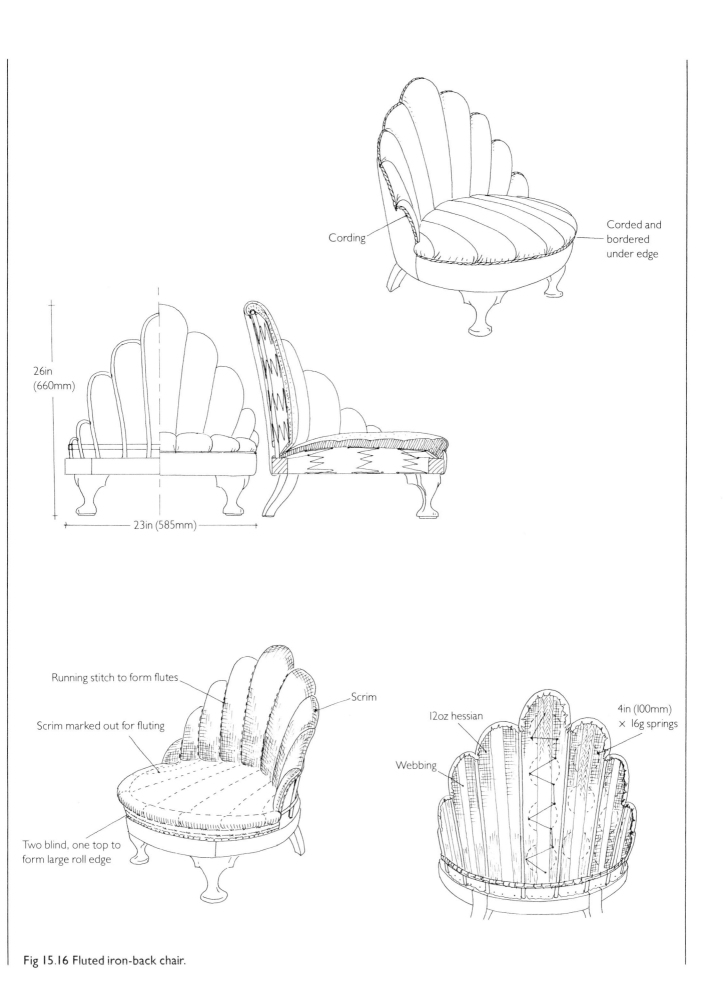

Cording

Corded and
bordered
under edge

26in
(660mm)

23in (585mm)

Running stitch to form flutes

Scrim

Scrim marked out for fluting

12oz hessian

4in (100mm)
× 16g springs

Webbing

Two blind, one top to
form large roll edge

Fig 15.16 Fluted iron-back chair.

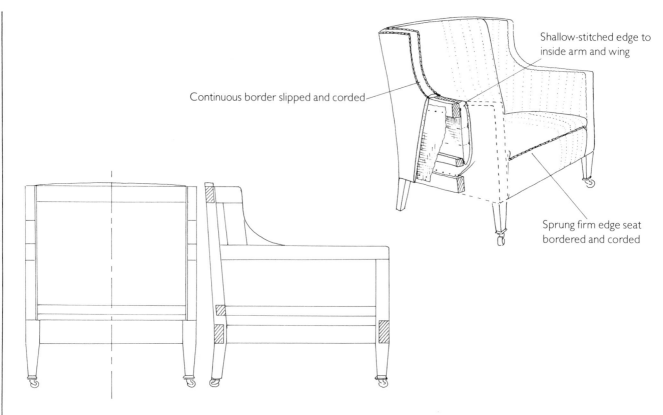

Continuous border slipped and corded

Shallow-stitched edge to inside arm and wing

Sprung firm edge seat bordered and corded

Fig 15.17 Small Edwardian armchair.

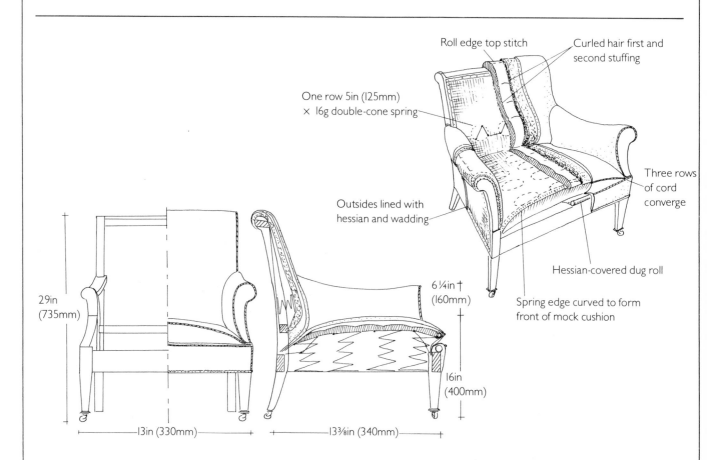

Roll edge top stitch

Curled hair first and second stuffing

One row 5in (125mm) × 16g double-cone spring

Three rows of cord converge

Outsides lined with hessian and wadding

Hessian-covered dug roll

Spring edge curved to form front of mock cushion

29in (735mm)

6¼in † (160mm)

16in (400mm)

13in (330mm)

13⅜in (340mm)

Fig 15.18 Drawing-room chair with mock cushion seat.

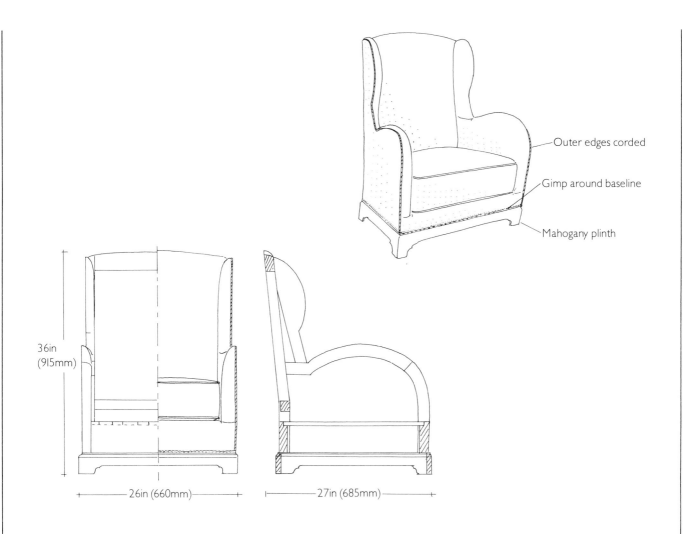

36in
(915mm)

26in (660mm)

27in (685mm)

Outer edges corded

Gimp around baseline

Mahogany plinth

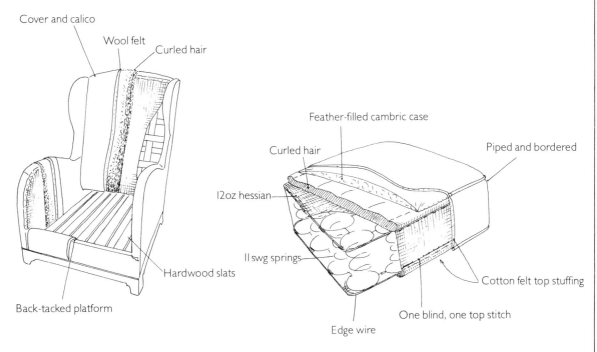

Cover and calico

Wool felt

Curled hair

Feather-filled cambric case

Curled hair

Piped and bordered

12oz hessian

Hardwood slats

11 swg springs

Cotton felt top stuffing

Back-tacked platform

Edge wire

One blind, one top stitch

Fig 15.19 Small wing chair with spring cushion seat on
wood slats, c. 1925.

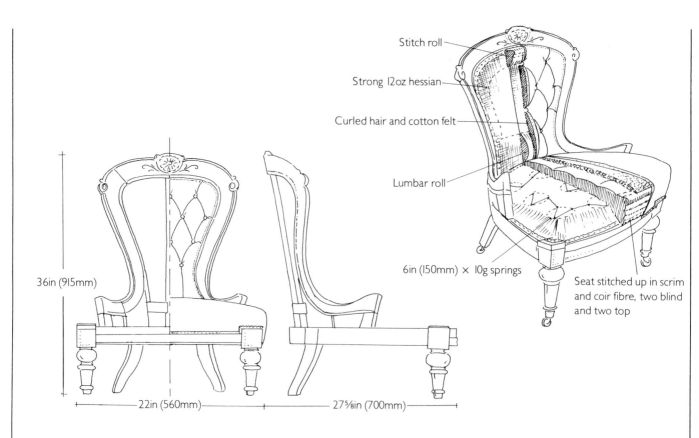

Stitch roll

Strong 12oz hessian

Curled hair and cotton felt

Lumbar roll

36in (915mm)

6in (150mm) × 10g springs

Seat stitched up in scrim and coir fibre, two blind and two top

22in (560mm)

27⅝in (700mm)

Fig 15.20 Button back chair.

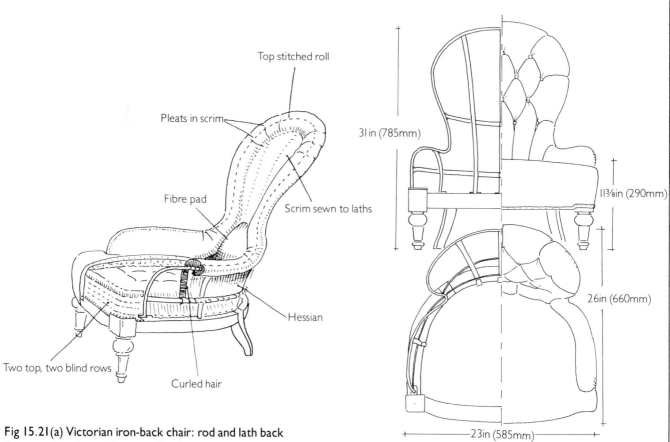

Top stitched roll

Pleats in scrim

Fibre pad

Scrim sewn to laths

Hessian

31in (785mm)

11⅜in (290mm)

26in (660mm)

Two top, two blind rows

Curled hair

23in (585mm)

Fig 15.21(a) Victorian iron-back chair: rod and lath back frame on beech seat frame and mahogany legs.

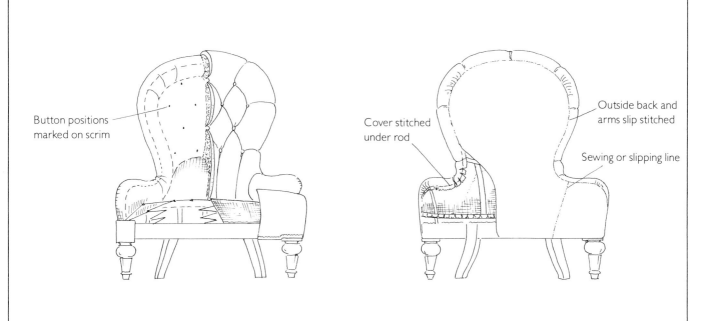

Button positions marked on scrim

Cover stitched under rod

Outside back and arms slip stitched

Sewing or slipping line

Fig 15.21(b)

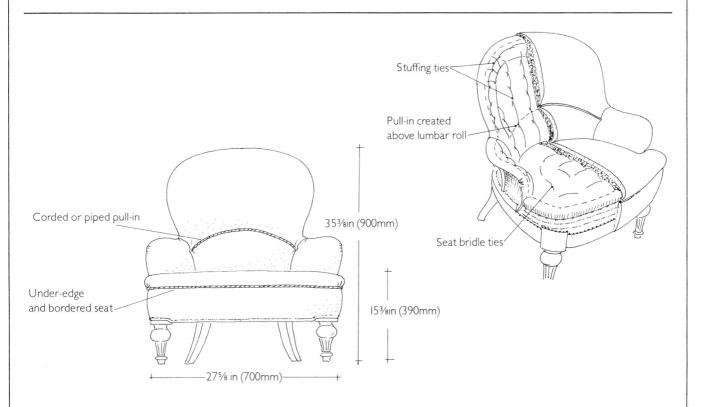

Stuffing ties

Pull-in created above lumbar roll

Corded or piped pull-in

35³⁄₈in (900mm)

Under-edge and bordered seat

Seat bridle ties

15³⁄₈in (390mm)

27⁵⁄₈ in (700mm)

Fig 15.21(c) An alternative upholstery method for the larger iron-back chair.

Bed Heads and Ends c. 1910

Tall, elegant upholstered bed heads and ends show interesting styles typical of the Edwardian era. They were constructed from hardwoods and designed to support metal bedsteads or box-spring bases.

Coverings Embossed leather and printed linens, decorated with hammered and brass nails.

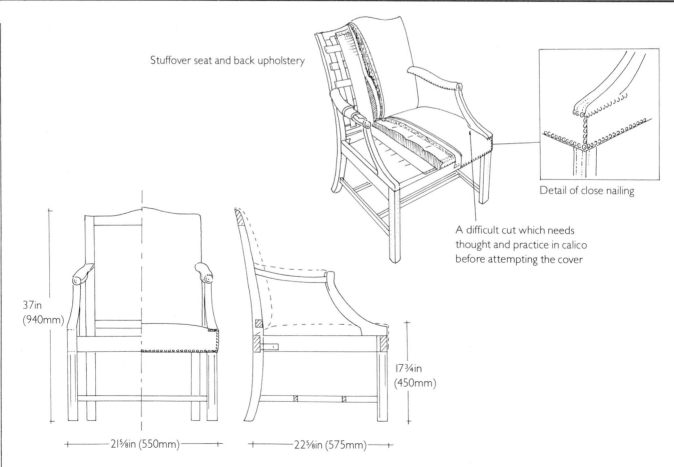

Stuffover seat and back upholstery

Detail of close nailing

A difficult cut which needs thought and practice in calico before attempting the cover

37in
(940mm)

17¾in
(450mm)

21⅝in (550mm)

22⅝in (575mm)

Fig 15.22 Gainsborough desk or library chair.

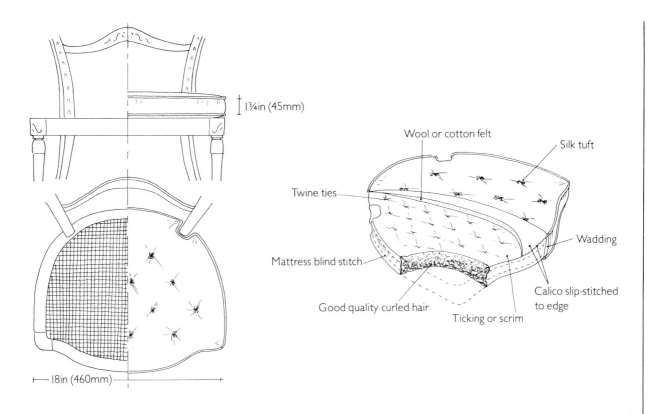

1¾in (45mm)

Wool or cotton felt

Silk tuft

Twine ties

Mattress blind stitch

Wadding

Good quality curled hair

Calico slip-stitched to edge

Ticking or scrim

18in (460mm)

Fig 15.23 Bedroom chair with painted frame and squab cushion.

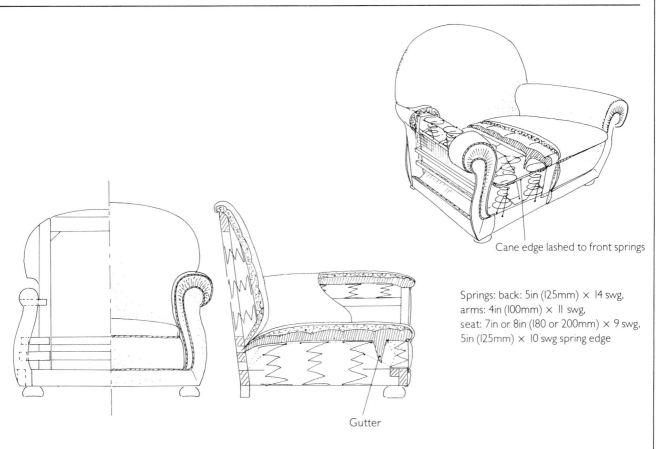

Cane edge lashed to front springs

Springs: back: 5in (125mm) × 14 swg,
arms: 4in (100mm) × 11 swg,
seat: 7in or 8in (180 or 200mm) × 9 swg,
5in (125mm) × 10 swg spring edge

Gutter

Fig 15.24 Easy chair with sprung arms and spring-edge seat.

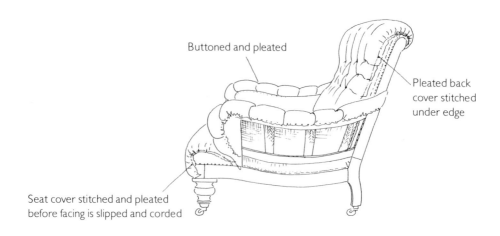

Buttoned and pleated

Pleated back
cover stitched
under edge

Seat cover stitched and pleated
before facing is slipped and corded

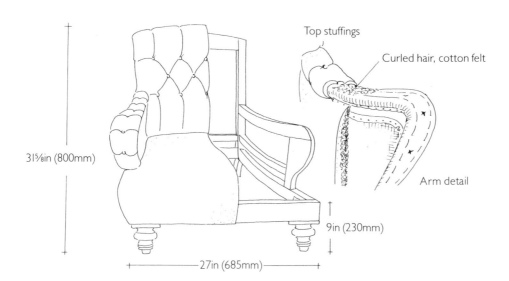

Top stuffings

Curled hair, cotton felt

Arm detail

31⅝in (800mm)

9in (230mm)

27in (685mm)

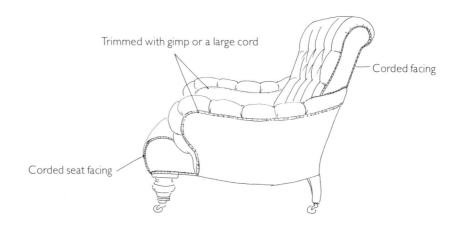

Trimmed with gimp or a large cord

Corded facing

Corded seat facing

Fig 15.25 Late nineteenth-century lounge chair.

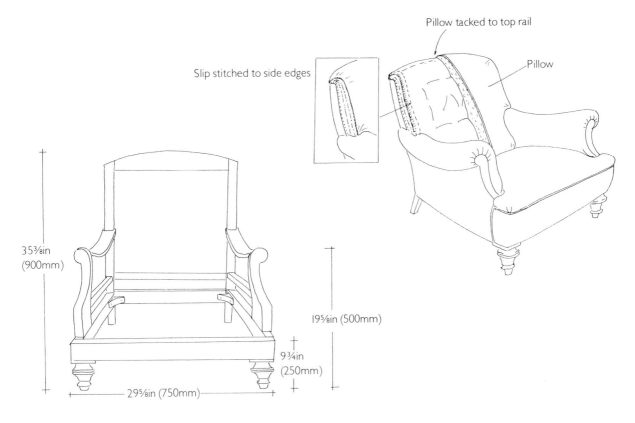

Pillow tacked to top rail

Pillow

Slip stitched to side edges

35⅜in (900mm)

19⅝in (500mm)

9¾in (250mm)

29⅝in (750mm)

Fig 15.26 Lounge chair with fixed feather pillow back.

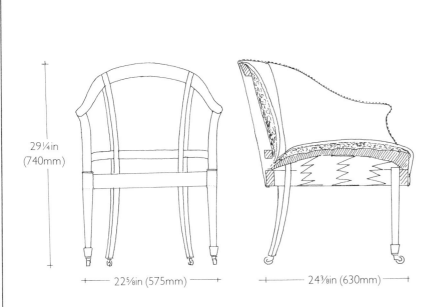

29¼in (740mm)

22⅝in (575mm)

24⅜in (630mm)

First and second stuffings throughout are good quality curled hair; top stuffings are of wool felt; outer linings of skin wadding; finished and decorated with close brass nailing; outside back turned and space nailed; seat front stitched up with two top and three blind rows.

Fig 15.27 Early twentieth-century tub chair in hide.

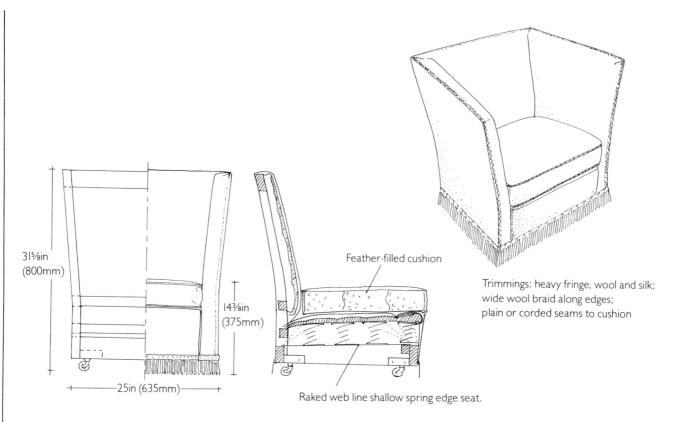

31⅝in
(800mm)

14⅜in
(375mm)

Feather-filled cushion

Trimmings: heavy fringe, wool and silk;
wide wool braid along edges;
plain or corded seams to cushion

◀——25in (635mm)——▶

Raked web line shallow spring edge seat.

Fig 15.28 Chair in the Knole style, c. 1930.

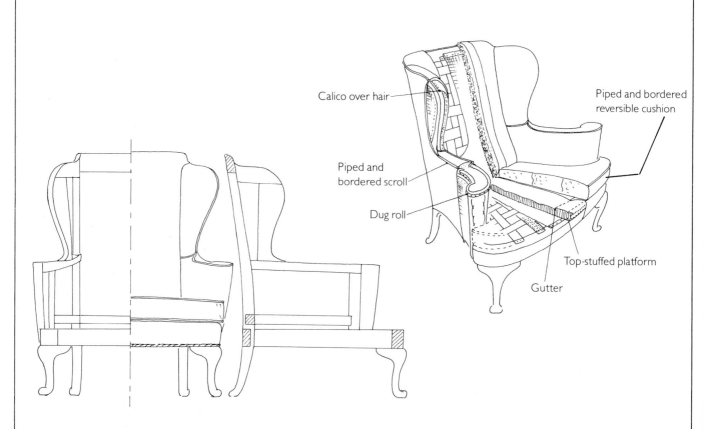

Calico over hair

Piped and bordered
reversible cushion

Piped and
bordered scroll

Dug roll

Top-stuffed platform

Gutter

Fig 15.29 Georgian wing armchair.

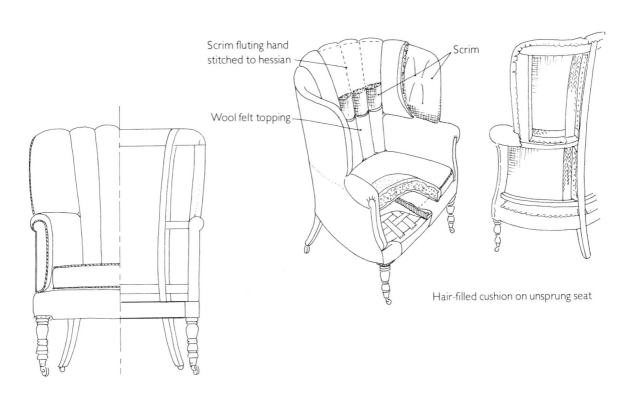

Scrim fluting hand stitched to hessian

Scrim

Wool felt topping

Hair-filled cushion on unsprung seat

Fig 15.30 Fluted wing chair, late eighteenth century.

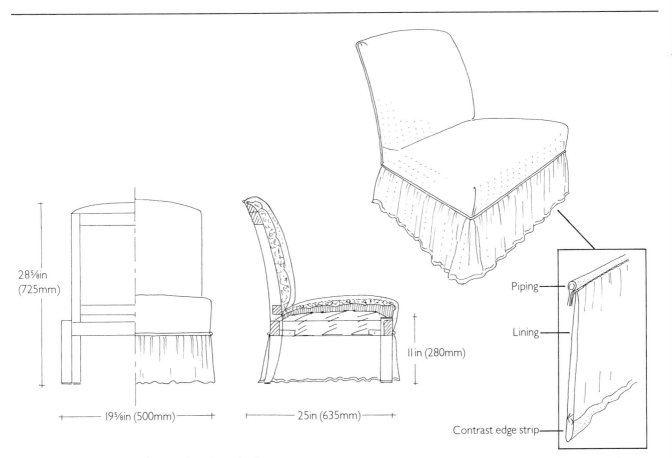

28⅝in (725mm)

11in (280mm)

Piping

Lining

Contrast edge strip

19⅝in (500mm)

25in (635mm)

Fig 15.31 Small bedroom chair with gathered valance.

Chapter Sixteen

Hand-sprung Upholstery

Since the middle of the nineteenth century, when sprung seating first became popular, the upholsterer has been hand-building sprung chairs and settees in an attempt to create comfortable furniture. By the end of the century the skill of springing up had become specialised and was carried out by a tradesman called a springer.

Today, in the factory situation, things have changed very little; the springer works in the spring shop where chair frames are prepared before being conveyed and stored ready for upholstery. Most traditional work done now, however, is carried out by the upholsterer, beginning with webbing and springing, followed by stuffing, stitching-up and covering.

There are many variations of hand-sprung work but all basically rely on a good webbed base and the correct choice of springs. It is probably true to say that the 6in (150mm) 10swg hourglass spring is the most used for average seating purposes. All other sizes and gauges are judged from this, being larger or smaller, heavier or lighter. By using this spring as a mean or average, the choice of which type to use is made easier and provides a basis from which to work. As an example, those seats which are obviously larger and deeper than average, will need 7in or 8in (175mm or 200mm) springs with perhaps a slight increase in gauge. It is not always good practice to make a seat firmer simply because it is larger. The end use must always be born in mind; it must, after all, be comfortable and acceptable to the user.

When fixed and lashed in place, the hourglass spring should be a minimum of 2in (50mm) above the rail edges. This allows comfortably for the springs to work in compression adequately and not become strained. The number of springs put into any area of seating can also have a bearing on the feel and comfort of a seat or back. Nine 6in (150mm) springs is a good number for a seat of average proportions. An extra row of three will need to be added if the seat is fairly deep. The same rule will apply if the seat is wider than normal. When the number of springs in a seat is increased, the seat will become firmer to the feel without actually

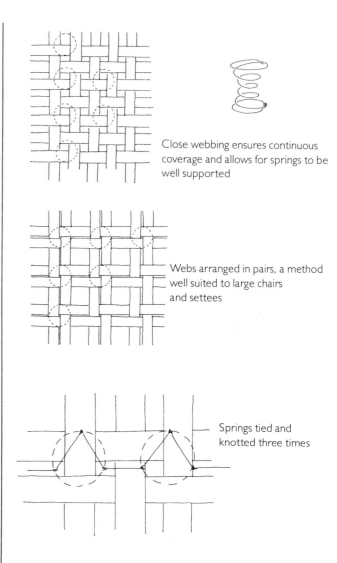

Close webbing ensures continuous coverage and allows for springs to be well supported

Webs arranged in pairs, a method well suited to large chairs and settees

Springs tied and knotted three times

Fig 16.1

increasing the wire gauge of the springs. However, the height of a spring will usually determine its gauge. Availability will also influence the choice being made. It can be said that generally springs for seating fall into the range of 8swg to 10swg, and their height from 5in to 8in (125mm to 200mm). Springs chosen for large armchairs will be in the 10swg to 12swg range, with a height of 4in or 5in (100mm or 125mm).

The choice for chair-back springs is always in the lighter gauge ranges. Traditionally upholstered chairs and settees, which have been hand sprung, need not be hard and unyielding. Research has shown that only 20 per cent of a sitter's weight is ever born by a chair back rest. A group of 11swg springs will produce a very firm back rest, so wire gauges should be generally well above this. When only a single row of back springs is needed for a lumbar support then 11 and 12 gauge are suitable. For a fully sprung back, however, gauges in the range of 14 to 16swg are ideal. The more springs used of course will automatically influence the feel and firmness.

Hourglass springs in the lighter 14 to 16 gauge ranges are produced mainly for the bedding industry. In mattresses, for example, large numbers of 16-gauge springs are grouped together as a unit. These are either as open units or as pocketed spring interiors. These light soft springs are ideal for chair back upholstery. The hourglass springs should be used rather than the barrel types, and tied in at about 6in (150mm) centres. Slightly heavier gauge springs are used at the base of a chair back if extra support is needed. Although there are no hard and fast rules regarding the selection of springs for chair work, the following table is given as a guide:

	Gauge (swg)	Height (in)	Type
Seats	8½	8–9 (200–225mm)	d/cone or hourglass
	9	6–7 (150–175mm)	ditto
	10	5–6 (125–150mm)	ditto
Arms	11	5 (125mm)	ditto
	12	4–5 (100–125mm)	ditto
Backs	12	6 (150mm)	ditto
	14	5–6 (125–150mm)	ditto
	16	4–5 (100–125mm)	ditto

The degree of comfort produced in a fully sprung chair is difficult to assess. The way in which springs are lashed down can have an effect on the comfort of a seat or back. Equally, the amount and the type of stuffing used can change the general feel and comfort. A good example of this is the use of curled hair as first stuffing in a seat, as compared with a fibre first stuffing. Hair will produce a slightly softer and more resilient foundation.

Experienced upholsterers will agree that they have their own preferences and will mostly stick to a routine that they have found to be satisfactory for their own style of work.

Fully sprung seats tend to fall into two separate categories. They are either firm edge or spring edge. Frame design generally determines which of these is to be used. The 'English' spring edge has a gutter and the front row of springs is fixed on to a wide front-seat rail. French and American spring edges are built up in a different way. Fig 16.2 shows the main differences.

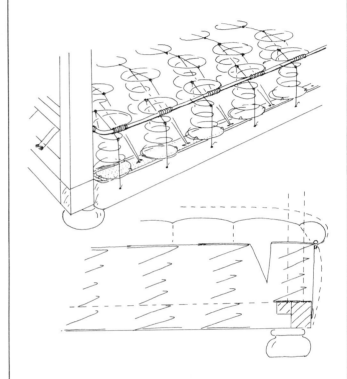

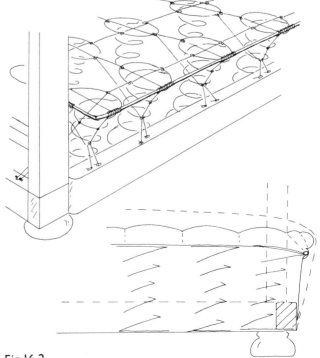

Fig 16.2

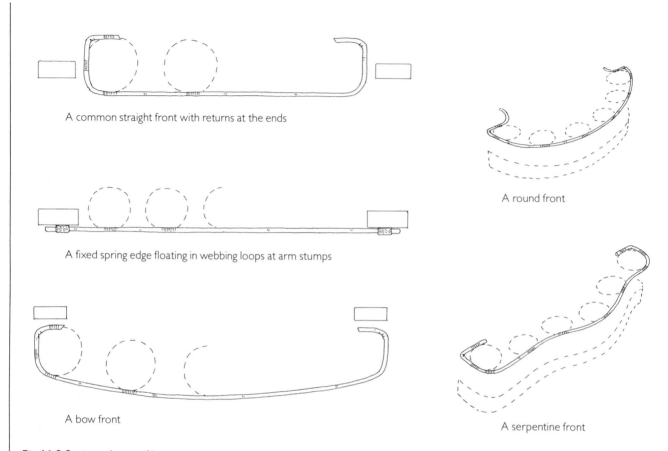

A common straight front with returns at the ends

A fixed spring edge floating in webbing loops at arm stumps

A bow front

A round front

A serpentine front

Fig 16.3 Spring edge profiles and shapes.

Tub Chair c. 1925

A combination of stippled show-wood and striking fabric design illustrates the decorative style of the 1920s.

Upholstery Hand-built on a strong heavy beech frame. The back and seat are sprung, with fillings of curled hair and wool flock.

The multi-coloured tapestry was piped and finished with decorative brass nails.

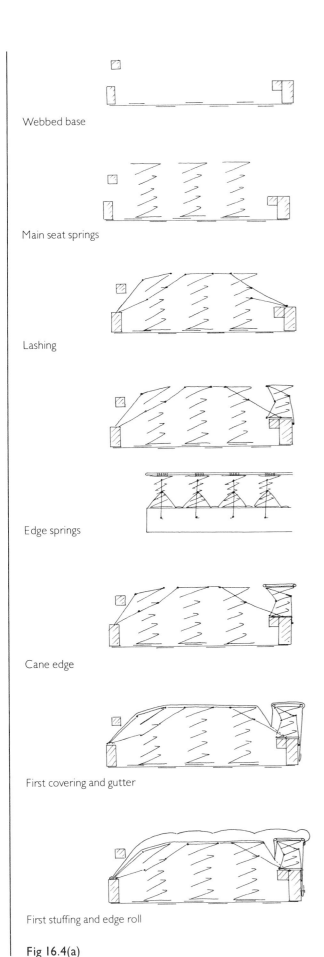

Webbed base

Main seat springs

Lashing

Edge springs

Cane edge

First covering and gutter

First stuffing and edge roll

Fig 16.4(a)

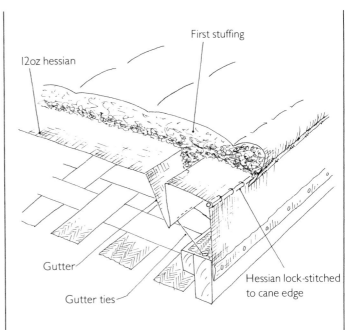

First stuffing

12oz hessian

Gutter

Gutter ties

Hessian lock-stitched to cane edge

Fig 16.4(b)

The spring edge is often referred to as the cane edge, which takes its name from the slim bamboo cane lashed along the front edge to hold the springs together and hold them in line. Since Victorian craftsmen first used this technique a flexible cane of about ⅜in (10mm) thickness is still the ideal material. When cane is not available a length of 8swg spring wire makes a good substitute. The wire does have some advantages, it is slightly cheaper to buy and can be bent and shaped more easily which is useful when serpentine and shaped fronts are being produced. Some spring edge shapes are shown in Fig 16.3.

There are occasions when a cane edge is formed around the whole perimeter of a seat, giving the seat a precise shape, often used in tub chairs and D-shaped seats. However, its main use is for seat fronts and top edges on chair and settee backs. Fig 16.4(a) illustrates the order in which a typical spring edge seat is built.

At this point the scrim work is complete and the choice of covering work has to be made. This choice depends on the style and shape of the job. Four typical variations are: a fixed seat with under edge and border, a cushion seat with platform and gutter, a cushion seat with under edge and borders, and an interesting variation using buttoned upholstery (Fig 16.5).

Producing a well-built spring edge relies on the correct positioning of springs, and an ability to tie and lash firmly. Providing the correct sequence is followed and care is taken at each stage to ensure that all the components line up and relate to the frame shape, the result will be good. It is helpful to stand back from the work occasionally, or move the chair to floor level and take a careful look at the work from different views. Any part that is badly out of line will then be obvious.

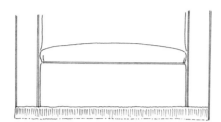

Fixed seat with under edge and border

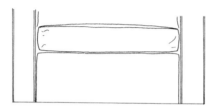

Cushion seat with platform and gutter

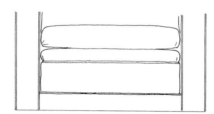

Cushion seat with under edge and borders

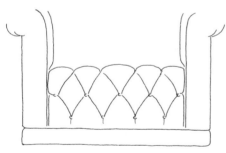

Using buttoned upholstery

Fig 16.5

Firm edge springing is a much simpler technique and is more generally used than the spring edge. A good webbed base is fitted, usually to the underside of the rails and the springs arranged and sewn on to the webbing. Spring arrangements depend on the size and shape of the area to be sprung. In most cases an hourglass spring has a base diameter of 3½in to 4in (88mm to 100mm) and these should be placed at about 6in (150mm) centres. This will produce a space of about 2½in (63mm) between springs. This can be reduced or increased to suit a particular seat or back.

As the springs are being spaced out and arranged on the webbing, the lashing operation should be kept in mind so that, where possible, straight lines of lashing will take in all the springs. Some typical arrangements

of springs are shown in Fig 16.6. Good lashing is important if a seat is to remain sound and comfortable. Springs are usually lashed with laid cord which is a very strong and stable material. When lashed into place a group of springs will be reduced in height by about 1¼in (30mm). Pulling the springs down any more than this is unnecessary and merely creates a very hard piece of work.

In a well-lashed seat the outer springs should be slightly tilted towards the outer edges of the frame and the centre springs should remain upright. Fig 16.7 shows the sequence of building firm edge sprung seating: webbing, springs, lashing and hessian covering and first stuffing.

LASHING

There is a variety of methods used to lash springs into place. Basically, the springs should be held in compression and not allowed to move or 'chatter' or become stressed in use. Plain lashing is produced with two lines of cord, one running front to back and the second running from side to side. A further two rows of cord can be added to form the second method called star lashing. The extra two are put in diagonally. The diagonal rows may run simply from corner to corner only or may be put in along all the diagonal rows of springs.

Plain lashing and star lashing are applied over the surface of the springs and link the tops of all the springs in two or three directions. A third method is centre lashing; this may be used as an addition to the other two or may be used as an alternative. When used as an addition it is only necessary to centre lash when spring heights reach 8in (200mm) or more. This helps to stabilise the group and stop distortion. Centre lashing can, however, be used as an alternative in place of the other two top lashed methods, on any size of spring. This method would be chosen when a softer and fairly flat seat is required. By lashing through the centre of a row of springs the top half is left free and relatively soft, the springs being stabilised from their centres (Fig 16.8). The above methods are all generally used and are adequate for most types of sprung upholstery work.

SPRUNG ARMS

Using 11- or 12-gauge springs the traditional spring arm is typical of Victorian and Edwardian upholstery. Frame design is important, the main arm rail needs to be wide enough and set low to provide adequate space for the springs. As with all springs that are mounted on to rails, an insulator of cloth or webbing is first stapled to the rail. The springs are then positioned and fixed over this. Wire staples are used, three per spring, or

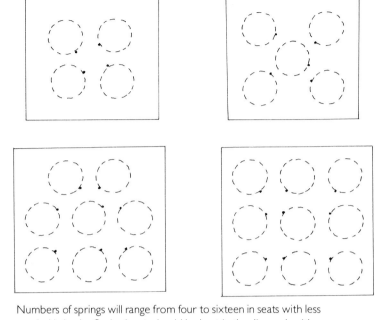

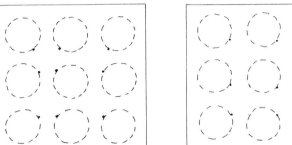

Numbers of springs will range from four to sixteen in seats with less needed in backs. Spring knots should be kept in the diagonal, with outer edges always clear.

Fig 16.6(a) Typical spring arrangements.

Spring layout for a large chair seat

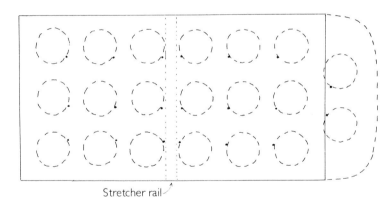

An extra row of three may often be placed over the stretcher rail for the longer seat. Two extra springs are added for a *chaise-longue* end.

Stretcher rail

Fig 16.6(b) An average layout for a settee seat.

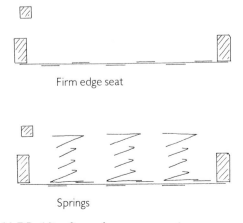

Firm edge seat

Springs

Fig 16.7 Building firm edge sprung seating.

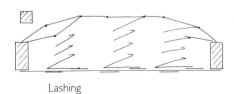

Lashing

Hessian covering and first stuffing

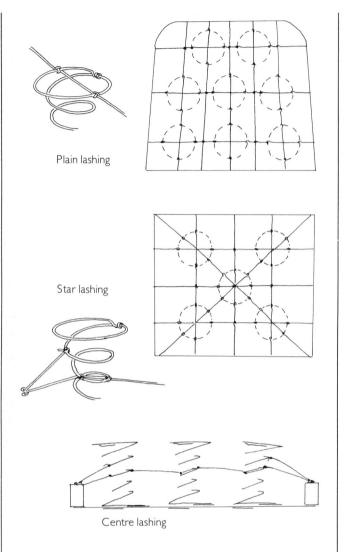

Plain lashing

Star lashing

Centre lashing

Fig 16.8 Types of lashing.

Fixing springs with webbing and tacks

Springs insulated from frame and fixed down with wire staples

Fig 16.9 A typical arm frame with good depth for springing.

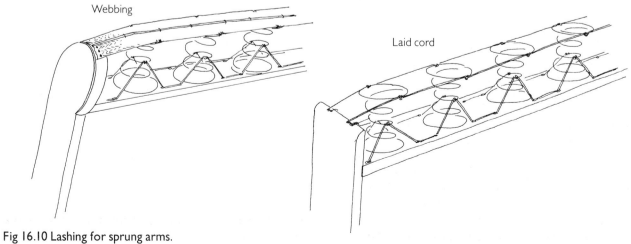

Webbing

Laid cord

Fig 16.10 Lashing for sprung arms.

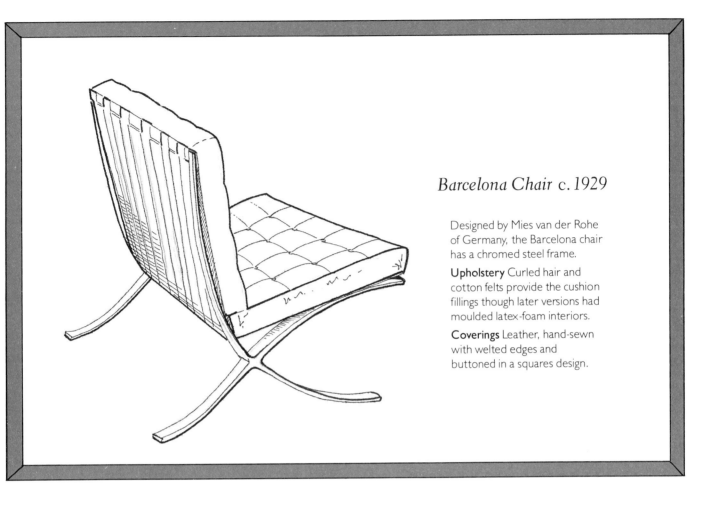

Barcelona Chair c. 1929

Designed by Mies van der Rohe of Germany, the Barcelona chair has a chromed steel frame.

Upholstery Curled hair and cotton felts provide the cushion fillings though later versions had moulded latex-foam interiors.

Coverings Leather, hand-sewn with welted edges and buttoned in a squares design.

strips of webbing with tacks neatly set around the spring base (Fig 16.9).

Two methods of lashing are shown: using webbing as the main link between springs, and using laid cord (Fig 16.10). Lightly stitched edges are created with the first stuffing, which may be fibre or hair. Arm shape will determine the amount and position of the stitching necessary. Scroll arms need a large roll or 'Chesterfield' stitch to support and hold the fillings. Arms that are more square or flat in section will normally require a sharper and smaller edge stitch along each side of the springing (Fig 16.11).

Three interesting pieces of spring work which use the basic techniques, with the introduction of shape and guttering, are the Chesterfield arm sofa, the sprung pouffe and a large easy armchair. The Chesterfield-style settee has three or sometimes four rows of 11swg double-cone springs. The top row sits upright on the frame while the second row is bent and angled over the frame edge and the subsequent rows are sewn into webbing to form the inside back rest. There are many variations for sofas of this kind, some of which have buttoned upholstery and some plain. When a job of this kind is to be buttoned, it is best not to web too densely so that access is available at the back

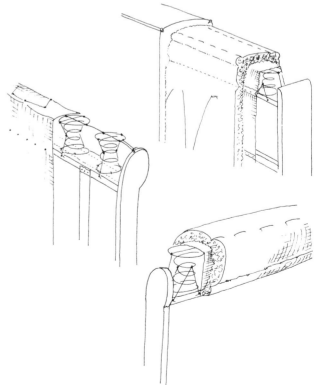

Fig 16.11 Creating shape with lightly stitched edges on square and scroll arms.

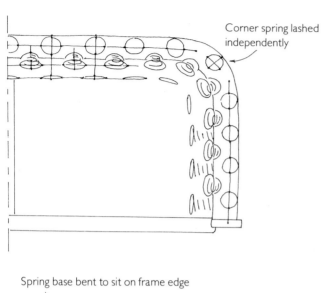

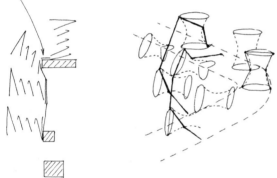

Fig 16.12 A fully sprung Chesterfield-style sofa.

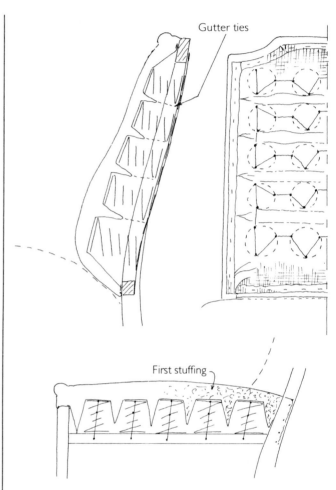

Fig 16.13 Guttering techniques on a large chair and on a sprung arm.

for tying off buttons. Fig 16.12 shows a plan and end view of the spring layout. A cane edge is sometimes used along the top back edge to help form a good outline and link the outer springs together.

The guttering technique is used in chair back upholstery to create independent rows of springing. A soft and luxurious back rest can be created using this method with curled hair first stuffing on 12- and 14-gauge springs. Gutters are formed horizontally with hessian tied down between each row of springs. These are then filled with stuffing and the back is bridled between the rows. An 11-gauge spring may be used in the base of the back (Fig 16.13).

Spring pouffes or floor seats have hardwood base frames and sprung edge tops. Two shapes are shown in Fig 16.14, each with nine 10swg springs. The appearance or style and finish of the seats can be made interesting and imaginative by careful selection of cover and trimmings.

In contrast, some interesting but much smaller pieces of upholstery are described with annotated drawings to conclude the following chapter, all of which illustrates the diverse range of work produced and restored by the upholsterer.

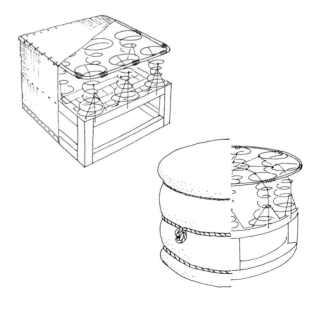

Fig 16.14 Sprung pouffes using nine 10-gauge springs and a cane-edge construction.

— *Chapter Seventeen* —

Settees and Other Pieces

The settee or sofa has long been associated with the lounge areas of houses and large buildings. As a piece of furniture it has always fascinated designers and architects, and down the ages many have extended its function and reshaped its outline to suit different social and architectural conditions.

A couch or *chaise longue* with its long seat and open end provides a seat for reclining and resting during the day, as well an occasional seat for two or three people. The modern settee, in a similar way, can be multi-functional. The sofa bed quickly converts from lounge seating to a double bed for night-time use.

During the early twentieth century, it became fashionable to provide seating for a small group of people in a quiet corner of a room. This became known as a 'cosy corner' and provided warmth and quiet in

houses and halls where rooms were generally large and draughty. The cosy corner was upholstered and draped with fabrics and was created and furnished by the upholsterer as a miniature interior.

The Knole settee is perhaps one of the earliest fully upholstered pieces of seating which is notable for its particular style. It has been copied and restyled many times, particularly by the Victorians. The Knole provdes an enclosed area for two or three people sitting together, with a high back and ends which are

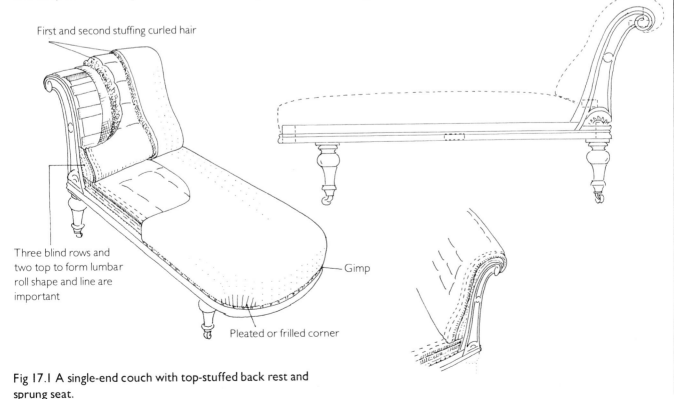

First and second stuffing curled hair

Three blind rows and two top to form lumbar roll shape and line are important

Gimp

Pleated or frilled corner

Fig 17.1 A single-end couch with top-stuffed back rest and sprung seat.

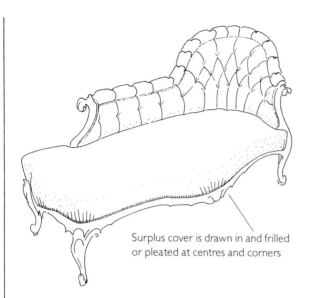

Surplus cover is drawn in and frilled or pleated at centres and corners

Fig 17.2 Mid-Victorian *chaise-longue* with buttoned and pleated edging.

Section of back rest, well regulated and top-stitched only

View of scrim and stitch work with button positions marked

adjustable. Basically simple but very functional, it quickly converts to a long lounger for day or evening use.

Another settee, which is very different in style but nonetheless impressive, is the Chesterfield. This was and still is made for club and domestic use. Not so much a piece of furniture to hide away in, but a low, opulent, styled sofa that one would wish to be seen

using. The Chesterfield can have a drop end or drop arm, which adapts easily for lounging and reclining.

Settees, long chairs, and couches are seen and enjoyed at their best where plenty of space is available. A large hall or foyer or a spacious lounge allow these larger pieces of upholstery to breathe and show their comfort and splendour.

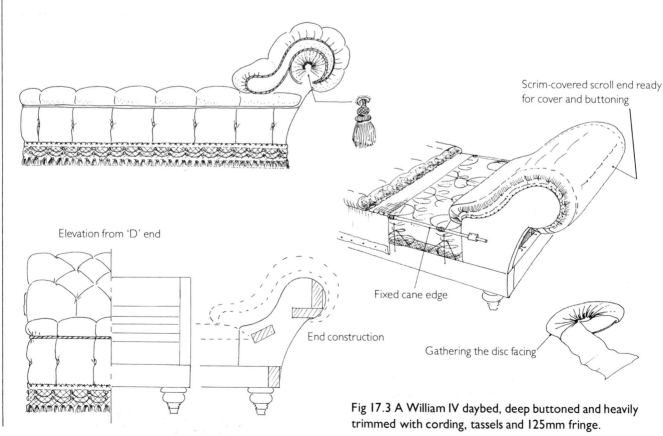

Scrim-covered scroll end ready for cover and buttoning

Elevation from 'D' end

Fixed cane edge

End construction

Gathering the disc facing

Fig 17.3 A William IV daybed, deep buttoned and heavily trimmed with cording, tassels and 125mm fringe.

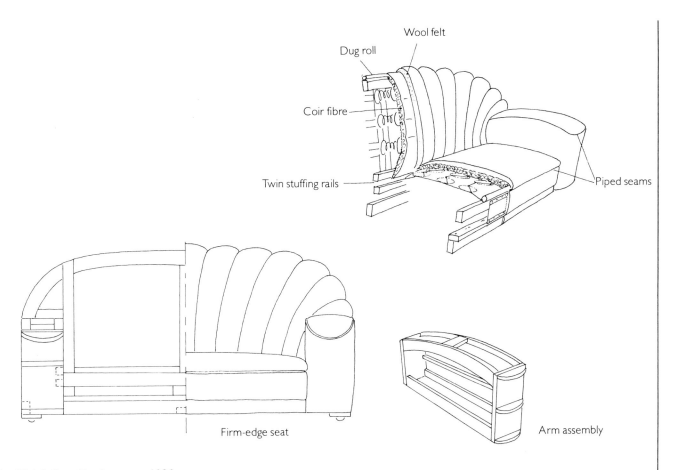

Wool felt

Dug roll

Coir fibre

Twin stuffing rails

Piped seams

Firm-edge seat

Arm assembly

Fig 17.4 A fluted back settee, 1930.

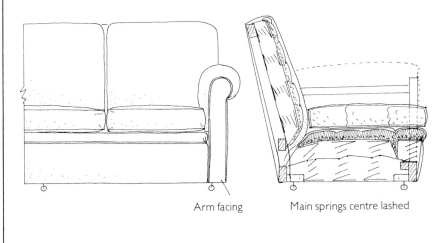

Arm facing

Main springs centre lashed

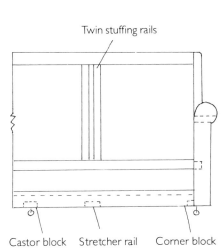

Twin stuffing rails

Castor block   Stretcher rail   Corner block

Fig 17.5 A large cushion settee with fixed spring-edge back cushions and loose feather-filled seat cushions. Curled hair, coir fibre and wool felts are used for first and second stuffings.

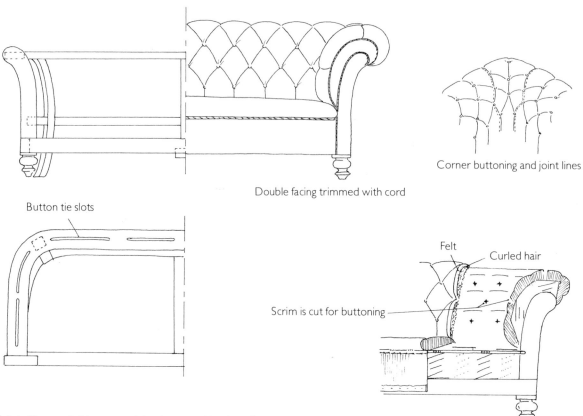

Corner buttoning and joint lines

Double facing trimmed with cord

Button tie slots

Felt

Curled hair

Scrim is cut for buttoning

Fig 17.6 A Chesterfield settee with a buttoned back and plain sprung-edge seat.

Tube Chair Art Deco
c. 1932

A comfortable tube-frame chair typical of its period. It is a mixture of chromed-steel tube and dark-coloured leather cloth, with a soft cantilever action.

Upholstery The chair back and seat are hand sprung on a beech frame. The fillings used were coir fibre, curled hair and a variety of flocks.

Coverings Moquettes and nitro-cellulose leather cloths were used, depending on whether the chair was for domestic or club use.

Hall or Lounge Stool

I The well-worn original upholstery is stripped and removed. Grass fibre and coloured webbings show evidence of age.

2 A webbed base is the first stage of restoration, using 2in (50mm) brown jute webbing and ½in (13mm) fine tacks (see pages 167–168).

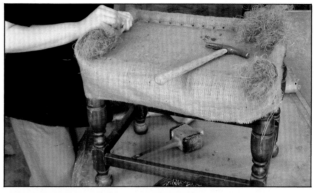

3 Strong hessian is used to line up the stool, cut with a large margin left to overhang all edges. Coir fibre is tightly rolled up and tacked to create the dug roll edge (see page 174).

4 The dugging or tack roll is run through with a top stitch to make it firm and sharp. A good dense layer of curled hair is strung in to form the first stuffing (see page 174).

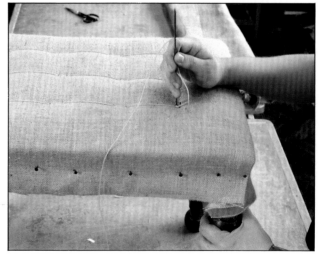

5 Fine jute scrim is temporary tacked over the first stuffing and bridle stitched to hold and set the hair in place (see page 170).

6 One or two layers of cotton felt or wool felt form the second stuffing over the scrim and are then pulled down in calico, with the corners neatly pleated. The scrim and the calico are tacked and trimmed without turnings.

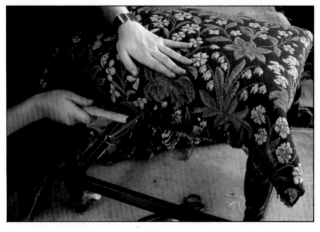

7 The heavy blue tapestry (which was an original covering taken from an old sofa) is set on and temporary tacked to give the best arrangement of pattern.

8 The borders of new cotton velour are pinned and slip stitched in place over a soft filling of cotton skin wadding (see page 120).

9 Upholstery cord is bound at the end and tucked down into the corner of the border before being slipped in place to trim the top edge (see page 215).

10 Tassel fringe completes the trimming, which is glued or back stitched along the border edge. A bottom lining is added to finish the underside of the stool.

Project Four
Mid-Victorian Dining Chair with Buttoned Seat

1 After careful stripping and cleaning, the bare chair frame is ready for reupholstery. The show-wood has been revived and waxed (see page 268).

3 10oz or 12oz hessian is fixed and turned to form a tight covering over the webbings. Chamfered outer edges are kept clear. Stuffing ties are then looped into the new hessian (see page 165 and Fig 13.6).

2 Reupholstery begins with new English webbing, set three by three and interwoven. The webbing should be tight but not overstrained (see Fig 13.2, page 167).

4 A first stuffing of coir fibre or Algerian grass is strung in and teased to a good even thickness over the seat (see pages 167–8).

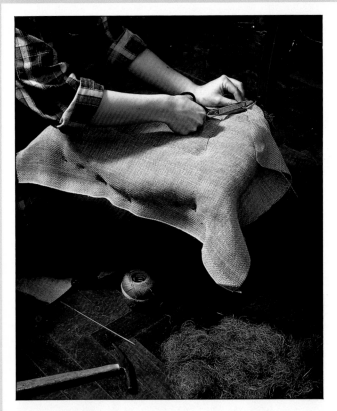

5 Fine 7oz scrim is temporary tacked and bridled down over the stuffing. The corners are folded back and cut around the two back legs (see Fig 13.9).

6 A small, even, stitched edge is formed around the seat using one blind stitch and one row of top stitches. At the pre-marked button points the scrim is cut (see Figs 13.13, 13.14 and 13.20).

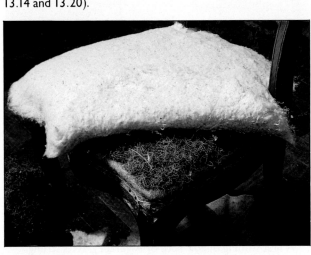

7 Soft even layers of curled hair and cotton felt combine to make the top stuffings (see Fig 13.21).

8 The long double point bayonet needle with flax twine is used to pull in the centre button to half depth. Diamond pleats begin to form as the buttoning continues (see Figs 13.23 and 13.24).

9 Pleats are straightened and adjusted with regulator and fingers before the buttons are tightened to full depth. Upholstery gimp finishes and decorates the curved seat edges (see pages 176–7, and Fig 13.25).

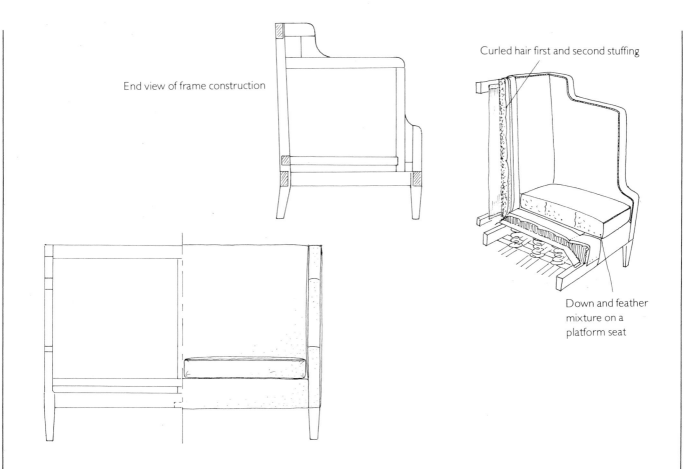

End view of frame construction

Curled hair first and second stuffing

Down and feather mixture on a platform seat

Fig 17.7 A tall-back settle-style settee.

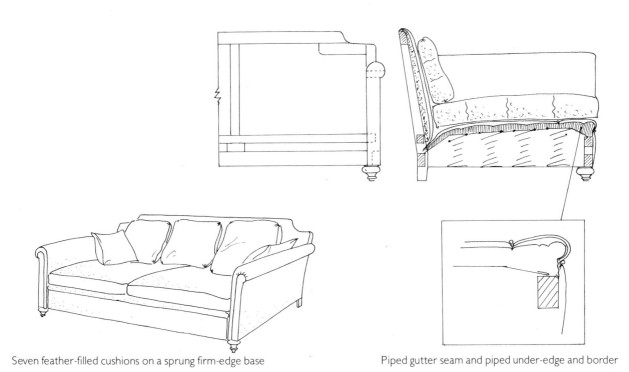

Seven feather-filled cushions on a sprung firm-edge base

Piped gutter seam and piped under-edge and border

Fig 17.8 A long, deep-seated sofa.

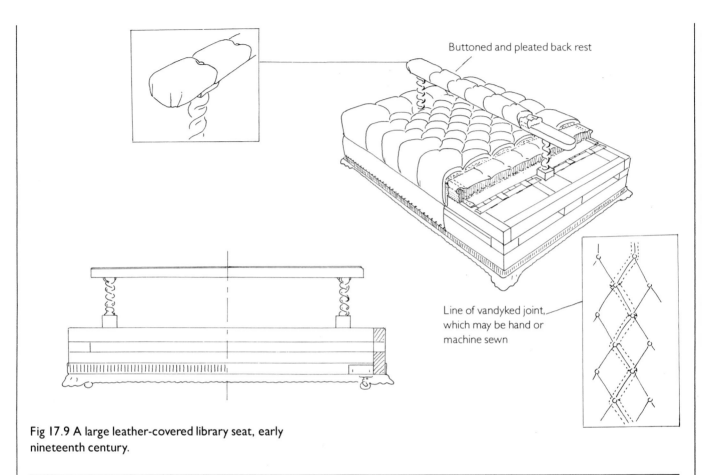

Buttoned and pleated back rest

Line of vandyked joint, which may be hand or machine sewn

Fig 17.9 A large leather-covered library seat, early nineteenth century.

Back frame is removed for upholstery, then refixed with dowel and screw fittings

Hair-filled bolster stitched up in scrim or ticking

Webbing and hessian

Wadding and calico

Bolster ends, hair or feather filled

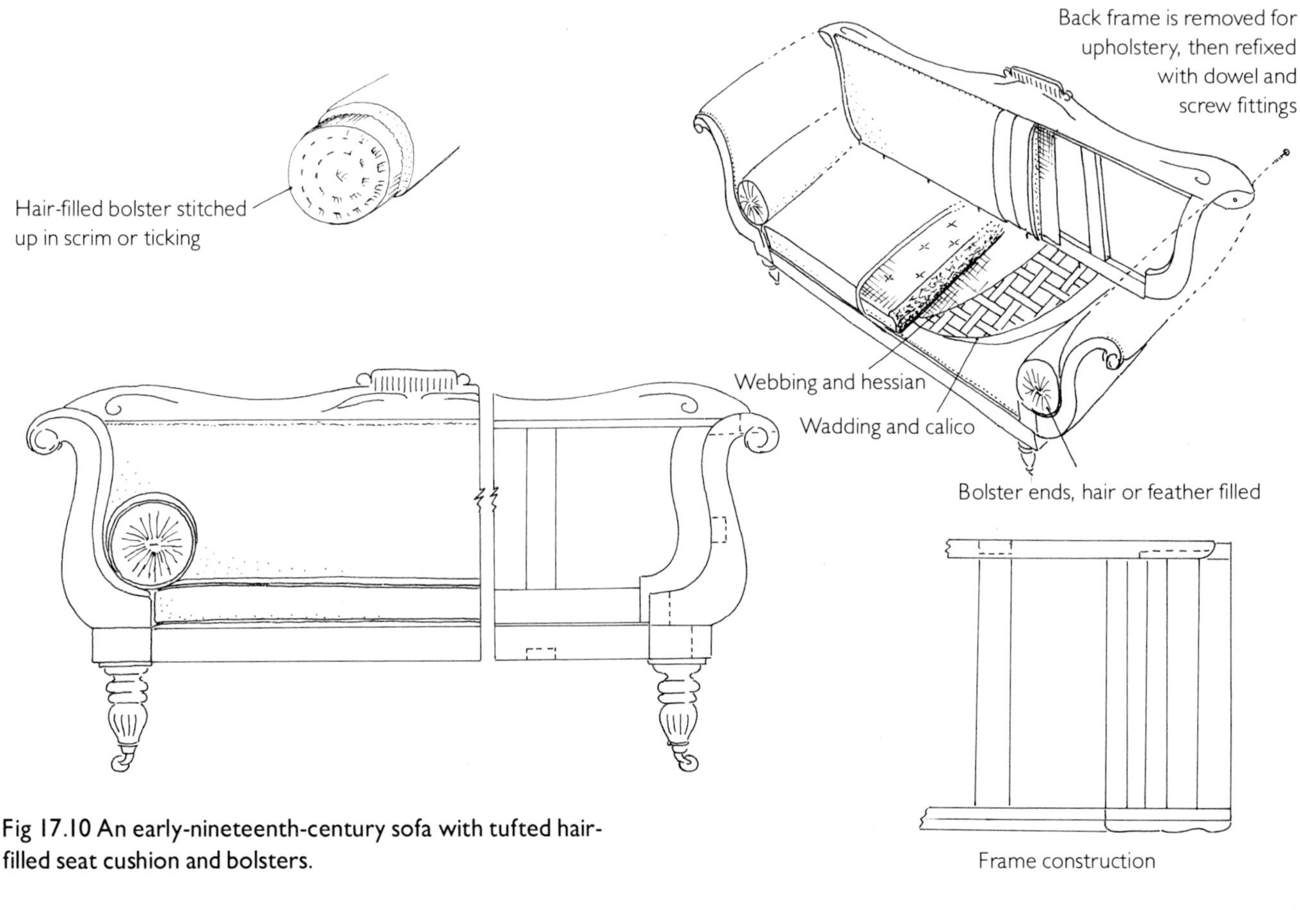

Fig 17.10 An early-nineteenth-century sofa with tufted hair-filled seat cushion and bolsters.

Frame construction

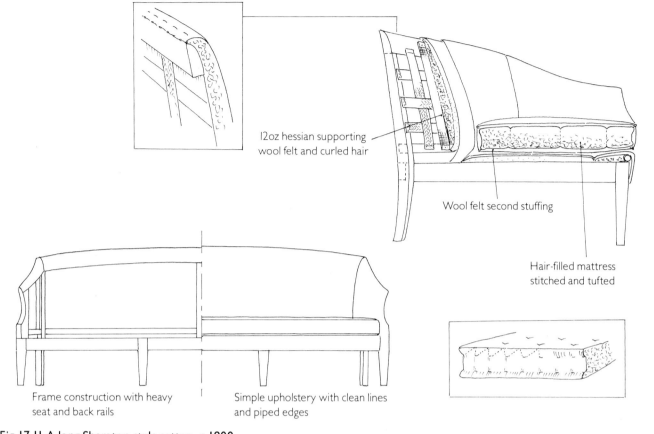

12oz hessian supporting
wool felt and curled hair

Wool felt second stuffing

Hair-filled mattress
stitched and tufted

Frame construction with heavy
seat and back rails

Simple upholstery with clean lines
and piped edges

Fig 17.11 A long Sheraton-style settee, c.1800.

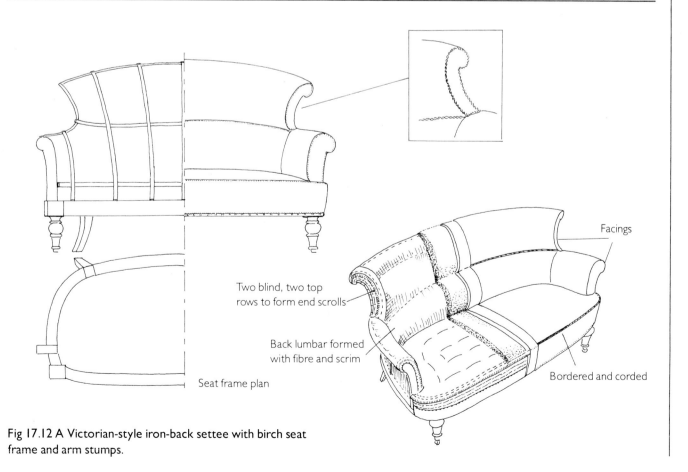

Facings

Two blind, two top
rows to form end scrolls

Back lumbar formed
with fibre and scrim

Seat frame plan

Bordered and corded

Fig 17.12 A Victorian-style iron-back settee with birch seat
frame and arm stumps.

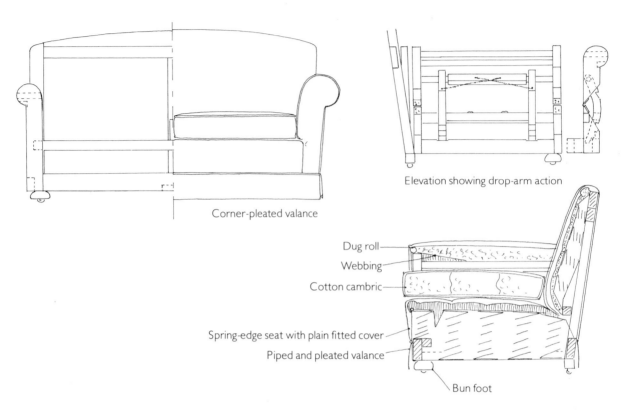

Corner-pleated valance

Elevation showing drop-arm action

Dug roll

Webbing

Cotton cambric

Spring-edge seat with plain fitted cover

Piped and pleated valance

Bun foot

Fig 17.13 A large, comfortable two-and-a-half-seater settee with drop arm.

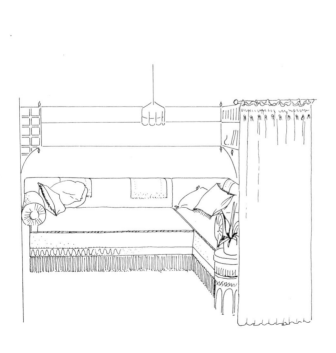

Fig 17.14 A 'cosy corner' using two settees, c.1900. Turkish-and-Moorish-style furnishings became popular towards the end of the Victorian period.

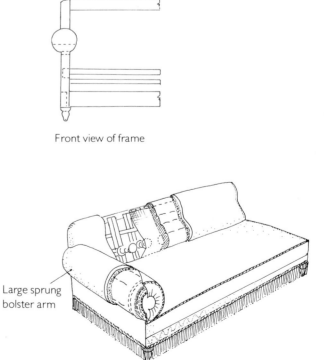

Front view of frame

Large sprung bolster arm

Cane-edge seat with corded and fringed borders

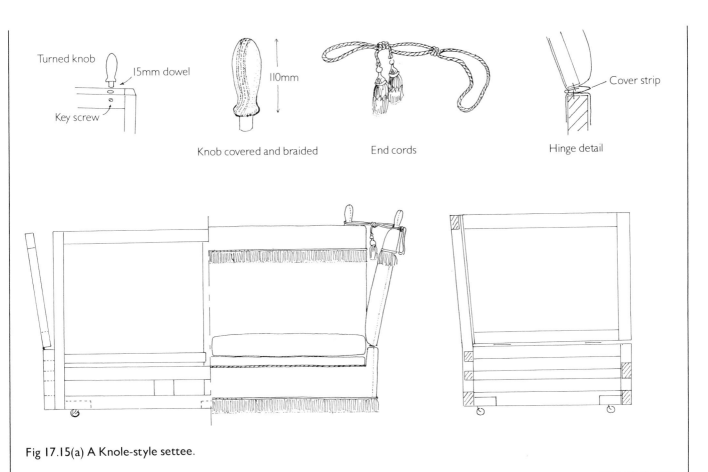

Turned knob

15mm dowel

Key screw

Knob covered and braided

110mm

End cords

Cover strip

Hinge detail

Fig 17.15(a) A Knole-style settee.

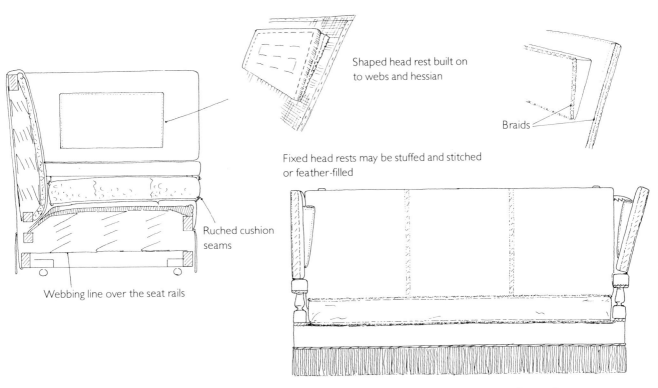

Shaped head rest built on to webs and hessian

Braids

Fixed head rests may be stuffed and stitched or feather-filled

Ruched cushion seams

Webbing line over the seat rails

Back and seat have been sprung for comfort

Fig 17.15(b) An earlier-style Knole which resembles more closely the original seventeenth-century settee.

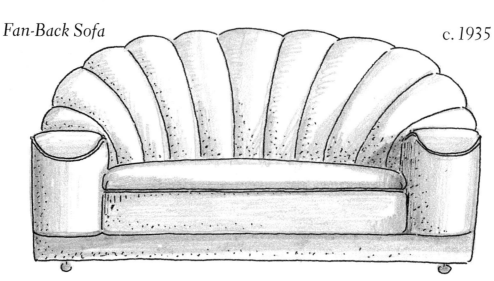

Fan-Back Sofa
c. 1935

An outstanding post-Deco design with typical sunray-fluted upholstery on a hardwood birch frame. Seats were often double sprung with lip front.

Upholstery Always firm and tightly stretched to hold the sharp outlines. These designs were produced in suites of three and four pieces.

Coverings Curly-pile moquettes, hides and coated cloths.

Seaming and fluting were machine-sewn.

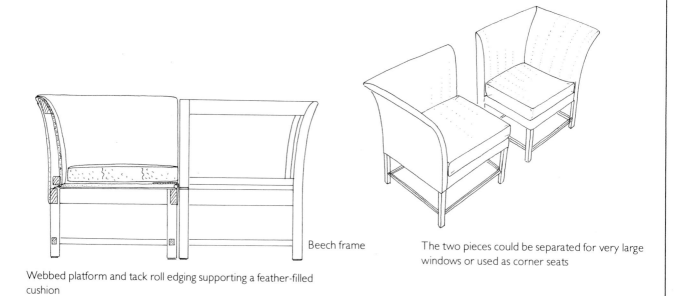

Webbed platform and tack roll edging supporting a feather-filled cushion

Beech frame

The two pieces could be separated for very large windows or used as corner seats

Fig 17.16 An early-nineteenth-century window seat.

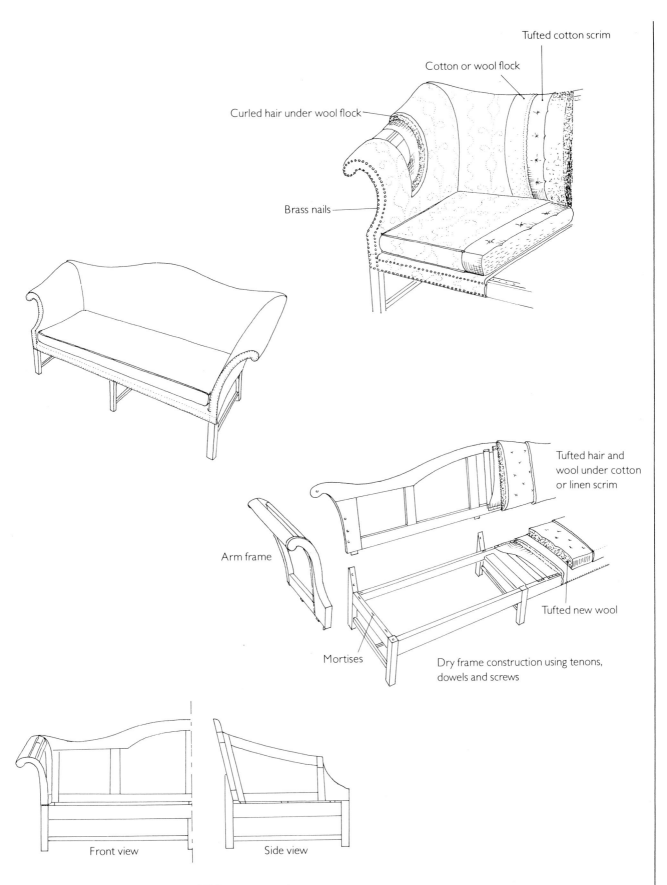

Tufted cotton scrim

Cotton or wool flock

Curled hair under wool flock

Brass nails

Tufted hair and wool under cotton or linen scrim

Arm frame

Tufted new wool

Mortises

Dry frame construction using tenons, dowels and screws

Front view

Side view

Fig 17.17 A Chippendale-style settee, *c.*1790, constructed on a mahogany seat frame with detachable arm and back supports.

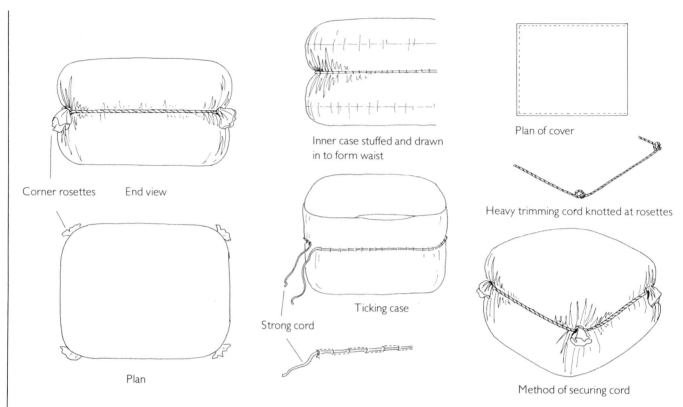

Corner rosettes   End view

Plan

Inner case stuffed and drawn in to form waist

Ticking case

Strong cord

Plan of cover

Heavy trimming cord knotted at rosettes

Method of securing cord

Fig 17.18 An Edwardian pouffe or footstool stuffed with straw, woodwool or flock.

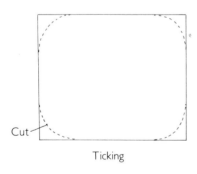

Cut

Ticking

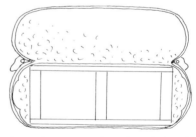

An alternative construction using a timber frame in the lower half

The inner case of strong calico or ticking forms the main construction and shape of the pouffe. This is made up to the size required with a base and top and a border or wall; a filling gap is left in the top edge.

A strong draw cord is fitted and anchored around the centre or just above the centre of the border. The case should be well filled and the draw cord gradually drawn to create a waisted shape. When the filling has settled the cord should be tied off and the filling gap sewn up.

Covering: Slide the completed inner into the sewn cover and slip the opening. Tuck the cover seams into the waist, draw up the corners and stitch in place.

Trimming: Secure the waist with heavy trimming cord, pulling tightly and knotting around the drawn up corners. Form the rosettes and secure with a few stitches.

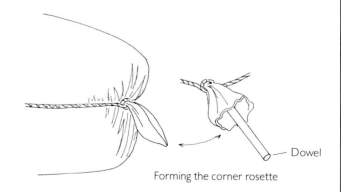

Dowel

Forming the corner rosette

Fig 17.19

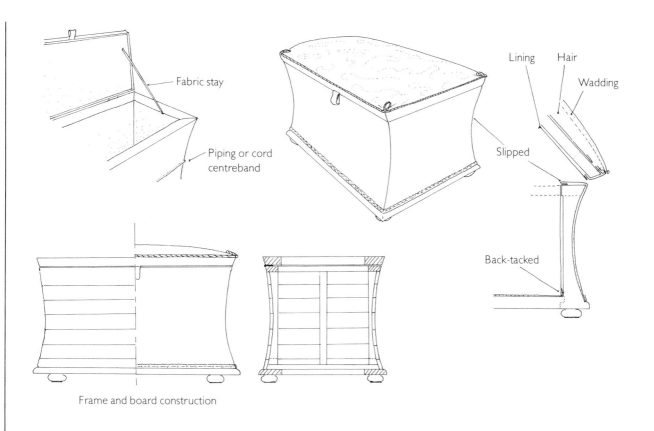

Fig 17.20 A late nine-nineteenth-century box ottoman.

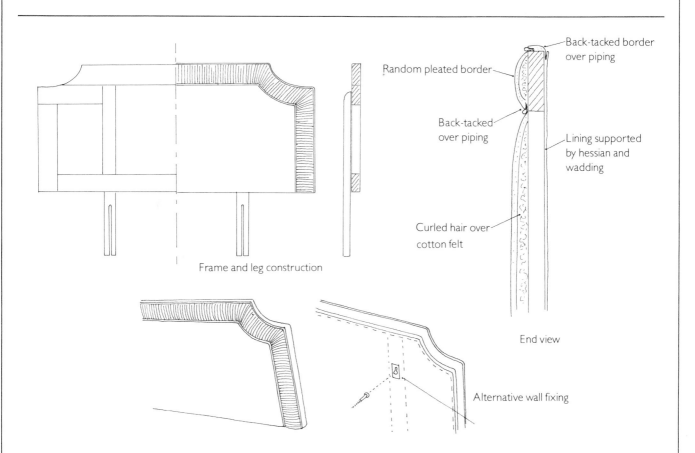

Fig 17.21 A double-bed headboard in a traditional style.

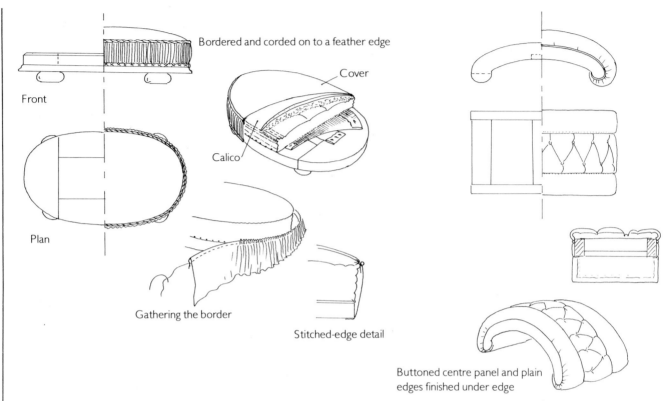

Bordered and corded on to a feather edge

Front

Cover

Calico

Plan

Gathering the border

Stitched-edge detail

Buttoned centre panel and plain edges finished under edge

Fig 17.22 Two nineteenth-century footstools.

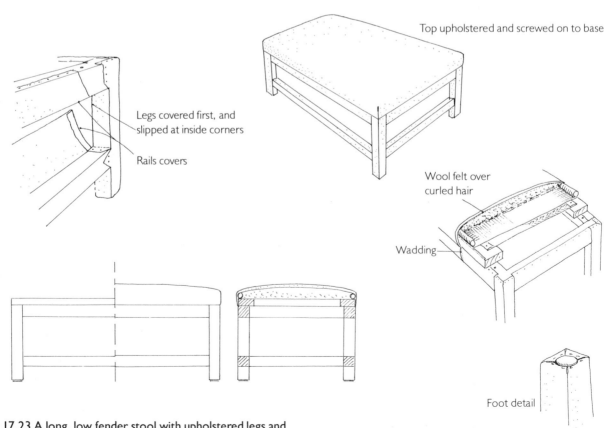

Top upholstered and screwed on to base

Legs covered first, and slipped at inside corners

Rails covers

Wool felt over curled hair

Wadding

Foot detail

Fig 17.23 A long, low fender stool with upholstered legs and underframe.

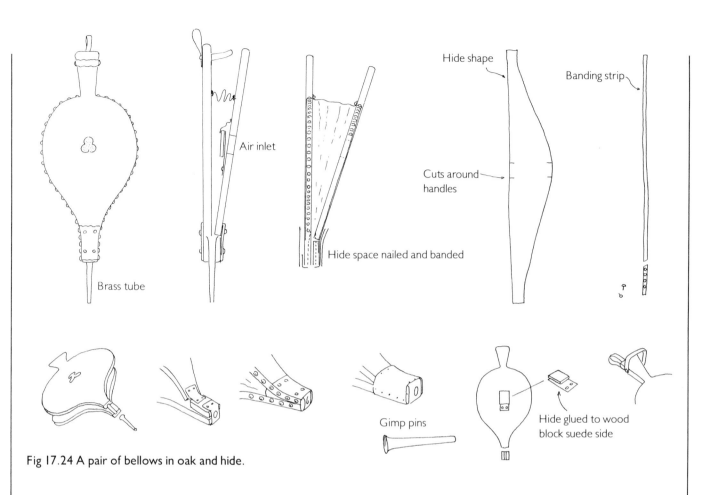

Brass tube

Air inlet

Hide space nailed and banded

Hide shape

Banding strip

Cuts around handles

Gimp pins

Hide glued to wood block suede side

Fig 17.24 A pair of bellows in oak and hide.

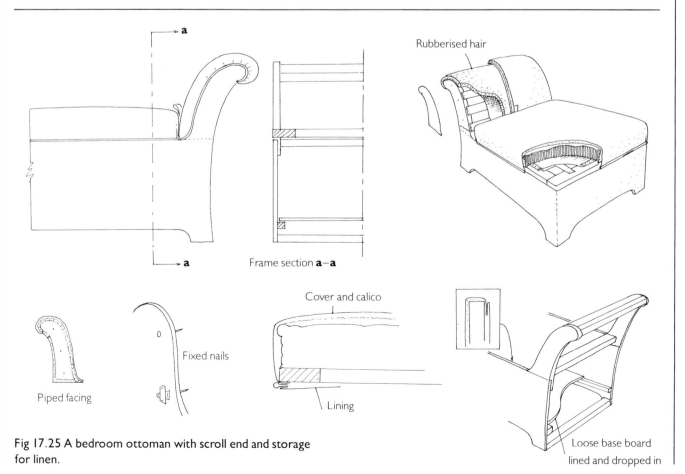

a

a

Frame section **a–a**

Rubberised hair

Piped facing

Fixed nails

Cover and calico

Lining

Loose base board lined and dropped in

Fig 17.25 A bedroom ottoman with scroll end and storage for linen.

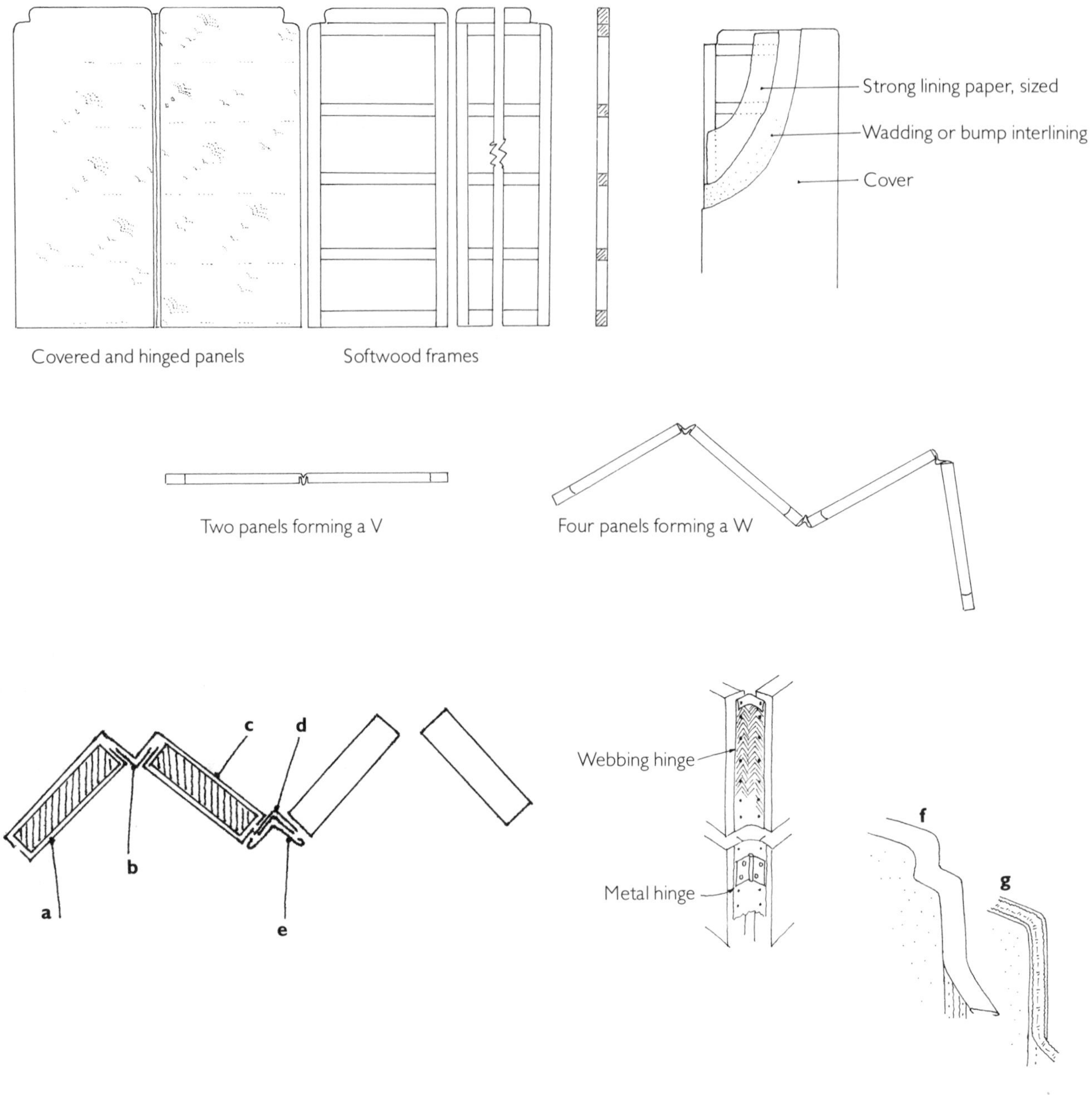

Covered and hinged panels   Softwood frames

Strong lining paper, sized

Wadding or bump interlining

Cover

Two panels forming a V   Four panels forming a W

Webbing hinge

Metal hinge

Fig 17.26 An upholstered four-fold screen.

The upholstered screen should be both functional and attractive. To ensure that a screen of this type is completely draughtproof, the frames are lined with strong Kraft paper or lining paper and then sized for added strength. Skin wadding or bump interlining is used as a padding.

Two V panels are made up first by covering and hingeing. The face covering **a** is applied, followed by the cover strip **b**, and then the hinge, which may be webbing or three metal hinges. The back covering **c** is fixed in place ensuring a good allowance is made into the hinge recess; at this point the cover is stitched, glued or gimp-pinned in place.

The two completed V panels are then brought together and the hinge is fixed; this is then covered by the cover strip **e**, which is slipped to the leading edges and glued or stitched to the back of the hinge.

Any trimming method may be used to finish all the edges of the screen, e.g. as in **f** and **g**.

Chapter Eighteen

Beds and Bedding

The bed is almost certainly one of the oldest pieces of furniture used by people. Beds and the making of them have a long and fascinating history, and the earliest recorded inventory included a bed, a chest and an oak bench.

In the year 1600 a bed in its simplest form was basically an oblong timber frame with rope or leather strips stretched and woven across it. The rope created a crude but flexible support for a long fabric bag stuffed with any available soft filling. The frame and its simple overlay were supported above floor level by wooden legs which were easily removable. Two other methods of support used stone work at a suitable height, or two small wooden chests, which provided storage and, at the same time, supported each end of the bed frame.

In the same period and in complete contrast to this simple piece of furniture, beds provided in palaces and manor houses were much more grand. These were of a much more permanent nature and mostly built-in as part of a bedroom or room corner. Generally, the main differences between the two types of bed were the size and the way in which the bigger bed was furnished. Curtains, drapes and covers were relatively lavish and expensive, for those who could afford them. In many cases beds in large houses were distinguished particularly by the textile coverings placed upon them. Mattresses or overlays, however, were basically the same but almost always filled with feathers. Very often the large bed would have two mattresses, the lower filled with wool and the upper with feathers and down.

Later in the period, enclosed sleeping places were

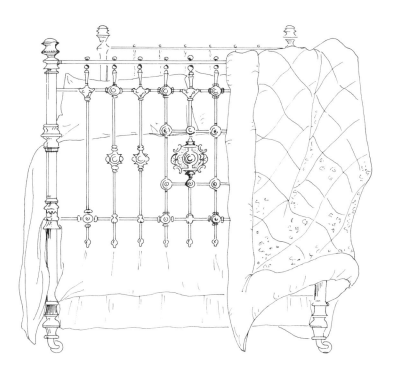

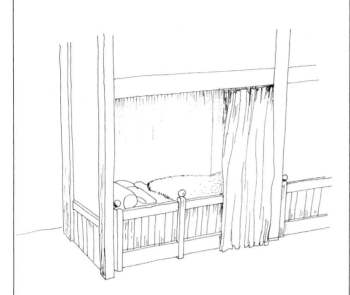

Fig 18.1 A Saxon bed, built in as a cabin made completely from locally grown timber, and furnished with animal skins and simple curtaining.

created either in an alcove or with wood panelling. Drapes and curtains hung in front of the sleeping area made a warm comfortable compartment. By the year 1660 it is evident from engravings and paintings that most beds and sleeping areas were relatively well furnished and well made. The bed base or frame remained simple, with the additional forms of support being either stretched canvas or rows of wood slats.

Suspending drapes and curtains was popular, with poles protruding from walls high above the bed or hung from a frame suspended from the ceiling with rope. Some were cantilevered from an end wall, again with

Fig 18.2 A Norman bed which was timber framed; long metal rods supported the draught-proof curtains.

heavy ropes or chains. These bed constructions remained in use for many years until they were eventually superseded by the canopy and the tester, which were carried by the bed itself. This meant that the larger bed became more mobile and had developed as a free-standing piece of furniture. Beds of this kind could be dismantled when necessary and rebuilt elsewhere. Style and colour could also be changed easily by removing the drapes and having a new set made and fixed by the house staff or by the upholder.

Attendants and those who worked in service had similar beds but on a smaller, less luxurious scale. However, it was often found that these took up too much room. A solution was found in the truckle bed. This was built very low and was as lightly framed as possible, being easy to move, and was stored under the large bed when not in use.

A few beds dating from early in the seventeenth century had four posts, although they did not have a fixed tester or upper frame. Posts at this time, and leading up to the eighteenth century, were very large and heavy and ornamented with emblems bearing family initials and crests. Testers became elaborately carved and heavily moulded.

For a time, in the early part of the eighteenth century, textile hangings and drapes became less fashionable and increasingly were replaced by ornamentation in timber work. Bed heads and ends and also posts were made of mahogany and walnut, and were exposed and carved in a variety of motifs and subjects in many different styles.

As Renaissance forms of decoration spread, so the bed became more architectural in appearance. The bed stock or frame was made to tenon into the head and the foot ends to be supported by short carved legs. Mattresses made from coarse canvas remained feather filled, but were slip covered with finer linen cloths.

During the early and mid-eighteenth century, European influences in design, materials and craftsmanship meant the fully draped and well-furnished four poster became a more common design. The posts supported the four tester rails or tester frame, and the large headboard was upholstered or draped. The mattresses were of wool or feathers or a wool and hair mixture. These mixture types were produced with a box-shaped linen or cotton cover and were tufted and edge stitched all along the outer edges. This formed a mattress very similar to the shape that we are familiar with today, i.e. the bordered mattress.

Drapes and covers were produced in sets made from calico, fine weave linens and, in some cases, silk. Printed linens and cottons were also available and became a popular alternative. The tester rails carried the main hangings with an outer and an inner valance or pelmet. A separate and often elaborate drape was fixed behind the headboard, and a ceiling or tester cloth completed the main furnishing. On the bed base and exciting classical design using the best materials available. Particular design influences at the time were Gothic, French and Chinese, reflected by movements and tastes in architecture. A fine example of Chippendale's work was the bed designed for the actor David Garrick, which was beautifully furnished with Chinese hangings in silk, and the woodwork painted in green and cream. Beds designed by Thomas Sheraton could usually be recognised by their elaborate draperies and his use of imported colourful textiles and their trimmings.

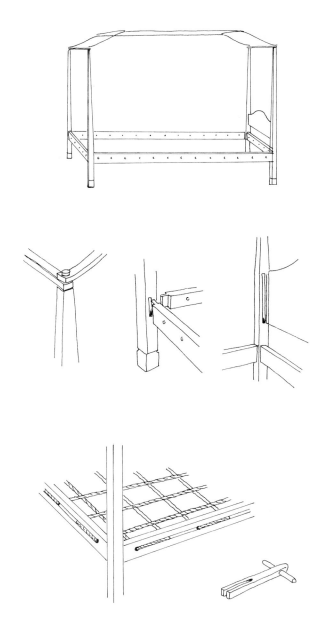

Fig 18.3 A simple country bed of the late eighteenth century, which was easily dismantled and transported when the need arose. Dry tenon joints held the main frame and the small head board and strong rope supported the mattresses. A wooden turnkey was used as a tightening device at regular intervals, keeping the bed rigid and the occupants well supported, hence the saying 'sleep tight'.

Fig 18.4 A large four-poster bed in the Chippendale style with a strong architectural influence; heavy wood slats formed the support for the mattresses.

a valance was occasionally fitted to hide the area below the frame, and a large bed cover placed over the mattress and linens would drape to the floor. A large feather-filled bolster was often included in the furnishing set. This would be cylindrical or oval in shape and would run the full width of the bed.

The long Georgian period saw many fine beds produced, mainly in the four-poster tradition. Mahogany and satinwood were the principal timbers employed by designers such as Thomas Chippendale and Thomas Sheraton. It was a period of extravagant

Country-made beds at this time were relatively simple in design, but nonetheless well furnished. Oak, mahogany and available local woods were used. Mattresses at the end of the century were still largely supported by slats of timber notched into the heavy side rails of the bed frame. This construction allowed for movement in the timber itself and for turning and replacement.

Although nineteenth-century beds remained generally large and cumbersome they were more open and built lower. The production of the four poster was decreasing. Regency styles in the early part of the century were well decorated with mounts of brass and wood inlay. Rosewood was used although mahogany was still the favourite timber for veneers and general bed construction.

The basic elements of supporting frame and stuffed mattress remained unchanged. Feather-filled overlays combined with heavy covers and bolsters provided the warmth and comfort required. The four-poster and the half-tester styles returned to fashion for a short while in the Victorian period. Drapes and textiles for these were relatively lightweight and mainly decorative.

Fig 18.5 A luxuriously furnished four-poster bed of the Georgian period which had festooned and gathered drapes, an upholstered head and heavy lined curtains at the four corners.

Fig 18.7 A mid-nineteenth-century bed made partly of wood but mostly of metal; metal rods formed the half-tester canopy and papier mâché panels were used to decorate the head and foot ends.

The second half of the century saw a radical change in bed construction and design. Iron and steel gradually replaced timber as the principal materials. The development of the coil spring was to have a marked effect on the manufacture of the bed and its general style and comfort. The factory-made bed was made almost completely from metal. Bed heads and

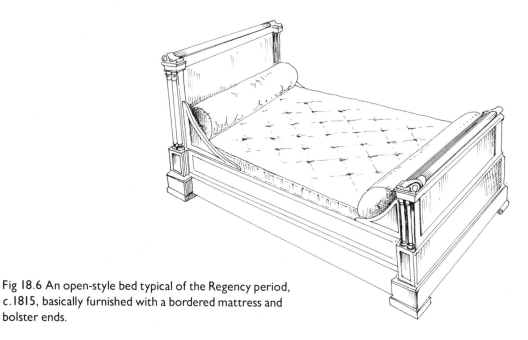

Fig 18.6 An open-style bed typical of the Regency period, c. 1815, basically furnished with a bordered mattress and bolster ends.

Fully Sprung Armchair
c. 1940

A fine example of stuffover sprung upholstery, typical of the pre-war years. Beech frame, wide arms and generous length of seat.

Upholstery Mostly hand-built with coir fibre and wool-felt fillings over sprung arms, seat and back. Seat cushions were either pocket-spring interior or feather.

Covering Wool moquette, cotton and rayon tapestry. Many were produced in hide for clubs or institutions. Such chairs were often loose covered for summer use which prolonged the life of the original covers.

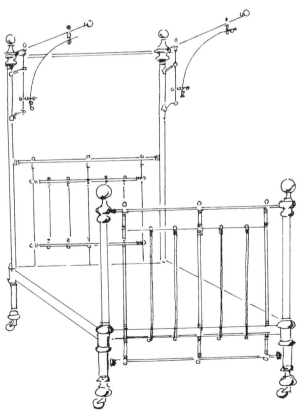

Fig 18.8 A Victorian brass bed in the Italian style — lightweight and mobile, with half-tester rods from which net and sheer curtains could be hung.

ends were formed from tube and steel rod with cast supports and joints. Angle iron and U-section rails became the main frame structure. Half testers made from curtain rod were an integral part of the bed-head-end frame. The metal bedstead was light and strong, with steel lath supports for the mattress and its bedding. Ingenious devices were designed and produced to adjust the laths and keep them taut and flat. The adjustable box spring was another Victorian innovation; it had a heavy pitch pine frame supporting a fine wire mesh. This was kept under tension with turn screws and simply dropped into the angle iron bedstead base. Coil springs were combined with wire mesh to make a comfortable base for curled hair and washed flock mattresses.

With the mass production of the metal bed, the bed chill was another interesting development. This enabled manufacturers to produce the easily transportable, knock-down bed. The 'chill' was a simple and effective jointing method which linked the bedstead to the head and end frames. The mattress was the fourth component in an easily assembled and transported piece of furniture. The term chill took its name from the newly invented iron moulds which were used to cast dovetail corner joints for beds. This process was known as chill casting, because of the rapidly chilled iron which produced exceptionally hard though rather brittle castings. This effective method of bed production had developed from the earlier

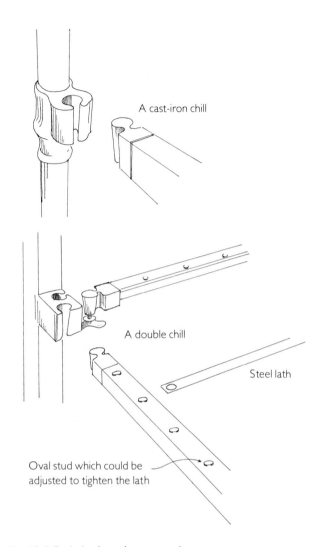

A cast-iron chill

A double chill

Steel lath

Oval stud which could be
adjusted to tighten the lath

Fig 18.9 Early bedstead construction.

Victorian types of metal bed made mainly by the
blacksmith, who forged and cast the parts by hand
methods.

The metal bed was a very functional piece of
furniture and was considered much more hygienic to
use and maintain. Designs were quite ornate and
elaborate, with the use of casting patterns, brass
mounts, wrought-iron work and copper and glass
inlays. Papier mâché panels were also used to enhance
the heads and ends. The continued use of the box
spring mattress, as it was known, and its improved
comfort were eventually to lead to the wooden divan
base as we know it today. Beds generally were
becoming more compact and more lightweight, and
standard sizes were beginning to emerge.

The early part of the twentieth century saw steady
production of both types of bed base, the box spring
and the metal bedstead. Development also took place
to find new ways to support the hair and flock
mattresses. Mattress fillings became softer and more

The three-piece combi-
nation bedstead which
was sprung with woven
diamond mesh, kept taut
with rows of tension springs

Fig 18.10 The simple and functional metal bedstead with steel
lath interwoven supports for a flock- or hair-filled *palliasse*.

Fig 18.11 Late-Victorian beds for children made in large
numbers in the early part of the twentieth century from
metal rod and tube with decorative brass mounts.

blends were introduced, such as washed woollen flock, mixed hair and white wool, as well as feather and down mixtures, known as 'shake-up' beds.

The French overlay was considered a high quality soft mattress compared with the other types being produced at that time. It consisted of a fine, quality bordered ticking case which was carefully hand filled. A layer of white wool was followed by a layer of best curled hair, which was again covered with wool. These and many other bed designs were to be seen by visitors to the Great Exhibition of 1851. New cotton fabrics were produced, particularly for use in mattress and box-spring upholstery. Ticking was produced from strong cotton very closely woven in a twill weave formation. Made in plain and stripe patterns, it was to remain the best type of fabric for containing loose fillings for mattresses, pillows and bolsters. The word 'tick' comes from a Greek term meaning 'case', and the cloth itself was referred to as 'ticken'. Eventually the term changed to ticking and is the textile definition still used today for proof, twill and jacquard fabric used universally in the bedding trade.

Since the end of the nineteenth century the manufacture of beds has become a very specialised business. Whereas previously the upholsterer was involved in bed-making, this was no longer possible. Bedding had become a production area mostly separated from other types of upholstery work.

During the years between the First and Second World Wars, bedstead design developed further with

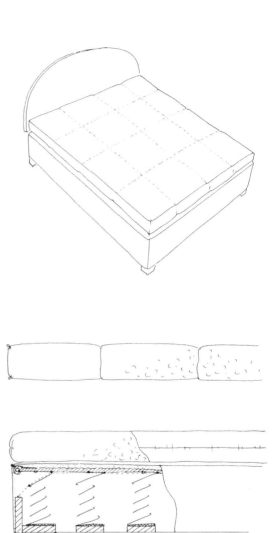

A section through a flexible edge divan with French feather-filled overlay

Fig 18.13 A large double-size, spring-edge divan with a bordered and sectioned feather overlay.

the diamond wire mesh base and the square link wire support, both of which incorporated rows of strong tension springs which kept the mesh taut and flexible. Woven wire mattresses, which were all machine-made, were particularly suited for institutional and contract use. They remain almost unchanged to this day except for the addition of the cone spring. However, for the domestic bedding market they were all eventually to be replaced by the reintroduction of the wooden bed in a completely new form.

The fully upholstered divan bed with its spring interior mattress or latex foam mattress arrived during the 1950s. The wooden divan bed base was a development of the upholstered box spring with the

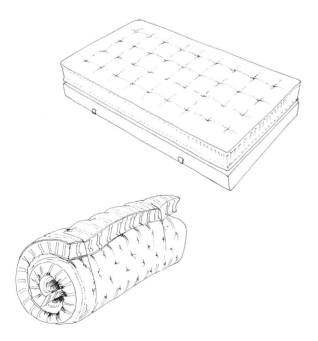

Fig 18.12 The upholstered box-spring based designed to drop into an angle iron bedstead. A soft, unsprung mattress covered in striped ticking, the surface is tufted and the borders are hand-stitched.

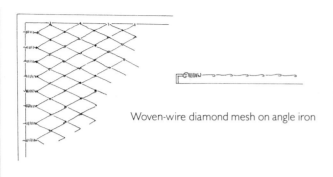

Woven-wire diamond mesh on angle iron

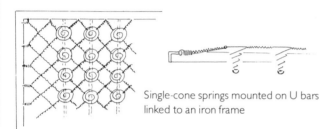

Single-cone springs mounted on U bars linked to an iron frame

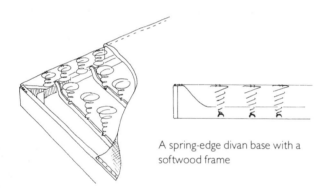

A spring-edge divan base with a softwood frame

Fig 18.14 Three sprung bed bases typical of the mid-twentieth century.

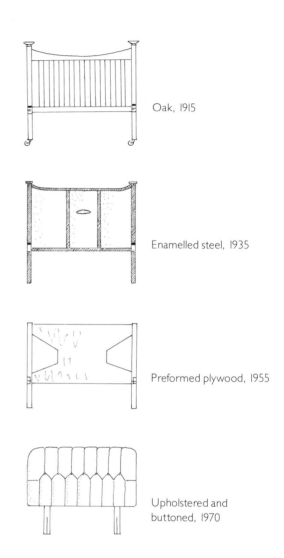

Oak, 1915

Enamelled steel, 1935

Preformed plywood, 1955

Upholstered and buttoned, 1970

Fig 18.15 Bed-head design 1915–1970.

addition of legs or castors. Fully upholstered headboards replaced the rather heavy wood and metal head and end supports, typical of the 1930s and '40s.

The standard sizes for beds and bedding were laid down by the British Standards Institution. Bed lengths were mainly 6ft 6in and widths were 2ft 6in and 3ft for singles and 4ft 6in and 5ft for double beds. These remained unchanged until the metrication of British measurements in 1971. Beds became a few centimetres longer but widths stayed about the same. However, the range of sizes increased which appeared to be in line with accepted European and American standards.

Metric bed sizes:

Small standard 90cm×190cm
Standard single 100cm×200cm
Compact single 75cm×190cm
Small standard double 135cm×190cm
Standard double (queen) 150cm×200cm
King sizes 180cm wide and above

Post-war changes in manufacture and materials saw the development and introduction of the Dunlopillo mattress. Soon to become a household name, these were made from the new moulded latex rubber foams. Invented in 1929 and later marketed as a foam for bedding and upholstery, latex mattresses were produced for the contract and domestic market, and competed successfully alongside the spring interior. A typical advertisement for the new foam mattresses stated: 'The new interiors are odourless, germ resisting, completely hygienic and free from dust creating material; require no shaking or turning.'

The second half of the twentieth century has seen many technical developments in the design of beds and the divan and its mattress. Production techniques have brought about improvements both in comfort and the wide choice of bed types available. Research into sleeping habits has increased the production of firm and orthopaedic beds. Hygiene has played an important part in the development of the modern bed. Standards of cleanliness for fillings and bed making materials were subject to BSI standards and government legislation in 1952 and 1953.

Foam manufacture was developed further and, in the 1960s, plastic foams made from polyurethane gradually began to replace rubber foams. Urethane foams proved to be generally more acceptable and easier to adapt and engineer. Their place in the bed making industry has resulted in a useful blend of foam fillings with the more conventional filling and the addition of polyester fibres. The 'all foam' urethane mattress has competed successfully with other types, not as a substitute but as an alternative. It is lighter in weight, self ventilating and has a different feel. The foam bed with its mattress and base are very practical in terms of maintenance and versatility in use.

During the period from 1963 to 1990, standards for bedding and bed manufacture have been monitored, improved and recommended. These improvements include:

    Use of fillings and their cleanliness
    Construction and proofing of tickings
    Spring types and the construction of spring interiors
    Flammability of foams and bed-covering fabrics
    Recommendations for fitting of handles and breathers for mattresses
    Safe beds and cots for young children
    Standard sizes

During the same period the duvet or continental quilt has largely replaced the eiderdown and the heavy woollen blanket as bed coverings. The duvet is lightweight, warm and hygienic and is available with a variety of quilted fillings, ranging from pure goose down and duck feathers to Holofil polyester fibres.

THE MODERN BED BASE

In very general terms there are five different kinds of bed base.

The spring-edge base

This is the most luxurious type produced, with springs mounted over the wooden base, which provide sprung support right out to the edges. It is a construction which gives a greater sleeping area and a better degree of comfort.

The firm-edge base

This is a shallower bed base in which the springs are set within the wooden frame. Springs are held in place by lashing or webbing from edge to edge in all directions. Both the spring edge and the firm edge are fully upholstered.

The solid-top base

This base has no springs and is very firm, and should be

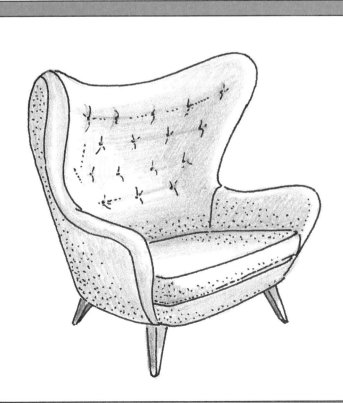

Wing Chair c. 1955

A typical curved-wing chair of the late 1950s with beech frame on tapering lacquered legs.

Upholstery Tension springs are used in the seat and back, and coir filled pads with wool and cotton felts provide the fillings. The loose seat cushion is latex foam or rubberised hair wrapped in kapok.

Covering Fabrics were a variety of wool moquette with an uncut loop pile. Two-tone colours with light insides and dark outside accentuated the chair's shape.

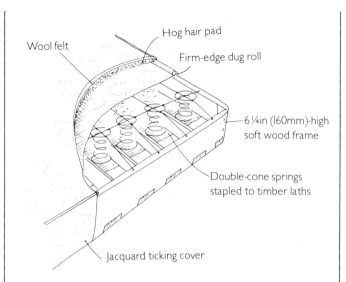

Wool felt

Hog hair pad

Firm-edge dug roll

6¼in (160mm)-high
soft wood frame

Double-cone springs
stapled to timber laths

Jacquard ticking cover

Fig 18.16 A divan base interior.

used with a mattress which is particularly well
constructed and designed to withstand the impact of a
non-yielding base surface. Some bases do have a
flexible layer of filling, usually foam, which provides
some resilience below the mattress. This base
construction method is often used in conjunction with
storage bases, which have a storage space in the form of
an empty box or sliding drawers below the mattress
level.

The slatted base

Generally a firm bed and designed on the traditional
bedstead principle, with the mattress supported on
springy hardwood slats. In good examples the slats are
located and cradled in flexible fixings. The slats run
from side to side suspended from strong timber side
rails.

The metal-frame base

Designed on the bedstead principle, these are made
mainly as single-bed sizes for particular areas of the
market, such as bunk beds, some children's beds and
for institutional use. Angle iron is the normal rail
construction and wire link mesh with tension springs
support the mattress.

THE MODERN MATTRESS

The spring interior

This type of mattress contains a machine-made spring
unit, which is made up from 13½-, 14- or 16-gauge
springs of the double cone type. Helical wires and edge
strips combine to hold the springs in line and in place.
Variations in the number of springs and their wire
gauges produce different degrees of support and feel.
The unit is surrounded by various grades of filling, with
a firm insulating pad laid over the springs and clipped
to the unit edges. This is followed with combinations of

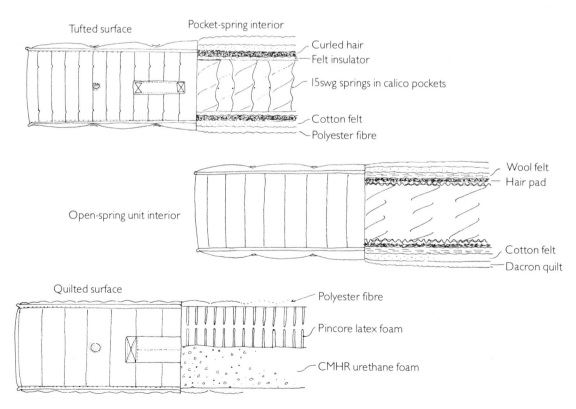

Tufted surface

Pocket-spring interior

Curled hair
Felt insulator

15swg springs in calico pockets

Cotton felt
Polyester fibre

Open-spring unit interior

Wool felt
Hair pad

Cotton felt
Dacron quilt

Quilted surface

Polyester fibre

Pincore latex foam

CMHR urethane foam

Fig 18.17 The modern mattress.

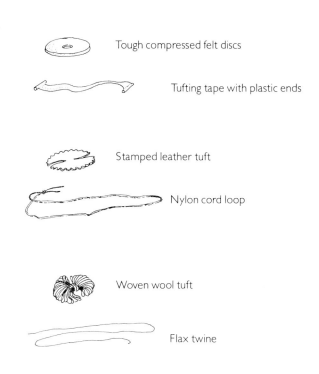

Tough compressed felt discs

Tufting tape with plastic ends

Stamped leather tuft

Nylon cord loop

Woven wool tuft

Flax twine

Fig 18.18 Tufts used for mattresses and bases.

new cotton felt, polyester fibre or wool felts. The outer layer in most good spring mattresses is a quilted layer or tufted layer of soft wadding. The mattress edges or borders are usually quilted and have breathers and fitted handles. The tufted types are usually hand finished with a blind mattress stitch which forms a firm, well-finished edge, and stabilises the border.

Pocket-spring mattresses

Generally the pocket-spring interior is considered to be the best method of springing a mattress. This differs from the open unit in the way that the springs are formed, and also in the mattress construction. The individual springs are cylindrical and not cone shaped and each spring is individually encased in a calico pocket. The rows of pocketed springs are then linked and clipped together to form the whole unit. An edge wire or metal strip which is fitted to the outer edge of the unit completes the interior. Fillings are arranged over the unit in the same order as for the open unit, except that a heavy insulating pad is not necessary in the same way, and may be a more lightweight type of compressed jute or felted cotton. Once again, good quality mattresses of this type are well worth the extra expense of hand finishing, with blind-mattress-stitch edging using polished waxed linen threads. The surfaces of the whole mattress are finally tufted with wool tufts or felt tufts adjusted to depth. These are an important part of any good mattress and help to hold and stabilise the ticking and fillings.

Foam mattresses

Basically simple, but carefully engineered, the all-foam mattress can be manufactured from latex foam or polyurethane CM foams. Many of the best mattresses of this type are made from a combination of these two foams. Different feel and support factors are produced by careful layering, and by varying the thicknesses of the foam layers.

CM foams are used as the base support foam, and latex provides the upper, softer layer. Thickness and density are important, and are varied to give more or less support and different degrees of comfort. The comfort and support qualities of a mattress cannot, of course, be judged in isolation, but must be assessed when the mattress is in combination with its bed base. Mattress densities are therefore produced to suit firm-edge, spring-edge or solid divan and bed bases.

An alternative construction is made up from CM foam to a thickness of 6in (150mm). A 2in (50mm) thick wall of reconstituted foam is then bonded to the outer edge of the main foam to form a supporting edge. Very often the foam unit is then overlaid with a softer topping to complete the interior. Most good foam mattresses are fitted with covers which have quilted panels and borders. Tufting is optional, but does help to keep the mattress and its cover stable, avoiding the possibility of shift or excessive movement of the cover over its interior. Unlike a spring interior or a soft unsprung mattress, in a foam mattress the number of tufts makes very little difference to the feel.

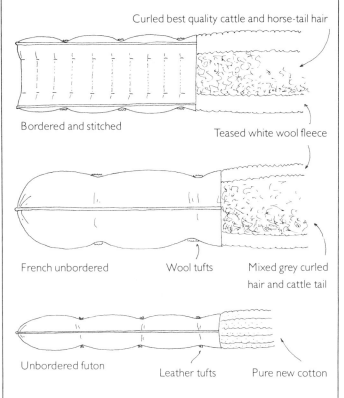

Curled best quality cattle and horse-tail hair

Bordered and stitched

Teased white wool fleece

French unbordered   Wool tufts   Mixed grey curled hair and cattle tail

Unbordered futon   Leather tufts   Pure new cotton

Fig 18.19 Soft, unsprung mattresses.

The soft unsprung mattress

The soft mattress is produced and upholstered using the best natural materials and fillings available. Variations are based on traditional bordered and unbordered styles. The techniques of filling and making up are done entirely by hand, and are varied to produce different degrees of support and warmth. The main ingredients are curled grey hair, white cattle and horse-tail hair, new cotton felts and sheep and lamb's-wool fleece. A typical arrangement would be layers of curled grey hair, overlaid with white tail hair, to form the core of the mattress. Surrounding the core are layers of teased white fleece wool. The bordered ticking case is then sewn up and tufted in diamond formation, with white wool tufts. To support the edges a side stitch or mattress stitch is worked around the top and bottom edges. As an alternative, a mattress may be made up using cattle- and horse-tail hair only as the filling, combined with extra tufting; this produces a mattress which is cooler to use and firmer to the feel.

The feather mattress and the shake-up mattress

A soft, warm overlay mattress is made from good downproof cambric or ticking with blended goose, duck and poultry feathers. The mattress is bordered and partitioned or sectioned to hold the lightweight filling in place. Regular turning is recommended to keep the fillings lively and well distributed.

The shake-up mattress is feather-filled and may be without borders. Very soft and very warm, this type should be regularly turned and shaken to keep the interior buoyant and evenly spread. A good quality case is necessary and is usually slip-covered with an easily detachable cover.

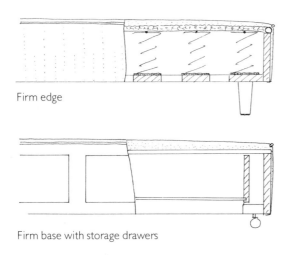

Firm edge

Firm base with storage drawers

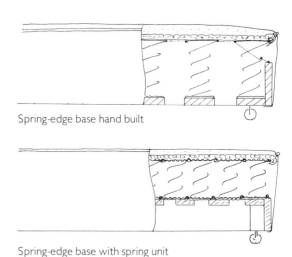

Spring-edge base hand built

Spring-edge base with spring unit

Fig 18.20 Divan bed bases.

Chapter Nineteen

Restoration

The reupholstery of traditional and relatively modern pieces of furniture is a continuous form of restoration. By nature, upholstery is an area of the furnishing business in which repair and replacement go on all the time. If a chair or sofa is of value, either aesthetically or sentimentally or in commercial terms, then it is worth restoring.

This may mean complete reupholstery or simply recovering. Very old pieces of furniture should be treated with great care and restored sympathetically. Each job that is undertaken has to be assessed individually, taking into account the age, the condition and the client's preferences. Costs and values also have to be considered.

The conservation of upholstered furniture has become an important area of the craft and applies especially to very old pieces of perhaps the eighteenth century and earlier. Upholstery techniques were very different in those times and so the methods used to conserve old and fragile seating are rather different from reupholstery of the commercial kind. The upholstered remains of some very old pieces can tell us a great deal about a particular period in history, and its craftsmen and the way in which they worked.

A chair will require restoration for a number of reasons. Firstly the covering may be very frail and dirty, faded, or completely worn out and no longer suitable. The upholstery itself will probably be sagging, or collapsed and no longer comfortable. The frame of a chair will often be weak, because joints have opened and rails are cracked and broken. Complete restoration may well involve most of these problems in some way.

During the twentieth century particularly, much good work from the past has been lost, either by reupholstery of the wrong kind or because economically careful restoration has not been possible. The upholsterer does have a responsibility to ensure that, wherever possible, important and interesting pieces of work are faithfully restored in the mode of the period in which they were originally designed and made. There are two quite different ways of approaching this kind of work. Both have the same aim

and will hopefully result in restoring the original condition. In most cases this is perhaps more important than just recreating something that can be used.

The first method is basically simple and yet is probably the most difficult to achieve. The piece to be restored is completely stripped of all its upholstery. The bare frame is carefully checked and, if necessary, repaired and strengthened. Repolishing may also be necessary, but in the case of anything remotely antique cleaning and reviving is all that is normally recommended. Basic cleaning and rewaxing with plenty of elbow grease can do wonders for most polished surfaces of any great age.

Using all new materials, which should be as near to original type as possible, the piece can then be reupholstered. The shape and style of the new upholstery should be carefully chosen to suit the period of a particular piece of work. Some research may be necessary if the period or style is not obvious or is unknown.

The second method requires a rather different approach, and is based on conserving as much of the original as is practical. This is only practical if the basic fillings are of good quality and they have survived in a reasonably good condition. Animal-hair fillings will generally outlast those that are vegetable based. Curled hog hair, cattle tail and horse mane and tail are good examples. Wool felts and flocks can also be included in this list. Vegetable fibres, such as coir husk or leaf, grass and seaweed, tend to dry out and become brittle much sooner. These are all reusable but much less likely to survive than the animal types. It is usually true to say that the better quality the original work, the more likely it will contain a high percentage of animal-hair filling.

Knock-Down Chair
c. *1960*

A chair designed and made with mass production in mind. Construction was KD for production purposes only, with preformed plywood arm components.

Upholstery Machine-made spring units in the back and seat, and latex-foam reversible seat cushion.

Coverings In moquette or bouclé.

Assuming that some or all of the original upholstery is still evident, then a careful examination will be the first job. It will be necessary to remove part or all of the top covering to assess the possibilities. Quite often a second or third covering will still be in place. Where this is obvious, then each one can be removed and stripped off with care, until the original upholstery is found.

With the covers removed and the original work exposed a true assessment can be made. The main supporting materials, such as webbings, springs and hessian, generally have to be replaced or reinforced. Seat areas are usually the first to fall victim to age, and can, in most cases, be removed and renewed. First and second stuffings can often be restored and reused. Soft overlay fillings, such as cotton waddings and felts, will almost certainly be matted and stained and will not be worth keeping.

The arm and back upholstery on the majority of chairs and settees will be in a much better condition than the seats. These can usually be conserved, cleaned and kept intact. However, some restoration will always be necessary.

MAKING THE CHOICE

The decision to restore by completely reupholstering, or to restore by conserving and rebuilding, will depend largely on the age of the piece, the upholsterer's preference and the costs that may be involved. Such decisions will be influenced further by the condition and quality and the proportions of the existing work.

Where these are basically good, and where with care they can be brought to life again, conservation is always an interesting possibility.

Shape and proportion are important, particularly in good antique work. Where these exist they should be retained and given new life. Fresh calico, with felts and waddings, will then enhance the new covering to complete the restoration. If this method of working is not possible then good reupholstery of the right kind will be necessary.

KEEPING A RECORD

Keeping a record of good restoration work is always interesting and will prove invaluable. This builds up a portfolio which can be referred to in the future. Take photographs or make sketches both before, during and after restoration. So often similar situations occur when shapes are to be built, or fabrics and trimmings have to be chosen both for period and modern work. A comparative reference is always useful for the future, both for the upholsterer and for future clients.

TECHNIQUES

Stripping
The stripping off of old upholstery can be a lengthy and tiring business, but it pays to take care and give a little more time where frames and showwood are obviously delicate. Timber frames can be very dry and

brittle. Wherever possible, use the ripping chisel in the grain direction of the timber. When it is necessary to rip across the grain then a levering technique should be adopted, using short arm taps with the mallet, rather than long, swinging blows. Some other essential tools will be the staple lifter, a trimming knife, pincers or snips and scissors.

Most chairs and settees can be stripped in the reverse order to which they were upholstered, beginning with the bottom lining under the seat, followed by the outside back, outside arms, outside wings, and facings, etc. This allows access to the seat, then the inside arms and, finally, the inside back. Once the outside covers are removed, then the main fixings between tacking rails and seat rails are released. All the other edges can then be loosened and the covers only removed. This exposes the calico coverings. At this stage the sprung seat of an armchair, for example,

could be completely stripped out, if necessary, by continuing to rip all its coverings and linings until the spring hessian and the lashing are exposed. If the seat is to be completely removed, then this can be concentrated on until the spring lashings are released from around the top of all four seat rails. To complete the stripping of the seat the chair can be turned upside down and the webbings ripped, allowing the remainder of the seat to fall out.

Now the chair can be looked at more closely and the condition of the arm and back upholstery inspected. At the same time dust and excess rubbish is cleaned away. With the chair in its calico cover and minus the seat, further stripping can be done depending on its condition and how much the arm and back upholstery requires restoring. Quite often this will mean removal of calico and waddings and sometimes top or second stuffings.

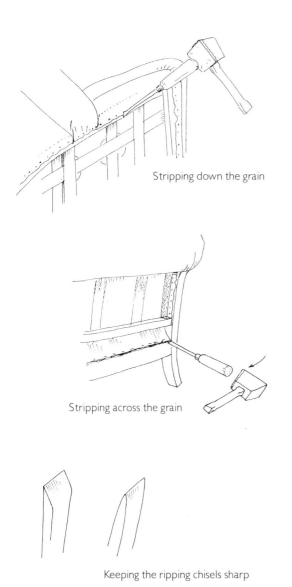

Stripping down the grain

Stripping across the grain

Keeping the ripping chisels sharp

Fig 19.1

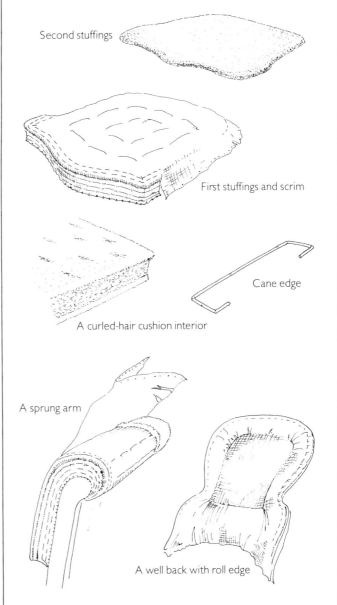

Second stuffings

First stuffings and scrim

Cane edge

A curled-hair cushion interior

A sprung arm

A well back with roll edge

Fig 19.2 Some of the items worth preserving and reusing.

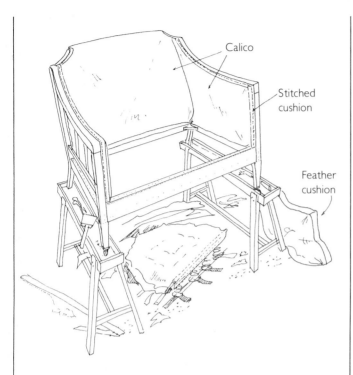

Fig 19.3 A chair with the cover removed and the sprung seat stripped out.

The seat upholstery which has been completely removed can be dismantled. Items such as cane edges and first stuffings are quite often reusable, whereas webbing, springs and top stuffings will almost certainly need replacing. Top covers can usually be disposed of unless they are of particular interest, or in part may be needed as patterns for special shapes. This may be the case if the work is of historical interest or is particularly rare. Old hand-embroidered fabrics or hand-stitched tapestries are quite often worth keeping and, having been cleaned, may be reused on small stools or cushions, for example. Antique textiles have a charm and value of their own and can be sold or kept for reuse. Any fabric that is in reasonable condition and is at least fifty years old or more is worth consideration before being thrown out.

Where the upholstery is unsprung, such as in dining chair and side chairs, arm upholstery and some inside backs, then only webbings and perhaps their hessian linings will need to be considered for replacement. The same will apply for platforms, either seats or backs which are unsprung, and merely support cushions.

Cleaning

When all stripping work is done the existing upholstery and the frame can be thoroughly cleaned. A suction cleaner can be used to get rid of as much dust and powdered fillings as possible. At the same time any very rough frame edges can be lightly sanded with coarse grade paper. Chamfered rails can also be rerasped in preparation for the rebuilding of the upholstery.

Repairs to frames

After cleaning, frame repairs that are only minor can be dealt with and are best done before any cleaning and reviving of showwood. Major repairs to framework will also have to be done at this stage. This may mean removal of all upholstery and, in some cases, will have to be entrusted to a chairmaker or furniture restorer. The following is a list of frame repair problems which are typical and crop up regularly in the upholstery workshop: loose and broken castors, castor holes becoming too large, breakout of timber on feet and legs, short grain splits and breaks, dry joints, broken dowels and tenons, split rebates, nailed joints becoming loose, housed tacking rails becoming loose, rusty screws or nails breaking, cracking on scrolls, corner blocks loosening and twisting, causing bad levelling. Where the main frame structure is not affected by any of these problems, they can mostly be dealt with in the upholstery workshop.

Reviving showwood

Cleaning is the first job, to remove accumulated dirt and grease. There are a number of cleaning fluids and recipes available. A well-tried and tested potion is a mixture of turpentine and linseed oil. This is applied with fine 000 grade steel wool, working gently over the surface and deeply into corners and carved areas. Care must be taken not to remove the polished surface or change the colour and patina which makes an old piece of furniture look mellow and attractive. After cleaning the surface will take on a dull appearance, which can then be revived. A good wax finish is effective and

Fig 19.4

Sacco Chair c. 1960 and All-Foam Chair c. 1970

Two chairs produced almost completely from oil-based plastics. The Sacco chair is very much like a large bean bag filled with partially expanded polystyrene beads.

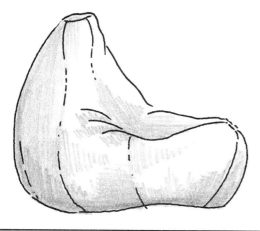

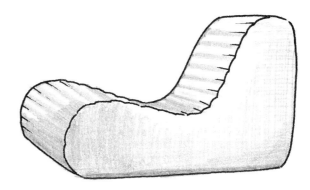

All foam chairs have little or no rigid frame or structure, and are made from cut polyurethane foam on a plywood-base board.
 Coverings are in canvas, coated fabrics and tweeds.

brings out the characteristics of a timber. A natural or dark furniture wax should be applied generously to the surface and left to harden. The final finish can then be produced with a soft clean rag, rubbing well in the direction of the grain. On carved and turned surfaces a soft brush will help to burnish and bring out a good satin finish. The same job can be done with a reviving cream or emulsion, which will clean and revive. When rubbed over, the polished surface becomes transparent, leaving the surface clean and bright. Surplus cream must be removed carefully and then finished off with a soft, clean duster.

Restoring the upholstery

By restoring any piece of good upholstery, the upholsterer seeks to reproduce the original feel of comfort, combined with good line and proportion, bringing back the firmness and the softness just where these are needed. This may be simply in a loose seat for a dining chair or on a large, sprung scroll arm for a sofa. The proportion and shape of the restored upholstery are equally important for both. Over stuffing is a common fault. A low tight-stitched edge is far more attractive and often more appropriate than something too heavy or too bulky. For this reason the conserving of first stuffings and foundation shapes, with or without stitched edges, is good practice.

Scrim coverings in reasonable condition can be left in place, or alternatively very carefully removed and replaced with new. Surface upholstery over first stuffings such as buttoning and fluting can be built up by adding extra filling to the existing top stuffings or, in the case of fluting, the new flutes will automatically be filled with new filling, but over the surface of a rebuilt base filling.

Work can begin on arms and backs by carefully removing webbings one at a time and replacing them, or by completely removing the whole of the first stuffings and renewing the foundation. The first stuffing can then be replaced and refixed using fresh bridle stitches and a tack stitch around the edges. This secures the filling and brings the edges back in line with the rails. Where the scrim has been renewed, then fresh rows of top stitching will help reform any lost shape.

The tack stitch is used a great deal in this kind of work; it is basically a blind stitch in which the twine is tacked down on to the edge of the rail after each stitch has been formed. This technique can be used effectively to move and readjust existing first stuffings and stitched edges, which are not being stripped. Using a regulator and the tack stitch, where it is necessary edges can be reset. Examples include arm fronts, back facings and the top of inside backs. This can also apply to seats when they are not being renewed.

The rebuilding continues with a new top stuffing, or reuse of the old by carding and teasing and tying this back into place as a new filling. At this stage new cotton felts or wool felts may be used before pulling down in calico. There may be a preference for the alternative method of covering the first stuffing with calico and applying felts after. New skin waddings may also be used to complete the filling before covering.

In recent years, thin polyester waddings of 4oz and 5oz weights have been used increasingly as a top filling before covering. There are several alternatives of this kind which help to give a smooth and even finish to all types of covering work. Staple fixings may also be preferred to tacks in some areas of chair work, particularly when frames are delicate and old or are liable to splitting near short-grain edges and in rebates.

Covering and finishing

There is basically little difference in the covering of a piece of work which has been reupholstered and one which has been restored by conserving. The same choices of fabric and trimming and finishing apply to either. However, it is often the small details of the covering and finishing work which stand out and indicate when an antique piece of upholstered furniture has been very well restored. Generally, it takes much longer to produce interesting detail and will cost more to use a range of attractive high quality trimmings. An ordinary fabric of medium price can look outstanding with the use of good trimmings and with interesting upholstery treatments.

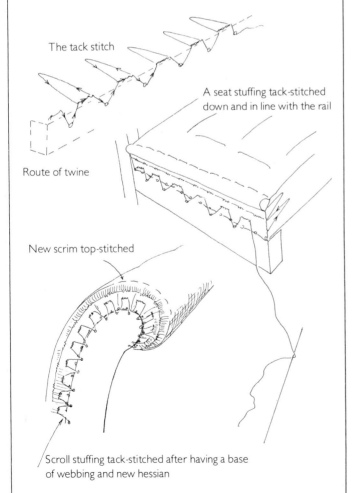

The tack stitch

Route of twine

A seat stuffing tack-stitched down and in line with the rail

New scrim top-stitched

Scroll stuffing tack-stitched after having a base of webbing and new hessian

Fig 19.5

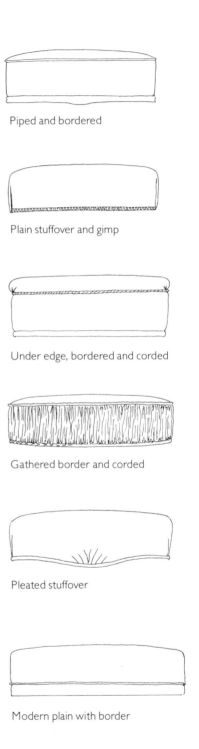

Piped and bordered

Plain stuffover and gimp

Under edge, bordered and corded

Gathered border and corded

Pleated stuffover

Modern plain with border

Fig 19.6 Seat front treatment.

Seat fronts, for example, can be plain stuffover, bordered or under-edge. Each of these has a quite different appearance, and each can be treated to make them attractive and interesting. Arm fronts and arm facings can be treated with a capped or an inset facing. Scroll facings can be treated in many different ways, by pleating, gathering or fan pleating, and then finished with piping, cording or ruche. Whichever method is chosen this will normally repeat itself on other parts of the job so that there is a balanced and uniform

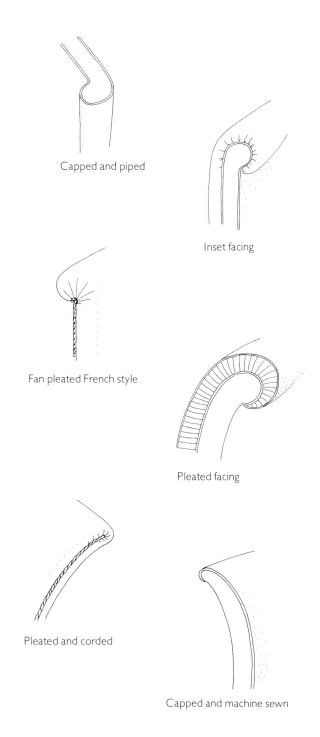

Capped and piped

Inset facing

Fan pleated French style

Pleated facing

Pleated and corded

Capped and machine sewn

Fig 19.7 Trimmings: arms and facings.

appearance. The amount of treatment needed will depend generally on the fabric being used and particularly on the style or period of the job.

Both modern and traditional methods of closing and finishing should be used on chairs and settees of any age. However, the slip stitch is still the most versatile and the most widely used. Frame design does vary so much and modern techniques such as back tacking and tacktrim depend much on good timber rails being the right shape and in the right place. Slip stitching of

outside arms and outside backs does allow the upholsterer the freedom to stitch and finish the work wherever it is easiest, and where the cover will turn and hug the frame shape best.

Whenever possible, the outside areas should be well lined and padded. This is always good practice and helps to give the well-upholstered appearance. Both skin wadding and cotton felts should be used generously before closing and final covering. The use of bottom and under-seat linings will vary according to type of work. Very often, early unsprung work was not under-lined. Where frames have become particularly rough or where restoration is difficult, it may be best to line and cover up the undersides. Generally, webbed and sprung upholstery, which is upholstered in the traditional way, is finished and lined with hessian or black cotton lining, hessian being the more traditional choice.

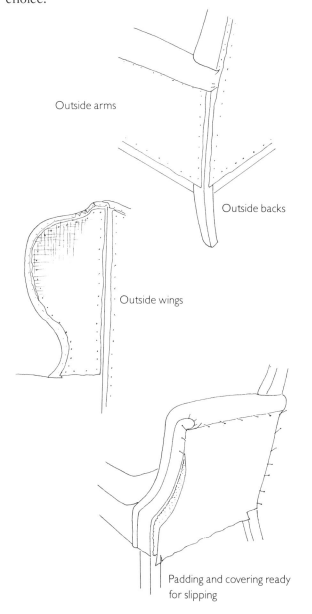

Outside arms

Outside backs

Outside wings

Padding and covering ready for slipping

Fig 19.8 Lining the outsides.

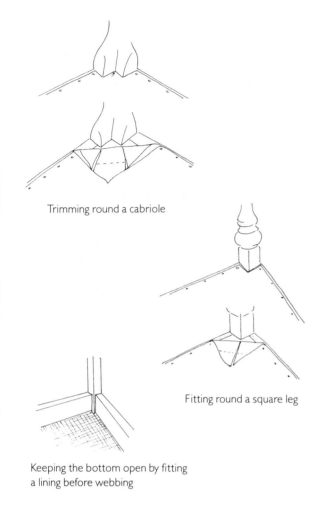

Trimming round a cabriole

Fitting round a square leg

Keeping the bottom open by fitting
a lining before webbing

Fig 19.9 Fitting the bottom linings.

Cushion work

Cushion fillings were fairly limited in type in early
upholstered furniture. Very old examples will be rare,
but when they do appear they will contain very basic
raw materials, such as sea grass, straw or wool, none of
which is very likely to stand reuse. Cushions, bolsters
and squabs or pads will have been very well used and
are unlikely to survive to any great age. Where they
have, then replacement of the fillings will almost
certainly be best.

Later examples, produced within the last one
hundred years, are more likely to have fillings such as
curled hair and waddings, feather or feather and down,
and wool or rag flocks. Even later examples will be
spring pattern interior, kapok or latex rubber foam.
Very few seat or back cushions are worth preserving,
with perhaps just one or two exceptions: hair-filled
bolsters and some back cushions which have been well
made and are still in good shape can be remade.

Removal of the covering and waddings will reveal the
ticking or calico case. If this is reasonably clean and still
strong, it can be removed carefully by cutting out all
the tufts and the edge stitching. The old interior

should be cleaned and a fresh layer of new hair applied
all round it as it is being replaced in a new ticking case.
After closing, the cushion can then be retufted and
restitched to strengthen and support the outer edges. A
new layer of wool felt or cotton felt will complete the
work ready for covering.

Loss of shape and resilience is normally the result of
hard use and most seat and back cushions suffer from
this over a period of time. A well-restored chair, couch
or sofa generally deserves new cushions and bolsters if
it is to give good service and to look refurnished and
inviting.

Seat, back and loose cushions for restored upholstery
should generally be well filled and even slightly over
filled, initially, in particular feather and down interiors.
All fillings, whether traditional or modern, have a
settling period, and will reduce slightly in height and
size after initial use. Width is less important, but in
height and depth, proportions and fillings should be
generous. This allows for the reduction and ensures
that the cushions will not appear flat or skimpy after
settling. Shape, finish and trimming will add interest
and style to cushions, especially when a suite or a sofa

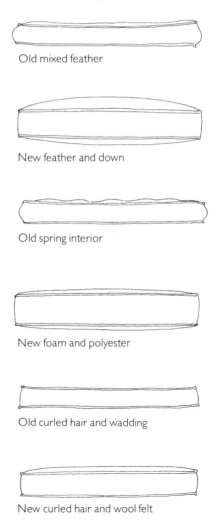

Old mixed feather

New feather and down

Old spring interior

New foam and polyester

Old curled hair and wadding

New curled hair and wool felt

Fig 19.10 Seat cushions.

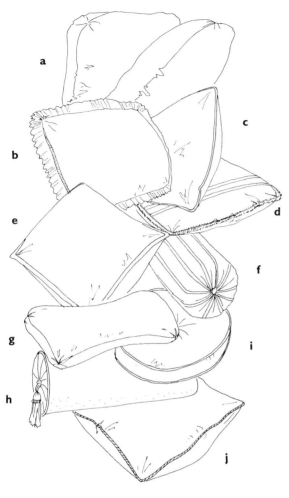

a Plain sewn with pleated corners
b Gathered strip sewn in
c Piped seams
d Ruched seams
e Top-stitched edging
f Plain shape pleated ends
g Saddle shape pleated corners
h Traditional bolster, piped and trimmed
i Circular bordered and piped
j Plain with corded seams

Fig 19.11 Cushions.

is fully cushioned. The upholsterer is often left to make the choice, particularly when original cushions are missing. This provides an opportunity to experiment and try different methods of make up and types of trimming. A library of records, pictures and books is essential and will often provide the background and the ideas when needed.

Trimming
Trimmings in upholstery usually refer to the decorative gimps, cords and fringes, etc., which are bought and used to decorate and finish period and conventional work. The term is in fact much broader and can be used to describe any method by which fabrics are worked or made up to produce design features and create style. It is the furnisher's way of presenting and finishing a piece of work and given the choice everyone will do it differently. Trimming has to be an interesting balance between personal taste and a true period style. For example, it would be completely wrong to trim the cushion on a Regency sofa with a ruche. But on an early Georgian wing chair, for instance, a dark colour ruche sewn into the edge of a rich tapestry would be very acceptable. The do's and don'ts soon become obvious with experience and sometimes with a little necessary research.

Trimmings do not necessarily have to be bought in as proprietary items, they can be made up using self or contrast fabrics. A loose cushion can be trimmed with self or contrast piping, a gathered or pleated strip sewn into the edge in the same way. Bias binding can be bought or made up and effectively used to edge an overlay, or a fixed cushion.

Valances and skirts are another example of trimming. Box pleated, plain or gathered valances can add

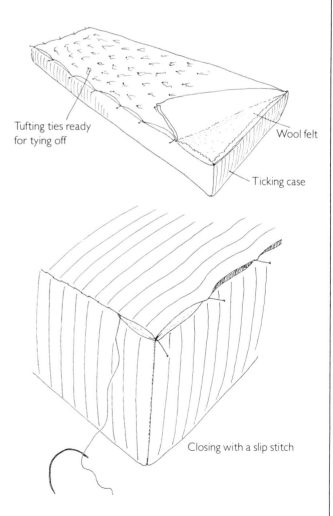

Tufting ties ready for tying off

Wool felt

Ticking case

Closing with a slip stitch

Fig 19.12 Restoring a large hair-filled cushion.

interest and style to bedroom and drawing room chairs. Such treatments are usually part of an interior or furnishing scheme. Valances on furniture are very often blended in to match similar trimmings on beds and windows. There are long periods in the history of interior decoration when trimmings and such decorative effects were not fashionable and were very little used. The upholsterer needs to be aware of these so that the work produced can be reasonably true to the period.

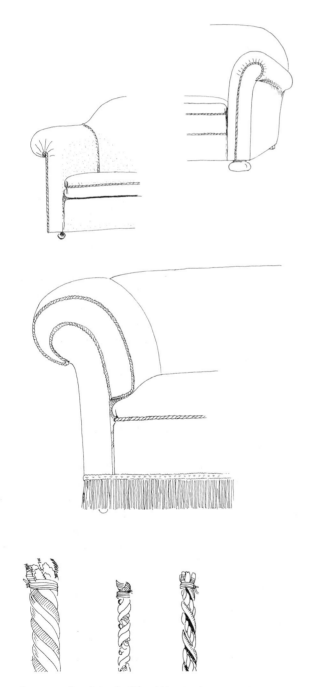

Large, small and standard furnishing cords

Fig 19.13 Trimmings.

How long will it take?

The time taken to restore and finish upholstered furniture can only be estimated in hours, based very generally on previous recorded work times with allowances for difficult or unusual pieces.

Assuming the average working day to be eight hours and a half day to be four hours, then a working week will range between forty and fifty hours.

Conditions and work content will vary enormously. For example, a small fully upholstered armchair will take about two hours to strip and clean up ready for rebuilding, so the most part of a morning should be allowed for jobs of any size, and a little longer for a couch or settee. Work of this kind should not be rushed but done methodically and with care.

Rebuilding and restoring the chair will begin with inside arm and inside back upholstery. About three to four hours should be allowed to bring the inside arms and inside back up to the calico stage. If covering fabric is available then work can continue, but if not then the new seat can be webbed and sprung and built up. A new seat with fixed sprung upholstery and a stitched front edge will take approximately three hours. The whole chair will then be covered completely in calico and ready for covering.

In most types of traditional chair work the arm coverings are done first, followed by the inside back and then the seat cover. The whole of the inside covering will be done in three to four hours, or an average morning or afternoon.

Borders, facings, pipings, etc. can then be made up and fitted. This always takes rather longer than at first seems likely. A good allowance should be made, perhaps an hour or more. An average of at least one and a half hours should be allowed for the lining and covering of the outside areas of the chair – a good finish is important – and this will include the underlining of the seat. Hand slipping and trimming will in many cases add another hour's work to complete the job.

A *summary of time taken*

Stripping: 2½ hours
Inside arms and back to calico: 3 hours
New seat: 3 hours
Covering the insides: 3½ hours
Borders, facings, etc: 1 hour
Lining and covering outsides: 1½ hours
Slipping and trimming: 1 to 3 hours

As a very general guide the restoring and upholstery of a small stuffover armchair would take approximately 15½ hours. A little extra time should be added for cover cutting and possibly small amounts of machine sewing. The chair used as an example would therefore be completed in about two days.

Chapter Twenty

The Furniture Industry:
opportunities, training, associations

'Think of a house, a large country house or a tiny one-up-one-down, then imagine that house without any fabric furnishing of any kind.'

The furniture industry offers a wide and interesting range of work opportunities. The industry is made up of a diverse range of crafts and skills, from computer-aided design to the management of large production units, and from the cutting of a dovetail to the sewing of a leather cushion. Job satisfaction and personal achievement will be found at all levels, and make a career in furniture making interesting and worthwhile.

The manufacturing side of the industry is made up of three distinct areas which serve to provide the furnishing needs of the country. The contract side offers a service to architects, surveyors and interior designers who may be engaged in the building and furnishing of non-residential buildings.

The residential or domestic market is extremely well served through the high street shops, and by another area of the industry in the form of direct sales and their direct sales shops. Mail-order buying accounts for another growing outlet to the consumer. Collectively, alongside the manufacturing sector, the small businesses in the United Kingdom provide an ever-growing and valuable service to the general public. This section of the industry designs, makes and restores much of the nation's best and most valuable furniture and furnishings.

As in many other manufacturing industries, good craftsmen and women and those people who become highly skilled as specialists are always at a premium and are always in demand. Financially, all the skilled areas of the industry are very rewarding. Wages and salaries are currently high and have been in the top twenty league since 1945. A normal week's work is 39 hours with a minimum of twenty-two days paid holiday per year. It is now true to say that working conditions are very good and completely unrelated to the traditional view of the furniture factory. A safe and healthy working environment exists and is enjoyed by some 74,000 people in 1,650 different companies. Many others are employed on the fringes of the industry and in the large and small businesses associated with it. The vast and loyal band of outworkers must number several thousand, who make, restore, gild, polish, paint, sew, upholster, carve, cane and rush.

As a very general guide, the principal upholstery production areas are London, Nottingham, High Wycombe, Leeds, Manchester, Bristol, South Wales and Glasgow.

EDUCATION AND TRAINING
Examining bodies
The City and Guilds of London Institute
The City and Guilds of London Institute, more widely known as City and Guilds, is Britain's leading technical testing and qualifying body. An independent organisation founded in 1878 and operating under a royal charter, it enjoys wide support from industry and works closely with the education service and government agencies. City and Guilds certificates are available for all the main sectors of industry, including furniture. Subjects are available at three career levels to complement industrial training and experience.

Progressive pattern of City and Guilds awards
The following is a typical example of certificates and awards made by City and Guilds to those passing through an industrial training programme linked to work experience and industrial experience in a factory or a small workshop. However, the scheme is flexible

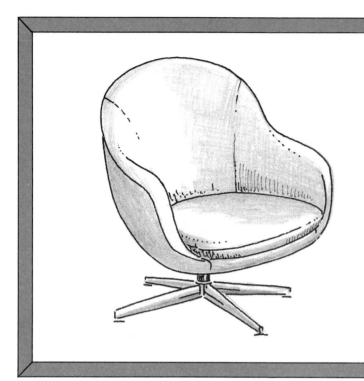

Moulded Shell Chair
c. *1965*

A moulded plastic shell chair of the type produced in large quantities during the late 1960s. Swivel, tilt and rocking actions were usually incorporated in the metal base.

Upholstery Polyurethane foam fillings throughout, with fixed foam seat cushion.

Coverings In coated fabrics, wool, tweed or acrylic velvet.

enough to allow mature people to opt in and out at the different levels, and awards may be gained in part- or full-time education.

Level I	Furniture Craft Certificate, Part I
Level II	Furniture Craft Certificate, Part II, internal or external
Level III	Furniture Advanced Studies Advanced Craft, Advanced Design and Construction, Advanced Industrial Studies
Career extension level	Management, teaching and technician certificates and awards
Licentiateship of the City and Guilds	LCG Awarded at and beyond career extension level, with relevant industrial experience
City and Guilds Insignia Award	Senior line and research management CGIA recognises technical excellence and application

City and Guilds is happy to work with employers and training organisations of all types and sizes. It recognises the importance of tailoring solutions to suit individual circumstances and to fit in with particular clients' requirements. Any technical college, the Careers Advisory Service or Local Education Authority office will be able to provide up-to-date information about City and Guilds' courses. The City and Guilds handbook is available on request.

Write to the Sales section, **City and Guilds of London Institute,** 76 Portland Place, London W1N 4AA.

The Business Training and Enterprise Council (BTEC)
BTEC courses are offered in Furniture Studies at National and Higher National level and are available at a number of colleges throughout the country, including London College of Furniture; Rycotewood College, Oxford; Basford Hall, Nottingham; Leeds; Manchester; and Bolton.

For information write to **The Business Training and Enterprise Council,** Central House, Upper Woburn Place, London WC1H 0HH.

The National Association of Retail Furnishers (NARF)
National Furnishing Diploma/Interior Design and Furnishing Merchandising Certificate: the two courses above are merged into a one-year intensive course, validated by NARF and offered by the **College for the Distributive Trades,** Back Hill, Clerkenwell, London EC1R 5E. Subjects covered include: interior and decorative design, floor coverings, soft furnishings, furniture upholstery, beds and bedding, history of furniture and business practices.

NVQs (National Vocational Qualifications)
These relatively new qualifications were introduced in 1990, and are supported by the DoE (Department of Employment), the CBI (Confederation of Business and Industry) and the TUC (Trades Union Congress).

The NVQ framework has five levels of achievement, beginning with Level 1 and developing into professional qualifications at Levels 4 and 5. All NVQs are based on standards developed by industry and commerce, and are available in almost every area of work within the manufacturing and service industries. Their highly vocational nature has meant that they are highly valued by many employers.

There are no fixed paths to developing the skills necessary to pass an NVQ. Some candidates will have learned their subject on a college course, combined with some work experience, others through a modern apprenticeship and so on. All candidates must have reached a standard whereby they can demonstrate to the assessor that they are able to meet the required standards, set out clearly in the literature that accompanies each unit.

NVQs are a worthwhile qualification to have, being of great benefit to the candidate and to prospective employers.

NVQs in the furniture industry

Assembled Furniture Production	Level II
Upholstered Furniture Production	Level II
Wood Machining	Level I
Wood Machining	Level II
Hand-Crafted Furniture	Levels I, II, III
Traditional Upholstery	Level III

Awarding bodies: G & G (City and Guilds), BTEC (British Training and Enterprise Council), RSA (Royal Society of Arts).

Governing body: BFM (British Furniture Manufacturers)

For further information please contact:
NCVQ (National Council for Vocational Qualifications)
222 Euston Road
London
NW1 2BZ
Tel: 0171 387 9898

Upholstery courses in full-time education
Colleges situated mainly in the principal upholstery-producing areas offer full-time courses in upholstery up to fine craft diploma level. Taking up a course of this kind is an alternative route into the craft, which should, if possible, be combined with some part-time industrial or workshop experience. In order to gain the technique and speed that are needed at a competent level, there is no real substitute for commercial workshop experience. However, the broad base in design, construction and making provided in a full-time course is an ideal stepping stone to a career in any part of the industry.

The courses available vary a great deal, from one year intensive practice to three year BA (Hons) degrees. The following are some good examples: one year, full-time intensive practice and study, for people nineteen years old and over; two year, full-time, in upholstery with some related studies, for people sixteen years old and over; three year, full-time, at college diploma level, with related studies for people eighteen years and over.

To generalise, the one- and two-year courses lead up to City and Guilds qualifications at advanced level (level III) and may include some associated subjects. The longer courses generally lead to diploma and degree level qualifications, and include City and Guilds certificated subjects at the second-year stage. A three-year course allows specialisation in a chosen craft, with additional subjects such as furniture design, construction, history, restoration and business studies.

Such courses may be studied at **Central Manchester College,** Manchester; **Buckinghamshire College of Higher Education,** High Wycombe; **London Guildhall University,** London E1 1LA; **Basford Hall College of Further Education,** Nottingham, **Burnley College,** Lancs; and **Brunel College,** Bristol.

A new and unique course is also available in this area. This is the BA (Hons) degree in furniture restoration at the Buckinghamshire College of Higher Education, High Wycombe. In this course of study, upholstery can be the chosen specialism, and for those who seek the ultimate in craftsmanship training, this is an ideal course.

ASSOCIATIONS AND SOCIETIES

The associations and societies listed provide advice and training, and offer essential services to the industry and those working in the industry.

Association of Master Upholsterers and Soft Furnishers
The Association has flourished and grown since it was founded in 1947 and it now has a large membership. Its main aims are to promote and maintain high standards of craftsmanship and materials in both modern and traditional upholstery. Membership is open to upholstery companies and self-employed upholsterers, and branches of the Association exist in most regions of the country. Every two years the Association presents the Francis Vaughan award to the winner of a competition for young upholsterers. All members have an opportunity to meet at a three-day conference which is held during the autumn of each year. The Association can be contacted at the **Association of Master Upholsterers and Soft Furnishers,** Francis Vaughan House, 102 Commercial Street, Newport, Gwent, NP9 1LU.

Rural Development Commission

The Rural Development Commission is England's rural development agency. In April 1988 the Development Commission merged with its agency CoSIRA (the Council for Small Industries in Rural Areas) to become the Rural Development Commission. Former CoSIRA county offices now form a network of thirty-one Rural Development Commission–Business Service offices throughout the country. As the Government's main agency for sympathetic rural development, the Rural Development Commission leads the way in supporting rural communities and representing their interests. The Development's Business Service provides local information and advice, technical and professional advice, and business management and financial help. The service also includes help for small firms and training courses for employees and the self employed.

These courses, of which there are many, include furniture and antique furniture restoration, upholstery, loose cover making, sewing machine maintenance and application. The courses are open to apprentices, improvers, journeymen and mastermen employed in rural industries. **Rural Development Commission** at 11 Cowley Street, London SW1P 3NA (071 276 6969) and 141 Castle Street, Salisbury, Wiltshire SP1 2TP (0722 336 255).

Furniture, Timber and Allied Trades Union

A trade union or trade society has existed in the industry since the early part of the nineteenth century. As the title suggests, the union currently represents a number of industries which are allied to the furniture and wood-working industries. Membership is open to anyone employed in the furniture and timber industries or any other woodworking or allied industries. Members pay a weekly contribution and are encouraged to become actively involved. FTAT is a democratic organisation, and all of its full-time officers and members are elected by postal ballot of its membership. Policy is determined by biennial conference. Union branch and workplace meetings are held regularly, and members may keep themselves up-to-date by taking the union journal, the *FTAT Record*.

Fourteen district offices exist throughout the UK, with a head office in London: **Furniture, Timber and Allied Trades Union,** 'Fairfields', Roe Green, Kingsbury, London NW9 0PT (081 204 0273/4).

Furniture Industry Research Association

The Furniture Industry Research Association provides an essential portfolio of service to the furniture industry. Its research, testing and information sections are available to help members and non-members solve problems associated with all aspects of furniture making. FIRA enjoys a membership of over 800 drawn from all corners of the industry and currently has a turnover of two million pounds.

FIRA is able to offer a wide range of courses based on comprehensive knowledge and experience gained from day to day work within research, testing, marketing, technical design and management services. The courses are designed for people with technical or managerial skills who need to increase their knowledge of a particular aspect of furniture. A technical library and information service is available from the **Furniture Industry Research Association,** Maxwell Road, Stevenage, Herts SG1 2EW (01722 366255).

Guild of Traditional Upholsterers

The new Guild of Traditional Upholsterers was formed in 1987, and for the first time the craft of traditional upholstery has its own guild. Formed by an enthusiastic group of qualified upholsterers, its main

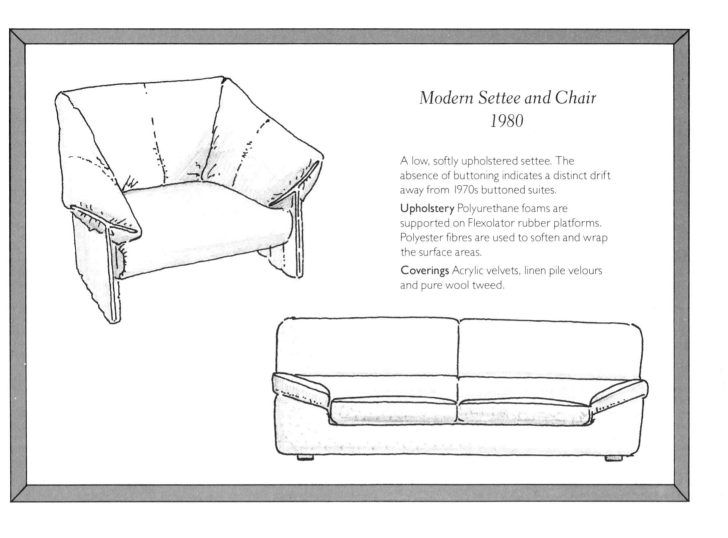

Modern Settee and Chair
1980

A low, softly upholstered settee. The absence of buttoning indicates a distinct drift away from 1970s buttoned suites.

Upholstery Polyurethane foams are supported on Flexolator rubber platforms. Polyester fibres are used to soften and wrap the surface areas.

Coverings Acrylic velvets, linen pile velours and pure wool tweed.

aim is to protect both the customer and the future of the traditional upholsterer and the craft. The organisation exists in order to uphold standards of excellence.

The Guild insignia features an upholstered X-frame chair with the motto *'Festina lente'*. Admission to the Guild is by evidence of practical competence and by interview. Members meet twice yearly, and a Guild magazine is circulated periodically. The GTU is growing steadily and already has a strong and enthusiastic membership.

For information and enquiries contact:

Guild of Traditional Upholsterers
Membership Secretary
Loosehanger Park
Redlynch
Salisbury
Wiltshire SP5 2PS

Other useful organisations

The Worshipful Company of Furniture Makers
30 Harcourt Street
London W1H 2AA

The Textile Institute
10 Blackfriars Street
Manchester M3 5DR
(0161 834 8457)

The Natural Filling Trades Association
Central House
32–66 High Street
Stratford
London E15 2PS

The National Bedding Federation
251 Brompton Road
London SW3 2E2

British Standards Institute
2 Park Street
London W1A 2BS
(0171 629 9000)

Enquiry Service
BSI
Linford Wood
Milton Keynes
MK14 6LE

The British Manmade Fibres Federation
24 Buckingham Gate
London SW1E 6LB
(0171 828 0744)

British Rubber Manufacturers Association
(Flexible Foam Group)
90–91 Tottenham Court Road
London W1P 0BR
(071 580 2794)

The Design Council
28 Haymarket
London SW1Y 4SU
(0171 839 8000)

The Crafts Council
44a Pentonville Road
Islington
London N1 9BY
(0171) 806 2500

The Guild of Master Craftsmen
166 High Street
Lewes
East Sussex BN7 1XU
(01273 478449)

The British Leather Confederation
Kings Park Road
Moulton Park
Northampton NN3 1JD
(01604 494131)

British Furniture Manufacturers Federation (BFM)
30 Harcourt Street
London W1H 2AA
(0171 724 0854)

Member associations of the BFM
High Wycombe Furniture Manufacturers Society
Wycombe House
9 Amersham Hill
High Wycombe
Bucks HP13 6NR
(01494 532484)

London and South Eastern Furniture Manufacturers Assocations
93 Great Eastern Street
London EC2A 3JB

Midlands and North-West Furniture Manufacturers Association
263A Monton Road
Monton
Eccles
Manchester M30 9LF

Northern Furniture Manufacturers Association
32 Scott Green
Gildersome
Morley
Leeds LS27 7AT

Scottish Furniture Manufacturers Association
Merchants House Buildings
30 George Square
Glasgow G2 1EG

West of England and South Wales Furniture Manufacturers Association
First floor
York House
Bond Street
Bristol BS1 3LQ

NCVQ (National Council for Vocational Qualifications)
222 Euston Road
London NW1 2BZ
(0171 387 9898)

Museums, National Trust houses, and privately owned stately homes

Where to see important collections of historic furniture and furnishings. The buildings listed below are just a few of the many hundreds of interesting places where period upholstery and furnishings can be seen, in historic settings.

Victoria and Albert
Museum, London
Geoffre Museum, London
Knole House, Kent
Ham House, Surrey
Waddesdon Manor,
Buckinghamshire
Kew Palace, London
Royal Pavilion, Brighton
Parnham House, Dorset
Aston Hall, Birmingham
Heaton Hall, Manchester
Chirk Castle, North Wales
St Fagans, South Wales
Temple Newsam, Leeds
Castle Howard, York
Dunrobin Castle, Golspie,
Sutherland
Scone Palace, Perth

Periodicals

The Cabinet Maker and *Retail Furnisher*
Benn Publications
Sovereign Way
Tonbridge
Kent TN9 1RW

Furniture Manufacturer
Magnum Publications
110–112 Station Road East
Oxted
Surrey

The World of Interiors
Condé Nast Publications
234 Kings Road
London SW3 5UA

The FIRA Bulletin
Furniture Industry Research Association
Maxwell Road
Stevenage
Herts SG1 2EW

Furniture & Cabinetmaking
Guild of Master Craftsman Publications
166 High Street
Lewes
East Sussex BN7 1XU

Bibliography

Practical Upholstery Clarence Howes, Evans Bros
First Stages in Upholstery; Traditional Hand Made Hilary Clare, Warne
Practical Upholstery and the Cutting of Loose Covers Frederick Palmer, Benn
Upholstery; a Practical Guide Desmond Gaston, Collins
Tapisserie D'Ameublement Claude Ossut, Editions H. Vial, Eyrolles
Upholstery in America and Europe Edward S. Cooke, Jr, Norton
Upholstery Styles Gillian Walkling, Quarto Publications
Which Way to Repair and Restore Furniture Consumer's Association
English Period Furniture Charles H. Hayward, Evans
Discovering English Furniture John Bly, Shire Publications Ltd
The Woodworkers' Pocketbook Charles H. Hayward, Evans
American Furniture in the Metropolitan Museum of Art Morrison Heckscher, Random House Publications, NY

Glossary

American cloth
An early form of leathercloth. Made from plain woven cotton coated on one side with linseed oil and other materials which made it waterproof.

Antimacassar
Detachable cover for the backs of chairs and settees, originally used as a protection against Macassar hair oil.

Armchair
Armed or arming chair as distinguished from a single or side chair having no arms.

Back stool
An early single chair or side chair which developed from the stool and the chest. Later examples were upholstered.

Ball fringe
A decorative trimming in which small balls, overwound with fine cord, hang at intervals among the long threads of the fringe.

Balloon back chair
A name given to Victorian chairs with round or oval backs, mostly mahogany or rosewood, and upholstered seats.

Bedford cord
A strong, finely corded fabric with a plain weave in which the cords run lengthwise. Often used as a platform cloth.

Bergère
Louis XIV and XV style armchairs with upholstered backs and sides and squab cushion seats. Later designs often have cane backs and sides.

Binding
A narrow fabric used to support and finish an edge, such as a tape or a bias cut strip.

Bolster arm
Large upholstered arm in a bolster shape – typical late nineteenth century.

Bouclé
French name for a cloth with a rough textured surface, produced by using a fancy yarn.

Border
A long strip or wall of fabric used to form the sides or boxing on a cushion or mattress, for example.

Box ottoman
A divan or couch with a hinged upholstered lid forming the seat and storage space under.

Braid
A flat, narrow woven fabric, used to decorate and finish upholstery, cushions and curtains.

Bridling
A stitch used to hold down and stabilise scrim coverings, usually over first stuffings. A bridle stitch is a large running stitch, which penetrates and sets the depth of stuffing.

Buckram
A material stiffened by the use of 45 per cent weight of some agent such size or glue. Base cloths are usually jute or cotton.

Bun foot
A turned, bun-shaped foot fitted to chairs and sofas – early twentieth century.

Calico
A white or unbleached cotton fabric with no printed design.

Cambric
A fine, plain-weave cotton fabric, often glazed on one side, and used as a down-proof casing.

Canapé
The French name for a divan or sofa of Louis XV period or design.

Cane edge
A sprung edge built on to a chair or bed using hour glass springs and a flexible cane.

Canvas
A strong, heavyweight, plain-weave fabric, traditionally made from flax or cotton. Also a term often used by upholsterers to describe the first covering over webbings or springs.

Casement
A plain-weave, even-textured, lightweight all-cotton fabric. Traditionally used for sun curtains on south-facing windows.

Chair bed
A low chair made from wood or metal which is dual function. The seat and back frames are completely adjustable for use as a single bed, with a minimum of three loose cushions.

Chaise-longue
French term for a couch or day bed with an upholstered back.

Chenille
A pile fabric in which the weft thread is specially prepared and twisted by machinery, or woven and cut, before being woven into the yarn to form the pile. Cotton chenille is used in upholstery.

Chill
The cast iron jointing block mounted on the head and foot ends of a metal bedstead. A chill, which may be single or double, has a tapered slot and supports the angle iron bed frame.

Chintz
A fine calico 90 or 120 centimetres wide, usually roller or screen-printed and glazed or semi-glazed. Quilter chintz: Indian word meaning brightly coloured.

Circ
A commonly used abbreviation for the small circular needles used for hand sewing and slip stitching of upholstery and soft furnishings.

Collar
A strip of cover sewn into an inside back to provide a pull-in around an arm.

Cosy corner
A seat with a high upholstered back which could be fitted into a corner and enable two or more people to sit together.

Counterpane
A bed cover concealing bedding.

Couch
A long upholstered seat with a back and one or two ends. Originally a double arm chair.

Cretonne
Originating from the French village of Creton and traditionally a copper-roller-printed cotton fabric. A term now more generally used to describe almost any type of lighter-weight floral printed cotton.

Damask
Figured Jacquard fabric, the weft forming the design and the warp composed of a comparatively fine yarn making the background.

Denier
The weight in grammes of 9000 metres of filament yarn, e.g. silk.

Divan chair
Fully upholstered arm chair with long seat, often with scroll arms; late nineteenth century.

Dogs
Large iron staples with sharpened ends. Used to brace and strengthen timber chair frames.

Drop
A curtain measurement, taken from the fixing or hook level down to the hem. Headings and turnings are added to the drop.

Duck
A strong closely woven cloth of cotton or flax, similar to canvas. An average weight would be 10oz per square yard.

Dug roll
Sometimes called a tack roll or thumb roll, it is formed around frame edges using small amounts of stuffing rolled up in hessian. Preformed dugging is produced from compressed paper or reconstituted chipfoam.

Dyeing
Application of a permanent colour to textile fibre, yarn or cloth.

Easy chair
Originally the name given to winged upholstered arm chairs, introduced about 1700, but now applies to upholstered arm chairs generally.

Embossing
A technique used on thick cloths and leathers to create relief patterns.

Farthingale chair
An armless chair of the Stuart period, then used to accommodate ladies' hooped skirts.

Feather down
The fine downy fibres cut and stripped from the quills of large feathers and used as a filling mixture.

Feather edge
A fine top stitch applied to a stitched edge to create a sharp edge line.

Fibre identification
Yarns taken from the warp and weft of a cloth and tested by burning, staining or microscopy to identify composition.

Field bed
A canopy type of bed easily dismantled.

Filament
A very fine, long and usually continuous textile fibre. Several filaments of silk for example are spun together to produce one strong yarn.

Flax
Strong, lustrous bast fibre taken from the stalk of the flax plant and woven into linen cloth.

Fly piece
A narrow strip of fabric sewn to the edge of inside backs, inside arms or seats to economise on cover.

Foldstool
A folding stool provided with a cushion for kneeling. Similar to a camp stool.

French overlay
A soft, unsprung, unbordered mattress filled with layers of hair sandwiched between new wool.

French work
The upholstery of chairs in the French style, using techniques such as diagonal stitching, feather edging, rope work and deep squab seats.

Frise
An American term used to describe a moquette with cut or uncut pile woven from mohair.

Futon
A simple Japanese floor bed or mattress made from strong cotton fabric and filled with cotton waste, tufted and unbordered. A futon is easily adapted and folded for sitting.

Galoon
An old name for various kinds of braid used in upholstery.

Garnett machine
Produces felted fillings, such as cotton and wool, in layered and cross lapped form.

Genoa velvet
A heavy velvet with a smooth ground weave and a pile figure in various colours.

Gimp
Edgings as used in bedding and upholstery to decorate seams etc. Made from cotton, silk, rayons or mixtures.

Hair cloth
An upholstery covering material woven from the tail and mane hairs of horses, with cotton and rayons added. Plain and damask weaves are typical.

Hessian (burlap)
A plain-woven cloth of flat yarns, usually jute, and made in 7 to 12oz weights.

Hogrings
Small steel open-ended rings which are clinched to fix materials and pads to spring edges and units.

India tape
Twill-woven 100 per cent cotton tape similar to webbing and used to bind or reinforce edges.

Kanaf
A natural textile fibre used as a substitute for jute and claimed to be rot-proof and very strong. Grown in the USA, Cuba and Russia.

Knitting chair
An armless upholstered chair with a wooden drawer fitted under the seat.

Knock down (KD) furniture
Pieces of furniture which may be easily folded, broken down or flat packed for distribution.

Knock up
A mass-production system producing upholstered components for assembly and fitting before despatch.

Laid cord
A very strong lashing cord in which the plies are laid together and not twisted.

Line
The long, lustrous fibres stripped from the bast or stalk of the flax plant.

Linters
Very fine cotton fibres taken from the seed after staple cotton has been removed.

Lit
The French name for a bed or mattress.

Loose cover
A slip cover used over upholstered furniture. Traditionally employed in the summer season and made from cool linen union fabrics.

Loose seat
Also called a slip seat, drop-in seat or pallet. An upholstered frame forming the seat of a dining chair supported on rebated rails.

Love seat
The name given to a small seat on which two people can sit close together.

Lug chair
Early English term for the wing type of easy chair.

Mohair
The long fine hair of the Angora goat. Also describes an upholstery velvet made with a cotton base and a short mohair pile.

Moiré
A fine ribbed fabric with a 'watered' surface produced by heated pressure rollers, creating a reflective surface.

Monks' cloth
For upholstery, a rough basket-weave fabric of cotton or jute.

Monofilament
A fine continuous thread, usually synthetic. Transparent types are used as sewing threads.

Moquette
Hard-wearing pile fabric, traditionally with a wool pile and cotton ground. Moquettes may be plain, figured, cut, uncut or frise.

Morocco hide
Soft goat-skin leather, distinguished by its fine grain and texture. Much used by eighteenth century upholsterers and cabinet makers.

Morris chair
Early twentieth-century Arts and Crafts style chair with adjustable back, padded wooden arms and loose seat and back cushions.

Motifs
The decorative figures in a pattern applied to or woven in a cloth.

Nap
The surface of a fabric raised by combing or with abrasive rollers.

Nursing chair
A nineteenth-century term for a single chair with a low seat 13in to 15in high (325mm to 375mm) high.

Orris
Crimp used in upholstering laces of various designs in gold and silver.

Ottoman
A long low seat without a back which originates from Turkey.

Palliasse
A mattress stuffed with natural filling such as chaff or straw.

Piece
An accepted unit length of fabric, ranging from 30 to 100 metres.

Pile fabric
Fabric with a plain ground and an extra warp or weft, which projects to give the surface a fibrous nap.

Pinstuffed
Shallow padded seat or back set into a rebated show-wood frame.

Piping
Narrow strip of fabric folded and sewn into a seam. Used with or without a cord.

Plain weave
A simple weave in which each warp thread interlaces over and under each weft thread. Also known as Tabby weave.

Plush
A general term for pile fabrics which have a longer pile than velvet and are less closely woven.

Pouffe
A stuffed footstool which stands high enough to be used as a seat.

Presspahn
A strong, narrow strip of compressed cardboard used for back-tacking and reinforcing edges.

Prie-dieu chair
A low-seated praying chair with a tall back and a narrow shelf.

Pull-in upholstery (taped)
A fly or tape sewn into a covered surface and pulled in to create a waisted effect. May also be hand-stitched through the cover surface.

Ramie
China grass, providing a strong lustrous fibre resembling silk.

Repp
A heavy and firmly woven wool fabric with transverse ribs; used for upholstery.

Rollover arm
A style of easy-chair arm upolstery with a strong rollover scroll shape.

Ruching
Narrow knitted decorative trimming with a heading and a cut or looped surface. Used generally in place of piping around cushions and edges.

Scrim
Plain open-weave cloth with hard twisted yarns, woven from jute, cotton or flax. Used in upholstery to cover first stuffings.

Scrollover arm
An arm which curves inwards from the seat of a chair in the form of a double scroll, breaking into a convex sweep before curving back to form an arm rest.

Seating
Upholsterers' term for hard-wearing cloths, for example haircloth.

Settee
A name derived from the seventeenth-century settle. It is usually made from wood with a high back, large enough for several people.

Shadow fabric
A cloth in which the warp yarn is printed prior to the cloth being woven.

Skiving
A technique used to trim leather with a knife to a fine feather edge and produce a scarf joint. Thin skivers of leather are used to trim surfaces in cabinet work.

Slip cover
Alternative name given to a loose or detachable cover.

Smokers' chair
A club easy chair, covered in leather, with a D or tub shape.

Sofa
This term appeared in the late seventeenth century and described a couch for reclining.

Spinneret
The stainless steel nozzle drilled with fine holes through which synthetic fibre filaments are formed by extrusion, e.g. Rayon, Nylon, Terylene.

Spoon back
The shape of a chair back, Queen Anne style, curved to fit the shape of the body.

Squab
A loose cushion.

Stitch up
A stuffed and shaped edge, reinforced with rows of blind and top stitches.

Stuffover
The name given to a chair or settee frame which is almost entirely covered with upholstery.

Tapestry
The original term applies to a wool fabric woven by hand, and later to power woven imitations, figured upholstery fabrics, and to fabric where designs are partly or wholly formed by the warp.

Tester
A canopy built or suspended above a bed as a frame or rails to support curtains.

Trimming
The applying or forming of decorative effects using fabrics.

Tub chair
A large easy chair with a concave back.

Tufting
The technique of bridling and compressing stuffed areas in chairs, cushions and mattresses to hold fillings in place and set a depth and firmness of feel.

Turkey work
Hand-knotting of wool into canvas to produce fabrics and carpets.

Upholstery
Fabric furnishings, upholstery as we know it, began as a craft in chair making and bed making at the end of the sixteenth century.

Valance
A length of fabric which may be pleated or gathered and used to conceal a rail or frame. Generally associated with bedding.

Vandyke
The term used in upholstery to describe a type of sewn joint in deep buttoning work. Traditionally, a hand stitched joint used in fine leather work and carefully hidden in the pleating between buttons.

Velours
A fine cotton velvet originating in France.

Velveteen
A very fine, lightweight cotton pile fabric with a weft pile; not of upholstery weight.

Warp
A yarn which runs in the length direction of a cloth.

Weft
A yarn which forms the cross threads in a cloth, selvedge to selvedge.

Welt
To conceal or decorate a fabric or leather joint. It also increases strength.

Worsted
Made from long wool yarn fibres, combed and twisted hard.

X-frame chair
Early seventeenth-century chair, upholstered and decorated with nails and fringe. Became popular during the reign of James I.

Metric Conversion Table

inches to millimetres

¼″	—	6mm	6″	—	150mm	26″	—	660mm
⅜″	—	10mm	6⅛″	—	155mm	27″	—	685mm
½″	—	13mm	6¼″	—	160mm	28″	—	710mm
⅝″	—	16mm	6½″	—	165mm	29″	—	735mm
¾″	—	19mm	6¾″	—	170mm	30″	—	760mm
⅞″	—	22mm	7″	—	178mm	31″	—	785mm
1″	—	25mm	7″	—	180mm	32″	—	815mm
1⅛″	—	30mm	7¼″	—	185mm	33″	—	840mm
1¼″	—	32mm	7½″	—	190mm	34″	—	865mm
1⅜″	—	35mm	7¾″	—	195mm	35″	—	890mm
1½″	—	38mm	8″	—	200mm	36″	—	915mm
1⅝″	—	40mm	8¼″	—	210mm	37″	—	940mm
1¾″	—	45mm	8½″	—	215mm	38″	—	965mm
2″	—	50mm	8¾″	—	220mm	39″	—	990mm
2⅛″-2¼″	—	55mm	9″	—	230mm	40″	—	1015mm
2⅜″	—	60mm	9¼″	—	235mm	41″	—	1040mm
2½″	—	63mm	9½″	—	240mm	42″	—	1065mm
2⅝″	—	65mm	9¾″	—	250mm	43″	—	1090mm
2¾″	—	70mm	10″	—	255mm	44″	—	1120mm
3″	—	75mm	10⅛″	—	257mm	45″	—	1145mm
3⅛″	—	80mm	11″	—	280mm	46″	—	1170mm
3¼″	—	83mm	12″	—	305mm	47″	—	1195mm
3½″	—	88mm	13″	—	330mm	48″	—	1220mm
3⅔″	—	93mm	14″	—	355mm	49″	—	1245mm
3¾″	—	95mm	15″	—	380mm	50″	—	1270mm
4″	—	100mm	16″	—	405mm	51″	—	1295mm
4⅛″	—	105mm	17″	—	430mm	52″	—	1320mm
4¼″-4⅜″	—	110mm	18″	—	460mm	53″	—	1345mm
4½″	—	115mm	19″	—	485mm	54″	—	1370mm
4¾″	—	120mm	20″	—	510mm	55″	—	1395mm
5″	—	125mm	21″	—	535mm	56″	—	1420mm
5⅛″	—	130mm	22″	—	560mm	57″	—	1450mm
5¼″	—	133mm	23″	—	585mm	58″	—	1475mm
5½″	—	140mm	24″	—	610mm	59″	—	1500mm
5¾″	—	145mm	25″	—	635mm	60″	—	1525mm

To obtain the metric size for dimensions under 60″, not shown in the above table, multiply the imperial size in inches by 25·4 and round to the nearest millimetre taking 0·5mm upwards.

e.g. 9⅛ × 25·4 = 231·8
          = 232mm

To obtain the metric size for dimensions over 60″ multiply the imperial size in inches by 25·4 and round to the nearest 10mm taking 5mm upwards.

e.g. 67″ × 25·4 = 1701·8
          = 1700mm

Index

Figures in *italic* refer to illustrations

acrylic 17, 22, Fig 7.6
Adam Brothers 13, 21
adhesives 45–6
Algerian fibre 72–3, Fig 6.14
all-foam chair 269, Fig 10.1
alternating feed mechanism 54, Fig 5.13
American cloth 14, 283
antimacassar 283
armchairs *19, 21, 23, 71, 97, 257*, 283, Figs 15.17, 15.18
arms of chairs 270–1, *232, 235*, Figs 6.4, 14.8, 16.9–16.11, 19.7
Art Deco style 15, 16, 22, *240*
Art Nouveau style 15, 22
Arts and Crafts Movement style 15, 22
Association of Master Upholsterers 277
automatic straight seamers 59, Fig 5.21

back stool 283, Fig 15.12
baize 20, 96
ball fringe 79, 283
balloon back chair 283
banding 79–80, Fig 6.26
Barcelona chairs *235*
battings 77, Fig 6.20
Baverstock folding chair *206*
bed hangings 13
bed heads and ends *222, 254, 257*, Figs 17.21, 18.7, 18.15
Bedford cord 68, 96, *282*, Fig 6.7
bedrooms
    chairs Figs 15.23, 15.31
    fabric used in 12, 13
beds 253–62; Figs 18.1–18.11
    base 261–2, Figs 18.14, 18.20
    mattress 262–4, Figs 18.17–18.20
bellows Fig 17.24
bench board 26, Fig 3.4
bergère chairs 283, Figs 15.6, 15.15
Berlin wool work 14, 20
binding 283
bleaching 94
blind stitch 171, Fig 13.13
boards 69, Fig 6.10
bolster arm 283
bolsters *132, 185, 255*, Figs 10.16, 13.42, 18.6
bolt croppers 39, Fig 4.13
border 283
bouclé 96, 283
box ottomans 13, 14, 283, Figs 17.18, 17.25
box-spring mattress 259, Figs 12.10, 18.12
braid 13, 283
brass nails 13

bridle stitches 169–70, Figs 13.9, 13.10
bridling 13, 169
British Standard stitch type *see* stitch types
brocade 20, 98
brocatelle 12, 98
buckram 69–70, 96, 283, Fig 6.11
bun foot 283
burlap 284
Business and Technician Education Council 276
button-back chairs 14, Figs 13.19, 15.20
button-fastening machines 61, Fig 5.27
button-making 28, 59–62, Figs 5.25–5.28
button-making presses 60, Fig 5.23
buttoning 14, 175–8, Figs 13.19–13.25, 14.20–14.25
    cushions 197–8, Fig 14.21
    patterns 178, Figs 13.26, 14.20
buttoning machines 59–62, Figs 5.23–5.28
buttoning tool 40, Fig 4.17
buttons 60, 175, Fig 5.24

cable cord 84
calico 22, 66–7, 96, 283, Fig 6.4
cambric 67, 96, 283
canapé 283
cane edge 15, *231*, 283, Figs 16.4, 17.15
cane work 18
canvas 89, 96, 283
carding 24
carding machines 15, 30, 48, Fig 5.2
carpeting 98–9
casement 283
chain-stitch machines 56, 117–18, Fig 5.16
chairs *19, 21, 23*, 138–44
    frame design and construction 138–44
    modern construction 188
    order of working 181–7
    restoration 268–71, Figs 19.5–19.9
    springs 228–9, 230–2, Fig 16.16
    stripping out 267–8, Fig 19.3
chaise-longues 23, 155, 283, Fig 17.2
channel work 14, 179–81, Figs 13.28–13.32; *see also* fluting
chenille 14, 22, 283
Chesterfield settee *194*, 235–6, *238*, Figs 16.12, 17.6
chintz 12, 20, 97, 283
Chippendale 13, 21, *255*, Figs 17.7, 18.4
City and Guilds of London Institute 275–6
cleaning 24
cloth *see also* fabric
    cutting 51–2, Figs 5.5, 5.6
    inspection 49–50, 100, Figs 5.5, 5.6
    measuring 49
    spreaders 50–1, Fig 5.7

coconut fibre 72
coil springs 13, 21, 151, Fig 12.1
coir fibre 72, Fig 6.13
collar 284
compasses 37, Fig 4.11
compound feed mechanism 54, Fig 5.13
compression tufting 62
cone springs 16, 152–3, Figs 12.3, 12.4
continuous zippers 59, Fig 5.22
conversation seats 14
cords 84, Figs 6.33, 6.34
corduroy 22, 98
cosy corner 163, 237, 283, Fig 17.15
cotton 89, Fig 7.3
cotton felt 73, Fig 6.15
couches 13, 21, 283, Fig 17.1
counterpanes 284
cover-laying machine 50, Fig 5.6
covers 182–3, 270–80, Figs 13.34–13.36
    cutting plans 114–16
    measuring 113
cow-tail hair 70
craftsmen 275
cretonne 98, 283
Cromwellian chair 32, Fig 15.8
curled hair 70–1
Curlifil 72
curtains 13, 254–5, 272–4, Figs 19.10–19.12
cushion covers 204–5, Figs 14.36, 14.37
cushion filler 48, Fig 5.4
cushion filling by machine 62, Figs 5.29, 5.30
cushions 13, 24, Figs 6.17, 6.18, 10.20, 10.21
    boxed 184–5, Figs 13.40, 13.41
    covers 204–5, Fig 14.37
    fillings 70–8, 185–7, 272
    interiors 203–4, Fig 14.34
    seams 206, Fig 14.38
    spring interior 186, Fig 13.43
    nosed edges 130, 132, Fig 10.11, 10.17
cutting 117, 182, Figs 9.13, 13.34
    foams 129–31, Figs 10.9–10.15
    frames 52
    patterns 115, Fig 9.9
    plans 113-16, Figs 9.6–9.9
    press 51–2, Figs 5.8, 5.9
    table 26–7, Figs 3.6, 3.7
cylinder bed machines 54, Fig 5.12

damask 12, 20, 98, 284
Danhauser sofas 21, 121
Danish influence 23
day bed 65, Fig 17.3
deep buttoning 198–9, Figs 14.23–14.25
denier 89, 284
denim 89, 96
differential feed mechanism 54, Fig 5.13
divan beds 259, Figs 18.13, 18.16, 18.20
divan chairs 201, 284
dogs 284
dolly sticks 36, Fig 4.9
down 75, Fig 6.18
drapes 254–5

drop 284
drop feed mechanism 54, Fig 5.13
drop-in seat 13, Figs 11.24, 15.1, 15.2
duck 96, 284
duck feathers 75, Fig 6.18
dug-roll 85, 174, Figs 6.34, 13.17
dust and fume extraction 30
duvets 261
dyeing 93, 284, Fig 7.12

easy chairs 284, Fig 15.24
edge rolls 174, 190–1, Figs 13.17, 14.7–14.9
Edwardian style 22, Fig 15.17
Edwardian suite 23, 211
eiderdown 75, 261
electric cloth cutters 46–7, Figs 4.30–4.34
electric drills 44, Fig 4.27
embossing 284
embroidered velvets 12, 20
equipment 25–9, Figs 3.1–3.9
estimating
    leather work 109
    reupholstery 110–12
extractor fans 30
eyelets 83, Fig 6.31

fabrics 87–100; *see also* cloth
    care of 99–100
Fabweb platform Fig 12.34
fan-back sofa 246
farthingale chairs 19, 36, 284
feather down 15, 284
feather edge 173–4, 284, Fig 13.16
feathers 75, Fig 6.18
    cushion filling 186–7, 204, 272, Figs 6.6, 6.18, 13.44, 15.6,
        15.15, 15.28, 27.8, 19.10
    mattresses 253, 255, 259, 264, Fig 18.13
Feltex 74
felts 73–4, Fig 6.15
fender stool Fig 17.23
Festival of Britain 16, 23
fibre identification 284
field bed 284
fillings 39-40, 70–8
    cleanliness 76
    Glossary of Terms 75
    restoration 265–6, 272
fire safety regulations 23, 100
    foams 137
firefighting equipment 29–30
first aid 30
flameproofing 95
flammability legislation 23, 100, 137
flat bed machines 53, Figs 5.11, 5.12
flax 89, 284, Figs 7.2, 7.3
Flexibead 80, Fig 6.26
flock filling 74, Fig 6.16
fluting 14, 179–81, 200, Figs 13.28–13.32, 14.26, 14.27
    chairs Figs 15.16, 15.30
    restoration 269
    settees 246, Fig 17.4
fluting stick 38, Fig 4.12

fly piece 134, 284, Fig 10.20
foam cutters 43, 129–31, Figs 4.24–4.25, 10.9–10.15
    maintenance 43
foam fabrication 132–6, Figs 10.16–10.22
foams 16–17, 125–37, Figs 10.2–10.22
    all-foam chair 269
    choice 136–7
    cushion interiors 203–4, Fig 14.34
    cutting 129–31, Fig 14.19
    gluing 28, 132, 196, Figs 14.16, 14.17
    manufacture 126–7, Fig 10.4
    mattresses 260–1, 263
    moulding 128, Fig 10.7
    working with 193–6, Figs 14.14, 14.15
foldstools 284
foot stools 14, Fig 17.22
four-poster beds 254–5, Figs 18.4, 18.5
framed and turned chair 29
frames 111, 138–44, Figs 11.1–11.25
    repairs to 268–9
French overlay 284, Fig 18.19
French work 284
fringes 13, 79, Fig 6.25
frise 284
furniture industry 275–81
Furniture Industry Research Association 278
Furniture, Timber and Allied Trades Union 278

Gainsborough chair Fig 15.22
galoon 284
garnett machine 73, 284
Genoa velvet 13, 284
Georgian style 13, 20
gimp 78, 284, Fig 6.23
gimp pins 80
Gimson, Ernest 15, 23
glue 45
gluing foams 28, 132, 196, Figs 14.16, 14.17
goose feathers 75, Fig 6.18
gout stools 14
Guild of Traditional Upholsterers 279
guttering 236, Fig 16.13

hair cloth 284
hair fillings 70–2, 186
hair pads 71, Fig 6.12
hammers 31, Fig 4.1
hand-sewn joints 119–20, Fig 9.16
hand-sprung upholstery 228–36, Figs 16.1–16.14
hand tools 31–40, Figs 4.1–4.17
headboard 222, Figs 17.21, 18.15
hemp 90
Hepplewhite 21, *111*
hessian 66, 97, 189–90, 284, Fig 6.2
    lining up in 167, Figs 13.4, 14.5, 14.6
hides 101–3, Figs 8.5, 15.8, 15.10, 15.27
    buying 108–9
    cutting 52
    defects Fig 8.6
    finishes 103–4, Fig 8.4
    marking out 107, Fig 8.7
    raw hide 101–2, Figs 8.1–8.3

hogring 284
hole cutters 37, Fig 4.10
hole punches 39, Fig 4.14
Holland linen 22, 68, 97
Hope, Thomas 21
horsehair 70
horsehair fabric 12, 14, 99
hot melt glue gun 44, Fig 4.26

India tape 284
insulating 188–9, Figs 14.3, 14.4
interior designers 13, 17
iron-back
    chairs *183*, Figs 11.4, 15.16, 15.21
    settees Fig 17.12
iron hands 33, Fig 4.4
Italian influence 23

job book 110–11, Figs 9.1, 9.2
joining 117–20, Figs 9.14–9.16
jute 90

KD furniture *see* knock down furniture
kanaf 284
kapok 74–5, Fig 6.17
knitted fabrics 92–3, Fig 7.11
knitting chair 284
knives 34, Fig 4.6
knock-down furniture 23, 144, 284, Fig 11.12
    chair 266
    fittings Figs 11.22, 11.23
knock up 285
Knole settees *15, 19,* 237, Fig 17.14
Knole style chair Fig 15.28
knots 167, Fig 13.5

ladies' chairs 23, *146*
laid cord 285
lashing 232, Fig 16.10
latex foam 16, 17, 23, 125, 260, Fig 10.1
    see also foams
lay of cover 113, Fig 9.3
laying up 51, Fig 5.7
leather 16, 20, 101–9
    buying 108
    cleaning 109
    estimating amounts 109
    furniture 105, Fig 8.5
    marking out 106–7, Fig 8.7
    properties of 104
    quilted Fig 14.33
    sewing 107
    tooling 104
    upholstery techniques 105–6
leather cloth 16, 22
library seats *21, 133*, Fig 17.9
line 285
linings 189–90, Figs 14.5, 14.6
linters 285
lit 285

lock-stitch sewing machines 52–4, 117, 123, Figs 5.10–5.12, 9.22
    feed mechanisms 54, 123, Figs 5.13, 9.23
    specialised machines 55, Figs 5.14–5.15
long-arm machines 55, 200, Fig 5.15
loose cover 285
loose cushions 181
loose curled hair 71, Fig 6.12
loose seat 285, Figs 11.24, 15.1
loose seat press 48, Fig 5.3
lounge chair Figs 15.25, 15.26
love seat 285
low-pressure adhesive spray gun 45, Figs 4.28–4.30
    maintenance 45
lug chair 285

Mackintosh, Charles Rennie 15, 23
machine sewing 120–4, Figs 9.22–9.24
machine threads 121–2, Figs 9.19–9.20
machines 30
mallets 34, Fig 4.5
man-made fibres 90–6, Fig 7.4
marking out
    fabric 115–16, Figs 9.9–9.12
    leather 106–7, Fig 8.7
Marot, Daniel's book 12, 13
materials 64–86
    preparation 110–24
mattresses 229, 262–4, Fig 6.16
    foam 260–1, 263
    history 253–5, 258–62, Fig 18.12
    sprung 152–3, 259, Figs 18.12, 18.17
    un-sprung 264, Fig 18.19
measuring
    for cover 113–16
    tapes 37–8, Fig 4.11
mercerisation 89, 94, 122
metals for chair frames 139–40, Fig 11.3
metal strainers 33, Fig 4.4
metre sticks 37, Fig 4.11
modern settee and chair 279
Modern style 16, 22
mohair 12, 285
moiré 99, 285
monks cloth 285
monofilament 122, 285
moquette 22, 89, 98, 285
Morocco hide 22, 285
Morris, William 15, 23
Morris chairs 23, 189, 285
motifs 285
moulded shell chairs 276
multi-lay cutting 117, Fig 9.13

nailed upholstery 13, 19
nails 81–2, Fig 6.28
nap 285
National Association of Retail Furnishers 276–7
needles 35–6, Fig 4.8
    for leather work 107–8
    for sewing machines 122, Fig 9.21
needlework coverings 12, 13

needlework tapestry 12
non-woven cloth 69, Fig 6.9
nursing chairs 14, 285

orris 285
ottomans 13, 14, 15, 285, Figs 17.18, 17.25
overedge machines 56, Fig 5.17
overedge upholstery Fig 15.5
ox hide 18

PVC cloths 22, 95, Fig 7.14
painted silk 12
palliasse 285
panelling leathers 105, Fig 8.5
papier-mâché 15
perforated patterns 116, Fig 9.10
petit-point 13
piece 285
pile fabric 285
pillows 184, Figs 6.5, 13.37, 13.38
pincers 37, 267, Fig 4.10
pins 37, 169, Figs 4.9, 13.8
pinstuffed 285, Figs 11.24, 15.3, 15.7
piping 285
piping cord 84, Fig 6.33
Pirelli platforms 160, Figs 12.33–12.35
plain weave 285
plastic foams 125–6
plastic for chair frames 140–1, Figs 11.5, 11.9
platform cloths 68, Fig 6.7
platform seats 191–3, Figs 14.10–14.13
plush 14, 98, 285
polyester
    fibre fillings 76–7, 204, Figs 6.19–6.21, 14.35
    foams 17, 125
polystyrene beads Figs 6.22, 11.5
polyurethane foams 16–17, 126–8, Figs 10.7, 10.8, 10.15
    fire regulations 137
Pop Art style 17, 22
post bed machines 54, Fig 5.12
pouffes 236, 249, 285, Figs 16.14, 17.19
power tools 28, 30, 40–7, Figs 4.18–4.34
Pratt, Samuel 21
prayer chairs 14
pre-formed fillings 16
press cutting 51–2, 116, Figs 5.8, 5.9, 9.12
presser feet 124, Fig 9.24
press-stud dies and punches 39, Fig 4.15
press-studs 82–3, Fig 6.29
presspahn 285
Prie-Dieu chairs 142, 285, Fig 15.9
printing fabrics 93, Fig 7.13
profile seamers 59, Fig 5.20
protective clothing 30, Fig 3.10
pull-in upholstery 285
puller feed mechanism 5, Fig 5.13
Pullmaflex units 158–9, Figs 12.18–12.21

Queen Anne style 13, 20
quilted fabrics 99
quilted panels 203, Fig 14.32

quilting 15, 200–1, Figs 14.28–14.30
   covers 202, Fig 14.31
   machine 58, Figs 5.18, 14.31
   panels 203, Fig 14.32

ramie 285
rasps 37, Fig 4.10
Regency style 13, 20
regulator 36, 170, Figs 4.9, 13.11
repp 68, 89, 97, 285
reupholstery 265–9
   estimating 110–12
ripping chisels 33–4, 267, Figs 4.5, 19.1
rocking chair Fig 15.7
roll edge 173, Fig 13.15
rollover arm 190, 285, Fig 14.7
rubber suspension 159–65, Fig 12.22
rubberised hair sheet 71–2, Fig 6.12
ruche 79, Fig 6.24
ruching 285
Rural Development Commission 278

Sacco chairs 23, 269
safety in the workshop 29–30, 63
satin tapestry coverings 12
scissors 31–3, 267, Fig 4.2
screen 252, Fig 17.26
scrim 66, 89, 97, 285, Fig 6.3
   restoration 269, Fig 13.1
scrollover arm 285, Fig 13.1
seams 117–20, Figs 9.14–9.16
   for cushion covers 206, Fig 14.38
   for quilting 203, Fig 14.32
seat edging 13, 170–4, Figs 13.12–13.18
seat fronts 270, Fig 19.6
seating 143, 285, Figs 11.11, 11.15
serpentine springing 154, Fig 12.13
set squares 37, Fig 4.11
set work 13, 18, 26, 286
settees *21, 23, 111,* 237–8, 286, Figs 17.1–17.17
   frame construction Fig 11.21

sewing chair Fig 15.13
sewing machine practice 120–4, Figs 9.22–9.24
sewing machine threads 121–2, Fig 9.9
sewing machines 15, 30, 48, Fig 5.1
   chain-stitch 56, Fig 5.16
   industrial 52–62, Figs 5.11, 5.12
   lock-stitch 52–5, Figs 5.10, 5.13–5.15
   maintenance 30
   overedge 56, Fig 5.17
   specialist uses 56, Fig 5.16
shadow fabric 286
shearing 94
shears 31–3, Fig 4.2
Sheraton 13, 255, Fig 17.11
side chairs *21,* 90, 103

silk 89, Fig 7.3
   brocade 89
   cords 15
   damask 13, 89
   embroidery 18
   plush 14
   velvet 18, 89
sisal 73
skewers 37, 169, Figs 4.9, 13.8
sleeping chairs 57
slip cover 286
slipper chair Fig 15.14
slipping thread 83–4, Fig 6.32
Smith, George 21
smokers' chairs 286
snips 33, 267, Fig 4.2
sofas 13, 286, Figs 13.1, 17.10
Soho tapestry 20
spoon back chairs 286
spring balance 39–40, Fig 4.16
spring edge work 14–15, 158, 229, 231, Figs 12.17, 16.2–16.4
spring units 153, Figs 12.6–12.10
springing 16, 151–9, Figs 12.1–12.21
   arrangements of Fig 16.6
   for mattresses 262–3, Fig 18.17
   hand-springing 228–36
   metal springs 152–9
   rubber suspension 159
sprung arms 232, 235, Fig 16.9
squab 286
squab cushions 13, 186, Figs 13.43, 15.23
staple guns 40–2, Figs 4.19–4.20
staple lifters 34, 267, Fig 4.7
staples 80–1, Fig 6.27
stitch up 286
stitch types 57, 117–20, Figs 9.16, 9.17
   BS 101 57
   BS 301 52–3, 57, Fig 5.10
   BS 304 57
   BS 401 56, 57, Fig 5.16
   BS 502 Fig 5.17
   BS 504 Fig 5.17
   BS 801 57
   for leather work 108, Fig 8.10
stitched edge upholstery 170–4, Fig 13.12
   edge types 173–4, Figs 13.15–13.18
stockinette 68, Fig 6.8
stools 13, 81, Figs 11.20, 11.25
stripping 266–8, Figs 19.1–19.3
stuffed upholstery 13–17
stuffing ties 167–8, Figs 13.6, 13.7
stuffings 13, 15
   restoration 265–6, 269, Fig 19.2
stuffover 286
   chairs 14, 151, Figs 12.2, 15.4
styrene foam *see* foams
suede 104
swing needle machines 55, Fig 5.14
swivel desk chair Fig 15.10

T-cushions 134, Fig 10.21
T-squares 37, Fig 4.11
table bench 26, Fig 3.5
tacking hammers 31, Fig 3.5
tacks 80, 168, Fig 13.8
tapestry 13, 18, 98, 286
tension springing 16, 23, 154, Figs 12.11 12.12
tester 286
ticking 67, 97, 259, Fig 6.5
timbers for chair frames 138–9, Figs 11.2, 11.6, 11.18
tooling leather 104
tools
    hand 31–40, Figs 4.1–4.17
    power 28, 30, 40–7, Figs 4.18–4.34
top stitch 173, Fig 13.14
tramline jigs 116, Fig 9.11
trestles 25, Figs 3.1–3.3
trimmings 13, 78–80, 286, Figs 6.23–6.33
    cord 79, 273, Figs 6.24, 19.13
trimming knife 267
trumeter measuring device 49
tub chairs 23, 230, 286, Figs 14.26, 15.11, 15.27
tube chairs 240, Figs 11.8, 11.17
Tudor style 12
Tufting 14, 286
Turkey chairs 171
Turkey work 13, 18, 286, 26
tussah 99
tweeds 22, 89
twin-head boxing machines 58, Fig 5.19
twines 83, 89
tying in 13

union 89, 98
Upholsterers' Guild 13
upholstery 286
    history 11–17
    leather 105
    nails 81–2, Fig 6.28
    restoring 269–74
    traditional methods 166–87, Figs 13.1–13.44
    twines 83, 89
Utility furniture 16, 23

valance 273–4, 286
vandyking 178–9, 199, Fig 13.27
velour 22, 89, 98, 286
velvet 12, 20, 89, 98
velveteen 98, 286
ventilators 83, Fig 6.30
Victorian style 13–15, 22
Voysey, C. F. 15
vinyl 17
Vitastretch webbing 164, Fig 12.32

waddings 74, 269–70, Fig 6.20
wall hangings 13
warp 92, 286, Fig 7.10
weaving 91, Fig 7.9
web strainers 33, Figs 4.3, 4.4

webbings 64–5, 89, 190, 228, Figs 6.1, 14.6, 15.10, 16.1
    basic techniques 166, Figs 13.2, 13.3
    rubber 159–65, Figs 12.22–12.35
weft 92, 286, Fig 7.10
well seat 170–1, Figs 13.12, 15.6
welt 286
whale bone 15
William and Mary style 13, 20
window seat 13, Fig 17.16
wing chairs 19, 21, 23, 57, 261
wire cutters 38–9, Fig 4.13
wire formers 39, Fig 4.13
wire hooks 39, Fig 4.13
wool 88–9, Fig 7.2
wool felt 73–4, Fig 6.15
wool plush 14, 22
woollen flock 74
workshop 14
    layout 28, Fig 3.8
    processes 24
    safety 29–30
    storage 27, Fig 3.9
worsted 88, 286

X-frame chair 11, 19, 286

yarns 91

zig-zag stitch 55, Fig 5.14
zips 121

TITLES AVAILABLE FROM
GMC Publications

◆

——————— BOOKS ———————

WOODTURNING

Adventures in Woodturning	*David Springett*	Practical Tips for Turners & Carvers	*GMC Publications*
Bert Marsh: Woodturner	*Bert Marsh*	Practical Tips for Woodturners	*GMC Publications*
Bill Jones' Notes from the Turning Shop	*Bill Jones*	Spindle Turning	*GMC Publications*
Carving on Turning	*Chris Pye*	Turning Miniatures in Wood	*John Sainsbury*
Colouring Techniques for Woodturners	*Jan Sanders*	Turning Wooden Toys	*Terry Lawrence*
Decorative Techniques for Woodturners	*Hilary Bowen*	Useful Woodturning Projects	*GMC Publications*
Faceplate Turning: Features, Projects, Practice	*GMC Publications*	Woodturning: A Foundation Course	*Keith Rowley*
Green Woodwork	*Mike Abbott*	Woodturning Jewellery	*Hilary Bowen*
Illustrated Woodturning Techniques	*John Hunnex*	Woodturning Masterclass	*Tony Boase*
Keith Rowley's Woodturning Projects	*Keith Rowley*	Woodturning: A Source Book of Shapes	*John Hunnex*
Make Money from Woodturning	*Ann & Bob Phillips*	Woodturning Techniques	*GMC Publications*
Multi-Centre Woodturning	*Ray Hopper*	Woodturning Wizardry	*David Springett*
Pleasure & Profit from Woodturning	*Reg Sherwin*		

WOODCARVING

The Art of the Woodcarver	*GMC Publications*	Wildfowl Carving Volume 1	*Jim Pearce*
Carving Birds & Beasts	*GMC Publications*	Wildfowl Carving Volume 2	*Jim Pearce*
Carving Realistic Birds	*David Tippey*	Woodcarving: A Complete Course	*Ron Butterfield*
Carving on Turning	*Chris Pye*	Woodcarving for Beginners:	
Decorative Woodcarving	*Jeremy Williams*	Projects, Techniques & Tools	*GMC Publications*
Practical Tips for Turners & Carvers	*GMC Publications*	Woodcarving Tools, Materials & Equipment	*Chris Pye*

PLANS, PROJECTS, TOOLS & THE WORKSHOP

40 More Woodworking Plans & Projects	*GMC Publications*	Sharpening Pocket Reference Book	*Jim Kingshott*
Electric Woodwork: Power Tool Woodworking	*Jeremy Broun*	Woodworking Plans & Projects	*GMC Publications*
The Incredible Router	*Jeremy Broun*	The Workshop	*Jim Kingshott*
Making & Modifying Woodworking Tools	*Jim Kingshott*		
Sharpening: The Complete Guide	*Jim Kingshott*		

TOYS & MINIATURES

Designing & Making Wooden Toys	*Terry Kelly*	Making Wooden Toys & Games	*Jeff & Jennie Loader*
Heraldic Miniature Knights	*Peter Greenhill*	Miniature Needlepoint Carpets	*Janet Granger*
Making Board, Peg & Dice Games	*Jeff & Jennie Loader*	Restoring Rocking Horses	*Clive Green & Anthony Dew*
Making Little Boxes from Wood	*John Bennett*	Turning Miniatures in Wood	*John Sainsbury*
Making Unusual Miniatures	*Graham Spalding*	Turning Wooden Toys	*Terry Lawrence*

CREATIVE CRAFTS

The Complete Pyrography	*Stephen Poole*	Making Knitwear Fit	*Pat Ashforth & Steve Plummer*
Cross Stitch on Colour	*Sheena Rogers*	Miniature Needlepoint Carpets	*Janet Granger*
Embroidery Tips & Hints	*Harold Hayes*	Tatting Collage: Adventurous Ideas for Tatters	*Lindsay Rogers*
Creating Knitwear Designs	*Pat Ashforth & Steve Plummer*		

UPHOLSTERY AND FURNITURE

Care & Repair	*GMC Publications*	Making Shaker Furniture	*Barry Jackson*
Complete Woodfinishing	*Ian Hosker*	Seat Weaving (Practical Crafts)	*Ricky Holdstock*
Furniture Projects	*Rod Wales*	Upholsterers' Pocket Reference Book	*David James*
Furniture Restoration (Practical Crafts)	*Kevin Jan Bonner*	Upholstery: A Complete Course	*David James*
Furniture Restoration & Repair for Beginners	*Kevin Jan Bonner*	Upholstery: Techniques & Projects	*David James*
Green Woodwork	*Mike Abbott*	Woodfinishing Handbook (Practical Crafts)	*Ian Hosker*
Making Fine Furniture	*Tom Darby*		

DOLLS' HOUSES & DOLLS' HOUSE FURNITURE

Architecture for Dolls' Houses	*Joyce Percival*	Making Period Dolls' House Accessories	*Andrea Barham*
The Complete Dolls' House Book	*Jean Nisbett*	Making Period Dolls' House Furniture	*Derek & Sheila Rowbottom*
Easy-to-Make Dolls' House Accessories	*Andrea Barham*	Making Tudor Dolls' Houses	*Derek Rowbottom*
Make Your Own Dolls' House Furniture	*Maurice Harper*	Making Victorian Dolls' House Furniture	*Patricia King*
Making Dolls' House Furniture	*Patricia King*	Miniature Needlepoint Carpets	*Janet Granger*
Making Georgian Dolls' Houses	*Derek Rowbottom*	The Secrets of the Dolls' House Makers	*Jean Nisbett*

OTHER BOOKS

Guide to Marketing	*GMC Publications*	Woodworkers' Career & Educational Source Book	*GMC Publications*

VIDEOS

Carving a Figure: The Female Form	*Ray Gonzalez*	Turning Boxes	*Chris Stott*
The Traditional Upholstery Workshop		Natural Edges & Hollow Forms	*Chris Stott*
Part 1: *Drop-in & Pinstuffed Seats*	*David James*	Decorative Effects and Colouring	*Chris Stott*
The Traditional Upholstery Workshop		Turning Bowls	*Chris Stott*
Part 2: *Stuffover Upholstery*	*David James*	ROUTING *with Roy Sutton*	
Hollow Turning	*John Jordan*	1. Basic Routing	*Roy Sutton*
Bowl Turning	*John Jordan*	2. Advanced Routing	*Roy Sutton*
TURNED BOXES *with Ray Key*		3. Safe Wood Machining	*Roy Sutton*
The Basic Box	*Ray Key*	4. Basic Spindle Moulding	*Roy Sutton*
The Capsule Box	*Ray Key*	5. Routing Jigs & Gadgets	*Roy Sutton*
The Finial Box	*Ray Key*	6. Developing the Router Workshop	*Roy Sutton*
Sharpening Turning & Carving Tools	*Jim Kingshott*	Turning Between Centres: The Basics	*Dennis White*
Sharpening the Professional Way	*Jim Kingshott*	Turning Bowls	*Dennis White*
Woodturning: A Foundation Course	*Keith Rowley*	Boxes, Goblets & Screw Threads	*Dennis White*
Colouring Wood	*Jan Sanders*	Novelties & Projects	*Dennis White*
Woodworks with Bertie Somme	*Bertie Somme*	Classic Profiles	*Dennis White*
Elliptical Turning	*David Springett*	Twists & Advanced Turning	*Dennis White*
Woodturning Wizardry	*David Springett*	Wood Finishing Tricks, Tips and Techniques	
Cutting and Sharpening for Woodturners	*Chris Stott*	Wood Finishing Techniques 2	

MAGAZINES

WOODTURNING ◆ WOODCARVING ◆ TOYMAKING
FURNITURE & CABINETMAKING ◆ BUSINESS MATTERS

◆

The above represents a full list of all titles currently published or scheduled to be published. All are available direct from the Publishers or through bookshops, newsagents and specialist retailers. To place an order, or to obtain a complete catalogue, contact:

GMC Publications, 166 High Street, Lewes, East Sussex BN7 1XU United Kingdom
Tel: 01273 488005 Fax: 01273 478606

Orders by credit card are accepted